# PENSION

# FUNDING

# &

# TAXATION:

# I M P L I C A T I O N S
# F O R
# T O M O R R O W

**EBRI**

EMPLOYEE
BENEFIT
RESEARCH
INSTITUTE

© 1994 Employee Benefit Research Institute
Education and Research Fund
2121 K Street, NW, Suite 600
Washington, DC 20037-1896
(202) 659-0670

**Library of Congress Cataloging-in-Publication Data**

Pension funding and taxation : implications for tomorrow.
    p.   cm.
  "An EBRI-ERF policy forum."
  Includes index.
  ISBN 0-86643-080-6 : $15.95
    1. Old age pensions—Taxation—United States—Congresses.
2. Pension trusts—Taxation—United States—Congresses.
I. Employee Benefit Research Institute (Washington, DC).
Education and Research Fund.
HD7105.35.U6P447   1994
331.25'2'0973—dc20

93-45511
CIP

# Table of Contents

**Part Two**
**What Are the Implications of Tax Policy Change?**

**List of Tables and Charts**

**Table**

**Chart**

# Preface

More than $5 trillion is now invested in American pension and retirement income programs. The U.S. tax system has extended special treatment to these funds by not subjecting either the contributions or the investment earnings to income tax until they are paid to the beneficiaries.

Beginning in the predepression era, and continuing until the enactment of the Employee Retirement Income Security Act of 1974, few limits were placed on the amounts that could be contributed to pension funds or the benefits that they could pay. Since 1974, Congress has acted many times to limit pension plans, with the passage of section 401(k) in 1978 and initial individual retirement account expansion in 1981 being the only two expansionary actions in the midst of many new requirements.

The trend toward reduction of tax preferences for retirement income programs was most pronounced in the Tax Reform Act of 1986, and it continued this year with provisions in the Omnibus Budget Reconciliation Act of 1993 (OBRA '93), which reduced compensation that can be considered for pension funding by more than 35 percent.

The federal deficit has been a factor in many of these actions, as lower contributions to pension plans are viewed as increasing current tax payments. During the heated debate before agreement on a tax or budget bill is reached, there is little time to undertake new analysis of long-term consequences—the costs and the benefits. The papers in this volume provide such analysis. They provide a basis for assessing where the pension system is today, the role that tax preferences have played in getting it there, and the implications of tax policy changes for future retirement income.

The papers were originally prepared for a policy forum of the Employee Benefit Research Institute Education and Research Fund (EBRI-ERF) held in Washington, DC on May 5, 1993, on the topic: "Pension Funding and Taxation: Achieving Benefit Security." The session included an active discussion among the authors and 100 invited participants with an interest in economic security issues.

The aging of the baby boom generation, the movement of this generation into positions of power, and the beginning hazy dreams of its retirement combine to guarantee a new intensity of interest in pension and retirement income issues. What will Social Security provide? Will I have a pension and how much will it provide? How much more will I have to save to live the life I want to live? Newspapers and magazines are beginning to be filled with these stories. Congres-

sional hearings have begun; presidential commissions cannot be far behind. This volume seeks to provide a basis for beginning to answer many of these questions.

## The Beginning

The introductory essay by Tom Paine pulls together the primary issues that need to be considered as we review and think about retirement income policy. Paine has just retired from a full career of designing employee benefit programs. He has been a practical scholar of retirement policy throughout his professional life, since working extensively with the 1962 Kennedy Commission on Retirement Income Policy. His breadth of experience comes through in this valuable first section.

## Where Is the Pension System Today?

This first section of papers begins with an overview of public and private pensions today by EBRI research analysts Celia Silverman and Paul Yakoboski. The paper documents the long-term growth of the system: the number and types of plans; the number of individuals working for organizations with plans, participating in plans, and entitled to benefits from plans; the assets accumulated and how they are invested; and the amount of money now flowing from plans to enhance economic security. The paper paints a picture of a system in which 40 million households are building benefits and which pays over $250 billion per year in benefits.

This overview is followed by a description of the present tax treatment of pensions by Richard Hubbard of Arnold & Porter. The paper takes the reader on a journey through the complex and ever-changing world of pension taxation. This summary, written to be understandable, allows one to avoid the thousands of pages of legislative and regulatory language while still coming into contact with the web of complexity faced by the pension technician. It makes clear why pension rules are not easy for pension participants to understand.

EBRI Fellow Jack VanDerhei then moves us into the complex worlds of tax law and actuarial science that provide the road map for pension funding. The picture painted by VanDerhei allows one to grasp why actuarial methods and assumptions about age, investment earnings, and life expectancy make such a difference in determining whether enough funds have been set aside.

My paper, "The Costs and Benefits of Pension Tax Expenditures," then seeks to pull much of this information together, looking at the level of support that tax preferences have provided, the allocation of these preferences between public- and private-sector pension plans, the present funded condition of the pensions promised by the federal government to its own employees, and the benefits flowing from the system to workers and retirees to enhance economic security.

This section of the volume ends with a paper by Sylvester Schieber and Gordon Goodfellow of The Wyatt Company that looks at who actually benefits from the tax preferences. It also presents a picture of the difference that labor force attachment makes in determining pension outcomes: those with little attachment to the work force will never get work-related pensions. This seemingly obvious fact, the authors note, is totally missed when analysis focuses on pensions without also considering Social Security and Supplemental Security Income. The paper then looks at the allocation of the tax benefit relative to taxes paid, underlining the fact that the pension system primarily benefits the middle class.

## What Are the Implications of Tax Policy Change?

Section Two of the volume turns to assessments of how changing the rules might affect pensions and benefit security. What are the possible costs and benefits of change?

Michael Gulotta of Actuarial Sciences Associates, Inc., begins with a review of recent changes in tax and funding rules and an assessment of the effect they have had on benefit security. He then reviews changes in OBRA '93 and proposals for reforms related to the Pension Benefit Guaranty Corporation. His paper underlines the degree to which changes in the law affect behavior.

Fiona Liston and Adrien LaBombarde of Milliman & Robertson then look at these issues for public employee pension plans in one paper and at the implications of changes in OBRA '93 in another, focusing on the sec. 401(a)(17) allowable compensation limit changes. Again, they underline the long-term nature of pension promises and the fact that, to meet a given pension income objective, one must either pay now or pay later: there is no free lunch.

Richard Ippolito of the Pension Benefit Guaranty Corporation then takes a leap into alternative futures, looking at pension tax policy relative to individuals' propensity to save versus consume. He empha-

sizes that Americans are not naturally motivated savers and that the tax treatment of pensions does make a major difference in individuals' decisions.

## What Do People Think It All Means?

The volume concludes with selected interactions and comments based on the proceedings of the policy forum. The section is organized by topic to make it more useful to the reader.

## Where Do We Go from Here?

The aging process for America is rolling forward relentlessly and along with it the number of individuals who must support themselves in retirement. If we manage to stay alive, each of us looks forward to the prospect of facing the retirement income challenge. Social Security, personal savings, and pension and retirement income programs will play a role for those who have worked. Understanding the role they can and will play, and the implications of policy change for each, can make a difference in consumption expenditures in the economy, the balance of trade, the number of Americans in poverty, and the balance between economic independence and reliance on welfare.

EBRI will continue an aggressive program of research, policy forums, public opinion surveys, and public education aimed at increasing understanding and enhancing preparation for the certainties and uncertainties that lie ahead.

With the publication of this book, we share the knowledge gained at the policy forum with a wider range of readers interested in the nation's retirement system. We wish to thank the speakers and participants and other authors for their substantial contributions to this book. We offer special thanks to the EBRI staff who contributed to the publication of this book: Laura Bos for her role in the organization and development of the policy forum; Deborah Holmes for copy editing the papers, Malaika Barnes and Leah Blaugrund for preparing the papers for publication, Cindy O'Connor for layout and design of the final publication, and finally to Nora Super Jones for planning the policy forum, overseeing the preparation of the papers and transcripts, and guiding the book through production.

The views expressed in this book are solely those of the authors and participants. They should not be attributed to EBRI.

Dallas L. Salisbury
President, EBRI
January 1994

# About the Authors

**Gordon P. Goodfellow** is an associate of The Wyatt Company's Research and Information Center. During his professional career he has specialized in the analysis of social security policy and private defined contribution plans. Before joining The Wyatt Company, he was with the Office of the Assistant Secretary for Planning and Evaluation as a senior policy analyst and project manager of the Panel Study of Income Dynamics.

**Michael J. Gulotta** is president and chief executive officer of Actuarial Sciences Associates (ASA), a New Jersey-based employee benefits consulting firm with a branch office in Boca Raton, Florida. Prior to the establishment of ASA, Mr. Gulotta held the position of Chief Actuary of AT&T. In that capacity, he was responsible for the actuarial allocation of the $54 billion of pension fund assets of the former Bell System pension plans. Formerly a Principle Actuary for New York City State, Mr. Gulotta was responsible for the actuarial audit of the New York Employees' Retirement System, the largest New York City retirement plan. Mr. Gulotta was graduated magna cum laude from Queens College of City University of New York and is a member of Phi Beta Kappa.

**Richard L. Hubbard** is a partner in the Washington, D.C. based law firm of Arnold & Porter. He is a member of Arnold & Porter's tax and employee benefits practice groups. He has been involved in a wide variety of federal and local tax matters and has particular expertise in federal income tax issues related to employee benefit plans, executive compensation, partnerships, tax-exempt organizations, and real estate. His practice involves both tax planning and tax controversy work. Mr. Hubbard joined Arnold & Porter in 1969 after a clerkship with Judge Arnold Raum on the U.S. Tax Court. He is a 1964 *magna cum laude* graduate of Williams College and a 1967 *magna cum laude* graduate of Harvard Law School.

**Richard Ippolito**, Ph.D., is the chief economist at the Pension Benefit Guaranty Corporation. His book, *An Economic Analysis of Pension Tax Policy in the U.S.*, was published by the Pension Research Council in 1990. Dr. Ippolito received his Ph.D. in economics from the University of Chicago in 1974.

**Adrien R. LaBombarde** is the research actuary in the employee benefits research department of Milliman & Robertson (M&R), Inc. Based in Washington, DC, he specializes in analysis of employee benefits, government regulations, and accounting rules. Mr. LaBombarde has served as consultant to the Pension Benefit Guaranty Corporation, the Social Security Administration, the General Accounting Office, and the Government Accounting Standards Board, as well as to M&R's private, public, and multiemployer clients. He is an expert in the development of personal computer simulation models and solutions for complex employee benefits problems. Mr. LaBombarde is an associate of the Society of Actuaries, a member of the American Academy of Actuaries, and an enrolled actuary under ERISA. He graduated *magna cum laude* from Drexel University with a B.S. in mathematics.

**Fiona E. Liston**, F.S.A., is a fellow of the Society of Actuaries, a member of the American Academy of Actuaries, and an enrolled actuary. She has over ten years of experience with consulting actuaries Milliman & Robertson, Inc., specializing in pension matters in both the public and private sectors. Ms. Liston's work includes producing actuarial valuations, financial accounting reports (FASB and GASB), and plan experience studies to test the appropriateness of actuarial assumptions.

**Thomas Paine** spent 35 years as an associate and partner in Hewitt Associates, most of this time as a consultant on employee benefits and compensation in New York. He retired from full-time work in 1990. Now living in California, he serves the firm on a part-time basis. His practice is confined to helping organizations develop strategy for human resources, compensation, and employee benefits.

**Dallas L. Salisbury** has been the president of EBRI since its establishment in 1978. Prior to joining EBRI, he served in senior employee benefits regulatory policy positions at PBGC and PWBA. Before entering the employee benefits field, Mr. Salisbury held public- and private-sector positions in Washington, DC and the State of Washington. He received a B.A. in Finance from the University of Washington and an M.A. in public administration from the Maxwell Graduate School in Syracuse.

**Sylvester J. Schieber**, Ph.D., is a vice president of The Wyatt Company and the director of its Research and Information Center in Washington, D.C. During his professional career he has specialized in the analysis of public and private retirement policy and health policy issues. Prior to joining The Wyatt Company in 1983, he served as the first Research Director of the Employee Benefit Research Institute in Washington, D.C. Before that, he served as the Deputy Director, Office of Policy Analysis, Social Security Administration, and Deputy Research Director, Universal Social Security Coverage Study, Department of Health and Human Services. He received a Ph.D. in economics from the University of Notre Dame in 1974.

**Celia Silverman** is a research analyst with EBRI, specializing in pension finance and retirement security issues. Her major EBRI projects have included EBRI's *Quarterly Pension Investment Report* and the *EBRI Databook on Employee Benefits*. Her current research efforts focus on pension plan and participation trends and future retirement income security. She has a B.A. in economics from the University of Pennsylvania.

**Jack VanDerhei**, Ph.D., is an EBRI Fellow and associate professor at Temple University. Dr. VanDerhei was a faculty member at the Wharton School of the University of Pennsylvania for eight years. He is a coauthor of the sixth edition of *Pension Planning*, published by Richard D. Irwin, and a member of the Pension Research Council. Dr. VanDerhei has served as a consultant for the Pension Benefit Guaranty Corporation, U.S. Department of Labor, and the International Foundation of Employee Benefit Plans. He holds a B.B.A. and an M.B.A. from the University of Wisconsin and an M.A. and a Ph.D. from the Wharton School.

**Paul Yakoboski**, Ph.D., is a research associate with EBRI. Before joining EBRI, he was a Senior Economist with the Human Resources Division of the U.S. General Accounting Office. He earned his Ph.D. in economics at the University of Rochester.

# I. Appraising Public Policy for Private Retirement Plans

BY THOMAS PAINE

## Introduction

In the last half century, the United States has followed retirement policies that employ multiple sources of support, governmental and private. Basic protection is provided by Old-Age, Survivors, and Disability Insurance (OASDI), the federal government's virtually universal program. Supplementation in the event of severe need is available from government programs for those whose income from other sources is insufficient. Funded retirement plans cover most employees of state and local governments and a majority of the work force employed in the private sector. Individual savings add to retirement security for many persons.

The role played by these various sources of income has remained quite stable for many years. OASDI provides the basic layer of security, emphasizing high pay replacement for low-income workers and a more modest replacement ratio for middle-income persons. The mechanisms of the formula assure that benefits for new retirees will rise to keep pace with changing levels of pay in the society. Major changes recently have concerned the portion of OASDI benefits that will be taxable income rather than any adjustment in the role the system plays. Stability may be threatened 20 or more years from now, when the number of beneficiaries will grow dramatically, but for the near future continuation of OASDI's present role seems likely.

Similarly, there has been continuity in private retirement plans. After a long period of gradual growth, further spread of these programs came to a halt in the 1980s. Defined benefit pensions actually started to decline in number, although assets in trust for future benefit payments continued to grow. In the last decade there has been a significant shift in popularity toward the defined contribution plan. By the end of the 1980s, 80 percent of all private-sector retirement plans were of the defined contribution type; these plans had 39 percent of the assets, received 65 percent of the contributions, and paid 49 percent of the benefits. A pattern has emerged among private, nongovernmental plans of a combination of defined benefit and defined contribution programs among large employers and solely a defined contribution plan for smaller organizations.

While the commitment among private plans is to "stay the course," the shift in relative emphasis toward defined contribution has some consequences for the provision of old-age income assurance.

- There is no benefit promise in a defined contribution plan. The benefit equals the sum of contributions made during the period of employment plus investment earnings on assets.
- The contribution in many cases is not specified in dollars or as a percentage of pay. It may vary with company profits or the amount of employee contributions.
- Upon termination of employment prior to retirement, defined contribution plans usually pay the worker the accumulated reserve in a lump sum. Some roll over these assets into an individual retirement account (IRA); many do not.
- Upon retirement, these plans usually permit the worker a choice between a lump sum and an annuity. Most workers choose cash.

All of these characteristics operate to diminish guaranteed retirement income. Many employers seem to be saying, "We'll do what we can" rather than "We'll do our share." So far, there has not been a broad public policy debate concerning whether these trends jeopardize the success of the employer-based leg of the three-legged retirement income stool. But that issue cannot be long postponed. The success of an advance-funded retirement system is measured over a long time period. Anything that jeopardizes retirement security today will have ramifications for at least two generations.

The federal government is much better equipped to analyze trends and raise policy issues today than it has been previously. An enormous amount of knowledge of retirement plans has developed in various agencies that have some role in overseeing private pensions. Research has improved on many issues. One might expect that possible solutions would be developed, consequences measured, and legislative proposals made on how best to assure old-age income security for tomorrow's retirees.

But long-term issues such as retirement income policy are given short shrift by a government seemingly transfixed by issues of current tax revenues and operating deficits. In the debates within government, short-term revenue considerations seem to have a veto power over any suggestions for reform.

An example can illustrate the problem. The new $150,000 limit on compensation that can be used in determining pension benefits is expressed in a way that lowers permissible funding for younger workers earning as little as $35,000 per year. Less funding means less retirement security. But it also means lower employer contributions and a smaller tax loss this year for the government.

Each year there are proposals to cut further into what private plans can do. It is doubtful that this succession of proposals amounts to a conscious attempt to cripple private retirement plans. But the sum total of many years of this effort is less future security provided by funded plans. There clearly is a need to get the debate into a forum where short-term revenue considerations do not constitute a veto power over all other public policy objectives.

In discussing issues of retirement policy, two major questions bear consideration. The first is whether the private retirement system delivers enough results to be worthy of receiving the tax breaks the law provides. If the answer to the first question is yes, the second question deals with what changes can be made in rules for these plans so that they maximize their contributions to old-age security.

## Do Private Plans Deserve the Tax Breaks They Receive?

The answer to this question depends on the perceived objectives of private retirement plans. These plans do not serve the purpose of helping the poor to avoid poverty in old age. They fail this objective in two ways.
- They do not cover the universe of private employment. They are found among large employers and less frequently among smaller ones. They concentrate their coverage among middle-income workers, with a smaller percentage of lower-paid workers covered. Economics is the primary reason why private plans never can attain universal coverage. No tax incentive will be able to entice marginal businesses into sponsoring a retirement plan.
- They do not slant their benefits toward helping the lower paid. Mostly, they provide payments that are proportionate to pay and length of service. Some plans for hourly paid workers are expressed as dollar per year of service, which helps the lower-paid worker proportionately more, but the income range of the covered groups is usually quite narrow and the weighting for lower-paid workers is limited.

Thus, if the justification for the private retirement system is helping the poor, it must be judged a

failure. However, that purpose has never been assigned to the private system because OASDI does such a good job accomplishing it. Our program of social insurance is virtually universal in coverage. Its benefit formula is heavily weighted toward lower-income workers. These two characteristics make OASDI well suited to the task of assuring minimum income for most aged poor. If economic circumstances change and this goal fails to be accomplished, it is more appropriate to increase OASDI benefits than to ask the private retirement system to take on that task.

Therefore, private pensions can only be justified as worthy of tax support if they fulfill other purposes. There are three reasons for their existence.
- The income they provide in retirement helps millions of persons maintain a decent living standard. The group helped most by private pensions is middle-income workers who are paid today between $20,000 and $50,000 per year. Without benefits from private plans, many of these workers would live closer to the poverty line. Some would become dependent on old-age assistance from government.
- Private pension plans are funded in advance during a person's working years. This changes the incidence of cost from what it would be if all retirement income were to be provided on a pay-as-you-go basis. Costs are assigned to periods when wages are earned rather than when benefits are paid. One can debate where the true incidence of these costs falls. But there are changes in the demographic distribution of the population over time and with it changes in the burden of unfunded payments. Having some of that burden funded through private plans produces an ameliorating effect on the cash burdens to society.
- Private provision for retirement is consistent with American values of economic independence, frugality, and foresight. We like not being dependent on government. While these values suggest individual rather than group action through an employer, the advantages of deferred taxes on employer contributions and trust fund earnings and the ability to underwrite mortality risk argue for employer-based plans.

Are these provisions sufficient to justify favorable tax treatment for private retirement plans? For the last 50 years, these reasons have been considered sufficient to include private plans as an integral part of public policy on retirement income. There seems to be little reason to change policy now. In fact, as the nation faces an increasing burden of OASDI benefits when the baby boom generation retires, having part of the job done by an advance-funded system looks very attractive.

If retirement income policy could be reaffirmed, it would serve as a way to measure the value of changes proposed from time to time. There should be some criterion other than the impact on the current federal budget and the deficit. Otherwise, we could inflict serious damage on the private system for the wrong reasons.

## How Can Retirement Income from Private Pension Plans Be Maximized?

Private retirement plans are never going to cover every employee in the economy. Maximizing the retirement income that can be generated from these programs means encouraging sponsorship by more employers and being sure that every dollar contributed stays in the system and purchases annuities. The trend toward defined contribution plans should not result in more money escaping in the form of lump-sum payments. Specifically, here are five suggestions for stretching private retirement plan money to provide maximum old-age income assurance.

- Simplify some of the rules applying to private plans. We want to assure that plans cover nondiscriminatory groups and the contributions are located fairly among participants. But the complexity of laws and regulations operates to discourage smaller employers from sponsoring plans. We should give up on perfect equity in order to have a simpler system that is more attractive to potential plan sponsors.
- When a worker changes jobs, no lump-sum payment should be permitted. The individual should roll the money into another employer plan or into an IRA. Those who hold several jobs during a career can have more adequate retirement income when all pieces of earned benefit are accumulated.
- The purposes of retirement plans are not fulfilled if the proceeds are paid in a lump-sum at retirement. A person can outlive his or her assets. All amounts should be paid in annuity form so that payments are guaranteed for life. If there is

objection to this suggestion as unnecessary, one could require annuity payment up to the minimum insured by the Pension Benefit Guaranty Corporation in the year of retirement, with any excess available as an annuity or in a lump sum.
- There are some respects in which the requirements of the Employee Retirement Income Security Act of 1974 (ERISA) have not been extended to participants in state and local government retirement plans. There appear to be no good reasons to continue special treatment such as less stringent funding requirements.
- Investment policies appropriate for use for retirement plans should be reviewed. The government is pressing to give employees more choice. Yet history shows that most people select fixed income portfolios, which will produce much less retirement income than a carefully managed equity portfolio when invested for a long period of time. And many employees who do choose stocks show an uncanny ability to buy high and sell low.

Probably investment choices should be maintained. But efforts should be made to put together attractive equity packages. If accumulating funds are invested in the same or similar portfolio as a fund of post-retirement assets, comparable retirement annuities can be purchased whether the market is high or low, because the value of both funds will move in similar fashion.

This has been a plea for a return to discussion of public policy for retirement benefits. There are things that need to be done to maximize the impact that funded private plans can make. The significance of the movement to defined contribution plans needs to be understood. The huge amount of spillage out of the system by lump-sum payments brings into question the public policy reason for tax support for private plans. We can see with certainty the hugh number of new retirees who will start receiving OASDI and private pension benefits soon after the turn of the century. We need to reappraise what steps we have to take to get ready.

Yet we are in a period in which short-term revenue considerations dwarf issues of long-term retirement policy. We must find a way to reorder our priorities.

# PART ONE

# WHERE IS THE PENSION SYSTEM

# II. Public and Private Pensions Today: An Overview of the System

BY CELIA SILVERMAN AND PAUL YAKOBOSKI

## Introduction

Pension plans—provided by both private and public employers—are a significant source of retirement income security for both current and future retirees. As such, they have served their social purpose quite well, yet issues remain that concern participants, providers, and policymakers. This paper serves two functions. One is to provide basic background information on the U.S. pension system, including coverage and participation rates among current workers and sources of income among today's elderly. The other is to highlight and clarify significant issues in the area of retirement income security by providing the most current data available regarding public and private defined benefit/defined contribution plan trends, plan funding levels, pension assets in the national economy, pensions as a part of individual savings, and total distributions from retirement programs and recipient rollover behavior.

## Pension Coverage and Participation

Retirement income from employment-based pension plans and the accrual of pension benefits during working years are integral parts of retirement income and savings for retirement in the United States. Employee Benefit Research Institute (EBRI) tabulations of the March 1990–1992 Current Population Surveys (CPS)[1] reveal that pension coverage[2] has risen gradually from 54.2 percent of the 119.1 million civilian, nonagricultural wage and salary workers in 1989 to 55.6 percent of the 119.8 million civilian, nonagricultural wage and salary workers in 1991. The percentage of the civilian, nonagricultural wage and salary work force who reported that they were participating[3] in an employer-sponsored pension or retirement plan grew slightly from 42.7 percent in 1989 to 43.4 percent in 1991 (table 2.1).

EBRI tabulations show that pension coverage and participation were higher than average among full-time workers and workers in the ERISA work force.[4] The percentage of full-time workers reporting pension participation grew from 50.9 percent in 1989 to 51.8 percent in 1991. The percentage of workers in the ERISA work force reporting pension coverage grew slightly between 1989 and 1991 from 65.7 percent to 66.6 percent. Pension plan participation among this work force was essentially unchanged, rising marginally from 58.3 percent to 58.5 percent over the same time period. Pension coverage and participation also vary by sector, firm size, work status, earnings, age, and gender (table 2.1).

Pension coverage and participation rates increase with income, but because of the income distribution of the population, most of those earning pensions are at lower and middle income levels. In 1991, among those earning less than $25,000 per year, 33.9 million were covered and 21.7 million participated. While this represents relatively low coverage and participation rates of 43 percent and 28 percent of all such persons, these workers represented 51.0 percent of all covered persons and 41.9 percent of all participants. Among those earning between $25,000 and $49,999 per year, 25.3 million were covered and 23.3 million participated. They represented 38.0 percent of those covered and 44.8 percent of participants. Among those earning $50,000 and over per year, 6.9 million participated, representing 13.3 percent of all participants.

Nineteen percent of workers employed by firms with fewer than 25 workers reported pension coverage in 1991, compared with 78.1 percent of workers employed by firms with 1,000 or more workers. The percentage of workers reporting that they were included in their employer's pension or retirement plan likewise increased with firm size, from 14.3 percent of workers in firms with fewer than 25 workers to

---

[1] The U.S. Department of Commerce, Bureau of the Census conducts the Current Population Survey monthly. The March survey provides supplemental data on work experience, income, noncash benefits, and migration.

[2] Workers reporting that their employer sponsored a pension or retirement plan for any of its employees in 1991.

[3] Workers reporting that they were included in their employer's pension or retirement plan in 1991.

[4] In 1974, Congress passed the Employee Retirement Income Security Act (ERISA), which set up specific pension participation standards. Generally, ERISA requires that a worker cannot be excluded from a plan because of age or service if he or she is aged 21 or older, has worked for the employer at least one year, and works 1,000 or more hours annually. Individuals who meet these criteria are more likely than workers in the general work force to accrue pension benefits and are classified as the ERISA work force.

### Table 2.1
**Employment, Pension Coverage, and Pension Plan Participation of the Civilian, Nonagricultural Wage and Salary Work Force and the ERISA Work Force, 1989–1991, and Characteristics of Plan Participants, 1991**

| | Employment (millions) | | | Employer Sponsors Plan[a] (percentage) | | | Employee Included in Plan[b] (percentage) | | | Characteristics of Employees Included in Plans—1991 | |
|---|---|---|---|---|---|---|---|---|---|---|---|
| | 1989 | 1990 | 1991 | 1989 | 1990 | 1991 | 1989 | 1990 | 1991 | (millions) | (percentage) |
| General Work Force | 119.1 | 119.3 | 119.8 | 54.2% | 55.3% | 55.6% | 42.7% | 42.9% | 43.4% | 52.0 | 100.0% |
| **Sector[c]** | | | | | | | | | | | |
| Private | 103.9 | 104.5 | 105.4 | 54.6 | 55.6 | 55.7 | 43.2 | 43.4 | 43.7 | 46.0 | 88.6 |
| manufacturing | 21.5 | 21.2 | 20.6 | 66.2 | 66.9 | 66.2 | 56.1 | 56.7 | 56.1 | 34.5 | 66.4 |
| nonmanufacturing | 82.4 | 83.3 | 84.8 | 51.5 | 52.7 | 53.2 | 39.8 | 40.0 | 40.7 | 11.6 | 22.2 |
| Public | 5.7 | 5.6 | 5.6 | 88.4 | 88.8 | 90.5 | 82.1 | 80.7 | 83.4 | 4.7 | 9.0 |
| Other | 9.5 | 9.2 | 8.8 | 29.8 | 32.2 | 32.4 | 14.0 | 4.5 | 14.3 | 1.3 | 2.4 |
| **Firm Size** | | | | | | | | | | | |
| Fewer than 25 workers | 28.2 | 28.7 | 28.5 | 18.5 | 18.6 | 19.2 | 13.6 | 13.6 | 14.3 | 4.1 | 7.9 |
| 25–99 workers | 16.9 | 16.5 | 16.7 | 38.3 | 41.2 | 40.5 | 29.4 | 31.2 | 30.7 | 5.1 | 9.9 |
| 100–499 workers | 18.1 | 18.3 | 18.3 | 57.8 | 59.5 | 59.6 | 45.8 | 45.6 | 45.9 | 8.4 | 16.1 |
| 500–999 workers | 7.3 | 7.0 | 7.2 | 69.9 | 70.9 | 70.8 | 54.8 | 54.6 | 55.7 | 4.0 | 7.7 |
| 1,000 or more workers | 48.6 | 48.7 | 49.1 | 76.7 | 78.0 | 78.1 | 61.3 | 61.5 | 61.8 | 30.3 | 58.4 |
| **Hours Worked** | | | | | | | | | | | |
| Part time[d] | 25.0 | 25.1 | 25.7 | 30.5 | 32.4 | 32.4 | 11.7 | 12.5 | 12.3 | 3.2 | 6.1 |
| Full time[e] | 94.0 | 94.2 | 94.1 | 60.5 | 61.4 | 61.9 | 50.9 | 51.0 | 51.8 | 48.8 | 93.9 |
| **Age** | | | | | | | | | | | |
| Under 25 years | 23.4 | 22.6 | 21.7 | 32.1 | 33.0 | 33.4 | 12.8 | 12.4 | 12.5 | 2.7 | 5.2 |
| 25–44 years | 62.5 | 63.1 | 63.6 | 58.7 | 60.0 | 59.2 | 47.9 | 48.2 | 47.6 | 30.3 | 58.2 |
| 45–64 years | 29.4 | 29.8 | 30.9 | 63.8 | 64.0 | 65.5 | 57.3 | 56.7 | 58.3 | 18.0 | 34.7 |
| 65 years and over | 3.7 | 3.8 | 3.6 | 42.4 | 43.4 | 42.3 | 28.4 | 27.9 | 26.6 | 0.9 | 1.8 |
| **Annual Earnings** | | | | | | | | | | | |
| Less than $10,000 | 38.2 | 36.8 | 36.1 | 27.9 | 29.1 | 28.9 | 10.7 | 10.3 | 10.1 | 3.6 | 7.0 |
| $10,000–$24,999 | 43.2 | 43.0 | 42.1 | 57.2 | 56.9 | 55.9 | 45.6 | 44.2 | 43.1 | 18.1 | 34.9 |
| $25,000–$49,999 | 30.1 | 31.2 | 32.4 | 77.5 | 78.0 | 78.1 | 71.6 | 71.2 | 71.8 | 23.3 | 44.8 |
| $50,000 and over | 7.6 | 8.3 | 9.2 | 77.1 | 78.3 | 80.1 | 73.1 | 74.0 | 75.6 | 6.9 | 13.3 |
| **Gender** | | | | | | | | | | | |
| Men | 62.1 | 62.1 | 62.3 | 56.1 | 57.2 | 57.1 | 44.6 | 46.9 | 46.8 | 29.1 | 56.1 |
| Women | 56.9 | 57.2 | 57.5 | 52.1 | 53.3 | 54.0 | 38.5 | 38.6 | 39.7 | 22.8 | 43.9 |
| ERISA Work Force[f] | 68.7 | 69.9 | 70.9 | 65.7 | 66.4 | 66.6 | 58.3 | 58.4 | 58.5 | 41.5 | 100.0 |

Source: Employee Benefit Research Institute tabulations of the March 1990, March 1991 and March 1992 Current Population Survey.

Note: Numbers and percentages may not add to totals due to rounding.

[a] Employees reporting that their employer had a pension plan or a retirement plan for any of its employees at any job they held in 1989, 1990, and 1991.

[b] Employees reporting that they participated in a pension plan or a retirement plan at any job they held in 1989, 1990, and 1991.

[c] Refers to longest job held during the year.

[d] Employees reporting that they usually worked fewer than 35 hours per week at this job.

[e] Employees reporting that they usually worked 35 or more hours per week at this job.

[f] Civilian, nonagricultural wage and salary workers aged 21 and older with at least one year of tenure who reported in the following March that they worked 1,000 or more hours in that year. A proxy for tenure was created because the March Current Population Survey does not include that variable. An employee is assumed to have at least one year of tenure if he or she reported having only one employer in the previous year and had worked 50 or more weeks during that year.

61.8 percent of workers employed by firms with 1,000 or more workers. While most plan participants were employed by large employers, 17.8 percent of pension plan participants worked for firms with fewer than 100 employees in 1991. The relatively low level of pension coverage among small firms figures significantly in assessing the prospects for the future of pension coverage. EBRI tabulations of the March 1992 CPS reveal that employers with fewer than 100 workers accounted for 37.8 percent of all workers in 1991. Policymakers would like small employers to establish pension plans, but even when marginal tax rates were high, regulation limited, and competition less strenuous most small employers did not sponsor plans. For these employers, the cost of Social Security is also a significant expense. As a result, it can generally be assumed that there will never be significant voluntary pension growth among small employers.

Workers in the 45–64 age group reported the highest rate of pension coverage for 1991 (65.5 percent). This compares with only 33.4 percent of workers under age 25 who reported coverage. Plan participation was also greatest among workers aged 45–64 (58.3 percent). Only 12.5 percent of workers under age 25 reported participating in their employer's plan. Pension plan participants aged 45–64 accounted for 34.7 percent of pension plan participants in 1991, while participants aged 25–44 accounted for 58.2 percent. The low coverage and participation rates among the young hold down the rates for the total work force, even though the inevitability of aging means that millions are likely to move into covered jobs and become participants.

## Pension Benefit Payments and the Income of Today's Elderly

Employer pensions are an important source of retirement income for current retirees. Pension plans paid more in benefits in 1990 ($238 billion) than Social Security retirement ($223 billion). The available data actually understate pension plans' contributions to retirement income because they do not include lump-sum distributions made prior to and at retirement. In spite of this, the number of retirees with pension income continues to grow. Forty-four percent of all aged households reported pension income in 1990 (Grad, 1992). According to the 1991 Advisory Council on Social Security, the percentage of elderly families receiving income from employer-sponsored pensions is expected to increase from the current 44 percent to 76 percent by the year 2018 (Reno, 1992). Among married couples currently aged 45 to 59, nearly 70 percent are earning a pension right, and others who are not now participating

in a pension plan report a pension right from a former employer (Goodfellow and Schieber, 1992).

In 1990, private pension benefits, estimated by the Department of Commerce at $143.9 billion, accounted for 31.2 percent of the $460.9 billion in total estimated retirement benefit payments (table 2.2). By comparison, private pension benefits totaled $7.4 billion and accounted for 16.0 percent of total retirement benefit payments in 1970. Combined with benefits paid by the federal civilian and military retirement system and state and local government employee retirement systems, employer payments of $237.9 billion accounted for 51.6 percent of total benefits in 1990. Social Security benefits for retirees and their spouses and dependents totaled $223.0 billion and accounted for the other 48.4 percent of total benefits (table 2.2).

Pension payments to individuals have increased over the years as the public and private pension systems have matured. Table 2.3 demonstrates the maturity of the pension system, with 44 percent of retirees reporting pension income in 1990, compared with 31 percent in 1976. In fact, with the exception of earnings and public assistance (excluding Social Security), the percentage of elderly persons receiving income from different sources has broadened since 1976. Social Security recipiency increased from 89 percent to 92 percent of single individuals and married couples aged 65 and over between 1976 and 1990. Additionally, 69 percent of these individuals and married couples received income from assets in 1990, up from 56 percent in 1976 (table 2.3).

Between 1976 and 1990, the relative composition of the elderly's aggregate income remained fairly stable except for income from assets and earnings. Income from private employer-sponsored pension plans accounted for 9 percent of the elderly's income in 1990, up from 7 percent in 1976. Income from pension plans sponsored by public employers accounted for 9 percent of the elderly's income, compared with 6 percent in 1976. Social Security benefits made up 36 percent of the elderly's income in 1990, down from 39 percent in 1976. Eighteen percent of the elderly's income was attributable to earnings in 1990, down from 23 percent in 1976. Income from assets accounted for 25 percent of the elderly's income in 1990, up from 18 percent in 1976 (table 2.4).

Again, these numbers represent annuity payments only, so that the billions of dollars now paid each year in lump-sum distributions and taken into income would result in earnings reported as asset income. As the pension system continues to change, it will become increasingly important to find a way to identify this pension-created wealth. The growth in the employment-based pension numbers discussed above

## Table 2.2
## Retirement Benefit Payments from Private and Public Sources, Selected Years 1970–1990

| Source of Benefit[a] | 1970 | 1975 | 1980 | 1985 | 1986 | 1987 | 1988 | 1989 | 1990 |
|---|---|---|---|---|---|---|---|---|---|
| | | | | | ($ billions) | | | | |
| Private Pensions | $7.4 | $15.9 | $36.4 | $97.7 | $120.2 | $120.8 | $124.1 | $131.7 | $143.9 |
| Federal Employee Retirement[b] | 6.2 | 14.5 | 28.0 | 41.1 | 42.2 | 44.9 | 48.1 | 50.6 | 53.9 |
| State and Local Employee Retirement | 4.0 | 8.2 | 15.1 | 25.5 | 28.4 | 31.2 | 34.1 | 36.9 | 40.1 |
| Subtotal | 17.6 | 38.6 | 79.5 | 164.3 | 190.8 | 196.9 | 206.3 | 219.2 | 237.9 |
| Social Security Old-Age and Survivors Insurance Benefit Payments[c] | $28.8 | $58.5 | $105.1 | $167.2 | $176.8 | $183.6 | $195.5 | $208.0 | $223.0 |
| Total | $46.4 | $97.1 | $184.6 | $331.5 | $367.6 | $380.5 | $401.8 | $427.2 | $460.9 |
| Total | 100.0% | 100.0% | 100.0% | 100.0% | 100.0% | 100.0% | 100.0% | 100.0% | 100.0% |
| | | | | | (percentage of total) | | | | |
| Private Pensions | 16.0 | 16.4 | 19.7 | 29.5 | 32.7 | 31.8 | 30.9 | 30.8 | 31.2 |
| Federal Employee Retirement[b] | 13.4 | 14.9 | 15.2 | 12.4 | 11.5 | 11.8 | 12.0 | 11.8 | 11.7 |
| State and Local Employee Retirement | 8.6 | 8.4 | 8.2 | 7.7 | 7.7 | 8.2 | 8.5 | 8.6 | 8.7 |
| Subtotal | 37.9 | 39.8 | 43.1 | 49.6 | 51.9 | 51.8 | 51.3 | 51.3 | 51.6 |
| Social Security Old-Age and Survivors Insurance Benefit Payments[c] | 62.1 | 60.3 | 56.9 | 50.4 | 48.1 | 48.3 | 48.7 | 48.7 | 48.4 |

Source: Employee Benefit Research Institute tabulations based on U.S. Department of Commerce, Bureau of Economic Analysis, *Survey of Current Business, January 1992* (Washington, DC: U.S. Government Printing Office, 1992); *The National Income and Products Accounts of the United States: Statistical Supplement, 1959–1988*, Vol. 2 (Washington, DC: U.S. Government Printing Office, 1992); and U.S. Department of Health and Human Services, Social Security Administration, *1991 Annual Report of the Board of Trustees of the Federal Old-Age and Survivors Insurance and Disability Insurance Trust Funds* (Baltimore, MD: Social Security Administration, 1991).
[a]Includes only employment-based retirement benefits.
[b]Includes civilian and military employees.
[c]Includes payments to retired workers and their wives, husbands, and children.

### Table 2.3
### Percentage of Single Individuals and Married Couples[a] Aged 65 and Over with Income from Specified Sources, Selected Years 1976–1990

| Source of Income[b] | 1976 | 1978 | 1980 | 1982 | 1984 | 1986 | 1988 | 1990 |
|---|---|---|---|---|---|---|---|---|
| | (millions) | | | | | | | |
| Number | 17.3 | 18.2 | 19.2 | 19.9 | 20.8 | 21.6 | 22.3 | 23.1 |
| Percentage with | | | | | | | | |
| Retirement benefits | 92% | 93% | 93% | 93% | 94% | 94% | 95% | 95% |
| Social Security[c] | 89 | 90 | 90 | 90 | 91 | 91 | 92 | 92 |
| Retirement benefits other | | | | | | | | |
| than Social Security | 31 | 32 | 34 | 35 | 38 | 40 | 42 | 44 |
| railroad retirement | 3 | 3 | 2 | 2 | 2 | 2 | 2 | 2 |
| government employee pensions | 9 | 10 | 12 | 12 | 14 | 14 | 14 | 15 |
| private pension or annuities | 20 | 21 | 22 | 23 | 24 | 27 | 29 | 30 |
| Earnings | 25 | 25 | 23 | 22 | 21 | 20 | 22 | 22 |
| Income from assets | 56 | 62 | 66 | 68 | 68 | 67 | 68 | 69 |
| Veterans' benefits | 6 | 5 | 5 | 4 | 5 | 5 | 5 | 5 |
| Public assistance | 11 | 10 | 10 | 16 | 16 | 7 | 7 | 7 |

Source: Susan Grad and Karen Foster, *Income of the Population 55 and Over, 1976*, U.S. Department of Health, Education, and Welfare, pub. no. 13-11865 (Washington, DC: U.S. Government Printing Office, 1979); Susan Grad, *Income of the Population 55 and Over*, 1978, 1980, 1982, and 1984, U.S. Department of Health and Human Services, Social Security Administration, pub. no. 13-11871 (Washington, DC: U.S. Government Printing Office, 1981–1985); and Susan Grad, *Income of the Population 55 or Older, 1986*, U.S. Department of Health and Human Services, Social Security Administration, pub. no. 13-11871 (Washington, DC: U.S. Government Printing Office, 1988); Susan Grad, *Income of the Population 55 or Older, 1988*, U.S. Department of Health and Human Services, Social Security Administration, pub. no. 13-11871 (Washington, DC: U.S. Government Printing Office, 1990); and Susan Grad, *Income of the Population 55 or Older, 1990*, U.S. Department of Health and Human Services, Social Security Administration, pub. no. 13-11871 (Washington, DC: U.S. Government Printing Office, 1992).

[a]Couples are included if they are married, living together, and at least one is aged 65 or over.

[b]Receipt of sources is ascertained by a yes/no response to a question that is imputed by the Current Population Survey for 1976–1986. A married couple is counted as receiving a source if one or both persons are recipients of that source. Data for 1988 and 1990 are from the Survey of Income and Program Participation.

[c]Recipients of Social Security may be receiving retired-worker benefits, dependents' or survivors' benefits, transitionally insured, or special age 72 benefits. Transitionally insured benefits are monthly benefits paid to certain persons born before January 2, 1987. The special age 72 benefit is a monthly benefit payable to men who reached age 72 before 1972 and to women who reached age 72 before 1970 and who do not have sufficient quarters of coverage to qualify for a retired worker benefit either under the fully or transitionally insured states provisions.

Table 2.4
**Composition of the Elderly's Income Over Time**

*Shares of Aggregate Income of Married Couples[a] and Unmarried Persons Aged 65 and Over: Percentage Distribution of Income from All Sources, Selected Years 1976–1990*

| Source of Income | 1976 | 1978 | 1980 | 1982 | 1984 | 1986 | 1988 | 1990 |
|---|---|---|---|---|---|---|---|---|
| Total Percentage | 100% | 100% | 100% | 100% | 100% | 100% | 100% | 100% |
| Percentage of Income from | | | | | | | | |
| Retirement Benefits | 55 | 54 | 55 | 54 | 53 | 54 | 55 | 55 |
| Social Security[b] | 39 | 38 | 39 | 39 | 38 | 38 | 38 | 36 |
| Railroad retirement | 1 | 1 | 1 | 1 | 1 | 1 | 1 | 1 |
| Government employee pensions | 6 | 6 | 7 | 7 | 7 | 7 | 9 | 9 |
| Private pension or annuities[b] | 7 | 7 | 7 | 6 | 6 | 7 | 8 | 9 |
| Earnings | 23 | 23 | 19 | 18 | 16 | 17 | 17 | 18 |
| Income from Assets | 18 | 19 | 22 | 25 | 28 | 26 | 25 | 25 |
| Public Assistance | 2 | 2 | 1 | 1 | 1 | 1 | 1 | 1 |
| Other | 2 | 2 | 3 | 2 | 2 | 2 | 2 | 2 |

Source: Susan Grad and Karen Foster, *Income of the Population 55 and Over, 1976*, U.S. Department of Health, Education, and Welfare, pub. no. 13-11865 (Washington, DC: U.S. Government Printing Office, 1979); Susan Grad, *Income of the Population 55 and Over*, 1978, 1980, 1982, and 1984, U.S. Department of Health and Human Services, Social Security Administration, pub. no. 13-11871 (Washington, DC: U.S. Government Printing Office, 1981–1985); Susan Grad, *Income of the Population 55 or Older, 1988*, U.S. Department of Health and Human Services, Social Security Administration, pub. no. 13-11871 (Washington, DC: U.S. Government Printing Office, 1990); and Susan Grad, *Income of the Population 55 or Older, 1990*, U.S. Department of Health and Human Services, Social Security Administration, pub. no. 13-11871 (Washington, DC: U.S. Government Printing Office, 1992).

[a]Couples are included if they are married, living together, and at least one is aged 65 or older.

[b]Recipients of Social Security may be receiving retired-worker benefits, dependents' or survivors' benefits, transitionally insured, or special age 72 benefits. Transitionally insured benefits are monthly benefits paid to certain persons born before January 2, 1987. The special age 72 benefit is a monthly benefit payable to men who reached age 72 before 1972 and to women who reached age 72 before 1970 and who do not have sufficient quarters of coverage to qualify for a retired worker benefit either under the fully or transitionally insured states provisions.

(tables 2.3 and 2.4) would be significantly greater if all income attributable to past pension distributions could be documented.

While 93 percent of the elderly married couples and 91 percent of elderly unmarried individuals receive Social Security benefits, the percentage receiving income from pensions and assets varies by marital status and income. Elderly married couples are more likely to receive income from pensions, earnings, and assets than elderly unmarried persons. Sixty-three percent of elderly married couples receive income from an employer pension, 34 percent receive income from earnings, and 79 percent receive income from assets. The corresponding figures for elderly unmarried individuals are 36 percent, 13 percent, and 63 percent. However, pension recipiency, earnings, and income from assets are more prevalent among those with higher incomes, regardless of marital status (table 2.5).

The composition of the elderly's income also varies by marital status and income. Retirement benefits amounted to 52 percent of total income for married couples and 60 percent of income for unmarried persons aged 65 and over in 1990. Social Security

provided 32 percent of aggregate income for married couples and 44 percent of total income for unmarried persons. Elderly married couples received 23 percent of their aggregate income from earnings, whereas unmarried persons received only 10 percent of their aggregate income from this source. Earnings and income from assets were a larger source of income for higher-income individuals and couples in 1990, while Social Security benefits and other public assistance programs contributed proportionally more to the total income of low-income elderly couples and individuals (table 2.6).

# Private and Public Plan Trends

## Definitions

Primary plan data reflect the number of pension plans intended to provide the primary source of employment-based retirement income. Active participants in these plans are the number of current employees that are participating in the plan. Use of primary plan active participant counts reduces double counting of employees that are in supplemental and primary plans or that

Table 2.5
## Sources of the Elderly's Income

*Income Sources by Levels of Total Income and Marital Status: Percentage of Married Couples and Unmarried Persons Aged 65 and Over with Income from Specified Sources by Quintile, 1990*

| Source of Income | Married Couples[a] (by quintile maximum) | | | | | | Unmarried Individuals (by quintile maximum) | | | | | |
|---|---|---|---|---|---|---|---|---|---|---|---|---|
| | Total | $13,066 | $19,573 | $27,680 | $41,881 | Greater than $41,881 | Total | $5,416 | $7,729 | $11,087 | $17,960 | Greater than $17,960 |
| Number (thousands) | 9,343 | 1,883 | 1,846 | 1,881 | 1,864 | 1,868 | 13,805 | 2,801 | 2,722 | 2,782 | 2,744 | 2,757 |
| Total Percentage | 100% | 100% | 100% | 100% | 100% | 100% | 100% | 100% | 100% | 100% | 100% | 100% |
| **Percentage with Income from** | | | | | | | | | | | | |
| Retirement benefits | 96% | 93% | 98% | 98% | 97% | 91% | 94% | 82% | 97% | 99% | 98% | 93% |
| Social Security[b] | 93 | 92 | 95 | 96 | 94 | 86 | 91 | 81 | 96 | 96 | 94 | 89 |
| railroad retirement[b] | 2 | 1 | 2 | 2 | 2 | 1 | 2 | c | 1 | 3 | 3 | 1 |
| government employee pensions[b] | 20 | 5 | 15 | 22 | 30 | 29 | 12 | 2 | 4 | 8 | 17 | 28 |
| private pensions or annuities[b] | 41 | 15 | 41 | 52 | 55 | 43 | 22 | 3 | 10 | 24 | 37 | 39 |
| Earnings | 34 | 12 | 25 | 34 | 43 | 57 | 13 | 4 | 6 | 10 | 19 | 27 |
| Income from assets | 79 | 46 | 73 | 84 | 94 | 98 | 63 | 27 | 43 | 65 | 84 | 94 |
| Public assistance | 3 | 10 | 3 | 1 | c | c | 9 | 26 | 13 | 6 | 1 | c |
| Veterans' benefits | 7 | 6 | 8 | 6 | 8 | 8 | 4 | 3 | 5 | 4 | 3 | 4 |

Source: Susan Grad, *Income of the Population 55 or Older, 1990*, U.S. Department of Health and Human Services, Social Security Administration, pub. no. 13-11871 (Washington, DC: U.S. Government Printing Office, 1992).

aCouples are included if they are married, living together, and at least one is aged 65 or over.
bAmounts of Social Security and railroad retirement are excluded from the separate items listed for persons receiving both sources because the Current Population Survey questionnaire asks for the combined amount. Similarly, amounts of government employee pensions and private pensions are excluded from the items listed for persons receiving both sources. All pension income is included in the retirement benefits category.
cLess than 0.5 percent.

## Table 2.6
## Composition of the Elderly's Income

*Shares of Aggregate Income of Married Couples and Unmarried Persons Aged 65 and Over by Levels of Total Income and Marital Status: Percentage Distribution of Income from Particular Sources by Quintile, 1990*

| Source of Income | Married Couples[a] (by quintile maximum) | | | | | | Unmarried Individuals (by quintile maximum) | | | | | |
|---|---|---|---|---|---|---|---|---|---|---|---|---|
| | Total | $13,066 | $19,573 | $27,680 | $41,881 | Greater than $41,881 | Total | $5,416 | $7,729 | $11,087 | $17,960 | Greater than $17,960 |
| Number (thousands) | 9,343 | 1,883 | 1,846 | 1,881 | 1,864 | 1,868 | 13,805 | 2,801 | 2,722 | 2,782 | 2,744 | 2,757 |
| Total Percentage | 100% | 100% | 100% | 100% | 100% | 100% | 100% | 100% | 100% | 100% | 100% | 100% |
| **Percentage of Income from** | | | | | | | | | | | | |
| Retirement benefits[b] | 52% | 85% | 79% | 68% | 58% | 32% | 60% | 79% | 86% | 82% | 68% | 42% |
| Social Security[b] | 32 | 79 | 62 | 46 | 32 | 14 | 44 | 77 | 82 | 72 | 49 | 21 |
| railroad retirement[b] | 1 | 1 | 1 | 1 | 1 | c | 1 | c | 1 | 2 | 2 | 1 |
| government employee pensions[b] | 9 | 2 | 6 | 9 | 12 | 9 | 8 | 2 | 2 | 4 | 8 | 12 |
| private pensions or annuities[b] | 10 | 3 | 9 | 12 | 13 | 9 | 7 | 1 | 2 | 5 | 9 | 9 |
| Earnings | 23 | 4 | 9 | 13 | 19 | 34 | 10 | 1 | 2 | 3 | 8 | 15 |
| Income from assets | 24 | 6 | 9 | 16 | 21 | 33 | 26 | 3 | 5 | 11 | 21 | 40 |
| Public assistance | c | 3 | 1 | c | c | c | 2 | 15 | 5 | 1 | 1 | c |
| Other | 2 | 2 | 3 | 2 | 3 | 2 | 3 | 2 | 2 | 2 | 3 | 3 |

Source: Susan Grad, *Income of the Population 55 or Older, 1990*, U.S. Department of Health and Human Services, Social Security Administration, pub. no. 13-11871 (Washington, DC: U.S. Government Printing Office, 1992).
aCouples are included if they are married, living together, and at least one is aged 65 or over.
bAmounts of Social Security and railroad retirement are excluded from the separate items listed for persons receiving both sources because the Current Population Survey questionnaire asks for the combined amount. Similarly, amounts of government employee pensions and private pensions are excluded from the items listed for persons receiving both sources. All pension income is included in the retirement benefits category.
cLess than 0.5 percent.

have left an employer and are participating in another employment-based plan. Employees that participate in multiple primary plans because they hold more than one job are still double counted in primary plan active participant counts. Active participant counts also consider only those employees currently working for an employer, allowing evaluation of work force trends.

Total counts of plans include both primary and supplemental pension plans. Total counts of participants count the participants in these plans, double counting participants for each plan in which they participate. Total counts of active participants include active participants in both primary and supplemental plans. Total counts of all participants include active, retired , and separated vested participants, and survivors in both primary and supplemental plans. These counts provide a picture of the number of total participants in a plan whether or not they are still employed by the plan sponsor.

## Private Plan and Participation Trends

Between 1975, when ERISA became effective, and 1989, the latest year for which these data are available, the total number of private tax-qualified employer sponsored plans more than doubled from 311,000 to 731,000. The total number of participants in these plans, including active workers, separated vested, survivors, and retirees rose from 45 million to 76 million over the same period (table 2.7). Data on active participants in private primary plans shows similar trends. The number of active participants increased from 31 million in 1975 to 43 million in 1989.

While the number of private employer-sponsored pension plans and plan participants has been increasing, proportionately fewer of these plans are defined benefit plans. An increasing number of employers have been offering primary and supplemental defined contribution plans, as well as a diverse array of plans combining features of defined benefit and defined contribution plans, or hybrid plans. The total number of private defined benefit plans increased from 103,000 in 1975 to 175,000 in 1983, decreasing to 132,000 by 1989. The total number of private defined contribution plans increased from 208,000 to 599,000 between 1975 and 1989, increasing from 67 percent to 82 percent of total private pension plans (table 2.7).

An increasing number and percentage of individuals are participating in private defined contribution plans relative to defined benefit plans. The total number of participants in all defined benefit plans was 33 million in 1975. Participation increased to 40 million in 1983 and has remained in the 40–41 million range since that time. Since 1975, the total number of participants in defined contribution plans increased from

12 million in 1975 to 38 million in 1987, decreasing to 36 million in 1989 (table 2.7). According to unpublished data by the U.S. Department of Labor, the decline in the total number of participants in defined contribution plans was due to the termination of several large supplemental employee stock ownership plans (ESOPs).

Active participants in private primary plans show trends similar to total participants. In 1975 and 1989, there were 27 million active participants in primary defined benefit plans. The number of active participants in primary defined benefit plans has remained in the range of 27 million to 30 million since 1975, gradually decreasing between 1984 and 1989 from 30 million to 27 million. Between 1975 and 1989, the number of active participants with a primary defined contribution plan significantly increased from 4 million to 15 million. Between 1975 and 1988, the number of active participants with a supplemental defined contribution plan increased from 6 million to 16 million (table 2.7).

More recent data from the Internal Revenue Service's (IRS) Office of Employee Plans and Exempt Organizations indicate a recent slowing of the defined contribution growth trend may be occurring. When requested, the IRS Office of Employee Plans and Exempt Organizations issues determination letters regarding the tax-favored status of private plans when they are established, amended, and terminated. Plans are not required by law to apply for these letters, and issuance of these letters may precede (or more commonly follow) the relevant plan transactions by a year or more. While IRS determination letter activity is at best an imperfect measure of plan starts and terminations, it gives some insight into more current plan and participant trends.

In fiscal 1990, the number of favorable letters issued regarding defined contribution terminations exceeded the number issued in response to initial defined contribution applications for the first time since the passage of ERISA.[5] The two were equal in fiscal 1991; however, the number of favorable applications for defined contribution plans in 1992 slightly exceeded the number of termination applications, with 14,000 initial applications and 11,000 termination applications (table 2.8).

IRS determination letter statistics also indicate that the decline in the number of defined benefit plans may be flattening. While the number of favorable letters issued regarding defined benefit plan applications has been declining since 1989, and the number of

---

[5]The fiscal year ends September 30.

## Table 2.7
## Private Plan Trends
### Summary of Private-Sector Qualified Defined Benefit and Defined Contribution Plan Trends, 1975–1989

| | 1975 | 1976 | 1977 | 1978 | 1979 | 1980 | 1981 | 1982 | 1983 | 1984 | 1985 | 1986 | 1987 | 1988 | 1989 |
|---|---|---|---|---|---|---|---|---|---|---|---|---|---|---|---|
| **Total Plans** *(thousands)* | 311 | 360 | 403 | 443 | 471 | 489 | 546 | 594 | 603 | 601 | 632 | 718 | 733 | 730 | 731 |
| Defined benefit[a] | 103 | 114 | 122 | 128 | 139 | 148 | 167 | 175 | 175 | 165 | 170 | 173 | 163 | 146 | 132 |
| Defined contribution[a] | 208 | 246 | 281 | 315 | 331 | 341 | 378 | 419 | 428 | 436 | 462 | 545 | 570 | 584 | 599 |
| Defined contribution as percentage of total | 67% | 68% | 70% | 71% | 70% | 70% | 69% | 71% | 71% | 73% | 73% | 76% | 78% | 80% | 82% |
| **Total Participation** *(millions)* | 45 | 48 | 50 | 52 | 55 | 58 | 61 | 63 | 69 | 74 | 75 | 77 | 78 | 78 | 76 |
| Defined benefit[b] | 33 | 34 | 35 | 36 | 37 | 38 | 39 | 39 | 40 | 41 | 40 | 40 | 40 | 41 | 40 |
| Defined contribution[b] | 12 | 13 | 15 | 16 | 18 | 20 | 22 | 25 | 29 | 33 | 35 | 37 | 38 | 37 | 36 |
| Defined contribution as percentage of total | 26% | 28% | 30% | 31% | 33% | 34% | 36% | 39% | 42% | 45% | 47% | 48% | 49% | 48% | 48% |
| **Active Participants** | | | | | | | | | | | | | | | |
| Primary plan is defined benefit | 31 | 32 | 33 | 34 | 35 | 36 | 37 | 37 | 39 | 40 | 40 | 41 | 42 | 42 | 43 |
| Primary plan is defined contribution | 27 | 27 | 28 | 29 | 29 | 30 | 30 | 29 | 30 | 30 | 29 | 29 | 28 | 28 | 27 |
| Percentage with primary defined contribution | 13% | 14% | 16% | 16% | 17% | 17% | 20% | 22% | 24% | 25% | 29% | 31% | 32% | 34% | 35% |
| Supplemental defined contribution[c] | 6 | 7 | 8 | 8 | 9 | 10 | 11 | 12 | 14 | 15 | 16 | 16 | 16 | 15 | d |
| Percentage with supplemental defined contribution[c] | 19% | 22% | 23% | 24% | 27% | 28% | 29% | 32% | 36% | 39% | 40% | 39% | 39% | 36% | d |
| **Assets** *($ billions)* | $260 | $298 | $325 | $377 | $445 | $564 | $629 | $789 | $923 | $1,045 | $1,253 | $1,383 | $1,402 | $1,504 | $1,676 |
| Defined benefit | 186 | 216 | 234 | 273 | 320 | 401 | 444 | 553 | 642 | 701 | 826 | 895 | 877 | 912 | 988 |
| Defined contribution | 74 | 82 | 91 | 105 | 126 | 162 | 185 | 236 | 281 | 344 | 427 | 488 | 525 | 592 | 688 |
| Defined contribution as percentage of total | 28% | 28% | 28% | 28% | 28% | 29% | 29% | 30% | 30% | 33% | 34% | 35% | 37% | 39% | 41% |
| **Contributions** | $37 | $43 | $47 | $56 | $61 | $66 | $75 | $80 | $82 | $91 | $95 | $92 | $92 | $91 | $105 |
| Defined benefit | 24 | 29 | 31 | 38 | 41 | 43 | 47 | 48 | 46 | 47 | 42 | 33 | 30 | 26 | 25 |
| Defined contribution | 13 | 14 | 16 | 18 | 21 | 24 | 28 | 31 | 36 | 43 | 53 | 58 | 62 | 65 | 80 |
| Defined contribution as percentage of total | 35% | 33% | 34% | 33% | 34% | 36% | 38% | 39% | 44% | 48% | 56% | 64% | 68% | 71% | 76% |
| **Benefits** | $19 | $21 | $23 | $27 | $29 | $35 | $45 | $55 | $65 | $79 | $102 | $130 | $122 | $119 | $138 |
| Defined benefit | 13 | 14 | 15 | 18 | 19 | 22 | 27 | 34 | 37 | 47 | 54 | 68 | 66 | 60 | 67 |
| Defined contribution | 6 | 7 | 8 | 9 | 10 | 13 | 17 | 21 | 28 | 33 | 47 | 63 | 56 | 58 | 71 |
| Defined contribution as percentage of total | 32% | 33% | 34% | 33% | 35% | 37% | 39% | 39% | 43% | 41% | 47% | 48% | 46% | 49% | 52% |

Source: Employee Benefit Research Institute tabulations based on John A. Turner and Daniel J. Beller, eds., *Trends in Pensions*, second edition (Washington, DC: U.S. Department of Labor, 1992); U.S. Department of Labor, *Private Pension Plan Bulletin*, Abstract of 1989 Form 5500 Annual Reports, Number 1, Winter 1993 (Washington, DC: U.S. Department of Labor, 1993).
aExcludes single participant plans.
bActive, separated vested, survivors, and retired. Not adjusted for double counting of individuals participating in more than one plan.
cPrimary plan may be either defined benefit or defined contribution.
dData not available.

Table 2.8

**Trends in Favorable Determination Letters Issued by Internal Revenue Service, 1975–1992[a]**

| | Defined Benefit | | Defined Contribution | |
|---|---|---|---|---|
| | New plans | Terminations | New plans | Terminations |
| | (thousands) | | (thousands) | |
| 1975 | b | b | b | b |
| 1976 | 3[c] | c,d | 19[c] | c,d |
| 1977 | 7 | 5 | 28 | 10 |
| 1978 | 10 | 5 | 56 | 11 |
| 1979 | 16 | 3 | 41 | 8 |
| 1980 | 19 | 4 | 50 | 9 |
| 1981 | 24 | 5 | 58 | 9 |
| 1982 | 28 | 5 | 57 | 10 |
| 1983 | 22 | 7 | 42 | 11 |
| 1984 | 13 | 9 | 28 | 11 |
| 1985 | 17 | 12 | 30 | 14 |
| 1986 | 22 | 11 | 45 | 15 |
| 1987 | 16[e] | 11[e] | 40[e] | 13[e] |
| 1988 | 17[f] | 12[f] | 46[f] | 13[f] |
| 1989 | 5[f] | 16[f] | 23[f] | 13[f] |
| 1990 | 2[f] | 16[f] | 11[f] | 17[f] |
| 1991 | d,f | 10[f] | 12[f] | 12[f] |
| 1992 | d,f | 9[f] | 14[f] | 11[f] |

Source: U.S. Department of the Treasury, Internal Revenue Service, Public Affairs Division, IRS determination letter statistics obtained from various IRS news releases, 1976-1992.
[a]By fiscal year. Fiscal years of plans vary.
[b]Data not available.
[c]Includes only letters issued under post-ERISA procedures. Some letters in 1976 were issued under pre-ERISA procedures.
[d]Fewer than 500.
[e]Transitional year comprised of the first three calendar quarters of 1987.
[f]Fiscal year beginning on October 1 of prior calendar year.

terminations applications still far exceed the number of initial applications for these plans, the number of termination applications decreased from 16,000 in 1990 to 10,000 in 1991 and was less than 500 in 1992.

## Defined Benefit Plans and Participants

Examining private primary defined benefit plan trends by plan size shows that the vast majority of plan terminations were very small plans, those with 2 to 9 active participants. Between 1985 and 1989, there was a net decrease in the number of primary defined benefit plans of 22 percent, or 36,823 plans. The net number of plans with 2 to 9 active participants decreased by about 28,000 plans, or 76 percent of the total reduction in defined benefit plans (table 2.9).

Between 1985 and 1989, the net change in the number of primary defined benefit plans was generally greater for plans with fewer active participants. While the number of mid-sized defined benefit plans declined between 1985 and 1989, the decline is lesser for larger plans. The number of defined benefit plans with 10 to 24 active participants decreased 26.7 percent between 1985 and 1989, while the number of defined benefit plans with 500 to 999 active participants decreased 14.2 percent (table 2.9). Some of the change in the number of plans by plan size is due to changes in individual plans' demographics. For example, a plan that had 400 participants in 1985 may have 600 participants in 1989.

The number of large primary defined benefit plans has remained stable between 1985 and 1989. In fact, the number of plans with 10,000 to 19,999 active participants increased 7.6 percent and the number of plans with 20,000 or more participants increased 1.7 percent. The number of primary defined benefit plans with 1,000 to 2,499 active participants decreased 5.9 percent between 1985 and 1989, while the number of plans with 2,500 to 4,999 active participants and 5,000 to 9,999 active participants remained relatively constant between 1985 and 1989, decreasing 1.7 percent and 1.1 percent respectively (table 2.9).

Since the majority of the decline in defined

Table 2.9
**Primary Defined Benefit Plan and Active Participant Trends**

| Active Participants | Primary Plans | | | | Active Participants (thousands) | | | | |
| --- | --- | --- | --- | --- | --- | --- | --- | --- | --- |
| | 1985 | 1989 | Net change | Percentage change | 1985 | 1989 | Percentage Distribution of Participants 1989 | Net change | Percentage change |
| 2–9 | 88,124 | 59,966 | –28,158 | –32.0% | 353 | 246 | 0.9% | –106 | –30.1% |
| 10–24 | 24,267 | 17,791 | –6,476 | –26.7 | 369 | 271 | 1.0 | –98 | –26.5 |
| 25–49 | 14,178 | 9,736 | –4,442 | –31.3 | 491 | 340 | 1.2 | –151 | –30.7 |
| 50–99 | 11,303 | 9,013 | –2,290 | –20.3 | 808 | 645 | 2.4 | –163 | –20.2 |
| 100–249 | 9,534 | 7,109 | –2,425 | –25.4 | 1,498 | 1,135 | 4.2 | –364 | –24.3 |
| 250–499 | 4,670 | 4,022 | –648 | –13.9 | 1,651 | 1,430 | 5.2 | –221 | –13.4 |
| 500–999 | 3,149 | 2,701 | –448 | –14.2 | 2,222 | 1,910 | 7.0 | –312 | –14.0 |
| 1,000–2,499 | 2,360 | 2,220 | –140 | –5.9 | 3,636 | 3,434 | 12.6 | –202 | –5.6 |
| 2,500–4,999 | 847 | 833 | –14 | –1.7 | 2,930 | 2,940 | 10.8 | 10 | 0.3 |
| 5,000–9,999 | 455 | 450 | –5 | –1.1 | 3,141 | 3,153 | 11.6 | 12 | 0.4 |
| 10,000–19,999 | 198 | 213 | 15 | 7.6 | 2,749 | 2,956 | 10.8 | 206 | 7.5 |
| 20,000 or more | 175 | 178 | 3 | 1.7 | 8,985 | 8,792 | 32.3 | –193 | –2.1 |
| None or None Reported | 10,280 | 18,485 | 8,205 | 79.8 | – | – | – | – | – |
| Total | 169,540 | 132,717 | –36,823 | –21.7 | 28,834 | 27,252 | 100.0 | –1,582 | –5.5 |

Source: Employee Benefit Research Institute tabulations of 1985 and 1989 Form 5500 annual reports filed with the Internal Revenue Service.

benefit plans occurred in primary plans with 2 to 9 participants, the decline in the number of employees covered by a primary defined benefit plans is lessened. Approximately 78 percent of active participants in 1989 participated in defined benefit plans with 1,000 or more active participants. Even if the 112,558 plans with fewer than 1,000 participants in 1989 were to terminate, 78 percent of active participants with primary defined benefit plans would continue to accrue benefits in their pension plans, while 22 percent of defined benefit participants (6.0 million) would have their pension benefits frozen. Many of these employees would still be covered by an existing defined contribution plan or contribute to another retirement arrangement.

Trends in the number of plans and active participants by active participant plan size are almost identical to those of primary plans because there are very few supplemental defined benefit plans (table 2.10). Trends in total participants show the same general trends, but reflect the greater stability in large defined benefit plans when all participants are included in the plan size count. The net change between 1985 and 1989 in the number of defined benefit plans is positive for all plans with more than 5,000 total participants, while the net change in defined benefit plans using primary active participant size definitions is not positive until the next size category—10,000 to 19,000 primary participant plans. There is also a greater increase in the net increase in large defined benefit

plans using total participants to define plan size because more plans move into larger plan size categories when retired, survivors, and separated vested participants are included in plan size. The number of plans with greater than 2,500 total participants increased by 105 plans, while the number of plans with greater than 2,500 primary active participants decreased by one plan.

## Defined Contribution Plans and Participants

Between 1985 and 1989, there was a net increase in the number of primary defined contribution plans of 67 percent, or 233,271 plans. However, the majority of the increase in private primary defined contribution plans was in very small plans, those with 2 to 9 active participants. The net number of plans with 2 to 9 active participants increased by 135,058 plans, or 58 percent of the total increase in primary defined contribution plans (table 2.11).

The net increase in the number of primary defined contribution plans decreased as plan size increased. Primary defined contribution plans with 10 to 24 active participants increased by 36,689 plans (52 percent), while plans with 100 to 249 active participants increased by 4,456 plans (50 percent). The increase in primary defined contribution plans with 1,000 or more active participants was 452 plans, or 0.2 percent of the total increase (table 2.11).

**Pension Funding and Taxation**

## Table 2.10
### Defined Benefit Plan and Participant Trends, by Total and Active Participant Size Classes

| | Total Plans | | | | Total Participants (thousands) | | | |
|---|---|---|---|---|---|---|---|---|
| | 1985 | 1989 | Net change | Percentage change | 1985 | 1989 | Net change | Percentage change |
| **Total Participants** | | | | | | | | |
| 2–9 | 85,222 | 56,245 | −28,977 | −34.0% | 348 | 229 | −119 | −34.1% |
| 10–24 | 25,813 | 18,904 | −6,909 | −26.8 | 398 | 279 | −119 | −29.9 |
| 25–49 | 13,799 | 9,862 | −3,937 | −28.5 | 487 | 328 | −159 | −32.6 |
| 50–99 | 10,737 | 8,184 | −2,553 | −23.8 | 772 | 560 | −212 | −27.5 |
| 100–249 | 10,286 | 8,224 | −2,062 | −20.0 | 1,648 | 1,288 | −360 | −21.8 |
| 250–499 | 5,502 | 4,596 | −906 | −16.5 | 1,953 | 1,611 | −342 | −17.5 |
| 500–999 | 3,728 | 3,368 | −360 | −9.7 | 2,645 | 2,338 | −307 | −11.6 |
| 1,000–2,499 | 2,943 | 2,843 | −100 | −3.4 | 4,534 | 4,342 | −192 | −4.2 |
| 2,500–4,999 | 1,124 | 1,120 | −4 | −0.4 | 3,875 | 3,810 | −65 | −1.7 |
| 5,000–9,999 | 607 | 623 | 16 | 2.6 | 4,237 | 4,609 | 372 | 8.8 |
| 10,000–19,999 | 298 | 362 | 64 | 21.5 | 4,117 | 4,806 | 689 | 16.7 |
| 20,000 or more | 254 | 283 | 29 | 11.4 | 14,625 | 15,757 | 1,132 | 7.7 |
| None or none reported | 9,859 | 17,853 | 7,994 | 81.1 | – | – | – | – |
| Total[a] | 170,172 | 132,467 | −37,705 | −22.2 | 39,639 | 39,957 | 318 | 0.8 |
| **Active Participants** | | | | | | | | |
| 2–9 | 88,250 | 59,967 | −28,283 | −32.0% | 353 | 247 | −107 | −30.2% |
| 10–24 | 24,338 | 17,792 | −6,546 | −26.9 | 370 | 271 | −99 | −26.8 |
| 25–49 | 14,204 | 9,738 | −4,466 | −31.4 | 492 | 341 | −152 | −30.8 |
| 50–99 | 11,342 | 9,023 | −2,319 | −20.4 | 812 | 646 | −166 | −20.4 |
| 100–249 | 9,567 | 7,123 | −2,444 | −25.5 | 1,503 | 1,137 | −366 | −24.4 |
| 250–499 | 4,691 | 4,034 | −657 | −14.0 | 1,659 | 1,435 | −224 | −13.5 |
| 500–999 | 3,160 | 2,712 | −448 | −14.2 | 2,230 | 1,917 | −313 | −14.0 |
| 1,000–2,499 | 2,377 | 2,234 | −143 | −6.0 | 3,658 | 3,453 | −205 | −5.6 |
| 2,500–4,999 | 854 | 833 | −21 | −2.5 | 2,955 | 2,940 | −15 | −0.5 |
| 5,000–9,999 | 458 | 452 | −6 | −1.3 | 3,165 | 3,166 | 0 | 0.0 |
| 10,000–19,999 | 201 | 214 | 13 | 6.5 | 2,781 | 2,967 | 185 | 6.7 |
| 20,000 or more | 175 | 178 | 3 | 1.7 | 8,985 | 8,792 | −193 | −2.1 |
| None or none reported | 10,309 | 18,827 | 8,518 | 82.6 | – | – | – | – |
| Total[a] | 169,926 | 133,127 | −36,799 | −21.7 | 28,964 | 27,310 | −1,654 | −5.7 |

Source: Employee Benefit Research Institute tabulations of 1985 and 1989 Form 5500 annual reports filed with the Internal Revenue Service and EBRI tabulations based on U.S. Department of Labor, Pension and Welfare Benefits Administration, *Private Pension Plan Bulletin,* Number 1 ( Winter 1993).

[a]Total plans for both active and total plan counts differ slightly due to use of different data sources.

The net increase in the number of active participants in primary defined contribution plans is most heavily distributed to plans with fewer than 250 participants. These plans accounted for 62.1 percent of the total net increase, or 3,244,000 active participants in primary defined contribution plans. The increase in plans with 250 or more active participants accounted for an additional 1,983,000 participants (table 2.11).

The difference between the total number of defined contribution plans and the number of primary defined contribution plans reflects trends in supplemental plans. Between 1985 and 1989, the number of supplemental plans decreased by 96,571 plans, most of which were very small plans (calculated from table 2.12).

There is little difference between the total number of participants and the number of active participants included in all defined contribution plans. Approximately 2,500 additional participants are in total participant counts, distributed across most plan size categories. These participants represent individuals other than active participants that are still included in the plan such as, retired participants, participants that have separated from service and are vested in the plan, or survivors. Fewer individuals remain participants in a defined contribution plan than remain in a defined benefit plan after terminating employment with the plan sponsor because most defined contribution participants receive lump sum distributions after leaving the employer.

## Table 2.11
### Primary Defined Contribution Plan and Active Participant Trends

| Active Participants | Primary Plans | | | | Active Participants (thousands) | | | | |
|---|---|---|---|---|---|---|---|---|---|
| | 1985 | 1989 | Net change | Percentage change | 1985 | 1989 | Percentage Distribution of Participants 1989 | Net change | Percentage change |
| 2–9 | 199,704 | 334,762 | 135,058 | 67.6% | 852 | 1,410 | 8.5% | 558 | 65.5% |
| 10–24 | 70,424 | 107,113 | 36,689 | 52.1 | 1,056 | 1,637 | 9.8 | 581 | 55.0 |
| 25–49 | 31,406 | 48,351 | 16,945 | 54.0 | 1,091 | 1,680 | 10.1 | 589 | 54.0 |
| 50–99 | 17,620 | 29,997 | 12,377 | 70.2 | 1,224 | 2,081 | 12.5 | 857 | 70.0 |
| 100–249 | 8,878 | 13,334 | 4,456 | 50.2 | 1,331 | 1,991 | 12.0 | 660 | 49.6 |
| 250–499 | 2,552 | 3,599 | 1,047 | 41.0 | 868 | 1,239 | 7.4 | 371 | 42.8 |
| 500–999 | 1,185 | 1,675 | 490 | 41.4 | 808 | 1,151 | 6.9 | 343 | 42.4 |
| 1,000–2,499 | 784 | 1,148 | 364 | 46.4 | 1,194 | 1,709 | 10.3 | 514 | 43.1 |
| 2,500–4,999 | 219 | 265 | 46 | 21.0 | 752 | 907 | 5.4 | 154 | 20.5 |
| 5,000–9,999 | 97 | 107 | 10 | 10.3 | 683 | 726 | 4.4 | 43 | 6.3 |
| 10,000–19,999 | 34 | 59 | 25 | 73.5 | 460 | 788 | 4.7 | 328 | 71.4 |
| 20,000 or more | 29 | 36 | 7 | 24.1 | 1,100 | 1,329 | 8.0 | 229 | 20.8 |
| None or none reported | 13,082 | 38,839 | 25,757 | 196.9 | – | – | – | – | – |
| Total | 346,014 | 579,285 | 233,271 | 67.4 | 11,420 | 16,647 | 100.0 | 5,227 | 45.8 |

Source: Employee Benefit Research Institute tabulations of 1985 and 1989 Form 5500 annual reports filed with the Internal Revenue Service.

## Federal, State, and Local Plan and Participation Trends

Among public employers, defined benefit plans remain the dominant primary retirement plan. In state and local governments in 1990, 90 percent of full-time employees participated in a defined benefit plan.[6] The number of active participants in the major federal pension systems, Civil Service Retirement System (CSRS), Federal Employee Retirement System (FERS), and the Military Retirement System (MRS), has increased from 4.8 million in 1980 to 6.5 million in 1990, decreasing slightly to 6.1 million in 1992. The total number of participants in these plans, including participants who are retired or have left federal employment but will receive a benefit at a later date, has increased from 8.0 million in 1980 to 10.9 million in 1992 (table 2.13). In 1987, the federal government established a supplemental plan called the thrift savings plan, an optional tax-deferred plan that is similar to a private sector 401(k) for employees covered by FERS and CSRS. By the end of 1992, there were approximately 2.9 million federal employees eligible to participate in the plan. Approximately 66 percent of those eligible to participate, or 1.9 million federal employees had active accounts and 45 percent, or 1.3 million made contributions to the thrift savings plan during that year.[7]

Defined contribution plans have also gained popularity at the state and local level. In 1990, 9 percent of full-time state and local employees participated in defined contribution plans compared with 5 percent of state and local employees in 1987.[8] A few state and local governments sponsoring defined benefit plans are currently considering establishing, or have already adopted, defined contribution plans as a primary pension plan. These governments believe defined contribution plans would enable them to better control liabilities, because they would not have to be concerned with plan underfunding and investment return. On July 1, 1991, the state of West Virginia established a defined contribution plan for all newly hired employees in the teachers' system while all

---

[6] U.S. Department of Labor, Bureau of Labor Statistics, *Employee Benefits in State and Local Governments, 1990* (Washington, DC: U.S. Government Printing Office, 1992).

[7] Unpublished data from the Federal Retirement Thrift Investment Board, 1992.

[8] U.S. Department of Labor, Bureau of Labor Statistics, *Employee Benefits in State and Local Governments, 1990* (Washington, DC: U.S. Government Printing Office, 1992); and U.S. Department of Labor, Bureau of Labor Statistics, *Employee Benefits in State and Local Governments, 1987* (Washington, DC: U.S. Government Printing Office, 1988).

## Table 2.12
## Defined Contribution Plan and Participant Trends, by Total and Active Participant Size Classes

| | Total Plans | | | | Total Participants (thousands) | | | |
|---|---|---|---|---|---|---|---|---|
| | 1985 | 1989 | Net change | Percentage change | 1985 | 1989 | Net change | Percentage change |
| **Total Participants** | | | | | | | | |
| 2–9 | 270,053 | 333,695 | 63,642 | 23.57% | 1,137 | 1,373 | 236 | 20.8% |
| 10–24 | 87,214 | 107,959 | 20,745 | 23.79 | 1,321 | 1,599 | 278 | 21.0 |
| 25–49 | 38,901 | 50,956 | 12,055 | 30.99 | 1,341 | 1,679 | 338 | 25.2 |
| 50–99 | 22,718 | 32,213 | 9,495 | 41.80 | 1,577 | 2,153 | 576 | 36.5 |
| 100–249 | 12,909 | 19,197 | 6,288 | 48.71 | 1,979 | 2,829 | 850 | 43.0 |
| 250–499 | 4,586 | 6,708 | 2,122 | 46.27 | 1,587 | 2,215 | 628 | 39.6 |
| 500–999 | 2,590 | 3,669 | 1,079 | 41.66 | 1,801 | 2,429 | 628 | 34.9 |
| 1,000–2,499 | 2,003 | 2,759 | 756 | 37.74 | 3,122 | 4,088 | 966 | 30.9 |
| 2,500–4,999 | 879 | 974 | 95 | 10.81 | 3,088 | 3,096 | 8 | 0.3 |
| 5,000–9,999 | 441 | 507 | 66 | 14.97 | 3,073 | 3,363 | 290 | 9.4 |
| 10,000–19,999 | 261 | 251 | –10 | –3.83 | 3,598 | 3,311 | –287 | –8.0 |
| 20,000 or more | 224 | 193 | –31 | –13.84 | 11,231 | 8,311 | –2,920 | –26.0 |
| None or none reported | 19,160 | 39,836 | 20,676 | 107.91 | – | – | – | – |
| Total[a] | 461,939 | 598,917 | 136,978 | 29.65 | 34,855 | 36,446 | 1,591 | 4.6 |
| **Active Participants** | | | | | | | | |
| 2–9 | 270,888 | 334,816 | 63,928 | 23.6% | 1,140 | 1,410 | 270 | 23.7% |
| 10–24 | 88,168 | 107,160 | 18,992 | 21.5 | 1,318 | 1,638 | 319 | 24.2 |
| 25–49 | 34,842 | 48,437 | 13,595 | 39.0 | 1,315 | 1,683 | 369 | 28.0 |
| 50–99 | 21,660 | 30,629 | 8,969 | 41.4 | 1,513 | 2,133 | 619 | 40.9 |
| 100–249 | 12,201 | 17,383 | 5,182 | 42.5 | 1,861 | 2,652 | 791 | 42.5 |
| 250–499 | 4,334 | 5,886 | 1,552 | 35.8 | 1,497 | 2,045 | 548 | 36.6 |
| 500–999 | 2,417 | 3,247 | 830 | 34.3 | 1,683 | 2,267 | 584 | 34.7 |
| 1,000–2,499 | 1,922 | 2,483 | 561 | 29.2 | 2,987 | 3,805 | 818 | 27.4 |
| 2,500–4,999 | 862 | 858 | –4 | –0.5 | 3,026 | 2,976 | –50 | –1.7 |
| 5,000–9,999 | 423 | 442 | 19 | 4.5 | 2,984 | 3,066 | 83 | 2.8 |
| 10,000–19,999 | 246 | 222 | –24 | –9.8 | 3,419 | 3,024 | –395 | –11.5 |
| 20,000 or more | 208 | 167 | –41 | –19.7 | 10,332 | 7,273 | –3,059 | –29.6 |
| None or none reported | 18,645 | 41,786 | 23,141 | 124.1 | – | – | – | – |
| Total[a] | 456,816 | 593,516 | 136,700 | 29.9 | 33,075 | 33,972 | 898 | 2.7 |

Source: Employee Benefit Research Institute tabulations of 1985 and 1989 Form 5500 annual reports filed with the Internal Revenue Service and EBRI tabulations based on U.S. Department of Labor, Pension and Welfare Benefits Administration, *Private Pension Plan Bulletin,* Number 1 (Winter 1993).
[a]Total plans for both active and total plan counts differ slightly due to use of different data sources.

previously hired employees still participate in the states' defined benefit plan. West Virginia's defined benefit plan for teachers does not have sufficient assets to pay benefits to current retirees. By offering the defined contribution plan to all new employees, the state is able to limit its future liabilities. Alaska and Michigan have made similar proposals, which have not yet been approved.

Nearly all state and local governments sponsor primary defined benefit plans. However, economic hardships have caused a few public employers to consider limiting their defined benefit plan coverage to current employees by providing defined contribution plan coverage to new employees, particularly for

underfunded pension plans. It is possible that more state and local governments would consider sponsoring primary defined contribution plans if the funding status of their defined benefit plans worsens and/or if investment returns worsen.

## Financial Trends

### Private Plans

During any particular year, the size of employer contributions to private defined benefit plans relative to payroll can vary considerably among employers. This variation arises from many sources, including the

## Table 2.13
## Public Plan Design Trends

*Summary of Selected Public-Sector Plan Trends, 1979–1991[a]*

| | 1979 | 1981 | 1983 | 1985 | 1986 | 1987 | 1988 | 1989 | 1990 | 1991 | 1992 |
|---|---|---|---|---|---|---|---|---|---|---|---|
| | | | | | | (thousands) | | | | | |
| **Plans** | | | | | | | | | | | |
| State and local retirement systems[b] | c | 3,075 | 2,564 | 2,589 | 2,580 | 2,414 | 2,416 | 2,387 | 2,387 | c | c |
| **Total Participation[d] (thousands)** | 4,533[e] | 21,095 | 22,785 | 23,825 | 24,122 | 24,975 | 26,041 | 27,321 | 27,593 | 10,843 | 10,860[f] |
| Federal Retirement Systems[g] | 4,533 | 6,408 | 8,321 | 8,591 | 8,695 | 9,882 | 10,264 | 10,636 | 10,735 | 10,843 | 10,860 |
| defined benefit | 4,533 | 6,408 | 8,321 | 8,591 | 8,695 | 8,860 | 8,947 | 9,190 | 9,110 | 9,143 | 8,960 |
| Civil Service Retirement System | 4,533 | 4,756 | 4,754 | 4,919 | 4,970 | 4,295 | 4,261 | 4,332 | 4,167 | 4,086 | 4,014 |
| Federal Employees Retirement System | h | h | h | h | h | 800 | 924 | 1,086 | 1,180 | 1,325 | 1,367 |
| Military Service Retirement System | c | 1,652 | 3,567 | 3,672 | 3,725 | 3,765 | 3,762 | 3,790 | 3,763 | 3,732 | 3,579 |
| defined contribution | | | | | | 1,022 | 1,317 | 1,446 | 1,625 | 1,700 | 1,900 |
| Thrift Savings Plan[j] | | | | | | 1,022 | 1,317 | 1,446 | 1,625 | 1,700 | 1,900 |
| defined contribution as percentage of total | | | | | | 10% | 13% | 14% | 15% | 16% | 17% |
| State and local retirement systems[b,k] | c | 14,687 | 14,464 | 15,234 | 15,426 | 15,093 | 15,777 | 16,684 | 16,858 | c | c |
| **Active Participants (thousands)** | 2,700[e] | 13,374 | 14,844 | 15,356 | 15,548 | 16,813 | 16,958 | 17,785 | 17,856 | 6,250 | 6,098[f] |
| Federal retirement systems[g] | 2,700 | 3,043 | 4,838 | 4,992 | 5,019 | 6,069 | 6,225 | 6,427 | 6,511 | 6,250 | 6,098 |
| defined benefit | 2,700 | 3,043 | 4,838 | 4,992 | 5,019 | 5,109 | 5,126 | 5,158 | 5,092 | 5,050 | 4,798 |
| Civil Service Retirement System | 2,700 | 2,755 | 2,690 | 2,800 | 2,800 | 2,080 | 2,011 | 1,918 | 1,826 | 1,726 | 1,654 |
| Federal Employees Retirement System | h | h | h | h | h | 800 | 919 | 1,052 | 1,136 | 1,260 | 1,276 |
| Military Service Retirement System[l] | c | 288 | 2,148 | 2,192 | 2,219 | 2,229 | 2,196 | 2,188 | 2,130 | 2,064 | 1,868 |
| defined contribution | | | | | | 960 | 1,099 | 1,269 | 1,419 | 1,200 | 1,300 |
| Thrift Savings Plan[j] | | | | | | 960 | 1,099 | 1,269 | 1,419 | 1,200 | 1,300 |
| defined contribution as percentage of total | | | | | | 16% | 18% | 20% | 22% | 19% | 21% |
| State and local retirement systems[b,l] | c | 10,330 | 10,005 | 10,364 | 10,529 | 10,744 | 10,732 | 11,357 | 11,345 | c | c |
| | | | | | | ($ billions) | | | | | |
| **Assets** | $226 | $294 | $400 | $529 | $622 | $732 | $825 | $922 | $1,047 | $367[f] | c |
| Federal retirement systems[g] | 64 | 83 | 110 | 154 | 186 | 219 | 262 | 289 | 326 | 367 | c |
| defined benefit | 64 | 83 | 110 | 154 | 186 | 218 | 260 | 284 | 318 | 355 | 394 |
| Civil Service Retirement System | 64 | 83 | 110 | 142 | 161 | 175 | 198 | 204 | 220 | 237 | 256 |
| Federal Employees Retirement System | h | h | h | h | h | 4 | 8 | 12 | 18 | 24 | 32 |
| Military Service Retirement System | n | n | n | 12 | 25 | 39 | 53 | 68 | 80 | 94 | 106 |
| defined contribution | | | | | | 1 | 3 | 5 | 8 | 12 | 16 |
| Thrift Savings Plan[j] | | | | | | 1 | 3 | 5 | 8 | 12 | 16 |
| defined contribution as percentage of total | | | | | | k | 1% | 2% | 2% | 3% | c |
| State and local retirement systems[b] | 162 | 210 | 290 | 374 | 437 | 513 | 563 | 633 | 721 | c | c |

(continued)

Table 2.13 (continued)
**Public Plan Design Trends**

| | 1979 | 1981 | 1983 | 1985 | 1986 | 1987 | 1988 | 1989 | 1990 | 1991 | 1992 |
|---|---|---|---|---|---|---|---|---|---|---|---|
| | | | | | ($ billions) | | | | | | |
| **Contributions** | | | | | | | | | | | |
| Federal retirement systems[g] | $38 | $50 | $57 | $90 | $95 | $97 | $100 | $104 | $108 | $65[f] | c |
|   defined benefit | | | | | | | | | | | |
|     Civil Service Retirement System | 16 | 22 | 25 | 54 | 56 | 56 | 58 | 60 | 61 | 65 | 64 |
|     Federal Employees Retirement System[h] | h | h | h | h | h | 2 | 3 | 4 | 4 | 5 | 6 |
|     Military Service Retirement System[i] | n | n | n | 27 | 28 | 29 | 29 | 28 | 27 | 28 | 28 |
|   defined contribution | | | | | | | | | | | |
|     Thrift Savings Plan[j] | j | j | j | j | j | 1 | 2 | 2 | 2 | 3 | 4 |
|   defined contribution as percentage of total | — | — | — | — | — | 2% | 3% | 4% | 5% | 6% | c |
| State and local retirement systems[b] | $21 | $27 | $32 | $37 | $39 | $42 | $43 | $44 | $46 | c | c |
| **Benefits** | | | | | | | | | | | |
| Federal retirement systems[g] | $34 | $45 | $54 | $62 | $67 | $71 | $77 | $83 | $89 | $57[f] | c |
|   defined benefit | | | | | | | | | | | |
|     Civil Service Retirement System | 23 | 32 | 37 | 40 | 42 | 44 | 47 | 50 | 53 | 57 | c |
|     Federal Employees Retirement System[h] | h | h | h | h | h | 0 | 0 | 0 | 0 | 0 | 0 |
|     Military Service Retirement System[l] | 10 | 14 | 16 | 17[p] | 18 | 18 | 19 | 20 | 22 | 23 | 25 |
|   defined contribution | | | | | | | | | | | |
|     Thrift Savings Plan[j] | j | j | j | j | j | 0 | 0 | 0 | 0 | 0 | 0 |
|   defined contribution as percentage of total | — | — | — | — | — | k | k | k | k | 1% | c |
| State and local retirement systems[b] | $11 | $14 | $17 | $22 | $24 | $27 | $30 | $33 | $36 | c | c |

Source: U.S. Department of Commerce, Bureau of the Census, *Finances of Employee-Retirement Systems of State and Local Governments*, selected years 1982–1990 (Washington, DC: U.S. Government Printing Office,1984–1992); U.S. Bureau of the Census, *1982 and 1987 Census of Governments, Employee Retirement Systems of State and Local Governments* (Washington, DC: U.S. Government Printing Office, 1983 and 1989); and unpublished data from the Office of Personnel Management, the Federal Retirement Thrift Investment Board, and the Department of Defense, Office of the Actuary.

a Data for the Civil Service Retirement System, Federal Employees' Retirement System, Military Service Retirement System, and state and local retirement systems are expressed in fiscal years. Data for the Thrift Savings Plan is expressed in calendar years.

b Excludes state and local plans that are fully supported by employee contributions.

c Data are not available.

d Includes active, separated vested, retired employees, and survivors.

e Excludes state and local, and military service retirement systems.

f Excludes state and local retirement systems.

g Includes the Civil Service Retirement System, Federal Employees' Retirement System, Military Service Retirement System, and Thrift Savings Plan.

h The Federal Employees' Retirement System was established June 6, 1986.

i Includes nondisability and disability retirees, surviving families, and all active personnel with the exception of active reserves.

j The Thrift Savings Plan was established April 1, 1987.

k Less than 0.5 percent.

l State and local plans are not adjusted for double counting of individuals participating in more than one plan.

m All active personnel excluding active reserves.

n The Military Retirement System was unfunded until October 1, 1984.

o Less than $0.5 billion.

p Benefits include only 11 months of payments. Beginning December 1984, benefits obligated for a month are paid at the beginning of the following month, rather than the end of the month of obligation.

plan's investment and actuarial experience, the relative generosity of the benefit formulas, age distribution of active participants and retirees, level of plan assets relative to future obligations, and plan sponsor's business needs.

Private defined benefit payments have been increasing at a faster rate than contributions since 1979, in part reflecting the maturity of the private pension system. In general for well-funded plans, the more retirees in a plan relative to active workers, the greater the plan's benefit payments and the lower the plans' contributions. In fact, contributions to private defined benefit plans have been declining since 1985 (chart 2.1, table 2.7). The full-funding limits in the Omnibus Budget Reconciliation Act of 1987 (OBRA '87) probably contributed to the declining contributions to defined benefit plans. OBRA '87 limited employer contributions to defined benefit plans with assets exceeding 150 percent of the plan's current liability measured as though the plan would terminate that year. Contributions to private defined benefit plans increased from $24 billion in 1975 to $48 billion in 1982 and decreased to $25 billion in 1989. Furthermore, strong investment performance over the mid- to late 1980s may have allowed employers to make lower contributions to their plans. At the same time, benefit payments from defined benefit plans generally increased between 1975 and 1989, increasing from $13 billion in 1975 to $68 billion in 1986, decreasing to

$60 billion in 1988 and increasing again in 1989 to reach $67 billion (table 2.7).

Contributions to private defined contribution plans have increased each year since the passage of ERISA, reflecting the increase in the number of defined contribution plans and the number of participants covered by these plans. Contributions increased from $13 billion in 1975 to $65 billion in 1988 and $80 billion in 1989. Benefit payments from defined contribution plans have also generally increased between 1975 and 1989, with a slight decrease in benefit payments between 1986 and 1988. Benefit payments increased from $6 billion in 1975 to $70 billion in 1989 (table 2.7).

## State and Local Plans

State and local pension plans have seen similar trends in recent years. While contributions and benefits have increased each year since 1980, benefits paid to pension recipients are increasing at a faster rate. Between 1986 and 1990, the excess of annual contributions over annual benefits declined from $15 billion to $10 billion (chart 2.2, table 2.13).

## Federal Plans

Benefit payments from federal pension funds far exceeded contributions until 1985 when the Department of Defense began making contributions to the

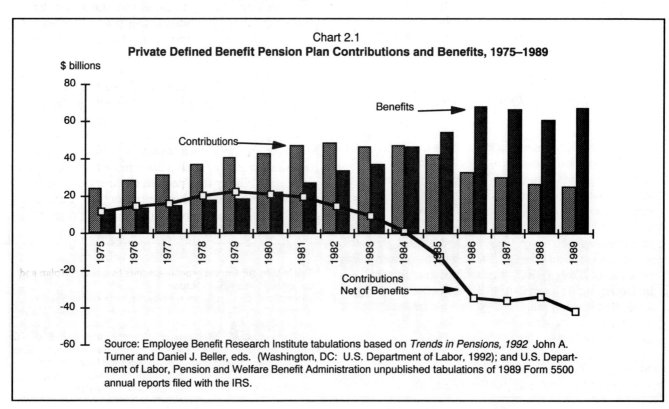

Chart 2.1
**Private Defined Benefit Pension Plan Contributions and Benefits, 1975–1989**

Source: Employee Benefit Research Institute tabulations based on *Trends in Pensions, 1992* John A. Turner and Daniel J. Beller, eds. (Washington, DC: U.S. Department of Labor, 1992); and U.S. Department of Labor, Pension and Welfare Benefit Administration unpublished tabulations of 1989 Form 5500 annual reports filed with the IRS.

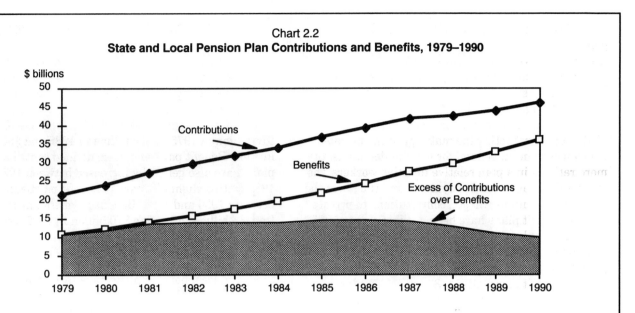

Chart 2.2
State and Local Pension Plan Contributions and Benefits, 1979–1990

Source: U.S. Department of Commerce, Bureau of the Census, *Finances of Employee-Retirement Systems of State and Local Governments*, selected years 1982–1989 (Washington, DC: U.S. Government Printing Office,1984–1991); and U.S. Bureau of the Census, *1982 and 1987 Census of Governments, Employee Retirement Systems of State and Local Governments* (Washington, DC: U.S. Government Printing Office, 1983 and 1989).

MRS. Benefits paid from the CSRS have been greater than contributions made to the fund each year since 1987, and benefits generally have been increasing at a faster rate than contributions. In 1979, contributions to the CSRS exceeded benefit payments by $1 billion, compared with 1992 when benefit payments from the CSRS exceeded contributions by $3 billion. The FERS has contributions in excess of benefits reflecting the low number of retirees relative to active workers. (chart 2.3, table 2.13)

## Funding Levels of Private Defined Benefit Plans

In the aggregate, defined benefit plans are well funded with $1.3 trillion in assets to back $900 billion in benefit liabilities. From 1977 to 1987, the funding status of single-employer defined benefit plans has significantly improved, rising from an average of 85 percent funded to 129 percent funded on a termination basis (table 2.14). Since 1980, defined benefit plans on average have been overfunded. The increase in funding ratios most likely reflects a combination of factors, including higher contribution rates needed to meet minimum funding standards, favorable investment returns on equity, and the use of higher interest rate assumptions to discount future benefits.

Available evidence suggests that approximately 85 percent of pension plans had assets equal to or exceeding 100 percent of liabilities in 1992, up from

45 percent in 1981, and 37 percent of plans had assets in excess of 150 percent of liability for accrued benefits in 1992 (table 2.15).[9] The percentage of plans that were fully funded on a termination basis increased every year between 1981 and 1987 and leveled off between 1987 and 1992. Survey findings also show that the percentage of plans funded at less than 75 percent of the level required for termination-basis sufficiency declined from 34 percent in 1981 to 4 percent in 1992 (table 2.15).[10]

Funding ratios of defined benefit plans vary depending on the formula used to determine benefit levels: final average pay, career average pay, or flat benefit pay. In 1992, plans with benefits determined by final average pay were adequately funded to meet liabilities on a termination basis more often than other plan types. Ninety-four percent of these plans had funding ratios greater than one, using the accrued benefit liability, compared with 84 percent of career

---

[9] The liability for accrued benefits assumes that both the plan and the sponsor are ongoing entities.

[10] Throughout this discussion termination basis refers to basing funding ratios on benefits accrued and assets accumulated at the end of the plan year—the assumptions plans would use to calculate liabilities for standard termination. Termination basis liabilities do not account for future salary increases. Termination basis funding does not refer to the Pension Benefit Guaranty Corporation's calculation of liabilities for underfunded terminations, using termination mortality and retirement age assumptions.

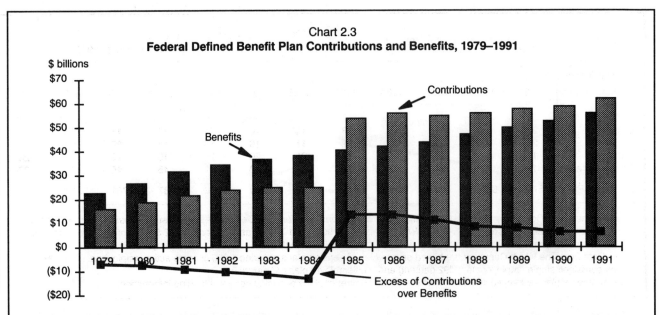

Chart 2.3
**Federal Defined Benefit Plan Contributions and Benefits, 1979–1991**

Source: Unpublished data from the Office of Personnel Management, the Federal Retirement Thrift Investment Board, and the Department of Defense, Office of the Actuary.
Note: Federal plans include the Federal Employee Retirement System, the Civil Service Retirement System, and the Military Retirement System.

Table 2.14
**Funding Ratios of Single Employer Defined Benefit Plans, 1977–1987**

| Year | Funding Ratio |
|------|---------------|
| 1977 | 85.0% |
| 1978 | 84.2 |
| 1979 | 91.0 |
| 1980 | 107.0 |
| 1981 | 106.9 |
| 1982 | 115.4 |
| 1983 | 124.7 |
| 1984 | 128.8 |
| 1985 | 136.3 |
| 1986 | 132.4 |
| 1987 | 128.6 |

Source: U.S. Department of Labor, Pension and Welfare Benefits Administration, John A. Turner and Daniel J. Beller, eds., *Trends in Pensions* (Washington, DC: U.S. Department of Labor, 1989).

average pay plans and 66 percent of flat benefit plans (table 2.15). Furthermore, 12 percent of flat benefit plans were less than 75 percent funded, compared with only 1 percent of final average pay plans and 2 percent of career average pay plans. Flat benefit plans are typically negotiated plans in which the benefit levels are increased periodically with inflation through negotiation with unions as part of a new contract. These plans are underfunded more often than career average or final pay plans due in part to the fact that the plans are not allowed to project increases in the fixed dollar amount when calculating their deductible contributions. The increases in the fixed dollar amount may be funded only after the benefit improvements have been negotiated. Plans with benefits determined by career average and final average formulas must account for projected salary increases.

While the defined benefit system is well funded in the aggregate, significant pockets of underfunding exist within the system. The Pension Benefit Guarantee Corporation (PBGC) estimates that there exists $40 billion in underfunding within single-employer plans. The underfunded plans have liabilities of approximately $162 billion and assets totaling approximately $122 billion. Thus they are 75 percent funded in the aggregate. According to PBGC, approximately 70 percent of the underfunding within the single-employer program (about $29 billion) is concentrated in plans sponsored by 50 companies, primarily in the automobile, steel, airline, and tire industries.

## Funding Levels of Federal Defined Benefit Plans

The federal government sponsors the military retirement programs and the civil service retirement programs for its workers. These programs represent a sizable liability to the federal government and thus ultimately to the American taxpayers (Salisbury, 1993). Budgeted outlays (inclusive of interest paid on bonds held as assets by the plans) for these employee pension programs grew from $21 billion in 1975 to $73 billion in 1991 and are projected to grow to $92 billion in 1997 (U.S. President, 1992).

The Civil Service Retirement and Disability Fund consists of two programs: the Civil Service Retirement System (CSRS) covers those hired as federal civilian employees prior to 1984, and the Federal Employee Retirement System covers those

hired after 1984. These programs represent a larger future obligation for taxpayers than cash outlays imply. These two programs had an unfunded liability of $870 billion in 1992, compared with $864 billion in 1991 (table 2.16). Combined contributions were just enough to cover benefit payments in both years, with the unfunded liability growing as a result of new benefit accruals. The unfunded liability of the two plans increased by $6 billion in 1992.

For the federal civilian plans, the actual contributions being made as a percentage of pay are substantial at 36.5 percent (table 2.16), compared with a reported 3.9 percent for private employers. However, the federal government would need to contribute 65.6 percent of pay in order to amortize the unfunded liability over 40 years. Funding for the value of one year's growth in promised benefits for present workers ("normal cost") requires a contribution equal to 21.3 percent of pay in the Civil Service Retirement Service and 12.9 percent of pay in the Federal Employee Retirement System (table 2.16).

MRS presents a future financial challenge for taxpayers and policymakers as well. However, the MRS's unfunded liability decreased slightly between 1991 and 1992. MRS had an unfunded liability of $633.1 billion at the end of FY 1992, compared with $627.0 billion at the end of FY 1991 (table 2.17). This decrease of $6.1 billion, when combined with the federal civilian pension plans' FY 1992 increase, resulted in a combined FY 1992 decrease in unfunded liabilities of $0.1 billion. The actual contributions to MRS were substantial—66.9 percent of pay, compared to MRS normal cost of 39.7 percent of pay. Funding the plan over the next 40 years would require contributions of 126 percent of pay. For FY 1992 this would have meant

## Table 2.16
### Civil Service Retirement and Disability Fund, September 30, 1991–September 30, 1992

| | CSRS[a] | FERS[b] | 9/30/92 Total | 9/30/91 Total |
|---|---|---|---|---|
| | ($ billions) | | | |
| Actuarial Value of Future Benefits | $1,031 | $128 | $1,159 | $1,126 |
| Assets | 256 | 32 | 288 | 261 |
| Unfunded Termination Liability | 774 | 96 | 870 | 864 |
| Normal Cost as a Percentage of Payroll | | | | |
|    Employer Civil Service Retirement System | | | 21.3% | 21.3% |
|    Employer Federal Employees Retirement System | | | 12.9% | 12.9% |
| Cost to Fund Plan as a Percentage of Pay (40 year amortization) | | | 65.6% | 68.1% |
| Actual Contributions as Percentage of Pay | | | 36.5% | 36.9% |
| Undercontribution as Percentage of Pay | | | 29.1% | 31.2% |
| Contributions | 30.1 | 5.7 | 35.8 | 34.1 |
| Investment Income | 21.9 | 2.3 | 24.2 | 22.7 |
| Benefit Payments | 32.8 | 0.3 | 33.1 | 33.1 |
| Participants (millions) | 1.8 | 1.3 | 3.2 | 3.2 |
| Annuitants (millions) | 2.2 | c | 2.2 | 2.2 |

Source: Employee Benefit Research Institute compilation from U.S. Office of Personnel Management, *An Annual Report to Comply with the Requirements of Public Law 95-595. Sept. 30, 1991, RI 10-27, March 1992.*
[a]Civil Service Retirement System.
[b]Federal Employees Retirement System.
[c]$29,900.

## Table 2.17
### Military Retirement System Actuarial Status Information as of September 30, 1992 and September 30, 1991

| | September 30, 1992 | September 30, 1991 |
|---|---|---|
| | ($ billions) | |
| Present Value of Future Benefits | $733.1 | $726.8 |
| Actuarial Value of Assets | $106.1 | $93.7 |
| Unfunded Termination Liability | $627.0 | $633.1 |
| Normal Cost as a Percentage of Pay | 39.7% | 40.6% |
| Cost to Fund Plan and Liabilities as Percentage of Pay (40-year amortization) | 126.0% | 129.0% |
| Actual Contributions as a Percentage of Pay | 66.9% | 66.2% |
| Underfunding as a Percentage of Pay[a] | 59.1% | 62.8% |
| Normal Cost Contribution | $16.3 | $17.2 |
| Investment Interest Income | $10.0 | $9.0 |
| Capital Gains | $6.7 | $8.6 |
| Unfunded Liability Amortization | $11.2 | $10.8 |
| Benefit Payments | $24.5 | $23.1 |
| Participants | 1.9 million | 2.1 million |
| Annuitants | 1.5 million | 1.5 million |

Source: Employee Benefit Research Institute compilation from *Chapter 95 of Title 31, U.S.C. Report on the Military Retirement System as of Sept. 30, 1992*, unpublished report.
[a]Underfunding is defined here as the difference between the contribution necessary to fund the plan in 40 years and the actual contribution made to the plan.

an added contribution of $24 billion.

Direct federal expenditures for retirement income are substantial. If taxpayers were funding these promises as fast as private employers must fund their plans as required by ERISA, the annual outlay—and either taxes or borrowing—would have to increase by at least $53 billion (Salisbury, 1993).

### *Funding Levels of State and Local Defined Benefit Plans*

Employer contributions to state and local retirement plans grew from $15 billion in 1975 to an estimated $46 billion in 1990. Most of these plans have been advance funded, resulting in significant investment earnings in addition to contributions. Total assets reached $988 billion in 1992. It appears that while state and local pension plans do not have sufficient assets to cover accrued liabilities in the aggregate, the aggregate underfunding is not severe. In a recent survey of state and local government pension systems, the value of assets as a percentage of the pension benefit obligation averaged 93 percent for the plans taken as a whole (Public Pension Coordinating Council, 1993). There were no significant differences in this ratio based on plan characteristics such as number of members; total assets; type of employees (i.e., general, teachers/school employees, police and firefighters); administrating jurisdiction (i.e., independent, state government, local government, special district); and geographical region.

Some state and local government and teachers' pension plans, however, are severely underfunded. According to a survey by Wilshire Associates in 1990, at least six public systems—including West Virginia, Oklahoma, Maine, and Washington, DC teachers' pension plans and the state employees' plans in Maine and Massachusetts—had insufficient assets to meet current retirees' benefit payments. Aging work force demographics, state budget deficits, and poor capital market performance may increase the likelihood that these plans will be unable to pay benefits in the future. In general, state and local employees retire earlier than workers in the private sector, with less than 8 percent of private employees expected to retire before age 60, compared with more than one-third of public employees. Currently, 75 percent of state and local employees are between the ages of 41 and 45 and therefore are close to retirement age.

## Investment Mix of Pensions

Pension assets grew from $1.6 trillion in 1983 to $4.4 trillion by the end of 1992 (table 2.18). Because the increased level of pension assets has drawn attention to the potential revenue that could be gained by removing the tax deferral on investment income of private pension trusts, it is important to analyze this amount on a disaggregated basis. At the end of 1992, private trusteed pension fund assets[11] made up more than one-half of the total assets in pensions. Private trusteed pension assets achieved an average annual growth rate of 12 percent between 1983 and 1992. Over this time period the allocation of private trusteed pension assets among plan types has shifted gradually, with single employer defined benefit plan assets growing an average of 10 percent annually, defined contribution plan assets growing 13 percent, and multiemployer plan assets growing 14 percent. Single employer defined contribution funds held 18.3 percent, or $286 billion, of all private and public pension assets at year-end 1983, increasing to 20.3 percent, or $891 billion, at the end of 1992. Multiemployer plans held 5.0 percent of all pension assets at year-end 1983, increasing slightly to 5.9 percent, or $260 billion by year-end 1992. Single employer defined benefit plan assets decreased as a percentage of total pension assets, declining from 33.6 percent, or $526 billion, of total assets in 1983 to 29.0 percent, or $1,276 billion, of total assets as of year-end 1992 (table 2.18).

Slightly less than 17 percent of total pension fund assets were in private insured pension funds at the end of 1991. These assets grew at an average annual rate of 13 percent from 1983 to 1991. The federal government retirement fund grew at an average annual rate of 12 percent from 1983 to 1992. At the end of that period, these assets made up 6.9 percent of total pension assets. State and local pension fund assets grew at an annual rate of 14 percent from 1983 to 1992 and at the end of that period represented 22.5 percent of total pension assets (table 2.18).

### *Private-Trusteed Investment Mix*

Asset allocation of private trusteed pension plans fluctuated between 1983 and 1992. At year-end 1992, 35.8 percent ($868 billion) of private trusteed pension assets was invested directly in equity, 17.7 percent ($430 billion) was invested directly in bonds, 9.7 percent ($237 billion) was invested directly in cash,

---

[11] The holdings of private pension plans are broadly categorized into two groups: trusteed funds and insured funds. These funds differ in who manages the fund's assets and who bears the investment risk. Trusteed pension funds are managed by a trustee appointed by the plan's sponsor. Insured pension funds are managed by life insurance companies. The assets of private pension plans may be held exclusively in either trusteed or insured funds or may be divided between the two types of funds.

## Table 2.18
## Financial Assets of Private and Government Pension Funds, 1983–1992

| Year | Single Employer | | Multi-employer | Private Insured | Federal Government Retirement | State and Local Government | Total |
|------|-----------------|--|----------------|-----------------|-------------------------------|----------------------------|-------|
| | Defined benefit | Defined contribution | | | | | |
| | | | | ($ billions) | | | |
| 1983 | $ 526 | $286 | $ 79 | $252 | $112 | $311 | $1,566 |
| 1984 | 535 | 322 | 81 | 291 | 130 | 357 | 1,716 |
| 1985 | 643 | 392 | 121 | 347 | 149 | 405 | 2,057 |
| 1986 | 739 | 447 | 143 | 410 | 170 | 469 | 2,378 |
| 1987 | 770 | 471 | 148 | 459 | 188 | 517 | 2,553 |
| 1988 | 857 | 522 | 170 | 516 | 208 | 606 | 2,879 |
| 1989 | 1,010 | 623 | 200 | 572 | 229 | 735 | 3,369 |
| 1990 | 965 | 584 | 194 | 636 | 251 | 752 | 3,382 |
| 1991 | 1,218 | 787 | 240 | 678 | 276 | 891 | 4,090 |
| 1992 | 1,276 | 891 | 260 | n/a | 304 | 988 | 4,397 |
| | | | | (percentage of total pension assets) | | | |
| 1983 | 33.6% | 18.3% | 5.0% | 16.1% | 7.2% | 19.9% | 100.0% |
| 1984 | 31.2 | 18.8 | 4.7 | 17.0 | 7.6 | 20.8 | 100.0 |
| 1985 | 31.3 | 19.1 | 5.9 | 16.9 | 7.2 | 19.7 | 100.0 |
| 1986 | 31.1 | 18.8 | 6.0 | 17.2 | 7.2 | 19.7 | 100.0 |
| 1987 | 30.2 | 18.5 | 5.8 | 18.0 | 7.4 | 20.3 | 100.0 |
| 1988 | 29.8 | 18.1 | 5.9 | 17.9 | 7.2 | 21.1 | 100.0 |
| 1989 | 30.0 | 18.5 | 5.9 | 17.0 | 6.8 | 21.8 | 100.0 |
| 1990 | 28.5 | 17.3 | 5.7 | 18.8 | 7.4 | 22.2 | 100.0 |
| 1991 | 29.8 | 19.2 | 5.9 | 16.7 | 6.7 | 21.8 | 100.0 |
| 1992 | 29.0 | 20.3 | 5.9 | n/a | 6.9 | 22.5 | 100.0 |

Source: Employee Benefit Research Institute, *Quarterly Pension Investment Report*, first quarter 1993 (Washington, DC: Employee Benefit Research Institute, 1993); Board of Governors of the Federal Reserve System, *Flow of Funds Accounts: Assets and Liabilities Outstanding Fourth Quarter 1992* (Washington, DC: Board of Governors of the Federal Reserve System, forthcoming).

19.7 percent ($478 billion) was directly held in other investments, and 17.1 percent ($415 billion) was invested in bank pooled funds (table 2.19). During the period between 1983 and 1992, direct investments in equity fluctuated between 34 and 36 percent of private trusteed assets, direct investments in bonds have generally declined from a high of 24.7 percent in 1984, direct investments in cash have ranged from the current low of 9.7 percent to a high of 11.1 percent in 1988. Bank pooled fund holdings and direct investments in cash have generally increased over the period (table 2.19).

The investment mix of trusteed funds varies by type of plan, with single-employer defined benefit plans and multiemployer plans allocating the greatest portion of their assets to direct equity investments in the aggregate. As of year-end 1992, single-employer defined benefit plans invested the greatest percentage of assets directly in equity, followed by multiemployer plans, and defined contribution plans (table 2.20). Single- employer defined benefit plans, however, decreased their direct holdings in equity from 40.2 percent in 1983 to 39.0 percent as of year-end 1992. Multiemployer plans held 27.6 percent of assets directly in equity in 1983, increasing to 34.3 percent by year-end 1992. Defined contribution plans increased direct equity investments from 31.0 percent in 1983 to a high of 33.3 percent in 1987, then decreased direct equity holding to 29.6 percent in 1990, increasing again in 1991 and 1992. However, single-employer defined contribution plans hold the greatest portion of their aggregate assets in investments other than directly held equity bonds and cash. Defined contribution plans' aggregate holdings in other investments, including bank pooled funds and mutual funds, increased from 32.7 percent of assets in 1983 to 40.9 percent in 1992 (table 2.20).

## Private-Insured Investment Mix

Asset allocation of private insured pension plans has also gradually shifted, with a greater proportion of separate account assets invested in equity, bonds, and

## Table 2.19
## Asset Allocation of Private Trusteed Pension Fund Assets, 1983–1992

| | Directly Held Assets | | | | Bank Pooled Funds | Total Assets |
|---|---|---|---|---|---|---|
| End of | Equity | Bonds | Cash Items | Other Assets | | |
| | ($ billions) | | | | | |
| 1983 | $322 | $209 | $ 90 | $160 | $106 | $ 886 |
| 1984 | 326 | 232 | 102 | 163 | 113 | 936 |
| 1985 | 414 | 268 | 121 | 194 | 159 | 1,156 |
| 1986 | 486 | 305 | 134 | 228 | 176 | 1,328 |
| 1987 | 491 | 296 | 144 | 248 | 210 | 1,389 |
| 1988 | 544 | 302 | 172 | 287 | 243 | 1,549 |
| 1989 | 661 | 341 | 191 | 348 | 292 | 1,833 |
| 1990 | 597 | 354 | 181 | 328 | 283 | 1,743 |
| 1991 | 798 | 409 | 222 | 436 | 381 | 2,245 |
| 1992 | 868 | 430 | 237 | 478 | 415 | 2,426 |
| | (percentage of total private trusteed assets) | | | | | |
| 1983 | 36.3 % | 23.5% | 10.1% | 18.0% | 12.0% | 100.0% |
| 1984 | 34.8 | 24.7 | 10.9 | 17.4 | 12.1 | 100.0 |
| 1985 | 35.8 | 23.2 | 10.4 | 16.8 | 13.8 | 100.0 |
| 1986 | 36.6 | 22.9 | 10.1 | 17.1 | 13.3 | 100.0 |
| 1987 | 35.3 | 21.3 | 10.3 | 17.9 | 15.1 | 100.0 |
| 1988 | 35.1 | 19.5 | 11.1 | 18.5 | 15.7 | 100.0 |
| 1989 | 36.0 | 18.6 | 10.4 | 19.0 | 16.0 | 100.0 |
| 1990 | 34.2 | 20.3 | 10.4 | 18.8 | 16.2 | 100.0 |
| 1991 | 35.5 | 18.2 | 9.9 | 19.4 | 17.0 | 100.0 |
| 1992 | 35.8 | 17.7 | 9.7 | 19.7 | 17.1 | 100.0 |

Source: Employee Benefit Research Institute, *Quarterly Pension Investment Report*, first quarter 1993 (Washington, DC: Employee Benefit Research Institute, 1993).

other investments and a smaller proportion invested in cash. Equity holdings increased from $3.8 billion in 1970 to $81.3 billion by year-end 1991 and increased as a percentage of total separate account assets, from 9.3 percent to a high of 12.0 percent in 1991. Private insurance company general account assets have increased dramatically since 1970, increasing from $36.0 billion to $519.2 billion by year-end 1991. General accounts have remained relatively stable as a percentage of private insured assets, decreasing from 88.3 percent in 1970 to 76.6 percent in 1991 (table 2.21).

### State and Local Government Funds Investment Mix

Asset allocation of state and local pension plans has also shifted toward equity and cash and away from bonds and other investments. Equity holdings increased from $10.1 billion in 1970 to $464.4 billion by year-end 1992, increasing from nearly 17 percent of state and local assets to 47 percent. State and local cash holdings increased from $0.6 billion in 1970 to $44.5 billion in 1992, increasing from 1 percent of state and local plan assets to nearly 5 percent of assets, reaching a high of 7 percent of assets in 1987 and 1988. While bond holdings decreased from 72 percent of state and local plan assets to 47 percent of assets, the assets increased from $43.7 billion to $459.1 billion (table 2.22).

## Pension Fund Holdings of Financial Assets in the Economy

### Equity Holdings

Private pension funds and state and local funds combined held $1,598 billion of equity by year-end 1992, increasing from $81 billion in 1970 and $1,061 billion in 1990. Private trusteed, private insured, and state and local pension funds have held a generally increasing percentage of the nation's equity since 1970 (chart 2.4). As of year-end 1992, private trusteed plans held 22.5 percent of the economy's equity and state and local funds held 9.9 percent. Private insured funds held

# Table 2.20
## Asset Allocation of Private Trusteed Pension Plans by Plan Type, 1983–1992

| | Single Employer Plans | | | | | | | | | | Multiemployer Plans | | | | |
|---|---|---|---|---|---|---|---|---|---|---|---|---|---|---|---|
| | Defined Benefit Plans | | | | | Defined Contribution Plans | | | | | | | | | |
| | Equity | Bonds | Cash Items | Other Assets | Total Assets | Equity | Bonds | Cash Items | Other Assets | Total Assets | Equity | Bonds | Cash Items | Other Assets | Total Assets |
| ($ billions) | | | | | | | | | | | | | | | |
| 1983 | $212 | $124 | $40 | $151 | $526 | $89 | $63 | $41 | $94 | $286 | $22 | $26 | $10 | $21 | $79 |
| 1984 | 202 | 136 | 46 | 150 | 535 | 101 | 70 | 46 | 105 | 322 | 23 | 28 | 9 | 21 | 81 |
| 1985 | 248 | 159 | 56 | 181 | 643 | 126 | 72 | 54 | 140 | 392 | 40 | 37 | 12 | 32 | 121 |
| 1986 | 293 | 178 | 60 | 208 | 739 | 148 | 79 | 60 | 159 | 447 | 45 | 48 | 14 | 36 | 143 |
| 1987 | 289 | 171 | 63 | 247 | 770 | 157 | 78 | 63 | 173 | 471 | 45 | 46 | 18 | 39 | 148 |
| 1988 | 323 | 176 | 72 | 286 | 857 | 168 | 80 | 75 | 199 | 522 | 53 | 47 | 25 | 45 | 170 |
| 1989 | 394 | 195 | 81 | 340 | 1,010 | 201 | 92 | 87 | 244 | 623 | 66 | 55 | 23 | 56 | 200 |
| 1990 | 362 | 202 | 76 | 325 | 965 | 173 | 96 | 83 | 231 | 584 | 62 | 56 | 22 | 54 | 194 |
| 1991 | 477 | 230 | 90 | 421 | 1,218 | 239 | 117 | 108 | 323 | 787 | 82 | 62 | 23 | 73 | 240 |
| 1992 | 498 | 233 | 95 | 450 | 1,276 | 281 | 128 | 118 | 364 | 891 | 89 | 69 | 23 | 79 | 260 |
| (percentage distribution) | | | | | | | | | | | | | | | |
| 1983 | 40.2% | 23.5% | 7.6% | 28.7% | 100.0% | 31.0% | 22.1% | 14.2% | 32.7% | 100.0% | 27.6% | 33.1% | 12.4% | 26.9% | 100.0% |
| 1984 | 37.8 | 25.5 | 8.7 | 28.1 | 100.0 | 31.3 | 21.9 | 14.3 | 32.5 | 100.0 | 28.5 | 34.2 | 11.8 | 25.5 | 100.0 |
| 1985 | 38.5 | 24.8 | 8.7 | 28.1 | 100.0 | 32.2 | 18.3 | 13.7 | 35.8 | 100.0 | 33.5 | 30.3 | 9.9 | 26.3 | 100.0 |
| 1986 | 39.6 | 24.1 | 8.1 | 28.2 | 100.0 | 33.1 | 17.7 | 13.5 | 35.7 | 100.0 | 31.4 | 33.4 | 9.9 | 25.3 | 100.0 |
| 1987 | 37.6 | 22.2 | 8.2 | 32.0 | 100.0 | 33.3 | 16.6 | 13.3 | 36.8 | 100.0 | 30.3 | 31.3 | 12.2 | 26.2 | 100.0 |
| 1988 | 37.7 | 20.5 | 8.4 | 33.4 | 100.0 | 32.2 | 15.2 | 14.4 | 38.1 | 100.0 | 31.0 | 27.4 | 14.9 | 26.6 | 100.0 |
| 1989 | 39.0 | 19.3 | 8.0 | 33.6 | 100.0 | 32.2 | 14.7 | 13.9 | 39.2 | 100.0 | 32.8 | 27.3 | 11.7 | 28.2 | 100.0 |
| 1990 | 37.5 | 20.9 | 7.9 | 33.7 | 100.0 | 29.6 | 16.5 | 14.2 | 39.6 | 100.0 | 32.0 | 28.9 | 11.3 | 27.7 | 100.0 |
| 1991 | 39.2 | 18.8 | 7.4 | 34.6 | 100.0 | 30.3 | 14.9 | 13.7 | 41.0 | 100.0 | 34.2 | 25.8 | 9.7 | 30.2 | 100.0 |
| 1992 | 39.0 | 18.2 | 7.5 | 35.3 | 100.0 | 31.5 | 14.4 | 13.3 | 40.9 | 100.0 | 34.3 | 26.5 | 8.8 | 30.3 | 100.0 |

Source: Employee Benefit Research Institute, *Quarterly Pension Investment Report*, first quarter 1993 (Washington, DC: Employee Benefit Research Institute, 1993).

## Table 2.21
## Asset Allocation of Private Insured Pension Funds, 1970–1991

| | Separate Accounts | | | | | General Accounts | Total Assets |
|---|---|---|---|---|---|---|---|
| | Equity | Bonds | Cash items | Other assets | Total separate | | |
| | | | ($ billions) | | | | |
| 1970 | $3.8 | $0.8 | $0.1 | $0.1 | $4.8 | $36.0 | $40.8 |
| 1975 | 8.7 | 2.4 | 0.1 | 0.4 | 11.5 | 58.5 | 70.1 |
| 1976 | 11.5 | 2.6 | 0.0 | 0.5 | 14.7 | 71.2 | 85.8 |
| 1977 | 10.2 | 4.3 | 0.0 | 0.9 | 15.4 | 82.0 | 97.5 |
| 1978 | 11.2 | 6.4 | 0.0 | 1.1 | 18.8 | 92.7 | 111.6 |
| 1979 | 12.6 | 9.0 | 0.0 | 1.4 | 23.0 | 108.7 | 131.7 |
| 1980 | 17.1 | 12.0 | 0.3 | 2.0 | 31.3 | 126.8 | 158.2 |
| 1981 | 16.4 | 17.7 | 0.3 | 3.4 | 37.9 | 144.7 | 182.5 |
| 1982 | 19.9 | 23.7 | 0.5 | 5.7 | 49.7 | 170.2 | 219.9 |
| 1983 | 24.0 | 26.1 | 0.5 | 8.1 | 58.8 | 192.9 | 251.7 |
| 1984 | 22.9 | 26.9 | 0.6 | 7.9 | 58.4 | 232.5 | 290.8 |
| 1985 | 31.6 | 31.6 | 0.6 | 9.8 | 73.7 | 273.0 | 346.7 |
| 1986 | 37.5 | 34.7 | 0.7 | 15.0 | 87.9 | 321.8 | 409.7 |
| 1987 | 41.0 | 31.6 | 0.6 | 14.9 | 88.0 | 370.7 | 458.7 |
| 1988 | 44.5 | 35.5 | 0.5 | 17.9 | 98.3 | 418.1 | 516.4 |
| 1989 | 56.0 | 36.9 | 0.3 | 21.6 | 114.7 | 457.7 | 572.5 |
| 1990 | 58.6 | 43.5 | 0.3 | 19.8 | 122.3 | 513.8 | 636.1 |
| 1991 | 81.3 | 56.0 | 0.3 | 21.3 | 158.9 | 519.2 | 678.1 |
| | | | (percentage distribution) | | | | |
| 1970 | 9.3% | 2.0% | 0.2% | 0.2% | 11.7% | 88.3% | 100.0% |
| 1975 | 12.4 | 3.4 | 0.1 | 0.6 | 16.5 | 83.5 | 100.0 |
| 1976 | 13.4 | 3.0 | 0.0 | 0.6 | 17.1 | 82.9 | 100.0 |
| 1977 | 10.5 | 4.4 | 0.0 | 0.9 | 15.8 | 84.2 | 100.0 |
| 1978 | 10.1 | 5.8 | 0.0 | 1.0 | 16.9 | 83.1 | 100.0 |
| 1979 | 9.6 | 6.8 | 0.0 | 1.0 | 17.5 | 82.5 | 100.0 |
| 1980 | 10.8 | 7.6 | 0.2 | 1.2 | 19.8 | 80.2 | 100.0 |
| 1981 | 9.0 | 9.7 | 0.2 | 1.9 | 20.7 | 79.3 | 100.0 |
| 1982 | 9.0 | 10.8 | 0.2 | 2.6 | 22.6 | 77.4 | 100.0 |
| 1983 | 9.6 | 10.4 | 0.2 | 3.2 | 23.4 | 76.6 | 100.0 |
| 1984 | 7.9 | 9.3 | 0.2 | 2.7 | 20.1 | 79.9 | 100.0 |
| 1985 | 9.1 | 9.1 | 0.2 | 2.8 | 21.3 | 78.7 | 100.0 |
| 1986 | 9.2 | 8.5 | 0.2 | 3.7 | 21.5 | 78.5 | 100.0 |
| 1987 | 8.9 | 6.9 | 0.1 | 3.2 | 19.2 | 80.8 | 100.0 |
| 1988 | 8.6 | 6.9 | 0.1 | 3.5 | 19.0 | 81.0 | 100.0 |
| 1989 | 9.8 | 6.4 | 0.1 | 3.8 | 20.0 | 80.0 | 100.0 |
| 1990 | 9.2 | 6.8 | 0.1 | 3.1 | 19.2 | 80.8 | 100.0 |
| 1991 | 12.0 | 8.3 | 0.0 | 3.1 | 23.4 | 76.6 | 100.0 |

Source: Employee Benefit Research Institute, *Quarterly Pension Investment Report*, first quarter 1993 (Washington, DC: Employee Benefit Research Institute, 1993).

## Table 2.22
### Asset Allocation of State and Local Pension Funds, 1970–1992

| Year | Equity | Bonds | Cash Items | Other Assets | Total Assets |
|------|--------|-------|-----------|--------------|--------------|
| | ($ billions) | | | | |
| 1970 | $ 10.1 | $ 43.7 | $ 0.6 | $ 5.9 | $ 60.3 |
| 1975 | 24.3 | 71.5 | 1.4 | 7.5 | 104.8 |
| 1976 | 30.1 | 81.2 | 1.4 | 7.7 | 120.4 |
| 1977 | 30.0 | 92.8 | 1.7 | 8.0 | 132.5 |
| 1978 | 33.3 | 109.2 | 2.7 | 8.6 | 153.9 |
| 1979 | 37.1 | 119.0 | 4.0 | 9.6 | 169.7 |
| 1980 | 44.3 | 138.6 | 4.3 | 10.9 | 198.1 |
| 1981 | 47.8 | 159.4 | 4.4 | 12.5 | 224.2 |
| 1982 | 60.2 | 181.6 | 7.0 | 13.8 | 262.5 |
| 1983 | 89.6 | 196.8 | 10.2 | 14.7 | 311.2 |
| 1984 | 96.5 | 230.8 | 14.0 | 15.3 | 356.6 |
| 1985 | 120.1 | 253.7 | 15.7 | 15.3 | 404.7 |
| 1986 | 150.2 | 284.7 | 18.9 | 15.6 | 469.4 |
| 1987 | 169.6 | 294.0 | 37.9 | 15.4 | 516.9 |
| 1988 | 219.7 | 330.7 | 40.0 | 15.6 | 606.0 |
| 1989 | 300.1 | 381.1 | 38.4 | 15.2 | 734.8 |
| 1990 | 296.1 | 397.3 | 40.3 | 17.8 | 751.5 |
| 1991 | 400.8 | 426.2 | 45.2 | 18.8 | 891.0 |
| 1992 | 464.4 | 459.1 | 44.5 | 19.8 | 987.8 |
| | (percentage) | | | | |
| 1970 | 16.7% | 72.4% | 1.0% | 9.8% | 100.0% |
| 1975 | 23.2 | 68.2 | 1.4 | 7.2 | 100.0 |
| 1976 | 25.0 | 67.4 | 1.2 | 6.4 | 100.0 |
| 1977 | 22.6 | 70.0 | 1.3 | 6.1 | 100.0 |
| 1978 | 21.6 | 71.0 | 1.8 | 5.6 | 100.0 |
| 1979 | 21.9 | 70.1 | 2.4 | 5.7 | 100.0 |
| 1980 | 22.4 | 70.0 | 2.2 | 5.5 | 100.0 |
| 1981 | 21.3 | 71.1 | 2.0 | 5.6 | 100.0 |
| 1982 | 22.9 | 69.2 | 2.7 | 5.2 | 100.0 |
| 1983 | 28.8 | 63.2 | 3.3 | 4.7 | 100.0 |
| 1984 | 27.1 | 64.7 | 3.9 | 4.3 | 100.0 |
| 1985 | 29.7 | 62.7 | 3.9 | 3.8 | 100.0 |
| 1986 | 32.0 | 60.7 | 4.0 | 3.3 | 100.0 |
| 1987 | 32.8 | 56.9 | 7.3 | 3.0 | 100.0 |
| 1988 | 36.3 | 54.6 | 6.6 | 2.6 | 100.0 |
| 1989 | 40.8 | 51.9 | 5.2 | 2.1 | 100.0 |
| 1990 | 39.4 | 52.9 | 5.4 | 2.4 | 100.0 |
| 1991 | 45.0 | 47.8 | 5.1 | 2.1 | 100.0 |
| 1992 | 47.0 | 46.5 | 4.5 | 2.0 | 100.0 |

Source: Employee Benefit Research Institute, *Quarterly Pension Investment Report*, first quarter 1993 (Washington, DC: Employee Benefit Research Institute, 1993).

1.9 percent of the economy's equity at year-end 1991, the latest year for which these data are available.

## Bond Holdings

Pensions holdings of bond funds have also steadily increased. Between 1970 and 1992, private trusteed pension plans bond holdings increased from $32.5 billion, or 5.9 percent of the economy's bond holdings, to $536.3 billion, or 8.0 percent of the economy's bond holdings (chart 2.5). Between 1970 and 1991, private insured funds' bond holdings increased from $0.8 billion to $56.0 billion, or from 0.2 percent of the economy's bond holdings, to 0.9 percent of the economy's bond holdings over the same period. Between 1970 and 1992, state and local funds' holdings increased from $41.7 billion to $458.2 billion but decreased from 7.6 percent to 6.8 percent of total bond assets in the economy.

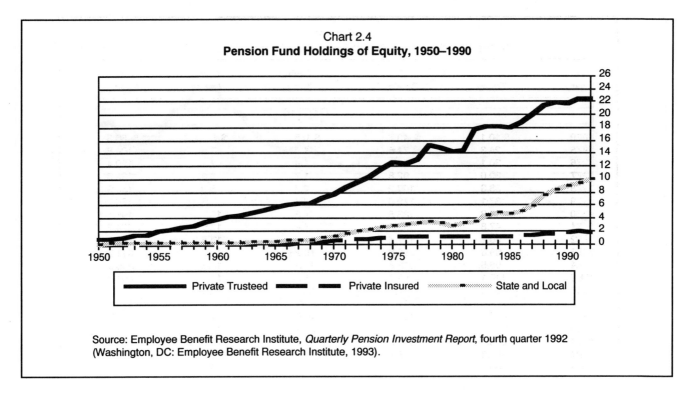

Chart 2.4
**Pension Fund Holdings of Equity, 1950–1990**

Private Trusteed ■■■ Private Insured ·········· State and Local

Source: Employee Benefit Research Institute, *Quarterly Pension Investment Report*, fourth quarter 1992 (Washington, DC: Employee Benefit Research Institute, 1993).

# Pensions and Saving

As measured by the National Income and Product Accounts (NIPA),[12] retirement programs represent a significant portion of personal savings. In 1982, while the personal savings rate was 8.6 percent of disposable income, employer contributions to private plans and government retirement benefits combined represented 4.7 percent of disposable income (chart 2.6). However, this figure decreased to 3.0 percent in 1991 as a result of high investment returns and new federal laws that have effectively reduced pension contributions. Personal savings experienced an even larger decrease during that period, reaching a rate of 4.7 percent in 1991. Most of the decline from 1982 to 1991 occurred in private plans, with employer contributions as a percentage of disposable income declining by 1.4 percentage points. Government retirement benefits as a percentage of disposable income decreased by

0.3 percentage points.

This analysis may actually underestimate the impact of retirement programs on savings because some components of pension savings are not separately identified in the national accounts. One component not included in chart 2.7 that has become increasingly important in recent years is the amount of employee contributions to pension plans. Although a recent estimate of this amount is not available, a good approximation for a conservative estimate is the amount of contributions to 401(k) plans for the year. This figure will not represent the entire amount of employee contributions to pension plans because it does not include contributions to other employment-based retirement savings vehicles, (e.g., after-tax employee savings accounts). Nevertheless, based on EBRI tabulations of the May 1988 Current Population Survey employee benefit supplement (CPS-EBS) for private-sector 401(k) plans, this component of pension

---

[12] The National Income and Product Accounts (NIPA) are maintained by the Bureau of Economic Analysis of the U.S. Department of Commerce. They show the value and composition of the nation's output and the distribution of income generated in its production. The accounts include estimates of gross domestic product (GDP), the goods and services that make up GDP, national income, personal income, and corporate profits.

There are inherent limitations in using NIPA data as a measurement of the impact of pensions on savings. Although the summation of contributions and investment income might account

for the increase in pension wealth for defined contribution participants, the relationship between these variables in a defined benefit pension plan is not nearly as precise. In fact, the Omnibus Budget Reconciliation Act of 1987 has prevented many overfunded defined benefit pension plans from making (tax-deductible) pension contributions for several years, although the growth in the participants' pension wealth has not been modified. Unfortunately, there is no separate treatment of defined benefit and defined contribution plans in NIPA.

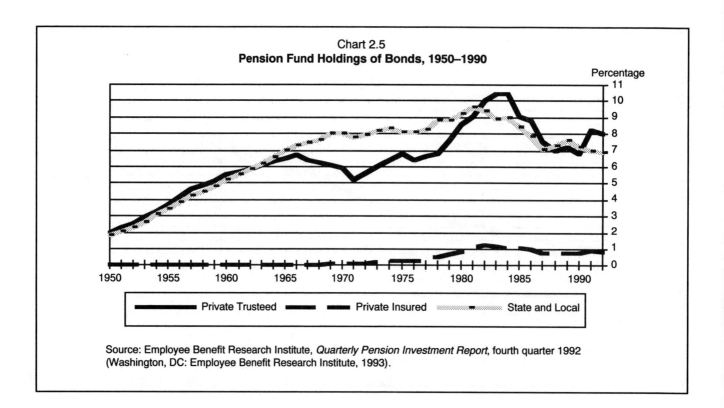

Chart 2.5
**Pension Fund Holdings of Bonds, 1950–1990**

Source: Employee Benefit Research Institute, *Quarterly Pension Investment Report*, fourth quarter 1992
(Washington, DC: Employee Benefit Research Institute, 1993).

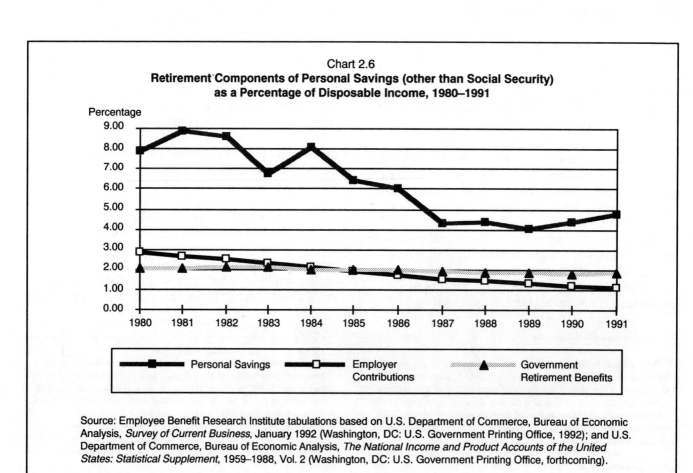

Chart 2.6
**Retirement Components of Personal Savings (other than Social Security)
as a Percentage of Disposable Income, 1980–1991**

Source: Employee Benefit Research Institute tabulations based on U.S. Department of Commerce, Bureau of Economic
Analysis, *Survey of Current Business*, January 1992 (Washington, DC: U.S. Government Printing Office, 1992); and U.S.
Department of Commerce, Bureau of Economic Analysis, *The National Income and Product Accounts of the United
States: Statistical Supplement*, 1959–1988, Vol. 2 (Washington, DC: U.S. Government Printing Office, forthcoming).

savings amounted to $19.3 billion (0.47 percent of disposable income in 1988).[13] Public-sector 401(k) contributions represent an additional $4.8 billion. Another $0.2 billion of contributions were made in 1988 by the 919,000 participants in the Federal Employee Retirement Savings program (Employee Benefit Research Institute, 1992).

Pension plans that are advance funded serve to expand total savings (VanDerhei, 1992). The magnitude has been debated, and studies show wide variation, from a low of $0.32 per $1.00 of pension savings to a high of $0.84. At either level, this translates into billions of dollars each year with total pension assets exceeding $4 trillion in 1991. As previously noted, federal pension plans have combined unfunded liabilities of more than $1.6 trillion as of FY 1991. If federal plan participants have saved less because of the pension income promise, then federal plans may have served to decrease personal savings, as private and state and local plans have served to increase personal savings with substantial advance funding.

Another way to assess the degree to which a pension plan assists individuals with total savings is to determine whether or not they report income other than earnings that would suggest other than pension savings. EBRI tabulations show that the lowest earners are likely to have only earned income. In 1991,

14.1 million persons with no interest income participated in their employer's pension plan, and 38.7 million persons with no dividend income participated (table 2.23). While these percentage participation levels and rates are lower than would be desirable, the number of people is significant. These individuals will likely be better off economically than the 36 million reporting no interest income and no pension participation, or the 61.1 million reporting no dividend income and no pension participation. Whether advance funded or not, for millions of individuals with an accrued pension benefit but no interest or dividend income, the pension may well be the only income producing savings they have as they approach retirement.

## Lump-Sum Distributions and Benefit Preservation

Defined contribution plans often involve explicit savings decisions by employees that directly impact their retirement income levels. These plans work best for participants when they elect to participate, invest plan assets appropriately, and preserve their benefits until retirement.[14]

The decision to participate in certain defined contribution plans, such as 401(k) plans, is generally voluntary and contingent on employee contributions.

---

[13] This estimate is conservative. It is based on the reported percentage of pay contributed, and earnings were limited to a maximum of $999 per week.

[14] A participant may be better off spending benefits before retirement if he or she would otherwise take out a loan with higher interest payments than the investment income gained by saving.

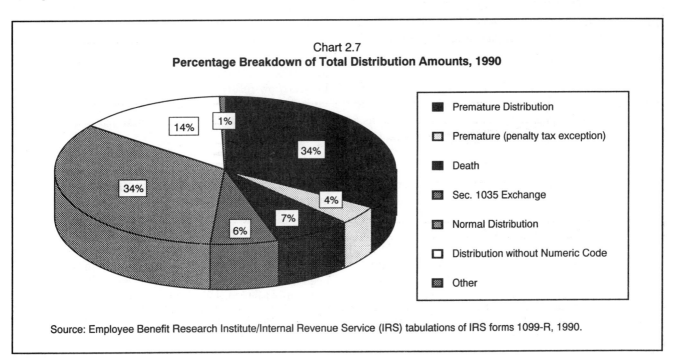

Chart 2.7
**Percentage Breakdown of Total Distribution Amounts, 1990**

- Premature Distribution
- Premature (penalty tax exception)
- Death
- Sec. 1035 Exchange
- Normal Distribution
- Distribution without Numeric Code
- Other

14% 1% 34% 34% 6% 7% 4%

Source: Employee Benefit Research Institute/Internal Revenue Service (IRS) tabulations of IRS forms 1099-R, 1990.

## Table 2.23
### Pension Coverage and Pension Participation of the Civilian, Nonagricultural Wage and Salary Work Force, by Earnings and Interest and Dividend Income, 1991

| | Total | Pension Coverage | | Pension Participation | |
| --- | --- | --- | --- | --- | --- |
| | (millions) | (millions) | (percentage) | (millions) | (percentage) |
| Total | 119.8 | 66.6 | 55.6% | 52.0 | 43.4% |
| Less than $10,000 | 36.1 | 10.4 | 28.9 | 3.6 | 10.1 |
| $10,000–$24,999 | 42.1 | 23.5 | 55.9 | 18.1 | 43.1 |
| $25,000–$49,999 | 32.4 | 25.3 | 78.1 | 23.3 | 71.8 |
| $50,000–$74,999 | 6.4 | 5.2 | 81.8 | 5.0 | 77.5 |
| $75,000–$99,999 | 2.7 | 2.0 | 76.1 | 1.9 | 71.5 |
| $100,000 or more | 0.1 | 0.1 | 75.8 | 0.1 | 64.8 |
| | | | | | |
| Without Interest Income | 50.1 | 20.8 | 41.5 | 14.1 | 28.1 |
| Less than $10,000 | 21.5 | 5.3 | 24.4 | 1.7 | 8.0 |
| $10,000–$24,999 | 19.7 | 9.4 | 47.6 | 6.9 | 34.9 |
| $25,000–$49,999 | 7.9 | 5.5 | 69.8 | 4.9 | 62.3 |
| $50,000–$74,999 | 0.7 | 0.5 | 69.6 | 0.5 | 62.3 |
| $75,000–$99,999 | 0.2 | 0.1 | 53.1 | 0.1 | 45.8 |
| $100,000 or more | 0.1 | a | 100.0 | a | 100.0 |
| | | | | | |
| Without Dividend Income | 99.8 | 51.6 | 51.8 | 38.7 | 38.8 |
| Less than $10,000 | 33.4 | 9.3 | 27.7 | 3.2 | 9.5 |
| $10,000–$24,999 | 37.6 | 20.4 | 54.3 | 15.5 | 41.2 |
| $25,000–$49,999 | 24.3 | 18.6 | 76.2 | 16.9 | 69.5 |
| $50,000–$74,999 | 3.4 | 2.6 | 78.5 | 2.5 | 73.1 |
| $75,000–$99,999 | 1.1 | 0.8 | 69.8 | 0.7 | 65.7 |
| $100,000 or more | a | a | 74.9 | a | 49.9 |

Source: Employee Benefit Research Institute tabulations of the March 1992 Current Population Survey.
aLess than 50,000.

According to EBRI tabulations of the May 1988 CPS-EBS, in 1988, 30.8 million workers, or 27 percent of nonagricultural wage and salary workers, were eligible for participation in a 401(k) plan. However, only 53 percent of those eligible contributed to their plan during that year. A recent EBRI/Gallup survey asked respondents whose employer sponsored a savings plan that allowed pre-tax employee contributions, such as a 401(k) plan, what percentage of their pay, if any, they contributed. Twenty-two percent said that they were not contributing to the plan; 17 percent contributed less than 5 percent of their pay, 15 percent contributed 5 percent of their pay; 14 percent contributed 6 percent to 9 percent of their pay; 18 percent contributed 10 or more percent of their pay; and 11 percent didn't know how much they contributed (Employee Benefit Research Institute/The Gallup Organization, Inc., 1992).

Participants in defined contribution plans tend to manage their funds conservatively, preferring low-risk, low-return investments. In recent surveys, 401(k) plan participants described themselves as conservative investors who prefer to direct their own investments toward insurance and bank contracts. Of those respondents to a June 1990 EBRI/Gallup survey who were employed, more than one-half (58 percent) expressed a preference for making their own investment decisions and 70 percent said they were more inclined to choose low-risk/low-return investments (such as bonds and guaranteed investment contracts) (Employee Benefit Research Institute/The Gallup Organization, Inc., 1990).

This preference for less risky and lower return investments may mean having less money available, and thus a lower standard of living, in retirement. In other words, many workers may have less retirement income than they need unless they diversify away from the options they currently favor or contribute a much larger proportion of their income (VanDerhei, 1992).

The growth in defined contribution plans has been accompanied by a growth in the availability of lump-sum distributions as all defined contribution plans provide such distributions. In addition, a significant number of defined benefit plans now offer lump-sum distributions. In a recent survey, 34 percent of the companies surveyed with defined benefit plans for salaried employees had a lump-sum option in the plan, and of these 67 percent made the option available to terminated vesteds, 72 percent to early retirees, and 75 percent to normal retirees (Hewitt, 1992).

EBRI/IRS tabulations show that the number of total distributions rose from 11.4 million in 1987 to 12.2 million in 1988 and then declined to 10.8 million in 1990 (table 2.24). (Note that these numbers consist not just of preretirement distributions upon job change, but include other distributions, such as retirement distributions, as well).[15] The number of distributions from defined benefit and defined contribution plans (non-IRA/ simplified employee pension (SEP) accounts) decreased from 8.8 million to 8.2 million over this time period, while the number of IRA/SEP distributions remained essentially constant at 2.6 million (table 2.24).

While the number of distributions declined over this period, the amount distributed increased steadily, implying a rise in the average amount distributed (table 2.24). The aggregate amount distributed rose from $80.3 billion in 1987 to $125.8 billion in 1990. This increase in the amount distributed was driven largely by the

increase in the amount distributed from non-IRA/SEP accounts from $65.9 billion in 1987 to $107.2 billion in 1990. By comparison, the amount distributed from IRA/SEP accounts rose a modest $4.2 billion. The average amount distributed was $11,656 in 1990 as opposed to $7,063 in 1987. The average distribution from non-IRA/SEP accounts rose by almost $6,000 over the four years, reaching $13,155 in 1990. The growth in the average IRA/SEP distribution was more modest over this period and totaled $7,035 in 1990 (table 2.24).

Thirty-eight percent, or $47.9 billion, of all funds distributed in 1990 were from premature distributions[16], i.e. distributions that occurred before the recipient reached aged 59 1/2[17] (chart 2.7). Thirty-four percent, or $43.0 billion, was accounted for by normal distributions, i.e. distributions where the recipient is at least aged 59 1/2. Fourteen percent, or $17.4 billion, of the funds distributed were not coded; these should be primarily excess contributions plus earnings/excess deferrals taxable in 1988 or 1989 (note that in years prior to 1990 a code was not required for normal distributions, therefore it is also possible that some proportion of these uncoded dollars are normal distribu-

---

[15] A total distribution is one or more distributions within one tax year in which the entire balance of the account is distributed. Lump-sum distributions (LSDs) are a subset of total distributions. An LSD is the result of one of the following: (i) on account of the employee's death, (ii) after the employee attains age 59 1/2, (iii) on account of the employee's separation from the service, or (iv) after the employee has become disabled. In addition to LSDs, a total distribution may be the result of a prohibited transaction, IRC Section 1035 exchange, excess contributions plus earnings/excess

deferrals, and PS 58 costs (premiums paid by a trustee or custodian for current life or other insurance protection). Most total distributions are LSDs; in 1990, 90 percent of all total distributions were LSDs and 79 percent of all funds distributed as a total distribution were due to an LSD.

[16] The appropriate code(s) indicating the type of distribution being made must be reported.

[17] These figures include premature distributions where an exception to the penalty tax applied. There were 0.3 million such distributions totaling $5.5 billion.

---

## Table 2.24
## Total Distributions from Tax Qualified Plans, 1987–1990

|  | 1987 | 1988 | 1989 | 1990 |
|---|---|---|---|---|
| Number of Distributions | (millions) | | | |
| Aggregate | 11.4 | 12.2 | 11.6 | 10.8 |
| Non-IRA/SEP | 8.8 | a | a | 8.2 |
| IRA/SEP | 2.6 | a | a | 2.6 |
| Total Amounts Distributed | ($ billions) | | | |
| Aggregate | 80.3 | 85.2 | 115.3 | 125.8 |
| Non-IRA/SEP | 65.9 | a | a | 107.2 |
| IRA/SEP | 14.4 | a | a | 18.6 |
| Average Amounts Distributed | ($ thousands) | | | |
| Aggregate | 7.0 | 7.0 | 10.0 | 11.7 |
| Non-IRA/SEP | 7.5 | a | a | 13.2 |
| IRA/SEP | 5.7 | a | a | 7.0 |

Source: Employee Benefit Research Institute/Internal Revenue Service tabulations of IRS Forms 1099-R, Statement for Recipients of Total Distributions from Profit-Sharing, Retirement Plans, Individual Retirement Arrangements, Insurance Contracts, Etc., 1987-90.
aNot available.

tion amounts). The remainder is divided up as follows: 7 percent are death distributions, 6 percent are Section 1035 exchanges,[18] and 1 percent are other (chart 2.7).[19]

Two points are highlighted by examining the ratio of the number of IRA rollover contributions to the number of total distributions along with the ratio of the amounts rolled over to the amounts distributed over the time period 1987-90. First, both ratios increased over the four years for which data are available. The ratio of the number of IRA rollovers to the number of total distributions rose from 0.23 in 1987 to 0.25 in 1989, after falling to 0.21 in 1988, and finally rose to 0.29 in 1990 (chart 2.8). The 1990 figure indicates that almost 30 percent of all total distributions were at least partially rolled over into an IRA in that year. The ratio of IRA rollover contribution amounts to total distribution amounts rose from 0.49 in 1987 to 0.54 in 1988, 0.55 in 1989, and finally to 0.57 in 1990 (chart 2.8). The 1990 figure indicates that 57 percent of all money distributed as a total distribution was rolled over into IRAs.

The second item of note is that the ratio of the rollover amounts is consistently larger than the ratio of the number of rollovers indicating that larger distributions tend to be rolled over. This is not surprising given that recipients of larger distributions, in particular,

those who are current workers, have more to lose from penalty taxation if they do not roll over into a tax qualified vehicle.

While the fraction of total distributions being rolled over into IRAs is increasing, as of 1990 it still stood at under 30 percent of total distributions, indicating that many recipients may not be thinking long term with their distribution money and thus may be jeopardizing their retirement income security. Undoubtedly, some people not rolling their distribution into an IRA are using the distribution for some other type of long term financial savings, such as an annuity purchase by retiring workers or a home purchase by younger workers, but many others are likely using the distribution to fund current consumption. In the May 1988 CPS/EBS, 34 percent of all preretirement distribution recipients reported having used the entire amount of their most recent distribution for consumption[20] and 40 percent reported using at least some of their most recent distribution for consumption (Piacentini, 1990). In such instances, some workers may be unwittingly sacrificing future consumption in retirement for consumption today. This may especially be a problem for lower wage earners who may need to use the distribution to cover expenses during a period of unemployment. As shown above, it is the larger, not

---

[18] Tax free exchange of insurance contracts under sec. 1035.

[19] This includes PS 58 costs excess contributions plus earnings/excess deferrals (and/or earnings) taxable in 1990, prohibited transactions, and disability distributions.

[20] Includes purchase of a car, education expenses, expenses incurred during a period of unemployment, and other uses.

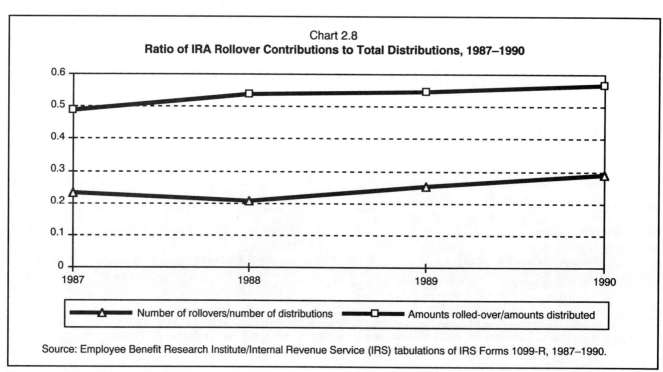

Chart 2.8
**Ratio of IRA Rollover Contributions to Total Distributions, 1987–1990**

Source: Employee Benefit Research Institute/Internal Revenue Service (IRS) tabulations of IRS Forms 1099-R, 1987–1990.

smaller, distributions that tend to be rolled over indicating that it is likely the lower wage earners who are sacrificing consumption in retirement for consumption today.

While further research is needed, it appears that there is a substantial potential for further retirement income gains from enhanced preservation. It is likely that preservation will be enhanced to some degree by the provision contained in the Unemployment Compensation Amendments of 1992 requiring employees to make a direct rollover of their qualified retirement plan distribution into another qualified plan or pay a mandatory 20 percent withholding fee on the lump-sum distribution.

# Conclusion

The employment-based pension system in the United States is a model for the rest of the world. It has contributed to the high economic status of the current generation of retirees and holds great promise for the future. It has provided a high return on investment for employers, individuals, and the government. However, there are gaps in employer-sponsored coverage, particularly in the small employer sector. A close eye on the implications of change, especially the trend toward greater use of defined contribution plans and the increasing occurrence of lump sum distributions, and a careful hand on adjustments that may be necessary to keep it on course should assure a sound pension future.

# Bibliography

Board of Governors of the Federal Reserve System, *Flow of Funds Accounts: Assets and Liabilities Outstanding Fourth Quarter 1992* (Washington, DC: Board of Governors of the Federal Reserve System, March 1993).

Employee Benefit Research Institute. *Databook on Employee Benefits.* Second Edition. Washington, DC: Employee Benefit Research Institute, 1992.

_____. *Quarterly Pension Investment Report*, fourth quarter 1992. Washington, DC: Employee Benefit Research Institute, 1992.

Employee Benefit Research Institute/The Gallup Organization, Inc. *Public Attitudes on Retirement Age and Planning, 1992*, G-35. Washington, DC: Employee Benefit Research Institute, 1992.

_____. *Public Attitudes on Retirement Benefits,* G-11. Washington, DC: Employee Benefit Research Institute, 1990.

Goodfellow, Gordon P., and Sylvester J. Schieber. "Death and Taxes: Can We Fund for Retirement Between Them?" Paper. Washington, DC: The Wyatt Company, 1992.

Grad, Susan. *Income of the Population 55 and Over*, 1978, 1980, 1982, and 1984. U.S. Department of Health and Human Services, Social Security Administration, pub. no. 13-11871. Washington, DC: U.S. Government Printing Office, 1981–1985.

_____. *Income of the Population 55 or Older, 1986*, U.S. Department of Health and Human Services, Social Security Administration, pub. no. 13-11871. Washington, DC: U.S. Government Printing Office, 1988.

_____. *Income of the Population 55 or Older, 1988*. U.S. Department of Health and Human Services, Social Security Administration, pub. no. 13-11871. Washington, DC: U.S. Government Printing Office, 1990.

_____. *Income of the Population 55 or Older, 1990*. U.S. Department of Health and Human Services, Social Security Administration, pub. no. 13-11871. Washington, DC: U.S. Government Printing Office, 1992.

Grad, Susan, and Karen Foster. *Income of the Population 55 and Over, 1976*. U.S. Department of Health, Education, and Welfare, pub. no. 13-11865 Washington, DC: U.S. Government Printing Office, 1979.

Pension Benefit Guaranty Corporation. *Pension Benefit Guaranty Corporation Annual Report, 1992*. Washington, DC: Pension Benefit Guaranty Corporation, 1993.

Piacentini, Joseph S. "Preservation of Pension Benefits." *EBRI Issue Brief*, no. 98 (Employee Benefit Research Institute, January 1990).

_____. "Preserving Portable Pensions," *EBRI Special Report* SR-7 (Employee Benefit Research Institute, June 1990).

Reno, Virginia P. "The Role of Pensions in Retirement Income: Trends and Questions." Paper. Washington, DC: National Academy on Aging, forthcoming.

Salisbury, Dallas. "Pension Tax Expenditures: Are They Worth the Cost?" *EBRI Issue Brief* no. 134 (Employee Benefit Research Institute, February 1993).

Turner, John A., and Daniel J. Beller, eds. *Trends in Pensions, 1989*. U.S. Department of Labor. Pension and Welfare Benefits Administration. Washington, DC: U.S. Department of Labor, 1989.

_____. *Trends in Pensions, 1992*. U.S. Department of Labor. Pension and Welfare Benefits Administration. Washington, DC: U.S. Department of Labor, 1992.

U.S. Department of Commerce. Bureau of the Census. *1982 and 1987 Census of Governments, Employee Retirement Systems of State and Local Governments* (Washington, DC: U.S. Government Printing Office, 1983 and 1989.

_____. *Finances of Employee-Retirement Systems of State and Local Governments*, selected years 1982–1990. Washington, DC: U.S. Government Printing Office, 1984–1992.

U.S. Department of Commerce. Bureau of Economic Analysis. *Survey of Current Business, January 1992*. Washington, DC: U.S. Government Printing Office, 1992.

_____. *The National Income and Products Accounts of the United States: Statistical Supplement, 1959–1988*, Vol. 2. Washington, DC: U.S. Government Printing Office, 1992.

U.S. Department of Defense. *Chapter 95 of Title 31, U.S.C. Report on the Military Retirement System as of Sept. 30, 1991*. Unpublished report.

U.S. Department of Health and Human Services. Social Security Administration. *1991 Annual Report of the Board of Trustees of the Federal Old-Age and Survivors Insurance and Disability Insurance Trust Funds*. Baltimore, MD: Social Security Administration, 1991.

U.S. Department of Labor. Bureau of Labor Statistics. "BLS Reports on Employee Benefits in Medium and Large Private Industry Establishments, 1991." News release, USDL 92-764, 9 December 1992.

_____. *Employee Benefits in Medium and Large Firms, 1989*. Washington, DC: U.S. Government Printing Office, 1990.

_____. *Employee Benefits in Small Private Establishments, 1990*. Washington, DC: U.S. Government Printing Office, 1992.

_____. *Employee Benefits in State and Local Governments, 1990*. Washington, DC: U.S. Government Printing Office, 1990.

U.S. Department of Labor. Pension and Welfare Benefit Administration. Preliminary Estimates of Participation and Financial Characteristics of Private Pension Plans, 1977. Washington, DC: U.S. Department of Labor, 1981.

U.S. Department of the Treasury. Internal Revenue Service. Public Affairs Division IRS determination letter statistics obtained from various IRS news releases, 1976–1992.

U.S. Office of Personnel Management. Retirement and Insurance Group. *An Annual Report to Comply with the Requirements of Public Law 95-595. Sept. 30, 1991, RI 10-27, March 1992*. Washington, DC: U.S. Office of Personnel Management, 1992.

U.S. President. Office of Management and Budget. *Budget of the United States Government: Fiscal Year 1993*. Washington, DC: U.S. Government Printing Office, 1992.

VanDerhei, Jack. "Pensions, Social Security, and Savings." *EBRI Issue Brief* no. 129 (Employee Benefit Research Institute, September 1992).

The Wyatt Company. *1989 Survey of Actuarial Assumptions and Funding: Detailed Survey Results Pension Plans with 1,000 or More Active Participants*. Washington, DC: The Wyatt Company, 1990.

_____. *1992 Survey of Actuarial Assumptions and Funding: Pension Plans with 1,000 or More Active Participants*. Washington, DC: The Wyatt Company, 1993.

Zorn, Paul. *Pendat: Survey of State and Local Government Employee Retirement Systems, Data Base User's Guide*. Chicago, IL: Public Pension Coordinating Council, 1993.

# III. The Tax Treatment of Pensions

BY RICHARD L. HUBBARD

## Introduction

The U.S. Congress recognized the need for tax incentives for private pension programs in the Revenue Act of 1921. This and statutes enacted since then, covering income from trusts and pension plans, were intentionally designed to encourage the expansion of pension coverage and increased saving levels and to provide a private source of retirement income in addition to Social Security. Today, private pension and retirement plans number more than 850,000.

The preferential tax treatment accorded more recently developed retirement and capital accumulation arrangements, such as individual retirement accounts (IRAs), simplified employee pensions (SEPs), section 401(k) arrangements, and Keogh plans for the self-employed, indicate a continued interest on the part of policymakers in increasing retirement savings.

The tax treatment accorded qualified plans provides incentives both for employers to establish such plans and for employees to participate in them. In general, a contribution to a qualified pension trust is immediately deductible in computing the employer's taxes, and the tax to the employee on the contributions is deferred until the employee subsequently receives a distribution from the plan. In the interim, investment earnings on the contributions are not subject to tax. This preferential tax treatment is contingent on the employer's compliance with nondiscrimination provisions governing employee coverage and benefit levels and other rules set out in the Internal Revenue Code (IRC) and in the Employee Retirement Income Security Act of 1974 (ERISA). These provisions depart significantly from the general principles inherent in the tax law and reflect longstanding policy decisions aimed at broadening pension coverage and strengthening the pension system.

## Legislative History

### Early History

Pension plans that provide employer tax deductions and the opportunity for the tax-deferred growth of investment earnings have long been permitted under the tax laws. Tax deductions for payments to retirement trusts for current costs were allowed even before specific legislation was enacted, provided the amounts represented reasonable compensation.[1] The Revenue Act of 1921 exempted the net interest income of stock bonus and profit-sharing plans from current taxation.[2] This exemption was extended to pension trusts in 1926.[3] Also beginning in 1921, employees were not taxed when they made contributions, but only when they received distributions from the pension trusts (to the extent that the benefits exceeded the employee's own contributions).[4]

Before 1928, the tax law did not permit an employer a deduction for the funding of pension liabilities for an employee's services that were performed before the effective date of the pension plan. Consequently, although many employers established balance sheet reserves (reserves that were not put into a separate fund) for this purpose, credits to these reserves were not tax deductible. Influenced by the number and size of these reserves, Congress enacted legislation in 1928 permitting employers to deduct a "reasonable" amount in excess of the amount necessary to fund the current pension liabilities.[5]

Not long afterward, lawmakers became concerned that the legislation governing pensions favored owners, officers, and selected employees without benefiting lower-paid employees. Of specific concern was the fact that a pension trust was not required to be irrevocable, so that a pension plan could be dissolved immediately after a sizable tax-deductible contribution had been made. The Revenue Act of 1938 addressed this concern by establishing the "nondiversion" rule and making pension trusts irrevocable. A pension trust is tax-exempt only if it is impossible, at any time prior to the satisfaction of all employee liabilities, for any part of the contributions or income to be used for a purpose

---

[1] *Elgin National Watch Co. v. Commissioner*, 17 B.T.A. 339, 358-60 (1929); *Hibbard, Spencer, Bartlett & Co. v. Commissioner*, 5 B.T.A. 464, 474 (1926). However, no deduction was permitted for additions to pension funds or reserves held by the employer until such amounts were actually paid to the employee. Also see Reg. 45, art. 108 (Revenue Act of 1918); Reg. 65, art. 109 (Revenue Act of 1924); and Reg. 69, art. 109 (Revenue Act of 1926).

[2] Revenue Act of 1921, § 219(f).

[3] Revenue Act of 1926, § 219(f).

[4] Revenue Act of 1921, § 219(f). Such a provision is currently codified in Code §§ 72 and 402.

[5] Revenue Act of 1928, § 23(q).

other than the exclusive benefit of employees or their beneficiaries.[6]

During World War II, pension plans became more widespread as federally imposed wage freezes induced employers and employees to negotiate compensation increases in the form of employer contributions to pension and other benefit plans. The growing number of pension plans drew attention to their potential misuse as a management tax-avoidance device. To address this problem, the Revenue Act of 1942 established nondiscriminatory employee eligibility rules for pension plan coverage, contributions, and benefits. Under these rules, a pension plan's eligibility requirements, benefits, and contributions may not discriminate in favor of officers, shareholders, or highly compensated employees. In addition, the act placed limitations on the allowable amount of the employer's deductions,[7] and rules were developed to integrate pension plans with the Social Security system.[8] These provisions of the Revenue Act of 1942 were incorporated in the IRC of 1954, and, along with modifications made by the Tax Reform Act of 1986 (TRA '86), today constitute the basic rules governing the qualification of pension plans.

### Recent History

In 1925, there were only about 400 private pension plans in operation, and approximately one-third of the total participants were employed by four of the country's largest corporations.[9] By 1954, there were about 25,000 pension plans with assets of $23.8 billion.[10] This increase aroused new concern over the potential for fiduciary abuse. The Welfare and Pension Plans Disclosure Act of 1958 (WPPDA)[11] sought to limit fiduciary abuse by establishing certain disclosure requirements. The WPPDA was more concerned with fiduciary standards than with employee rights. A 1965 report issued by President Kennedy's Committee on Corporate Pension Funds[12] expressed concern over the benefits denied because of unduly restrictive vesting and forfeiture provisions and the failure of some plans to accumulate and retain sufficient funds to meet their benefit obligations. In response to this concern and to the proliferation of pension plans (371,000 plans with net assets of $218.2 billion existed in 1974), ERISA was enacted.[13]

ERISA was intended to establish equitable standards of plan administration, create minimum vesting standards, establish standards of fiscal responsibility by requiring the amortization of unfunded liabilities, insure most vested but unfunded liabilities against premature plan termination, promote "a renewed expansion of private retirement plans" and increase the number of participants receiving private retirement benefits.[14] ERISA supplemented existing tax provisions by imposing contribution and benefit limits as well as comprehensive requirements for eligibility, vesting, employer deductions, and benefit accruals. However, the basic tax structure under ERISA was substantially the same as that which had existed since the Revenue Act of 1921.

## Tax Principles Governing the Deductibility and Funding of Retirement Plan Contributions

The deductibility of employer contributions to retirement plans is governed, in part, by the same tax principles that govern the deductibility of other business expenses under IRC sec. 162.[15] Under sec. 404(a), employer contributions are not deductible unless they are otherwise deductible as reasonable compensation for services rendered. In this respect, the tax laws governing the deductibility of pension contributions are narrower in scope than those governing the deductibility of other forms of compensation because they place specific statutory limits on the allowable deduction amount.[16]

Also, the rules governing the timing of business expense deductions are generally broader in scope than those applicable to the timing of deductions for pension contributions. A business expense deduction generally may be taken in the taxable year during which the

---

[6] Revenue Act of 1938, § 165(a).

[7] Revenue Act of 1942, § 162(b).

[8] Revenue Act of 1942, § 162(b), amending § 165(a) of the 1939 Code.

[9] U.S. Congress, Senate, Committee on Labor and Public Welfare, *Legislative History of the Employee Retirement Income Security Act of 1974 (P.L. 93-406)* (Washington, DC: U.S. Government Printing Office, 1976).

[10] Unpublished asset data, Employee Benefit Research Institute, *EBRI Quarterly Pension Investment Report* data base; and plan count from Internal Revenue Service periodic press releases compiled by Employee Benefit Research Institute.

[11] 29 U.S.C. § 301 (1976) (repealed).

[12] President's Committee on Corporate Pension Funds and Other Private Retirement and Welfare Programs, *Public Policy and Private Pension Programs: A Report to the President on Private Employee Retirement Plans* (Washington, DC: U.S. Government Printing Office, 1965).

[13] Unpublished asset data, Employee Benefit Research Institute, *EBRI Quarterly Pension Investment Report* data base; plan count from *EBRI Notes*, no. 12 (December 1987).

[14] H.R. 533, 93d Cong., 1st Sess. (1973).

[15] Unless otherwise indicated, all section references are to the Internal Revenue Code of 1986, as amended.

[16] §§ 415(b), (c).

expenses are paid or incurred (or in the year accrued by an accrual basis taxpayer).[17] By contrast, sec. 404 requires that contributions to qualified plans be paid in order to be deducted. This rule, which applies to plans that have ". . . the effect of a stock bonus, pension, profit-sharing, or annuity plan, or similar plan deferring the receipt of compensation,"[18] in effect, puts all employers on a cash-accounting basis for these purposes.[19] For nonqualified plans, amounts paid or contributed by the employer must be included in the employee's income for tax purposes in order to be deductible by the employer.[20]

## Qualified Plans

The statutory treatment of the deductibility of contributions to qualified plans is consistent with prestatutory rules governing deductions for payments to pension trusts. Prior to the Revenue Act of 1928, such deductions were permitted based on the theory that the employer had made actual payments to viable trusts as part of compensation, which, if reasonable, were deductible as ordinary and necessary business expenses.[21] The deduction was not in question, despite the fact that the amounts contributed could revert to the employer in the case of liquidation or revocation of the trust or that the employer retained the right to alter the provisions of the trust.

Subsequent statutory provisions made pension trusts irrevocable (Revenue Act of 1938) and restricted the conditions under which contributed amounts could revert to the employer. When a qualified plan terminates, only the excess amount resulting from "erroneous actuarial computations" may be returned to the employer,[22] and under the Omnibus Budget Reconciliation Act of 1990 (OBRA '90) an excise tax is imposed on the surplus assets reverting to the employer. This excise tax is at the rate of 20 percent if the employer either establishes a qualified replacement plan or amends the terminating plan to provide for benefit increases. Otherwise, the excise tax rate is 50 percent.[23]

In addition, the Omnibus Budget Reconciliation Act of 1987 (OBRA '87) provides that, with certain exceptions, amendments to pension plans permitting reversions to employers may not be made effective until five years after they are adopted.[24] In the case of plans that, as of December 17, 1987, had no provision relating to the distribution of plan assets to the employer, this new rule will apply only to amendments adopted after one year after the effective date of the law. Plan provisions adopted before December 17, 1987, and providing for distribution of plan assets to the employer are not affected. OBRA '87 also includes a provision that allocates excess plan assets between employer and employee contributions on a pro rata basis. In many circumstances, this will increase the portion of the excess that must be distributed to employees.

In addition to the deductibility of contributions under the reasonableness limits imposed by sec. 162, an employer sponsoring a qualified plan may deduct contributions only up to certain dollar limits set by statute. These limits may differ by (1) plan type (e.g., defined benefit, defined contribution, stock bonus, profit sharing); (2) whether employees are covered by more than one plan; and (3) whether the plan falls into a special plan category called top-heavy plans.

### Plan Types

*Defined Benefit Plans*—In a defined benefit plan, the employer agrees to provide the employee with a specified benefit amount at retirement and must arrange to fund this benefit in accordance with the actuarial principles under which the plan is managed.

Maximum Funding Limits—The IRC sets a maximum limit on the amount of contributions for which the plan sponsor may claim a tax deduction each year. This limit is the lesser of (1) the normal cost for the year plus amortization over a 10-year period of the initial unfunded actuarial liability and any increases due to changes or actuarial losses; or (2) 150 percent of the plan's current liability, which is defined as all liabilities to employees and beneficiaries under the plan, with the exception of liability for certain benefits that are contingent on certain unpredictable events. The U.S. Department of the Treasury may issue regulations that will adjust the 150 percent figure "in a budget neutral manner" to reflect plan participants' ages and lengths of service. Contributions in excess of the above limits are not deductible by the employer. In practice, employers generally contribute only that amount for which they will receive a deduction in the year of contribution. Additionally, there is a 10 percent excise tax on nondeductible employer contributions to

---

[17] § 162(a).

[18] U.S. Treasury, Reg. § 1.404(b)-1.

[19] With the limited exception that a deduction is permitted for a taxable year contribution made after the close of the taxable year but prior to the return filing date (including extensions). § 404(a)(6).

[20] § 404(a)(5).

[21] *Elgin National Watch Co. v. Commissioner*, 17 B.T.A. 339 (1929); *Hibbard, Spencer, Bartlett & Co. v. Commissioner*, 5 B.T.A. 464 (1926).

[22] U. S. Treasury, Reg. § 1.401-2(b)(1).

[23] §§ 4980(a), (d).

[24] ERISA, § 404(d).

qualified plans; this tax is imposed each year until a deductible contribution is permissible.[25]

In addition to general limitations, the tax deductibility of contributions is also limited on an individual participant basis under sec. 415. A defined benefit plan must provide that the annual benefit for an individual participant cannot exceed the lesser of $90,000, adjusted for the cost of living ($115,641 in 1993) or 100 percent of the participant's average compensation for his or her three highest earning years. There is also an overall limit on annual compensation that can be considered for contribution or benefit purposes.[26] This limitation, which first became effective for 1989, was originally $200,000, indexed for cost-of-living increases, and had reached $235,840 for 1993. The Omnibus Budget Reconciliation Act of 1993, however, reduced the limit, effective for 1994, to $150,000, again indexed for cost-of-living increases. Maximum benefits payable to individuals under private-sector defined benefit plans generally must be actuarially reduced if the beneficiary claims benefits before the Social Security normal retirement age, which is scheduled to rise gradually from age 65 to age 67 between the years 2000 and 2016.

If the plan provides for benefits in excess of the limits, the plan loses its tax qualified status, and any contribution to fund a benefit in excess of the limits is not deductible.[27]

Minimum Funding Limits—A defined benefit plan is also subject to minimum funding requirements.[28] In general, the minimum amount an employer must contribute to a defined benefit plan each year is the sum of the normal cost of the plan for the year and the amount necessary to amortize past service costs. This amount is then decreased by the amount necessary to amortize decreases in pension liabilities and experience gains.[29]

The minimum funding provisions for single-employer plans must be satisfied through a quarterly payment program.[30] The amount of any required installment is 25 percent of the required annual payment, which is the lesser of 90 percent of the minimum funding requirement for the year, or 100 percent of the minimum funding requirement for the preceding plan year. For plans on a calendar year basis, quarterly payments are due on April 15, July 15, October 15, and January 15. For noncalendar year

plans, payments are due 3.5, 6.5, 9.5, and 12.5 months after the close of the prior plan year.[31]

Any single-employer plan with an unfunded current liability (meaning a termination liability and not a projected liability) will have to pay an additional amount to force more rapid funding of liabilities that existed as of December 31, 1987; of new liabilities created after that date; and of liabilities arising from the occurrence of unpredictable contingent events such as a plant closing.[32]

The additional charge is limited to the amount necessary to increase the funded current liability percentage to 100 percent and is the amount of the minimum contribution subtracted from the new "deficit reduction contribution." The deficit reduction contribution is the amount required to amortize the pre-1988 unfunded liability over 18 years; plus the amortization of the new unfunded liability, which is a percentage that decreases with the amount of underfunding; plus amortization over no longer than 7 years for liabilities created by a contingent event.[33] A special rule allows for slower funding of past service liability in a new plan or a newly expanded plan. OBRA '87 also made changes in prior law that allowed more discretion for actuarial assumptions. For single-employer plans, each actuarial assumption must be reasonable individually, rather than in the aggregate, and special rules apply to interest rate assumptions. The plan must use an interest rate in the "permissible range," that is, not more than 10 percent above or below the average rate for 30-year Treasury bonds for the 4-year period ending on the last day before the beginning of the plan year for which the interest rate is being used. The Treasury Department may also specify a lower rate, under the appropriate circumstances, that is not less than 80 percent of the average rates described above. No rate outside of the "permissible range" is allowed.[34] Multiemployer plans are exempted from these interest rules, except as applied to the full-funding limitations. Also, for single-employer plans only, the amortization schedule for net experience gains and losses was reduced from 15 years to 5 years, and amortization for gains and losses attributable to changes in actuarial assumptions or methods was reduced from 30 years to 10 years.[35]

Failure to comply with these minimum funding requirements leads to the imposition of an excise tax

---

[25] § 4972.
[26] § 401 (a) (17).
[27] § 404(j).
[28] Id.
[29] § 412(b).
[30] § 412(m).

[31] Id.
[32] § 412(c).
[33] § 412(l).
[34] § 412(b)(5).
[35] §§ 412(b)(2)(iv), (v).

equal to 10 percent of the funding deficiency, and failure to correct the deficiency may result in an additional tax equal to 100 percent of the deficiency.[36] A lien may be imposed against all the assets of the plan sponsor and members of its controlled group for failing to meet any installment payments during the plan year as each payment is missed if the unpaid balance plus interest exceeds $1 million.[37]

The minimum funding requirements may be waived in certain situations, but minimum funding waivers for single-employer plans were restricted by OBRA '87. Funding waivers will be granted only if the plan sponsor demonstrates to the Secretary of the Treasury a temporary substantial business hardship for it and each member of its controlled group.[38]

Effective January 1, 1988, the maximum number of waivers granted in the 15 years after that date is reduced to 3 from 5 under prior law for single-employer plans.[39] Additional requirements are imposed on the submission of applications for waivers and on the amortization period and the interest rate to be used in computing the amortization charge for waived contributions. For multiemployer plans, hardship need not be temporary, and there need not be hardship at a contributing employer's controlled group level in order for a multiemployer plan to qualify for a funding waiver. Also, multiemployer plans may still obtain 5 funding waivers in a 15-year period.[40]

These minimum funding standards also apply to defined contribution plans that are money purchase plans (where contributions are expressed as a percentage of covered payroll), but not to profit-sharing or stock bonus plans.[41]

*Defined Contribution Plans*—In a defined contribution plan, the employer makes specified contributions to the employee's account and, on termination of employment, the employee is entitled to the value of the vested part of the account. A defined contribution plan thus requires the establishment of an individual account for each participating employee, because it is funded through the accumulation (including income and capital appreciation) of the contributions made on behalf of each employee.

There are several types of defined contribution plans: money purchase plans (where employer contributions are stated as a percentage of an employee's salary); target benefit plans (where contributions are scaled to achieve a specified retirement benefit); profit-sharing plans (including 401(k) arrangements), thrift plans, stock bonus plans, and employee stock ownership plans (ESOPs). In general, annual additions[42] to defined contribution plans may not exceed the lesser of 25 percent of an employee's compensation or $30,000.[43] The $30,000 limitation is subject to adjustment when the adjusted dollar limitation for a defined benefit plan exceeds $120,000. The dollar limitation for a defined contribution plan will then equal 25 percent of the dollar limitation for a defined benefit plan.[44] The IRC further limits the maximum deductible contribution to profit-sharing and stock bonus plans to an amount equal to 15 percent of the compensation of all participants.[45] The dollar limitation on the amount of annual compensation that can be considered in determining contributions applies to defined contribution plans.

*Participants in More Than One Plan*—In addition to limiting contributions to separate plans, sec. 415(e) imposes further contribution limitations when an employee participates in both a defined benefit and a defined contribution plan sponsored by the same employer. Sec. 404(j) denies any deductions for amounts contributed to fund or provide benefits in excess of the limits.

In general, sec. 415(e) provides that, if a participant is covered by both a defined benefit plan and a defined contribution plan maintained by the same employer, the sum of a defined benefit plan fraction and a defined contribution plan fraction may not exceed 1.0. These fractions are calculated as follows.

The numerator of the defined benefit plan fraction is the projected annual benefit of the participant determined at the close of the year. The denominator is the lesser of: (1) 1.25 multiplied by the maximum dollar limitation for a defined benefit plan; or (2) 1.4 multiplied by the percentage of compensation limit (for a defined benefit plan) for the year.

---

[36] § 4971.
[37] § 412(n)(3).
[38] § 412(d)(1).
[39] Id.
[40] Id.
[41] § 412(h).
[42] The term *annual addition* means the sum for any year of (1) employer contributions; (2) the employee's contribution; and (3) forfeitures. § 415(c)(2).
[43] § 415(c).

[44] Id.
[45] § 404(a)(3). Amounts contributed in excess of 15 percent of compensation may be carried over to a succeeding year, but the deductible amount in any taxable year shall not exceed 15 percent of the participant's compensation for the year. For contributions in any year beginning before January 1, 1987, the amount of the contribution in excess of the deductible amount for that year may be carried forward for deduction in a later year, but the later year deduction may not exceed 25 percent of the participant's total compensation for the year.

The numerator of the defined contribution plan fraction is the total annual additions to the participant's account through the close of the year. The denominator is the sum, for all years of the participant's service, of the lesser for each year of: (1) 1.25 multiplied by the maximum dollar limitation for a defined contribution plan; or (2) 1.4 multiplied by the percentage of compensation limit (for a defined contribution plan) for the year.

An additional limit is placed on the employer's deduction when one or more employees are covered by both a pension or annuity plan and a profit-sharing or stock bonus plan. If this is the case, the total deduction for contributions to all plans may not exceed either 25 percent of compensation paid or accrued to all plan participants during the taxable year or, if greater, the contribution necessary to satisfy minimum funding standards for that year. Excess amounts contributed may be deducted in succeeding taxable years subject to the 25 percent limit in the year deducted.[46]

*Top-Heavy Plans*—The Tax Equity and Fiscal Responsibility Act of 1982 (TEFRA) established a new category of plans known as "top-heavy" plans. A plan is top heavy if 60 percent or more of the accounts or accrued benefits under the plan are attributable to "key employees," defined as: officers (revised in 1988 to exclude those earning less than one-half of the dollar limit on contributions in a defined benefit plan); the 10 employees owning the largest shares of the employer and having annual compensation of more than the dollar limit on contributions in a defined contribution plan; owners of more than a 5 percent interest in the employer; or owners of more than a 1 percent interest in the employer who receive compensation from the employer in excess of $150,000.[47]

A top-heavy plan must satisfy certain requirements concerning the benefits or plan contributions for nonkey employees. The plan must meet one of two accelerated vesting schedules and certain minimum benefit or plan contribution requirements.[48] In determining plan contributions or benefits, only the first $150,000 of an employee's compensation (beginning in 1994) will be taken into account.

## Nonqualified Plans

The statutory treatment of employer deductions for deferred compensation under nonqualified plans differs substantially from prestatutory rules governing such deductions. Prior to the Revenue Act of 1942, unfunded noncontingent liabilities incurred to pay deferred compensation were tax deductible by an accrual-basis employer even though such amounts were paid and includable in the employee's gross income in later years.[49] Payments to trustees under deferred income plans were also deductible as long as the amount could revert to the employer only in situations beyond the employer's control.[50]

Under the Revenue Act of 1942, the employer was permitted a tax deduction only (1) on the payment of benefits (unfunded plans); or (2) if the employee's interest was nonforfeitable at the time the contribution was made (funded plans).[51] Although the Tax Reform Act of 1969 continued the rule governing unfunded plans, it substantially revised the treatment of funded plans by permitting the employer to take a deduction when the employee's interest became vested even though the employee's interest had been forfeitable at the time the contribution was made.[52] The IRS had previously taken the position that the employer was never entitled to a deduction for contributions in which an employee's interest was forfeitable when the contribution was made.[53]

Current statutory treatment of tax deductions for nonqualified plan contributions restricts their availability. Deductions are still available for employer liabilities calculated on an accrual basis if there is no deferral of compensation.[54] Contributions to nonqualified plans are deductible only when paid and included in the employee's gross income. This requirement is met in unfunded plans when payments are actually made to the beneficiary[55] and in funded plans when the employee's rights in employer contributions are not subject to a substantial risk of forfeiture.[56] In addition, in nonqualified plans, the employer's deduction is available only if separate accounts for each employee are maintained.

---

[46] § 404(a)(7).

[47] § 416(i).

[48] § 416(b).

[49] *Globe-Gazette Printing Co. v. Commissioner*, 16 B.T.A. 161 (1929), acq. IX-1 C.B. 20 (1930).

[50] *Surface Combustion Corp. v. Commissioner*, 9 T.C. 631, 655 (1947); Oxford Institute v. Commissioner, 33 B.T.A. 1136 (1936).

[51] Revenue Act of 1942, § 23(p)(1)(D). Also see U.S. Treasury, Reg. §§1.404(a)-12(b)(2), (c).

[52] § 404(a)(5); U.S. Treasury, Reg. § 1.404(a)-12(b)(1).

[53] U.S. Treasury, Reg. § 1.404(a)-12(c).

[54] *Lukens Steel Co. v. Commissioner*, 442 F.2d 1131 (3d Cir. 1971) (supplemental unemployment benefit plan); *Washington Post Co. v. United States*, 405 F.2d 1279 (Ct. Cl. 1969) (profit-incentive plan), nonacq. Rev. Rul. 76-345, 1976-2 C.B. 134.

[55] U.S. Treasury, Reg. § 1.404(a)-12(b)(2).

[56] §§ 83(a) and 402(b).

# Taxation of Employees on Plan Contributions

Under general tax principles, income is taxed when it is constructively received, i.e., when it comes into an individual's substantial control and discretion. In addition, as a general rule, when an employee receives a nonforfeitable interest in property in exchange for services, he or she is immediately taxed on the value of that property, even if he or she does not have immediate access to it, e.g., a vested interest in an irrevocable trust for his or her benefit. Under general tax rules, therefore, employer contributions to a pension or retirement plan would be taxable to the employee at the time the contribution vested and became nonforfeitable. Employee contributions also generally would be subject to tax because the funds contributed are initially within the employee's control. As discussed below, the IRC excepts from the general rules employer contributions to qualified plans and certain employee contributions.

## Employer Contributions

Whether employer contributions receive favorable tax treatment is determined by qualified plan status. Since the Revenue Act of 1921, the IRC has excepted employer contributions from the general rule stated above, and an employee has not been taxed on employer contributions to qualified plans until benefits are distributed to the employee.[57] This is true whether or not the employee is vested under the plan. Of course, before being vested the employee cannot be taxed on employer contributions because this interest is forfeitable; however, once vested, this interest is nonforfeitable and not subject to sufficiently substantial conditions as to preclude taxation under the general rule even though the benefits may not be payable until a later date (e.g., retirement or attainment of a certain age).

The general rule still applies to nonqualified plans. In funded nonqualified plans, the employee must include in income the value of the accrued benefits not subject to substantial risk of forfeiture.[58] There exists a "substantial risk of forfeiture" if the employee's right to

full enjoyment of the property is conditioned on his or her future performance of substantial services or other substantial conditions related to the purpose of the transfer of the property.[59] When such a risk does not exist, the employee's rights to the employer's contributions in a nonqualified plan are deemed vested and that amount is taxable.

In unfunded nonqualified plans, the employee is taxed on receipt of benefits because an unfunded plan does not set aside property for the benefit of the employee. Nonqualified plans have historically tended to be unfunded.[60] Nevertheless, most employers establish balance sheet reserves to cover the plans. ERISA established regulatory (nontax) funding standards for nonqualified plans but exempted many of the more usual types of nonqualified plans from these standards.[61]

Accrued benefits under unfunded plans are financed upon the employee's retirement either from current operating income or from previously established reserves, and the employer takes a tax deduction for payment of benefits at that time. Employees pay taxes on retirement income at their postretirement marginal tax rate, but run the risk of the employer's financial inability to pay benefits.

## Employee Contributions

Employee contributions are provided for by some plans both to increase retirement savings and to reduce the employer's plan costs. The IRC imposes limits on both the mandatory and the voluntary amounts employees may contribute to qualified plans. Limits on the mandatory contribution amount are aimed at eliminating the risk that the contribution requirements will result in prohibited patterns of discrimination. If employee contribution requirements are particularly burdensome, they could indirectly exclude employees from participation. The statutory limits on voluntary contributions, in turn, are aimed at preventing a qualified plan from offering excessive benefits to highly compensated employees in the form of savings accounts accruing tax-deferred interest.

***Mandatory Employee Contributions***—Employee contributions are considered mandatory if they are

---

[57] Prior to the Economic Recovery Tax Act of 1981 (ERTA), employees were taxed on amounts distributed or "made available" from a qualified plan. Sec. 314(c) of ERTA deleted reference to "made available." See § 402(a)(1)(repealed).

[58] §§ 83(a) and 402(b).

[59] U.S. Treasury, Reg. §§ 1.402(b)-1, 1.83-3(c).

[60] There are widespread reports that the growth of nonqualified plans has accelerated in response to legislation such as the Tax Equity and Fiscal Responsibility Act of 1982 and the Tax Reform Act of 1986.

[61] Exempted plans include unfunded deferred compensation plans for highly compensated employees and excess benefit plans. See ERISA §§ 301-306, particularly §§ 301(a)(3) and (9).

required as a condition of employment, a condition of plan participation, or a condition of receiving employer contributions. As a general rule, mandatory contributions cannot be so burdensome as to permit participation only by highly paid employees, thus discriminating against lower paid employees.[62] While most mandatory contributions are not deductible by the employee, earnings accumulated on these contributions are not taxed until distributed.

Mandatory employee contributions are found in relatively few private employer plans. In 1989, the most recent year for which U.S. government data are available, only 6 percent of participants in private defined benefit plans and 34 percent of participants in "retirement" defined contribution plans paid part of the cost of their plans.[63] Also, there is evidence that the relative importance of employee contributions in private employer plans had been declining sharply until the early 1980s. In a 1980 survey of 325 plans accounting for 8.2 million participants, Bankers Trust Company found that the number of contributory plans fell from 33 percent in 1975 to 19 percent in 1980.[64] This trend could reverse in the future, however, as sec. 401(k) arrangements continue to grow in popularity.

Unlike private-sector plans, public-sector plans are predominantly contributory. In 1990, 75 percent of governmental pension plan participants had to pay part of the cost of their defined benefit plans.[65] The typical plan requires contributions of 3 percent to 8 percent of salary. Employee contributions accounted for approximately 29 percent of total contributions to these plans in 1989–1990.[66] About 88 percent of the much smaller group of governmental participants (9 percent) in defined contribution plans paid part of the cost of their plans in 1990, although 17 percent of employees participated in separate, free-standing tax-deferred annuity (403(b)) plans that were not matched by employer contributions.

Federal civilian employees hired before January 1, 1984, contribute 7 percent of compensation annually to the Civil Service Retirement System. They also may make voluntary contributions (without a

match from the employer, the federal government) to a supplemental thrift plan. These federal employees are not directly covered by Social Security, but they do pay the Medicare Hospital Insurance payroll tax and are eligible for Medicare. Federal civilian employees hired on or after January 1, 1984, contribute to Social Security and Medicare; they are also covered by a noncontributory defined benefit plan; and they may also choose to contribute to a voluntary thrift plan that provides for matching contributions from the government. Beginning in fiscal year 1985, the federal government has made contributions for military retirement benefits on an accrual basis, but the plan continues to be noncontributory for military personnel.

*Voluntary Employee Contributions*—Generally, voluntary employee contributions to employer-sponsored plans are not tax deductible—they are made with "after-tax" dollars. Under special statutory rules, however, certain employee contributions may be made with "before-tax" dollars (thereby becoming, in effect, tax deductible). This is true despite the fact that in some cases (IRAs, for example), the employee has actually received the compensation being saved for retirement. In a cash or deferred arrangement under sec. 401(k), the employee exercises discretion and control by annually electing whether or not to forgo cash compensation in favor of deferred compensation that vests immediately, and amounts deferred are not included in the employee's gross income until actually received. Similar plans for certain nonprofit institutions and state and local governments are authorized under sec. 403(b). In addition, public-sector employees may participate in salary reduction arrangements under sec. 457. And a special arrangement is available to government plans, sec. 414(h)(2), in which employee contributions characterized as employer contributions are excludable from current gross income for federal income tax purposes.

The reason these special statutory rules depart from traditional tax principles is policy oriented. Congress believed that individual retirement saving was necessary to enable retirees to maintain preretirement standards of living and that the level of saving has not been adequate for that purpose. In addition to promoting individual retirement saving (a needed supplement to the Social Security system) and supplementing pension plans with deferred vesting schedules, tax deductible employee contributions remove the sole responsibility for retirement saving from the employer and provide added insurance for the employee against the possibility of early plan termination or the employee's involuntary separation from service by layoff or firing.

---

[62] U.S. Treasury, Reg. § 1.401(m)-1; Rev. Rul. 80-307, 1980-2 C.B. 136.

[63] U.S. Department of Labor, Bureau of Labor Statistics, *Employee Benefits in Medium and Large Firms, 1989* (Washington, DC: U.S. Government Printing Office, 1990).

[64] Bankers Trust Company, *Corporate Pension Plan Study: A Guide for the 1980s* (New York: Bankers Trust Company, 1980).

[65] U.S. Department of Labor, Bureau of Labor Statistics, *Employee Benefits in State and Local Governments, 1990* (Washington, DC: U.S. Government Printing Office, 1992).

[66] U.S. Department of Commerce, Bureau of the Census, *Finances of Employee Retirement Systems of State and Local Governments in 1989–90* (Washington, DC: U.S. Government Printing Office, 1992).

Thus, these special arrangements do not exist within the confines of accepted pension tax principles: they are, instead, Congress' response to the need for increased levels of private retirement saving.

# Special Retirement Arrangements

The following section describes the special arrangements Congress has authorized to allow employees to save more money on their own for retirement on a tax-deferred basis, as well as some other separate types of plans Congress has enacted to provide for the special needs of small businesses and the self-employed.

## Sec. 401(k)

The Revenue Act of 1978 authorized cash or deferred arrangements under sec. 401(k). An employee may elect to have a portion of compensation (otherwise payable in cash) contributed to a qualified profit-sharing or stock bonus plan. These contributions are not treated as distributed or available (taxable) income to the employee but as deductible employer contributions to the plan.[67] Sec. 401(k) arrangements have achieved considerable popularity since 1981, when the IRS published proposed and final regulations clarifying their implementation.

As long as the 401(k) arrangement meets specific participation and nondiscrimination standards, contributions and deductions are governed by the same rules as other defined contribution plans except that the maximum employee elective contribution cannot exceed a specified dollar limitation, adjusted for the cost of living, which is $8,994 for 1993. Because of a change made by TRA '86, a nonprofit organization cannot maintain a sec. 401(k) plan unless it was adopted before July 2, 1986, and a state or local government or political subdivision may not maintain such a plan unless it was adopted before May 6, 1986.[68]

## Sec. 403(b)

A special type of tax-deferred retirement arrangement under sec. 403(b) is available to certain nonprofit organizations and public schools, including public colleges and universities. In plan years beginning after December 31, 1988, tax deferred annuities (TDAs) must satisfy, with respect to contributions not made pursuant to salary reduction, essentially the same nondiscrimination rules and participation rules as qualified retirement plans. In addition, special nondiscrimination rules apply to elective contributions made by employees through salary deferrals.

Annual contributions to a TDA cannot exceed a maximum limit referred to as an exclusion allowance. The exclusion allowance is generally equal to 20 percent of the employee's includable compensation from the employer multiplied by the number of the employee's years of service with that employer, reduced by amounts already paid by the employer to purchase the annuity. In addition to the limit imposed by the exclusion allowance, there is a limit on employee contributions made through salary reduction of $9,500 annually or the limit on deferrals under 401(k) plans, as indexed. This limit is reduced by any deferrals on the employee's behalf to a 401(k) plan. The limit applies until the indexed 401(k) limit ($8,994 for 1993) reaches $9,500, at which time the TDA limit will also be indexed in the same manner as the 401(k) plan limit. If an employee is required to contribute a set percentage of compensation to a TDA as a condition of employment, the contribution does not count toward the annual limit. In addition, a special annual catch-up election, available for employees of educational organizations, hospitals, home health agencies, health and welfare service agencies, or churches or conventions of churches, allows larger salary reduction contributions for an eligible employee who has completed 15 years of service.

## Sec. 457

This section contains rules applicable to deferred compensation arrangements of state and local governments or agencies and instrumentalities of either. Deferred compensation plans for employees of tax-exempt organizations were made subject to sec. 457 by provisions of TRA '86.

Amounts of compensation deferred under a sec. 457 deferred compensation plan are not taxed to the employee as current income but are taxed as income when received. It is not required that a sec. 457 deferred compensation plan be offered to all employees on a nondiscriminatory basis. The plan must be unfunded. Among numerous requirements that a sec. 457 plan must meet, the amounts deferred are limited to no more than 33 1/3 percent of includable compensation or $7,500, whichever is less.[69] Any amounts being deferred under a sec. 403(b) tax-deferred annuity must be taken into account in determin-

---

[67] § 402(a)(8).
[68] § 401(k)(4)(B).

[69] § 457(b)(2).

ing whether the overall $7,500 limit has been exceeded.[70] The exclusion allowance of a sec. 403(b) tax-deferred annuity and the includable compensation on which it is figured are affected by amounts deferred under sec. 457.

## Sec. 414(h)(2)

Another arrangement under which pension plan participants may defer taxation on amounts contributed to a pension plan is available only to public employees under an arrangement known as "employer pick-up." Under retirement plans maintained by any state or political subdivision, sec. 414(h)(2) provides that the employing unit may "pick up" contributions that have been designated by the plan as employee contributions. When such contributions are picked up, they are treated as if they were made by the employer instead of by the employee. "Picked up" employee contributions are not currently taxable as income to the employee but are instead taxed later when received as pension income.

Amounts of employee contributions that are assumed by the employer under a pick-up arrangement must be taken into account in determining the exclusion allowance in setting amounts that may be additionally tax deferred through sec. 403(b) tax-deferred annuities. However, the overall limit of $9,500 for elective deferrals under tax-deferred annuities is not reduced by the amount of an individual's employer pick-up. Public employee, state teacher, or university retirement systems in at least 18 states currently use a pick-up arrangement.

## Individual Retirement Accounts

An IRA is a separate trusteed account in which an individual has a nonforfeitable interest. IRAs were established by ERISA in 1974. In establishing IRAs, Congress intended to offer workers who did not have employer-sponsored pension coverage an opportunity to set aside tax-deferred compensation for use in retirement. The 1981 Economic Recovery Tax Act (ERTA) extended the availability of IRAs to all employees (i.e., even those who already had employer-sponsored pension coverage). TRA '86 retained tax-deductible IRAs for those who are not "active participants" in employer-sponsored plans but restricted or eliminated the tax deduction for a taxpayer who is an active participant in an employer-sponsored retirement plan and has an income above specified levels.

A single worker can contribute and deduct from gross income up to $2,000 or 100 percent of earned income (whichever is lower) per year if he or she is not an active participant in an employer-sponsored plan or is an active participant and has an adjusted gross income (AGI) of less than $25,000.[71] Deductible contributions are phased out for AGI between $25,000 and $35,000.[72] Nondeductible contributions are allowed for the balance of the $2,000 maximum limit.

Where a husband and wife both earn income, each may contribute up to $2,000 or 100 percent of earned income (whichever is lower) per year.[73] A two-earner couple can therefore make a combined contribution of up to $4,000. Where a husband and wife file a joint return and either spouse is covered by an employer-sponsored plan, both are restricted in their eligibility to make deductible IRA contributions under the rules that apply to their combined AGI. They are each allowed fully deductible contributions up to $2,000 if their combined AGI is below $40,000.[74] Deductible contributions are phased out for a combined AGI between $40,000 and $50,000, and nondeductible contributions may make up the balance of the $2,000 limit. A $2,000 nondeductible contribution would be allowed for each working spouse if their combined AGI exceeded $50,000.

A married worker with a nonworking spouse can contribute up to $2,250 or 100 percent of the employed spouse's earned income (whichever is lower) per year only if the worker is not an active participant in an employer-sponsored plan or is an active participant but has AGI below $40,000.[75] The dollar limit on deductible contributions to a spousal IRA is phased out for active pension plan participants in accordance with the rules described above.

All taxable alimony received by a divorced person is treated as compensation for purposes of the IRA deduction limit, and the regular eligibility rules apply.

An employer can contribute to an IRA on behalf of the employee or also offer employee IRAs through payroll deduction arrangements.

The law permits individuals to roll over distributions of total or partial account balances from: (1) one IRA to another and (2) a qualified employer plan to an IRA. The transfer of assets from one account to another must be completed within 60 days.[76]

If an individual receives a distribution from an

---

[70] § 457(c)(2).
[71] §§ 219(b), (g)(2)(B)(i).
[72] § 219(g)(2)(A)(ii).
[73] § 219(b).

[74] § 219(g)(2)(B)(ii).
[75] § 219(c).
[76] § 408(d)(3).

IRA comprised of deductible contributions and earnings, the entire amount of the distribution is includable in his gross income and subject to tax. If an individual receives a distribution comprised in part of previously taxed nondeductible contributions, the amount of the distribution that represents nondeductible contributions is excludable from gross income. If an individual receives a distribution from an IRA before he attains age 59 1/2, a 10 percent penalty tax is imposed on the amount of the distribution includable in the individual's gross income.[77] This is in addition to the regular income tax on the portion of the distribution that is includable in gross income.

## Simplified Employee Pensions

SEPs are employer-sponsored plans that have some features in common with IRAs. In a SEP, the employer contribution is limited to the lesser of 15 percent of compensation or $30,000, which includes amounts that employees elect to contribute through salary deferrals.[78] An employer may contribute to a SEP in addition to contributing to other qualified pension plans, but the SEP contribution will count in the total deductible limit on employer contributions to all qualified plans.

The employer contribution is channeled into a retirement account maintained for the individual employee. For tax purposes, amounts contributed to a SEP by an employer on behalf of an employee and elective salary deferrals are excludable from the employee's gross income. Employees are fully and immediately vested in the employer's contributions and the investment earnings on the contributions.

TRA '86 expanded the possibilities for employee participation in a SEP by providing a salary reduction option, which is available to employees in firms with 25 or fewer employees if 50 percent of all eligible employees elect to participate.[79] The maximum deferral for 1993 is $8,994, reduced by any salary reduction contributions to a 401(k) or 403(b) plan. A special nondiscrimination test also applies whereby no single highly compensated employee can defer through salary reduction more than 125 percent of the average deferral percentage for all other eligible employees.

Employer contributions and employees' elective deferrals to a SEP are excluded from the employee's taxable income. Contributions and earnings in the SEP accumulate tax free until withdrawn.

The SEP plan must permit employer contributions to be withdrawn at any time by the employee, and continued employer contributions may not be conditioned on any portion of employer contributions remaining in the account.[80] Earnings accumulated on employer contributions are not taxed to the employee until distributed. SEPs are subject to the same penalties on premature withdrawals as IRAs.

As a result of TRA '86, an employee covered under a SEP may not be able to make fully deductible contributions to his or her own IRA unless his or her adjusted gross income falls below $25,000 (single) or $40,000 (married), as described above.

## Plans for the Self-Employed

Self-employed individuals and noncorporate employers can now establish retirements plans similar to those available to corporate employers.[81] Prior to the passage of TEFRA, Keogh, or H.R. 10, plans were subject to more stringent limits on contributions than were corporate plans. In addition, Keogh plans benefiting an owner-employee (a sole proprietor or partner whose partnership interest exceeds 10 percent) were required to meet special standards with respect to plan coverage, vesting, distributions, and other matters affecting the security of employee benefits. Reflecting the belief that the level of available tax incentives encouraging retirement savings should not depend on whether the employer is incorporated or not, TEFRA repealed the special rules for Keogh plans and generally eliminated the distinctions between qualified plans of corporate and noncorporate employers. Some of the special rules formerly applicable only to Keogh plans and intended to prevent abuse with respect to the provision of retirement benefits were retained, however, and made generally applicable to all tax-qualified plans. In addition, other rules formerly applicable only to plans for the self-employed were made applicable to all top-heavy plans.

Keogh plans are now on a par with corporate qualified plans with respect to limits on contributions and benefits. Furthermore, all qualified plans are now subject to the former Keogh rules relating to the timing of benefit distributions and the integration of defined contributions plans with Social Security. Top-heavy plans are subject to special limitations concerning includable compensation, vesting, distribution, and minimum nonintegrated benefits or contributions,

---

[77] § 72(t).
[78] § 404(e)(3)(a).
[79] § 408(k)(6).
[80] § 408(k)(4).

[81] Technically, contributions to Keogh plans are not employee contributions, because the self-employed individual is treated as an employer as well as an employee. In addition, the self-employed individual must make contributions to the plan on behalf of employees.

many of which formerly applied only to Keogh plans that benefited owner-employees.

## Taxation of Investment Earnings

Generally, applicable tax principles suggest that either the employer or the trust should be taxed on a qualified trust's investment earnings. Under the tax laws generally applicable to ordinary trusts, the employer would be taxed on a plan's investment income if it retained either a reversionary interest in plan assets due to vesting contingencies or substantial powers over the trust (such as the right to appoint trustees or to substantially alter the provisions of the trust). If the employer did not retain a reversionary interest or sufficient power over the plan, the trust would be taxed on trust income not distributed to participants.

Since the Revenue Act of 1921, however, the investment earnings of a qualified pension trust have not been subject to taxation until they are distributed. This rule applies even though, under current statutory provisions, an employer may retain the right to appoint trustees or to alter, amend, or terminate a pension plan.

In a nonqualified trust, the employer is taxed on investment earnings until the amounts become vested in the employees. At that time, the trust becomes taxable on earnings until the amount is distributed to the employees.

## Types of Retirement Plan Distributions and Tax Treatment

Under the statutory scheme, special rules govern the treatment of distributions from qualified plans. The rules are wide ranging: in some instances they automatically terminate the tax-deferred status of amounts distributed; impose a tax penalty for preretirement lump-sum distributions; impose a tax penalty on large distributions; and, in certain cases, provide further favorable tax treatment after distributions are completed.

As a general rule, distributions from a qualified trust that was previously funded with deductible employer contributions and enhanced tax-free earnings are includable in full in the gross income of the employee when received.

### Periodic Distributions from Accumulated Reserves in the Form of an Annuity

Because distributions are includable in the gross income of an employee when received, benefits payable in the form of an annuity are included in the employee's income only as payments are received.[82] If the employee contributes some of the amount necessary for the purchase of the annuity, the employee's previously taxed contributions may be recovered tax free, but on a pro rata basis over the term of the annuity. The earnings on annuities funded with employee contributions generally are subject to tax, even if these contributions are made with after-tax dollars. Contributions by (or on behalf of) the employee to IRAs, SEPs, and 401(k)s, however, are usually made with pretax dollars; accordingly, retirement benefits attributable to such contributions are fully taxable on receipt.

### Lump-Sum Distributions of Accumulated Pension Contributions and Earnings

A distribution to an employee may be entitled to special tax treatment if it is a lump-sum distribution. A lump-sum distribution is defined generally as a distribution of an employee's total accrued benefit made within a single taxable year and made on the occasion of the employee's death, attainment of age 59-1/2,[83] or separation from the employer's service. Self-employed individuals, however, may receive lump-sum distribution treatment only in the case of such a distribution made upon death, disability, or the attainment of age 59 1/2. A distribution of an annuity contract from a trust or an annuity plan may be treated as a lump-sum distribution.

TRA '86 substantially changed the tax treatment of lump-sum distributions. Under prior law, which is still applicable to certain individuals covered by a transition rule, favorable capital gains treatment and 10-year forward income averaging applied. Amounts distributed as a lump sum from a qualified plan were separated into pre-1974 amounts and post-1973 amounts. This computation was made by multiplying the amount distributed by a fraction: the numerator was the number of months of active participation in the plan before January 1, 1974, and the denominator was the total number of months of active participation.[84] The resulting sum was deemed the

---

[82] If the plan provides the employee with the option of receiving the amount as either a lump-sum distribution of benefits or an annuity in lieu of the lump sum, the employee must exercise the option to receive annuity payments within 60 days from the date when the lump sum first became payable or be treated as having constructively received the entire value (§ 72(h); see also Revenue Ruling 59-94, 1959-1 C.B. 25).

[83] § 402(d)(4)(A).

[84] In computing months of active participation before 1974, any part of a calendar year in which there was participation is counted as 12 months. When calculating months of participation after 1973, any part of a calendar month of participation is treated as one month.

pre-1974 portion and, in the absence of the election described below, was taxed as a long-term capital gain. Such treatment may have been favorable to the taxpayer because such capital gain was subject to a lower rate of tax. The balance of the lump-sum distribution was deemed the post-1973 portion and was treated as ordinary income.

An employee participating in the plan for 5 or more years prior to distribution could elect to use a special 10-year forward income averaging method to compute the amount of tax on the post-1973 amount. Under this special income averaging rule, a separate tax was computed at ordinary income rates on one-tenth of the post-1973 amount (less a minimum distribution allowance), and the resulting figure was multiplied by 10. Because of our progressive income tax rates and the fact that this tax was computed separately from the taxpayer's other income, the 10-year forward income averaging rule could result in substantial tax savings.

A separate election could be made to treat all pre-1974 amounts as ordinary income eligible for 10-year forward income averaging. Such an election could be advantageous since, depending on the amount of the distribution, 10-year forward income averaging might have produced a lower tax on the pre-1974 amount than would capital gains treatment. The election was irrevocable and applied to all subsequent lump-sum distributions received by the taxpayer.

TRA '86 phases out capital gains treatment for lump-sum distributions over 6 years beginning January 1, 1987, and eliminates 10-year forward averaging for taxable years beginning with December 31, 1986. Instead, TRA '86 permits a one-time election of 5-year forward averaging for a lump-sum distribution received after age 59 1/2. Under a transition rule, a participant who attained age 50 by January 1, 1986, is permitted to make one election of 5-year forward averaging or 10-year forward averaging (at 1986 tax rates) with respect to a single lump-sum without regard to attainment of age 59 1/2 and to retain the capital gains character of the pre-1974 portion of such a distribution. Under the transition rule, the pre-1974 capital gains portion is taxed at a rate of 20 percent.

Distributions from 401(k) plans are eligible for special lump-sum tax treatment. IRA and 403(b) distributions, however, are not.

A lump-sum distribution received in the form of employer securities or retirement bonds receives additional favorable tax treatment. In general, the net unrealized appreciation attributable to an employer's securities is not taxed on distribution but is taxed only when the securities are sold.[85]

A 10 percent additional tax is imposed on lump-sum distributions paid to individuals before age 59 1/2 from most tax-favored retirement plans.[86] The tax does not apply to the return of employee after-tax contributions (but it does apply to the earnings thereon) or to amounts rolled over to an IRA or other qualified plan. It also does not apply to distributions from sec. 457 plans of state and local governments or to certain distributions from an ESOP prior to January 1, 1990. The 10 percent penalty is not imposed if the distribution is received after an individual attains age 59 1/2 or is taken in the form of an annuity. Payments made after the participant has separated from service on or after age 55, used for payment of medical expenses to the extent deductible under federal income tax rules, or made to or on behalf of an alternate payee pursuant to a qualified domestic relations order are exempt from the penalty tax.

Distributions in any year exceeding $150,000 and lump-sum distributions in excess of $750,000 are subject to a 15 percent excise tax.[87]

## Estate and Survivor Benefits

The favorable treatment once afforded to estate and survivor benefits has been repealed. At one time, benefits attributable to employer contributions were wholly excludable from the decedent's gross estate. The exclusion was limited to $100,000 by TEFRA and was repealed by the Deficit Reduction Act of 1984. Retirement benefits remain excludable from a decedent's gross estate under the martial deduction provisions. Benefit payments from a qualified trust received by the beneficiaries or the estate of an employee are excludable from gross income for income tax purposes in an amount not to exceed $5,000.[88] Any amounts received during the lifetime of the decedent or attributable to amounts accumulated under nonqualified plans are includable in the decedent's estate. Similarly, a participant who has elected to provide a survivor benefit based on accrued benefits under the plan is deemed to have made a gift to the beneficiary to the extent that the survivor benefit is based on the employee's own contributions.

## Participant Loans

Loans to participants from qualified trusts are a use of pension assets that has received some policy attention in recent years. Prior to the passage of TEFRA, loans to

---

[85] § 402(e)(4)(B).
[86] § 72(t).
[87] § 4980A(c).
[88] § 101(b).

participants from plan assets were subject only to the rules governing other plan investments: the loan had to bear a reasonable rate of interest, be adequately secured, and provide a reasonable repayment schedule. Participant loans were generally secured by the portion of the participant's interest in the plan that was nonforfeitable at the time the loan was made. It was further required that plan loans be made available to all participants on a nondiscriminatory basis.

By 1982, Congress had become concerned that widespread borrowing from plan reserves could reduce the role of plans as retirement savings. At the same time, legislative debates reflected the concern that prohibiting loans entirely would discourage voluntary participation among employees who might need access to such funds during financial emergencies.[89]

In response to these concerns, TEFRA added new provisions restricting plan loans under sec. 72: loans are to be treated as plan distributions unless they meet certain requirements. The requirements were further tightened by TRA '86.

For loans after December 31, 1986, the amount of new loans plus the outstanding balance of all other plan loans cannot exceed the lesser of (a) $50,000, or (b) the greater of one-half of the present value of the employee's nonforfeitable accrued benefit under the plan or $10,000. As a result of TRA '86, the $50,000 limit is reduced by the excess of the highest outstanding loan balance during the one-year period ending on the day before the new loan is made, over the outstanding balance on the date of the loan. This was intended to prevent a plan participant from maintaining a permanent $50,000 loan through the use of balloon payments and bridge loans from third parties.[90]

Loans must be repaid within five years. A longer term is available only for loans to acquire the participant's principal residence. The loan must require substantially level amortization payments, payable at least quarterly. The deductibility of interest on plan loans follows the general income tax rules, except that interest on loans made to a "key employee" or attributable to elective deferrals under a 401(k) or tax-deferred annuity is never deductible. Nondeductible interest paid to the plan also does not increase the individual's basis in a plan or tax-deferred annuity. Loans from IRAs are treated as distributions under all circumstances, regardless of whether the requirements

applicable to qualified plan loans are met. Similarly, the pledging of an IRA as security for a loan will result in the amount being treated as if it were distributed.[91] In addition, loans to owner-employees from Keogh plans continue to be prohibited transactions.[92]

### Rollovers

Effective January 1, 1993, the rules on rollovers have changed. Under new law, a total or partial distribution of the balance to the credit of the employee under a qualified plan may be rolled over tax free into another qualified plan or IRA unless the distribution is one of a series of substantially equal payments made (1) over the life (or life expectancy) of the participant (or the joint lives or life expectancies of the participant and his or her beneficiary), or (2) over a specified period of 10 years or more.[93] The transfer must be made within 60 days of the participant's receipt of the distribution from the first plan. A qualified retirement or annuity plan must permit participants to have any distribution that is eligible for rollover transferred directly to another qualified plan or IRA. If a plan makes a distribution to an individual of a sum that is eligible to be rolled over, the plan must withhold 20 percent of the distribution even though the distribution, if rolled over within 60 days, would not be subject to tax.[94] If a plan transfers a distribution directly to another qualified plan or IRA, the withholding requirement does not apply.

If any portion of a lump-sum distribution is rolled over, forward income averaging is not available for a distribution of the balance. Similarly, if a distribution from a plan that is not a lump-sum distribution is rolled over, forward averaging is not available to a subsequent lump-sum distribution from that plan.

## Conclusion

The deductibility of employer contributions to qualified pension trusts under current law is consistent with prestatutory law governing such deductions. The statutory treatment of trust earnings and plan participants represents a departure from general tax principles and was inspired by the express policy goals of encouraging pension coverage and expansion, increasing saving levels, and providing a private, in addition to

---

[89] U.S. Congress, Joint Committee on Taxation, *General Explanation of the Revenue Provisions of the Tax Equity and Fiscal Responsibility Act of 1982*, Joint Committee Print (Washington, DC: Government Printing Office, 1982).

[90] For purposes of this limit, all of an employer's plans are treated as one.

[91] § 408(e)(4).

[92] § 4975(d).

[93] § 402(c).

[94] § 3405(c)(1)(B).

a public, source of retirement security. The tax-favored treatment of qualified pensions is thus not a recent development but rather was present in early statutory rules and prior nonstatutory law. The favorable treatment accorded IRAs, SEPs, 401(k)s, and 403(b)s is similarly intended to increase voluntary individual retirement savings.

# IV.  Funding Public and Private Pensions[1]

BY JACK VANDERHEI

## Introduction

This chapter is intended to provide the background necessary to fully grasp the technical details of many of the other chapters of this book. It is designed to acquaint the reader with the funding requirements faced by sponsors of both private and public defined benefit[2] pension plans.

This chapter deals with cash flow concepts (pension funding), not income and expense concepts (accounting). Sponsors of most large private plans must comply with Financial Accounting Standards Board (FASB) Statement No. 87, Employers' Accounting for Pensions (FASB 87), which establishes standards for financial reporting and accounting for an employer that offers pension benefits to its employees. Accounting requirements also exist for governmental plans. In November 1986, the Governmental Accounting Standards Board (GASB) issued its Statement No. 5: Disclosure of Pension Information by Public Employee Retirement Systems of State and Local Governmental Employers. This document provides direction to accountants as to how defined benefit pension information for public employee retirement systems (PERS) should be disclosed, as well as how that information should be handled for state and local governmental employers.

## Funding Private Pension Plans

A private defined benefit plan must meet specific tax law requirements for minimum funding and observe funding limitations in order to qualify for tax advantages. While many of these concepts apply to both single employer plans and multiemployer plans, there are some important differences. Since most of the

recent public policy debate has concerned the single employer plans (e.g., the solvency of the Pension Benefit Guaranty Corporation (PBGC) program for these plans), they will be the exclusive focus of this chapter.[3]

### The Spectrum of Prefunding Approaches

Various approaches have been used to finance private pension plans in the past, including the current disbursement approach and the terminal funding approach. Although they are not permitted by the Internal Revenue Code (IRC) for qualified plans, knowledge of these two approaches should provide a better basis for understanding advance funding required by law.

Under the current disbursement approach (commonly referred to as the pay-as-you-go approach), the employer pays each retired worker's monthly pension as it becomes due. The monthly pension outlays are provided out of current operating income and are treated as a part of wage costs. The cash flow consequences of this approach to the sponsor are relatively low for the first few years since the number of retired employees eligible for benefits is typically small. However, as the eligible population matures, the retirement benefits eventually become a significant percentage of compensation.

Under the terminal funding approach, the employer sets aside a lump-sum amount on the date of retirement sufficient to provide the monthly pension benefit promised for the employee under the plan. As a percentage of compensation, the contributions required under the terminal funding approach will tend to increase each year until a stable population is achieved.[4] Thereafter, the annual costs should remain constant (as a percentage of compensation) unless the

---

[1] Portions of this paper appeared previously in Everett T. Allen, Jr., Joseph J. Melone, Jerry S. Rosenbloom, and Jack L. Van Derhei, *Pension Planning: Pensions, Profit Sharing, and Other Deferred Compensation Plans*, seventh edition (Homewood, IL: Richard D. Irwin, Inc., 1992).

[2] In general, a defined benefit pension plan provides a formula that specifies the amount each participant will receive as a retirement benefit beginning at a specific age. Typically, the benefit amount will increase with both the number of years of participation and the participant's compensation. Sponsors generally do not earmark pension contributions to individual participants under this approach. In contrast, under the defined contribution approach a

plan sponsor provides a mechanism for determining the annual contribution for each participant (e.g., 3 percent of compensation). The participant's benefit is typically equal to the value of the accumulated account balance. Since the concept of over- or underfunding these plans is rarely a concern, they will not be dealt with in this paper.

[3] Readers interested in the technical differences in the funding requirements between the two types of plans are encouraged to see McGinn (1992).

[4] See McGill and Grubbs (1989), for a discussion of the basic concepts of plan population.

method of determining benefits and/or demographics of the participants change.

Like the current disbursement approach, terminal funding does not require the employer to make any contributions on behalf of employees who are still actively at work. As a result, annual pension costs under both of these approaches could be subject to extreme volatility as asset values fluctuate and different numbers of employees choose to retire each year.

In contrast, under advance funding, the employer (and the employee, under contributory plans) sets aside funds on some systematic basis prior to the employee's retirement date. If contributions are made on an advance funding basis, the accumulated assets in the pension fund will soon exceed the aggregate lump sums needed to provide benefits to those workers who are already retired. This excess of pension assets represents the advance funding of benefits that have been accrued or credited to the nonretired participants.

Advance funding of a pension plan serves several purposes:[5]

- **Security of benefits**—It should be noted that there is no accumulation of pension funds in an irrevocable trust or through a contract with an insurance company under the current disbursement method. As a result, the security of the retirement promise to the participants relies exclusively on the future financial strength of the employer. Although this lack of participant security can be mitigated under the terminal funding approach by the purchase of an annuity from an insurance company when a participant retires, it provides no protection for the active employees.

- **Protection of the PBGC**—PBGC insures that at least a specified portion of promises made by private defined benefit plans will be paid to the participants regardless of the status of the sponsor or the level of funds in the pension plan. Without the requirement for at least a minimum amount of advance funding for the covered sponsors, this government agency would undoubtedly be faced with increasing claims as financially-troubled firms began to reduce (or even eliminate) annual contributions for active employees.

- **Enforcement of fiscal responsibility**—The relatively even distribution of annual pension outlays under advance funding produces a more equitable allocation of the firm's cash flow over the years. This ensures that sponsors recognize the cost

of the active employees' eventual retirement benefits at the same time they benefit from their services.

Another advantage of advance funding is the financial flexibility that is provided to the sponsor. The accumulation of assets in a pension fund resulting from the advance funding of benefits serves as a buffer during periods of financial stress. During a period of low earnings or operating losses, an employer may find it advisable to reduce or eliminate pension contributions for a year or even a longer period. This can be done in those cases where the pension fund is of sufficient size that a temporary reduction of contributions does not violate the minimum funding requirements imposed by the Employee Retirement Income Security Act of 1974 (ERISA). It should be noted that this financing flexibility does not necessitate any reduction or termination of pension benefits.

## Steps in the Prefunding Process

Before explaining the technical details involved in complying with the minimum funding standards, it is important to understand the three basic steps involved in this process.

First, the sponsor must determine for a specified group of participants the likely value of the promised pension benefits. Quite simply this will depend on how many of the participants continue working with the sponsor until "retirement age."[6] The sponsor must make various assumptions to determine the probability that each of the current participants will receive a pension benefit. This will depend on estimates for preretirement mortality as well as those for disability and turnover. Assuming an employee reaches "retirement age," a sponsor with subsidized early retirement provisions may need to estimate the exact age at which the participant chooses to retire.[7] Because the participant's retirement benefit is based on his or her salary, in many defined benefit plans the sponsor often needs to estimate these values either for the participant's entire career or for the period immediately preceding retirement. Once the participant retires, the total value of the payments often depends on the life expectancy of the participant and perhaps his or her spouse. Therefore, the sponsor also needs to estimate postretirement mortality for the participants. The final computation in this process involves a calculation of the present value of each of the cash flows assumed to take

---

[5] McGill and Grubbs (1989), pp. 375-8.
[6] The description in this section obviously ignores the cost of terminated vested participants as well as those qualifying for death

or disability benefits under the pension plan. These details will be addressed later in the paper.
[7] This is explained under Rate of Retirement on p. 62.

place under the plan.

The second basic step takes the present value of promised benefits and allocates it to different years in such a manner that the needed assets will be accumulated eventually. This step relies on a computational device known as an actuarial cost method.

Finally, the sponsor needs to ensure that the

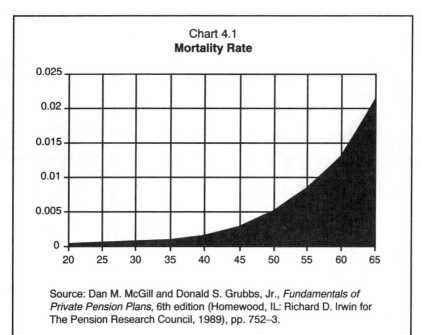

Chart 4.1
**Mortality Rate**

Source: Dan M. McGill and Donald S. Grubbs, Jr., *Fundamentals of Private Pension Plans*, 6th edition (Homewood, IL: Richard D. Irwin for The Pension Research Council, 1989), pp. 752–3.

for reasonableness. The primary concerns are that overly conservative estimates will lead to an increase in funding (with a consequent loss of revenue to the Treasury) while overly optimistic assumptions will reduce funding and perhaps threaten benefit security (or increase exposure of the PBGC).

*Mortality*— Participant mortality will impact the cost of the pension

actual experience under the plan does not differ from the assumptions made in the initial calculation by more than an allowable amount. In fact, the specific choice of original assumptions is not of overwhelming importance as long as they are adequately reviewed and revised in operation.[8]

## *Actuarial Assumptions*[9]

All costs, liability, rates of interest, and other factors under the plan must be determined on the basis of reasonable actuarial assumptions and methods. This standard has been met as long as the total plan contribution equals the contribution that would be obtained if each assumption and method were reasonable.

The types of assumptions that must be made include both demographic (employee mortality and disability, turnover rates and rates of retirement) and economic (interest rates and salary growth). Although no specific limits exist for most assumptions,[10] the Internal Revenue Service (IRS) does audit assumptions

plan in two ways. First, the higher the rate of mortality among active employees, the lower will be the cost of retirement benefits under the plan. However, preretirement death benefits will increase the cost of the plan.[11] Second, the rate of death among retired participants generally determines the duration of benefits.

Several mortality tables are available for pension cost calculations. Today the 1971 Group Annuity Mortality Table and the UP-84 Table are in many cases replacing the prior mortality tables.[12] Chart 4.1 provides an illustration of how mortality rates for employees increase from age 20 to 65 under the former table.

***Rate and Duration of Disability***—If a pension plan offers a disability benefit, cost projections for that plan should include a disability assumption. Disability rates are used to estimate both the number of employees eligible for the disability benefit and those who

---

[8] For a discussion of testing deviations and revising assumptions, see pages 27–29 of Schoenly (1991).

[9] The discussion in this section concentrates on ongoing, single-employer, trusteed plans. Special valuation considerations exist for insured plans, collectively bargained plans, and terminated plans. See pages 29–32 of Schoenly (1991).

[10] A notable exception exists for plans with funding ratios (based on termination liabilities) below 100 percent or above 150 percent. In those cases, the interest rate used to compute current liabilities is bounded by a 10 percent corridor around an historical average of 30-year Treasury bill rates. This is explained under OBRA '87 Minimum Funding Requirements for Underfunded Plans, p. 72.

[11] Since the passage of ERISA, all qualified plans must offer qualified joint and survivor (QJS) annuities to married individuals eligible for early retirement. The Retirement Equity Act of 1984 expanded that offer to all employees with vested benefits who have attained the age of 35. While the plan sponsor may pass the cost of such survivor benefit along to participant by means of a reduced benefit upon actual benefit commencement, many plans have incorporated the cost of the QJS benefit as an ancillary employer-provided benefit.

[12] For a description of these mortality tables, see Donald S. Grubbs, Jr., "Mortality Tables for Pension Plans," *Society of Actuaries Study Note*, 1992.

---

will not receive regular retirement benefits. Chart 4.2 provides an illustration of annual disability rate assumptions. It is important to note that the estimates used by a plan will be influenced by several plan provisions including the definition of disability and the waiting period before benefits begin.

*Turnover*— Employees who separate from service prior to the point at which their benefits are 100 percent vested represent a cost-reducing factor to a pension fund. Even when an employee has achieved full vesting under a final average pay plan, turnover will reduce the eventual cost of the plan because the participant's benefit will be based on a lower average salary.

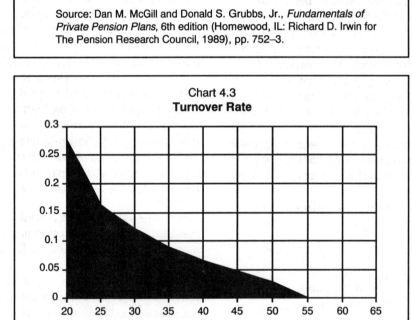

Chart 4.2
**Disability Rate**

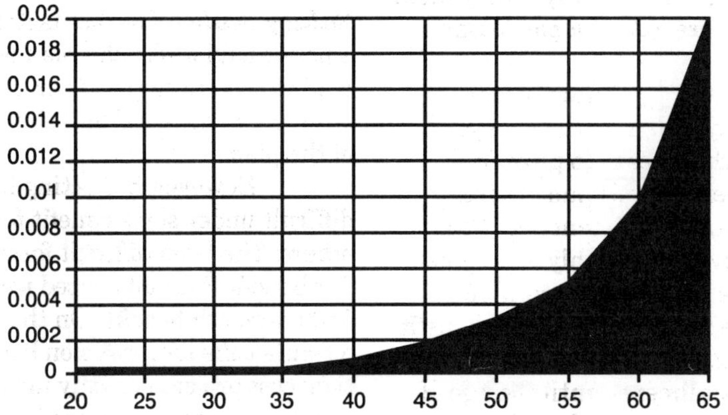

Source: Dan M. McGill and Donald S. Grubbs, Jr., *Fundamentals of Private Pension Plans*, 6th edition (Homewood, IL: Richard D. Irwin for The Pension Research Council, 1989), pp. 752–3.

Chart 4.3
**Turnover Rate**

Source: Dan M. McGill and Donald S. Grubbs, Jr., *Fundamentals of Private Pension Plans*, 6th edition (Homewood, IL: Richard D. Irwin for The Pension Research Council, 1989), pp. 752–3.

*Rate of Retirement*—Actuaries must often make an assumption regarding the likelihood of retirement at various ages. This is especially true when the plan provides some form of subsidized early retirement benefit (i.e., an early retirement benefit that is greater than the actuarial equivalent of the normal retirement benefit) and when it is expected that many employees will, in fact, retire early.

Defined benefit plans may offer early retirement subsidies through two different approaches. Sponsors may include subsidies on a permanent basis by writing them into the plan document. This type of subsidy will typically be triggered upon certain

Chart 4.3 provides an illustration of annual turnover rate assumptions in which the withdrawal rate is assumed to be a decreasing function of age. Although the age composition of the covered group has a significant impact on turnover rates, turnover rates also vary depending on the length of service of employees.

Turnover tables developed to guide pension consultants are of assistance for initial cost calculations, and adjustments in assumed turnover rates can be made as the actual experience under the plan evolves.[13]

events such as plan shutdown or job elimination. Alternatively, the early retirement window program is a temporary program instituted by the employer only when the expected additional retirement pattern will

---

[13] Schoenly (1991) points out that several considerations need to be factored into the use of sponsor's historical data including:
- the potential for nonrepresentative economic conditions and growth rates for the company's workforce,
- the installation of a plan may affect turnover rates,
- a change in the sponsor's business may affect the size and characteristics of the workforce, and
- the impact of downsizing and spinoffs on termination rates.

help achieve corporate goals. Instead of applying to all employees at a particular time, these plans allow employees to choose the enhancement only if they meet certain requirements and retire within a particular period of time.

Early window retirement program incentives can be paid out of a qualified plan in various ways.[14] One of the more popular techniques is to provide temporary supplements when a participant retires prior to Social Security normal retirement age. For example, the plan could provide a monthly supplement to the retiree until he or she reaches the age of 65, which would be equal to the full Social Security benefit that begins at age 65. The plan might also pay Social Security supplements in installments until the age of 62, equal to the reduced Social Security benefit to which the employee is entitled beginning at age 62.

Another popular method is to credit the employee with additional service and/or to impute additional years to the employee's age. For example, if an employee was age 55 with 15 years of service, for purposes of benefit delivery they would get the same benefit as if they were age 60 with 20 years of service.

Other techniques include:

- adding additional benefit forms (e.g., people who retire within a particular period of time get a lump-sum distrubution (LSD) that is not otherwise available),
- reducing or eliminating early retirement reductions,
- accelerating vesting,
- using a shorter final average pay period,
- using projected pay, rather than actual pay, and
- providing cost-of-living adjustments to the postretirement monthly benefits.

The valuation process for early retirement windows generally proceeds by valuing the options assuming all eligible participants elect the early retirement incentive to provide the maximum cost to the sponsor for the incentive program. Cost estimates can then be made assuming various levels of acceptance.

***Salary Scale***—The last factor affecting the total amount paid under the plan is the amount of pension paid to each retired worker. It goes without saying that the higher the benefit level, the greater will be the cost of the plan.

However, projecting benefit levels is more difficult under some benefit formulas than under others. The least difficult formula is one that provides a flat benefit[15] for all retired workers, for example, a $100-a-month benefit. On the other hand, if the benefit formula calls for a pension benefit related to compensation, cost projections may include an assumption regarding expected future increases in the salaries of covered employees. For example, if a plan provides a pension benefit of 1 percent of salary per year of covered service, future increases in salary will increase benefit levels and, therefore, the cost of the plan.

Salary increase assumptions usually consist of three components: inflation, productivity increases, and merit increases. Chart 4.4 illustrates a salary scale using a merit scale that decreases with age plus a 3.5 percent annual inflation rate and a 0.5 percent productivity increase assumption. The chart shows that under these assumptions a 20-year-old is expected to experience more than a 14-fold increase in salary by age 65.

***Investment Returns***—In a funding calculation, the investment return assumption is used as a discount factor in valuing the liabilities. The investment income earned on the accumulated assets of a funded pension plan reduces the ultimate cost of the plan. Thus, the higher the investment return assumption, other things being equal, the lower will be the projected cost of the plan. Chart 4.5 shows that for an individual age 20, approximately 7 cents would need to be invested to have accumulated $1 at age 65 assuming a 6 percent rate of return. However, if the rate of return assumption is increased to 8 percent, the initial contribution decreases to 3 cents. For a given plan, the impact of a

---

[14] It should be noted that the sponsor's flexibility in designing early retirement window programs may be constrained by several sections of the Internal Revenue Code. For example, the Section 415 limits provide for a steep reduction in the maximum amount of benefit that can be paid in an annuity form as employees retire at earlier ages. Furthermore, the regulations for the Section 401(a)(4) nondiscrimination requirements may limit the success of these programs in several respects. Under the benefits, rights, and features requirement of these regulations, the early retirement program will be in violation if it turns out that the effect of the program is really only to benefit highly compensated employees, which is a distinct possibility since many of the older employees eligible under the terms of the plan will be highly compensated

employees. Also plans forced to use the general rule to pass the amounts testing requirement will find that these window plans are considered in testing most valuable accrual rate. Again, if a significant number of highly compensated employees benefit under the subsidy, it may be difficult for the plan to pass this requirement.

[15] In the case of negotiated plans providing a flat benefit per year of service, there is generally no advance provision for future increases in the unit benefit amount, and, in fact, current IRS regulations do not allow an assumption of future increases. It is generally recognized that benefit levels will be increased periodically due to inflationary pressures, but recognition is not given to this fact in cost projections until increases are actually negotiated.

change in the investment return assumption on the estimated cost of the plan depends on the age distribution of participants and their relative benefit credits.

The investment return assumption[16] used should recognize the total anticipated rate of return including investment income, dividends, and realized and unrealized capital appreciation (or depreciation).

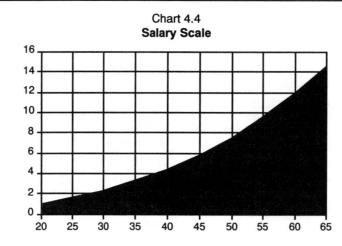

**Chart 4.4**
**Salary Scale**

Source: Dan M. McGill and Donald S. Grubbs, Jr., *Fundamentals of Private Pension Plans*, 6th edition (Homewood, IL: Richard D. Irwin for The Pension Research Council, 1989), pp. 756.

of that level of inflation.

***Expenses***—The expenses of administering the pension plan must be added to the benefits paid in arriving at the ultimate cost of the plan. The expense assumption used depends on the type of administration and the funding instrument involved. Under some insured plans, the insurance company includes a loading for expenses in the gross premiums charged for purchased benefits. In the case of trust fund plans, the employer may pay the actuarial, legal, administrative, and investment expenses associated with the plan separately from the contribution payments to the plan.

The choice of an appropriate rate of investment return is particularly difficult if a sizable portion of the assets is invested in common stocks, since these investments are subject to significant fluctuations in value.

According to Itelson (1991), the most common method of selecting interest assumptions has been called the Building Block Approach. Investment returns will include components for inflation, real risk-free return, and premium for risk and lack of liquidity or marketability. Each asset category (stocks, bonds, cash, etc.) will have its own anticipated real return. Taking a weighted average and then adjusting[17] for inflation provides an expected real yield. Another approach results in interest assumptions varying by year. Typically, these select and ultimate interest rates begin with high current yields and decline to a lower level in the future. This allows the actuary to recognize current returns but allows conservatism for possibly lower future rates. This is often justified on the assumption that the near-term results are more predictable than those in the distant future.

Even more important than the absolute level of the interest assumption is its interaction with the salary assumption. The two assumptions should reflect the same economic basis. For example, if price inflation of 4 percent is expected over the long term, the salary growth assumption should include the impact on wage

## Asset Valuation Methods

For a number of reasons, current market values of securities have seldom been used in actuarial valuations. Two of the most important reasons are: (1) market values will generally be relatively high in periods of high corporate earnings, thereby reducing the apparent need for contributions (and also the tax deductible limits) at times when the employer may be best able to make large contributions toward the pension fund (in periods of low corporate earnings the reverse will often be true, with required contributions and tax deductible limits increased at a time when the employer's capacity to contribute is at a minimum); and (2) because of market value fluctuations, to measure a plan's unfunded liabilities on any given date by the current market values of the fund's equities could produce a very irregular funding pattern—the antithesis of the orderly procedure, which is an essential characteristic of a satisfactory pension funding program.[18]

---

[16] Beginning with the 1988 plan year, the actuary must select an interest rate for calculations the plan's current liabilities (used for purposes of the deficit reduction contribution and the full-funding limitation described later) from a range of rates specified by the Secretary of the Treasury. The interest assumption must fall within a permissible range that runs from 90 percent to 110 percent of a four-year average of rates under 30-year Treasury securities.

[17] The author cautions against simply adding expected inflation to the anticipated real return since high inflation has generally resulted in low rates of return.

[18] William F. Marples, *Actuarial Aspects of Pension Security* (Homewood, IL.: Richard D. Irwin, 1965), p. 107.

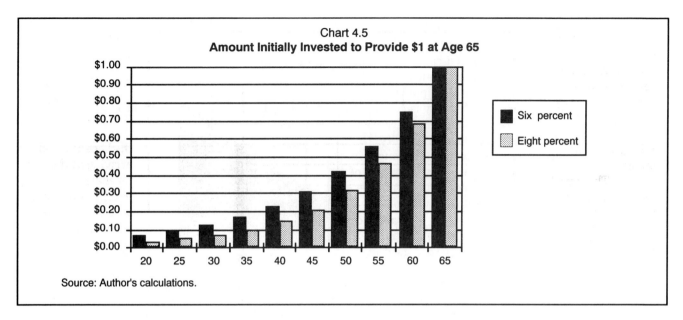

**Chart 4.5**
**Amount Initially Invested to Provide $1 at Age 65**

Source: Author's calculations.

In spite of the above objections, current market values are used in some situations. In fact, the IRC allows the value of a defined benefit plan's assets to be determined by any reasonable actuarial valuation method that takes fair market value into account.[19] Generally, the IRS has taken the position that this condition is satisfied if the asset valuation method generates an asset value that is between 80 percent and 120 percent of fair market value.[20] Obviously, fair market value alone would be an acceptable method.

A number of approaches have been developed to overcome the drawbacks noted above to the use of current market value. For example, to minimize the effects of short-term market fluctuations, a moving average (e.g., a five-year average) of market values may be used. Another method used to minimize such fluctuations is to recognize appreciation annually, based on an expected long-range growth rate (e.g., 3 percent) applied to the cost (adjusted for appreciation previously so recognized) of common stocks.

## Actuarial Cost Methods

There are six different actuarial cost methods, each producing different patterns of annual costs under the plan.[21] Some funding methods are designed to ensure that contributions are a relatively stable percentage of the plan sponsor's annual payroll cost. Others are designed for larger contributions in the early years of

the plan so that investment earnings pay a relatively large share of total pension benefits. Others are designed for small contributions early on and larger contributions later in the plan life when the plan sponsor will, theoretically, be well established and better able to make large contributions. All funding methods are designed to ensure that the plan eventually reaches a full-funding level.

Most actuarial cost methods break down the total actuarial cost into the *normal cost* and the *supplemental cost* of the plan. The *normal cost* of the plan is the amount of annual cost, determined in accordance with a particular actuarial cost method, attributable to the given year of the plan's operation.

Most plans provide credit for service rendered prior to the inception date of the plan. If the normal cost under the particular cost method is calculated on the assumption that annual costs have been paid or accrued from the earliest date of credited service (when in fact they have not), the plan starts out with a supplemental liability. At the inception of the plan, the supplemental liability (also known as the accrued liability) arises from the fact that credit for past service is granted, or part of the total benefit is imputed, to years prior to the inception of this plan. The annual contribution normally will be equal to the normal cost of the plan plus at least enough of a contribution to amortize the supplemental liability over a specified

---

[19] Money purchase plans must base assets solely on the basis of fair market value.

[20] For multiemployer plans, the valuation of assets rules do not apply to bonds (or other evidences of indebtedness) if a plan administrator makes a special election to value these instruments on an amortized basis.

[21] Although one of these (the accrued benefit cost method) is mandated by FASB 87 for *accounting purposes*, neither the IRC or the regulations require the use of a specific actuarial cost method for *funding purposes*.

period of time.[22] If it is desired to fund this supplemental liability in a more rapid manner (10 years is generally the minimum period over which it can be funded on a deductible basis), larger annual contributions will be required. The portion of the annual cost applied toward the reduction of the supplemental liability is referred to as the plan's *supplemental cost.* As the plan continues in operation, the size of the supplemental liability normally will change. In addition to normal changes in the supplemental liability that may occur as a result of the actuarial method being used, these changes in the size of the supplemental liability may result from variations in benefit formulas, deviations of actual from expected experience, and changes in the actuarial assumptions or in the actuarial cost method used in subsequent normal cost calculations. Offsetting any increase in the supplemental liability will be any unanticipated increase in the size of pension fund assets.

To illustrate the application of each of these methods, assume that an employer establishes a plan in 1993 and adopts a benefit formula that provides each employee with 50 percent of his or her final salary in a straight life annuity.[23] The employer adopts the actuarial assumptions listed in the Supplement and assumes that the purchase price of a straight life annuity paying $1 per year for life beginning at age 65 is $9.268. In an attempt to simplify the calculations, assume that the plan can be structured in such a manner that a participant must work with the sponsor until age 65 to be eligible for the pension. The employer has four employees with the following age, service and salary characteristics:

| Employee | Attained Age | Entry Age | Years of Past Service | Salary |
|---|---|---|---|---|
| A | 60 | 40 | 20 | $200,000 |
| B | 50 | 45 | 5 | 100,000 |
| C | 30 | 30 | 0 | 50,000 |
| D | 25 | 25 | 0 | 25,000 |
| | | | | 375,000 |

The first step under any of the actuarial cost methods involves a computation of the expected benefit for each employee, assuming he or she is still working for the sponsor at age 65. Multiplying the employee's current salary by the ratio of the salary scale[24] at age 65 divided by the salary scale at the employee's current (attained) age provides:

| Employee | (1) Salary | (2) Salary Scale (attained age) | (3) Salary Scale (age 65) | = (1) * ( 3 ) / 2 Projected Salary |
|---|---|---|---|---|
| A | $200,000 | 11.898 | 14.603 | $245,470 |
| B | 100,000 | 7.544 | 14.603 | 193,571 |
| C | 50,000 | 2.349 | 14.603 | 310,834 |
| D | 25,000 | 1.596 | 14.603 | 228,744 |

In other words, 60-year-old employee A would be expected to increase his or her salary from the current $200,000 to $245,470 at the end of five years. Once the final salary is known, it is multiplied by 50 percent to provide an estimate of the annual benefit:

| Employee | (1) Projected Salary | = (1) * 50% Projected Benefit |
|---|---|---|
| A | $245,470 | $122,735 |
| B | 193,571 | 96,786 |
| C | 310,834 | 155,417 |
| D | 228,744 | 114,372 |

*Accrued Benefit Cost Method*—An accrued benefit cost method is one under which the actuarial costs are based directly upon benefits accrued to the date of cost determination—such benefits being determined either by the terms of the plan or by some assumed allocation of total prospective benefits to years of service. To determine the actuarial cost of the plan for a given year, the method assumes that a precisely determinable unit of benefit is associated with that year of a participant's credited service. For example, for em-

---

[22] The minimum amortization amount will depend upon when the supplemental liability was created and may also depend upon the funding status of the plan. A detailed explanation is given later under Funding Standard Account, p. 71.

[23] It is important to note that these illustrations are used to demonstrate the basic calculations involved in determining normal costs and supplemental liabilities and do not reflect numerous restrictions and constraints beyond the scope of this paper. Two of the most important items ignored in these illustrations are the impact of the sec. 415 benefit limitations and the sec. 401(a)(17)

limit on includable compensation in qualified plans. For a technical description of these limitations, see Everett T. Allen, Jr., Joseph J. Melone, Jerry S. Rosenbloom and Jack L. VanDerhei, *Pension Planning: Pensions, Profit Sharing, and Other Deferred Compensation Plans,* seventh edition (Homewood, IL: Richard D. Irwin, Inc., 1992). For an analysis of the most recent changes in the sec. 401(a)(17) limit, see Jack L. VanDerhei, "Implications of Lowering the Compensation Limit for Qualified Retirement Plans, *EBRI Notes,* no. 5 (Washington, DC: Employee Benefit Research Insititute, May 1993).

[24] See column 2 in the Supplement.

ployee A above, the $122,735 projected benefit is split pro-rata among the 25 total years of service (20 years of past service and 5 years of future service until age 65). This results in an annual accrual of $4,909. Calculations for the entire plan follow:

| Employee | (1) Projected Benefit | (2) Years of Service | = (1) / (2) Annual Accrual |
|---|---|---|---|
| A | $122,735 | 25 | $4,909 |
| B | 96,786 | 20 | 4,839 |
| C | 155,417 | 35 | 4,440 |
| D | 114,372 | 40 | 2,859 |

The next step in the calculation of the normal cost under the accrued benefit cost method is to determine the present value of each participant's benefit credited during the year for which costs are being calculated. The cost per dollar of benefit is a function of the participant's attained age and of the mortality and interest assumptions for an individual of that age.

| Employee | (1) Annual Accrual | (2) Survival Percentage[25] | (3) Interest Discount[26] | (4) Annuity Factor | =(1)*(2)*(3)*(4) Normal Cost |
|---|---|---|---|---|---|
| A | $4,909 | 0.8592% | 0.7472582 | 9.268 | $29,213 |
| B | 4,839 | 0.6646 | 0.4172651 | 9.268 | 12,438 |
| C | 4,440 | 0.1416 | 0.1301052 | 9.268 | 758 |
| D | 2,859 | 0.0643 | 0.0972222 | 9.268 | 166 |
| | | | | | 42,575 |

The normal cost of the plan as a whole is simply the sum of the separate normal costs for the benefits credited for each participant during that particular year. Although the normal cost for a given participant increases over time under the accrued benefit cost method, the normal cost for the plan as a whole generally does not increase as rapidly, or may even remain fairly constant or decrease. The reason for this is that some older employees will die or terminate, and they will probably be replaced by much younger workers. If the distribution of current service benefit credits by age and sex remains constant, the total normal cost of the plan will remain constant.

At the inception of the plan, the supplemental liability under the accrued benefit cost method arises from the fact that either past service credits have been granted or a part of the benefits of the plan is imputed to past service. The supplemental liability at the

[25] See column 3 in the Supplement.
[26] See column 4 in the Supplement.

inception of the plan under the accrued benefit cost method is simply the present value of the accrued past service benefits credited as of that date. This can also be calculated by multiplying each employee's normal cost by his or her years of past service and summing the result:

| Employee | (1) Years of Past Service | (2) Normal Cost | = (1) * (2) Past Service Benefit |
|---|---|---|---|
| A | 20 | $29,213 | $584,264 |
| B | 5 | 12,438 | 62,188 |
| C | 0 | 758 | 0 |
| D | 0 | 166 | 0 |
| | | 42,575 | 646,452 |

Thus, the normal cost under the accrued benefit cost method for the first plan year is $42,575 and the supplemental liability is $646,452. As will be shown later in the paper, both of these figures are components of the plan's minimum required contribution for the year.

The remaining actuarial cost methods have as their objective the spreading of the costs of total projected benefits *evenly* over some future period.

***Individual Level Premium Method***—The normal cost accruals under this method are determined by distributing the present value of an individual's total projected benefits as a level amount or percentage of earnings over his or her assumed *future* period of coverage under the plan. Total projected benefits include past-service benefits, if any, as well as future-service benefits to be credited by retirement age. Thus, no unfunded supplemental liability is created under this cost method at the inception of the plan, since the present value of future benefits is exactly equal to the present value of future normal cost accruals. Thereafter, there is still no supplemental liability if contribution payments have been made equal to the normal costs that have accrued in prior years.

| (1) Employee | (2) Projected Benefit | (3) Survival Percentage | (4) Interest Discount | (5) Annuity Factor | =(1)*(2)*(3)*(4) Present Value of an Individual's Total Projected Benefits |
|---|---|---|---|---|---|
| A | $122,735 | 0.8592% | 0.7472582 | 9.268 | $730,330 |
| B | 96,786 | 0.6646 | 0.4172651 | 9.268 | 248,753 |
| C | 155,417 | 0.1416 | 0.1301052 | 9.268 | 26,536 |
| D | 114,372 | 0.0643 | 0.0972222 | 9.268 | 6,626 |
| | | | | | 1,012,246 |

This actuarial cost method requires, then, a projection of total benefits distributed by age at the inception of coverage and calculation of the normal cost based on a set of level premium deferred annuity rates. The latter may be determined by dividing the present value of an individual's total projected benefits by the present value of a temporary employee-based life annuity (TEBLA) running to normal retirement age. Since this method attempts to calculate a level dollar amount (as opposed to a level percentage of compensation), a TEBLA without a salary scale assumption is used:

| Employee | (1)<br>Present Value of an Individual's Total Projected Benefits | (2)<br>TEBLA (attained age without salary scale)[27] | (1) / (2)<br>Normal Cost |
|---|---|---|---|
| A | $730,330 | 4.253 | $171,721 |
| B | 248,753 | 8.75 | 28,429 |
| C | 26,536 | 7.059 | 3,759 |
| D | 6,626 | 5.737 | 1,155 |
| | | | 205,064 |

Thus, the first year's normal cost under this actuarial cost method is nearly five times larger than in the previous method; however, it does not generate a supplemental liability, and the amortization of this amount will obviously be zero. If there is no change in the projected benefits of any employee and the covered group remains constant, the normal cost under the plan will remain constant (subject to adjustment to the extent that actual experience deviates from the assumptions employed). Obviously, this will not prove to be the case in most plans. For example, if the benefit formula is related to compensation, employees will be entitled to larger projected benefits as they receive salary increases above those assumed in the salary scales. Also, new employees will become eligible for participation in the plan, and some currently covered workers will terminate their participation under the plan. Since the age and sex distribution and the benefit levels of new employees are not likely to be identical to those of terminated participants, there are bound to be variations in the annual contributions for the plan as a whole.

**Entry Age Normal Method**—This cost method is similar to the previous method except that the assumption is made, for the initial group of participants, that the period over which costs are spread begins with the first year they could have joined the plan had it always been in effect (the participant's entry age). In the case of the initial group of participants, a supplemental liability is automatically created because of the assumption that normal cost payments have been made prior to the inception date of the plan.

Using the example cited above, the present value of an individual's total projected benefits at entry age is computed. Note that these values will be different for employees A and B because the probability of survival and the interest discount apply to the entire period of time from when they were first hired until age 65.

| Employee | (1)<br>Projected Benefit | (2)<br>Survival Percentage (entry age) | (3)<br>Interest Discount (entry age) | (4)<br>Annuity Factor | =(1)*(2)*(3)*(4)<br>Present Value of an Individual's Total Projected Benefits at Entry Age (PVBEA) |
|---|---|---|---|---|---|
| A | $122,735 | 0.3809% | 0.2329986 | 9.268 | $100,953 |
| B | 96,786 | 0.5248 | 0.3118047 | 9.268 | 146,782 |
| C | 155,417 | 0.1416 | 0.1301052 | 9.268 | 26,536 |
| D | 114,372 | 0.0643 | 0.0972222 | 9.268 | 6,626 |

Once the present value of an individual's total projected benefits at entry age has been determined, it is divided by the present value of a temporary employee based life annuity running from the *entry* age until age 65. This differs from the previous method in both the duration of the annuity for employees with past service and in its use of a salary scale. This reflects the need for a normal cost that is a constant percentage of compensation for each employee. Since the sponsor assumes the employees' salaries will increase according to the salary scale, this information must be included in the present value of a temporary employee-based life annuity.

| Employee | (1)<br>PVBEA | (2)<br>TEBLA (entry age, with salary scale)[28] | = (1) / (2)<br>Normal Cost at Entry Age |
|---|---|---|---|
| A | $100,953 | 13.787 | $7,322 |
| B | 146,782 | 13.191 | 11,127 |
| C | 26,536 | 11.969 | 2,217 |
| D | 6,626 | 9.791 | 677 |

At this point we know that the normal cost for each employee at entry age. Before determining the normal cost percentage, we need to compute what the employee's salary was at that time (according to the salary scale):

---

[27] See column 5 in the Supplement.

[28] See column 6 in the Supplement.

| Employee | (1) Salary | (2) Salary Scale (entry age) | (3) Salary Scale (attained age) | = (1) * (2) / (3) Entry Age Salary |
|---|---|---|---|---|
| A | $200,000 | 4.446 | 11.898 | $74,735 |
| B | 100,000 | 5.853 | 7.544 | 77,585 |
| C | 50,000 | 2.349 | 2.349 | 50,000 |
| D | 25,000 | 1.596 | 1.596 | 25,000 |

Reviewing what we have calculated for employee A thus far may be useful. We know that at entry age (40) the employee had a normal cost computed of $7,322 and a salary (according to the salary scale) of $74,735. Since both of these values are determined at age 40 for the employee, we can use their ratio to determine the normal cost percentage for that employee:

| Employee | (1) Entry Age Normal Cost | (2) Entry Age Salary | = (1) / (2) Normal Cost Percentage |
|---|---|---|---|
| A | $7,322 | $74,735 | 9.80% |
| B | 11,127 | 77,585 | 14.34 |
| C | 2,217 | 50,000 | 4.43 |
| D | 677 | 25,000 | 2.71 |

Note that a different normal cost percentage is calculated for each employee (a potential nuisance that we will treat in the next actuarial cost method) and that once computed, an employee will generally have the same normal cost percentage for the remainder of his or her service with the employer.

The only remaining step in computing the normal cost of the plan is to multiply each employee's normal cost percentage by their current salary and sum the products:

| Employee | (1) Salary (attained age) | (2) Normal Cost Percentage | = (1) * (2) Normal Cost |
|---|---|---|---|
| A | $200,000 | 9.80% | $19,595 |
| B | 100,000 | 14.34 | 14,342 |
| C | 50,000 | 4.43 | 2,217 |
| D | 25,000 | 2.71 | 677 |
| | | | 36,832 |

Before determining the plan's supplemental liability under this actuarial cost method, it may be instructive to point out that the present value of benefits (PVB) can either be financed through the present value of future normal costs (PVFNC) or treated as a supplemental liability (SL):

$$PVB = PVFNC + SL, \text{ or}$$
$$SL = PVB - PVFNC$$

Since we have already calculated the present value of benefits as of each employee's attained age in the previous actuarial cost method, we only need to calculate the present value of future normal costs for the two employees with past service to determine the supplemental liability:

| Employee | (1) Normal Cost | (2) Present Value a Temporary Employee-Based Life Annuity (attained age, with salary scale) | = (1) * (2) Present Value of Future Normal Cost |
|---|---|---|---|
| A | $19,595 | 4.597 | $ 90,080 |
| B | 14,342 | 11.464 | 164,420 |
| | | | 254,500 |

Computing the difference between these two amounts for employees A and B provides the initial past service liability:

| Employee | (1) Present Value of Benefits (attained age) | (2) Present Value of Future Normal Costs | = (1) - (2) Initial Past Service Liability |
|---|---|---|---|
| A | $730,330 | $90,080 | $640,250 |
| B | 248,753 | 164,420 | 84,333 |
| | | | 724,583 |

The result, of course, is that the normal costs are lower under the entry age normal cost method than the level premium method. However, since the normal costs have not been paid for the prior years, there is a supplemental liability under the entry age normal method. Unlike the accrued benefit cost method, the initial supplemental liability under the individual cost method does not bear a precise relationship to past service benefits.

In valuations after the first year of the plan, the normal cost and supplemental liability would be calculated in the same manner as at the plan's inception. However, the annual contribution would be a payment of the normal cost and some payment toward the unfunded supplemental liability (the supplemental liability less any assets that have accumulated). The normal cost calculation would be affected by any changes in assumptions or plan provisions while the calculation of the unfunded supplemental liability would be affected not only by changes in assumptions or plan provisions, but also by any actuarial gains or losses since the plan actually started.

**Aggregate Cost Method**—The distinguishing characteristic of aggregate level cost methods is that the normal cost accruals are calculated for the plan as a whole without identifying any part of such cost accruals with the projected benefits of specific individuals. The cost accruals are typically expressed as a percentage of compensation.

| Employee | (1) Salary (attained age) | (2) Present Value of a Temporary Employee-Based Life Annuity (attained age, with salary scale) | = (1) * (2) Present Value of Future Normal Costs |
|---|---|---|---|
| A | $200,000 | 4.597 | $ 919,400 |
| B | 100,000 | 11.464 | 1,146,400 |
| C | 50,000 | 11.969 | 598,450 |
| D | 25,000 | 9.791 | 244,775 |
|  |  |  | 2,909,025 |

The normal cost accrual rate under an aggregate method can be determined by dividing the present value of future benefits for all participants (1,012,246—see Individual Level Premium Method) by the present value of the estimated future compensation for the group of participants calculated above ($2,909,025). This accrual rate (34.80 percent) is then multiplied by the total annual earnings ($375,000) to determine the initial normal cost of the plan ($130,488). Since there is no assumption that any normal costs have been accrued prior to the inception date of the plan, the above method does not create a supplemental liability.

In the determination of cost accruals after the inception of the plan under the above method, recognition must be given to the plan assets that presumably have been accumulated to offset prior normal cost accruals. Thus, for those years subsequent to the establishment of the plan, the accrual rate is determined by dividing the present value of aggregate future benefits, less any plan assets, by the present value of future compensation.

**Attained Age Normal and Frozen Initial Liability Methods**—The normal cost accrual can be calculated under an aggregate method to produce a supplemental liability. The actuary may simply use a supplemental liability generated by one of the individual cost methods. Under the attained age normal method, the unfunded supplemental liability generated by the accrued benefit cost method ($646,452) is subtracted from the present value of aggregate future benefits ($1,012,246) in the calculation of the normal cost percentage:

$$\frac{1,012,246 - 646,452}{2,909,025} = 12.57\%$$

This percentage is multiplied by the total current salary to produce the normal cost:

12.57% * $375,000 = $47,154

This obviously reduces the normal cost from that obtained under the aggregate method; however, the supplemental liability of $646,452 must now be amortized.

Under the frozen initial liability method, the unfunded supplemental liability generated by the entry age normal method is subtracted from the present value of aggregate future benefits in the calculation of subsequent normal cost percentages.

## Minimum Funding Standard

The basic minimum funding standard required by the IRC is that a pension plan having supplemental liabilities[29] must amortize such liabilities over a specified period of time in addition to the funding of normal cost. Because the actuary uses judgment in selecting actuarial assumptions, and because the plan sponsor can choose from a number of different funding methods, a specific minimum contribution is not required by ERISA.

In meeting the minimum funding standards, the liabilities of a pension plan must be calculated on the basis of actuarial assumptions and actuarial cost methods that are reasonable and that offer the actuary's best estimate of anticipated experience under the plan. Each individual assumption must be reasonable or must, in the aggregate, result in a total contribution equal to that which would be determined if each of the assumptions were reasonable.

For plans in existence on January 1, 1974, the maximum amortization period for supplemental liability is 40 years; for single-employer plans established after January 1, 1974, the maximum amortization period is 30 years. Moreover, experience gains and losses for single-employer plans must be amortized over a 5-year period (15 years for experience deviations occurring before 1988).[30] The shorter amortization period for gains and losses was designed to stimulate the use of realistic actuarial assumptions. Changes in supplemental liabilities associated with changes in

---

[29] It should be noted that, under variations of some actuarial cost methods (e.g., the aggregate cost method and the individual level premium method) the accrued liability is set equal to the value of the assets. Thus, by definition, there is no unfunded supplemental liability under these plans.

[30] As seen in the previous section, some actuarial cost methods do not generate experience gains and losses.

actuarial assumptions must be amortized over a period not longer than 10 years (30 years for assumption changes made before 1988).

An amortization period may be extended by the IRS for up to 10 years if the employer shows the extension would provide adequate protection for participants and their beneficiaries. Such potential extensions are advantageous for those cases where a substantial risk exists that unless such an extension were granted, a pension plan would be terminated, or greatly reduced employee benefit levels or reduced employee compensation would result.

The Treasury Department can also allow some flexibility in employers meeting the minimum funding standards of the IRC. In those circumstances where an employer would incur temporary substantial business hardships and if strict enforcement of the minimum funding standards would adversely affect plan participants, the Secretary of the Treasury may waive for a particular year payment of all or a part of a plan's normal cost and the additional liabilities to be funded during that year. The law provides that no more than three waivers may be granted a plan within a consecutive 15-year period; the amount waived, plus interest, must be amortized not less rapidly than ratably over 5 years (15 years for deficiencies waived before 1988).

To determine substantial business hardship, one must consider the following factors:[31]
- Is the employer operating at an economic loss?
- Is there substantial unemployment or underemployment in the trade or business and in the industry concerned?
- Are the sales and profits of the industry concerned depressed or declining?
- Is it reasonable to expect that the plan will be continued only if the waiver is granted?

The employer must have a reasonable chance to recover and meet the costs of the plan in the future, (including the amortization of the waived amount) for the Treasury to grant a waiver. The Treasury requires proof of the potential for recovery before granting any such request.[32]

There are certain exemptions from the mandated minimum funding standards. Generally, the minimum funding standards apply to pension plans (as opposed to profit-sharing and stock bonus plans) of private employers in interstate commerce, plans of employee organizations with members in interstate commerce, and plans that seek a qualified status under the tax laws. Exempt plans include government plans and church plans, unless they elect to comply with the requirements of the IRC. Fully insured pension plans (funded exclusively through individual or group permanent insurance contracts) are exempt from the minimum funding rules as long as all premiums are paid when due and no policy loans are allowed. Additionally, plans that are also exempt are arrangements designed to provide deferred compensation to highly compensated employees, plans that provide supplemental benefits on an unfunded, nonqualified basis, and those plans to which the employer does not contribute.

## Funding Standard Account

All pension plans subject to the minimum funding requirements must establish a "funding standard account" that provides a comparison between actual contributions and those required under the minimum funding requirements.[33] A determination of experience gains and losses and a valuation of a plan's liability must be made at least once every year.[34] The basic purpose of the funding standard account is to provide some flexibility in funding through allowing contributions greater than the required minimum, accumulated with interest, to reduce the minimum contributions required in future years.

For each plan year, the funding standard account is charged with the normal cost for the year and with the minimum amortization payment required for initial supplemental liabilities, increases in plan liabilities, experience losses, the net loss resulting from changes in actuarial assumptions, waived contributions for each year, and adjustments for interest in the preceding items to the end of the plan year.[35] The account is credited in each plan year for employer contributions made for that year, with amortized portions of decreases in plan liabilities, experience gains, the net gain resulting from changes in actuarial assumptions, amounts of any waived contributions, and adjustments for interest in the preceding items to the end of the plan year.[36]

If the contributions to the plan, adjusted as indicated above, meet the minimum funding standards,

---

[31] Sec. 412(d)(2).
[32] Rev. Proc. 83-41.
[33] A pension plan using a funding method that requires contributions in all years not less than those required under the entry age normal funding method can elect compliance under the "alternative minimum funding standard." For a detailed description, see Archer (1991).

[34] Under certain circumstances, the IRS may require an actuarial valuation more frequently. Sec. 412(c)(9).
[35] Plan sponsors are able to change their funding methods with the (sometimes automatic) approval of the IRS. See Rev. Proc. 85-29 and IRS Notice 90-63.
[36] In certain situations, the account will also be credited with a full-funding limitation credit. See Prop. Reg. Sec. 1.412(c)(6)-1(g).

Table 4.1
**Minimum Required Contribution without Deficit Reduction Contribution**

| | | |
|---|---|---|
| Normal Cost at January 1, 1990 | | $500,000 |
| Amortization Charges at January 1, 1990 | | |
|     Initial unfunded liability | $75,000 | |
|     Plan changes | $325,000 | |
|     Actuarial losses | $100,000 | |
| Total | | $500,000 |
| | | |
| Interest to Year End on Normal Cost and Amortization Charges at 9 percent | | $90,000 |
| | | |
| Total Charges | | $1,090,000 |
| Credit Balance at January 1, 1990 | | 0 |
| Amortization Credits at January 1, 1990 | | |
|     Plan changes | $150,000 | |
|     Actuarial gains | $250,000 | |
| Total | | $400,000 |
| | | |
| Interest to Year End on Credit Balance and Amortization Credits at 9 percent | | |
| | | |
| Total Credits | | $436,000 |
| Minimum Required Contribution | | $654,000 |

Source: Michael A. Archer, "Minimum Funding Requirements," in Martin Wald and David E. Kenty, eds., *ERISA: A Comprehensive Guide* (New York: John Wiley & Sons, Inc., 1991).

the funding standard account will show a zero balance. If the funding standard account has a positive balance at the end of the year, such balance will be credited with interest in future years (at the rate used to determine plan costs). Therefore, the need for future contributions to meet the minimum funding standards will be reduced to the extent of the positive balance plus the interest credited.

Table 4.1 provides an example of the calculation of the minimum required contribution for a plan with a 9 percent valuation interest rate.

*OBRA '87 Minimum Funding Requirements for Underfunded Plans*—The Omnibus Budget Reconciliation Act of 1987 (OBRA '87) established two new funding requirements for many underfunded single-employer plans,[37] effective beginning with 1989 plan years: an additional amortization total (AAT) based on a new concept referred to as a deficit reduction contribution (DRC) and an unpredictable contingent event amount (UCEA).[38] The additional funding charge is equal to the sum of the additional amortization total and the unpredictable contingent event amount. These additional charges only apply to the extent that the plan has unfunded current liabilities, defined as the difference between current liabilities[39] (CL) and the adjusted value of assets (AVA).[40] This can be expressed as:

new funding standard charge
= minimum (AAT + UCEA, CL - AVA)

The additional amortization total is equal to the excess of the deficit reduction contribution over the

---

[37] These rules do not apply to plans with fewer than 100 participants. If a plan has between 100 and 150 participants, the impact of the rules is phased in as a function of the number of participants.

[38] Although a complete description of the UCEA is beyond the scope of this chapter, it should be noted that the value of any unpredictable contingent event benefit (UCEB) is not considered until the event has occurred. UCEBs include benefits that depend on contingencies that are not reliably and reasonably predictable such as facility shutdowns on reductions in the work force. The UCEA is generally equal to the greater of (1) the sum of all amortization amounts for all unpredictable events that have occurred in the seven-year period including the current plan year, or (2) a UCEB cash flow amount, the effect of which is phased in through the year 2001.

[39] In general, the current liability is the plan's liability determined on a plan termination basis. Specifically, it is the present value of

accrued benefits projected to the end of the current plan year, but excluding the value of unpredictable contingent events that have not occurred. The present value of this liability is calculated using the plan's valuation interest rate, provided that it is between 90 percent and 110 percent of the weighted average of rates of interest on 30-year Treasury securities during the four-year period ending on the last day of the prior plan year. Furthermore, the interest rate should be consistent with current insurance company annuity rates. The IRS may, by regulation, extend this range downward if 90 percent of the weighted average is unreasonably high but to no lower than 80 percent of the weighted average.

[40] The adjusted value of assets is equal to the assets as valued for plan valuation purposes (see under Asset Valuation Methods, p. 64) minus any credit balance in the funding standard account (as defined in the previous section of this chapter).

Table 4.2
**Development of Deficit Reduction Contribution**

| | | |
|---|---|---|
| **A.** | **Unfunded Old Liability Amount** | |
| (1) | Current liability as of January 1, 1989 based on October 16, 1987 plan provisions | $10,000,000 |
| (2) | Actuarial value of assets as of January 1, 1989 (less credit balance) | $8,000,000 |
| (3) | Unfunded old liability[1] | $2,000,000 |
| (4) | 18-year amortization of unfunded old liability at the current liability rate of 9 percent | $209,564 |
| **B.** | **Unfunded New Liability Amount** | |
| (5) | Current liability as of January 1, 1990 | $12,000,000 |
| (6) | Actuarial value of assets as of January 1, 1990 (less credit balance) | $9,500,000 |
| (7) | Unfunded current liability[2] | $2,500,000 |
| (8) | Unamortized unfunded old liability[3] | $1,951,575 |
| (9) | Unfunded new liability[4] | $548,425 |
| (10) | Current liability funded percentage[5] | 79.2% |
| (11) | Percentage of unfunded new liability recognized[6] | 19.0% |
| (12) | Unfunded new liability amount[7] | $104,201 |
| **C.** | **Deficit Reduction Contribution** | |
| (13) | Sum of unfunded old liability amount and unfunded new liability amount[8] | $313,765 |
| (14) | Amortization changes and credits for initial unfunded and plan changes[9] | $250,000 |
| (15) | Deficit reduction contribution[10] | $63,765 |

Source: Michael A. Archer, "Minimum Funding Requirements," in Martin Wald and David E. Kenty, eds., *ERISA: A Comprehensive Guide* (New York: John Wiley & Sons, Inc., 1991).

[1] (1) − (2)        [6] 30% − .25 ((10) − (35%))
[2] (5) − (6)        [7] (11) * (9)
[3] (3) − (4) * 1.09    [8] (4) + (12)
[4] (7) − (8)        [9] 75,000 + 325,000 − 150,000
[5] (6) / (5)        [10] minimum ((13) − (14); (7))

net total of the following funding standard account amortization charges and credits (FSANET):

- Charge for the initial unfunded accrued liability
- Charges for plan changes
- Credits for plan changes

$$AAT = DRC - FSANET$$

The deficit reduction contribution is equal to the sum of the unfunded old liability amount (UOLA) and the unfunded new liability amount (UNLA):

$$DRC = UOLA + UNLA$$

The unfunded old liability amount is generally equal to an 18-year amortization ($ä18$) of the unfunded old liability (UOL):[41]

$$UOLA = UOL/ä_{18}$$

The UOL is simply the difference between the current liability and the adjusted value of assets as of the beginning of the first plan year to begin after 1988:[42]

$$UOL = (CL - AVA)$$

as of beginning of the first plan year to begin after 1988.

Panel A of table 4.2 illustrates how this concept is applied. Continuing with the example from table 4.1, assume that the current liability as of January 1, 1989 is $10 million based on a 9 percent discount rate. If the adjusted value of assets at that time is $8 million, the unfunded old liability will be equal to $2 million. At a 9 percent discount rate, the 18-year amortization factor is 10.48 percent. Multiplying this by $2 million produces an unfunded old liability amount of $209,564.

The unfunded new liability amount (UNLA) is determined as a percentage of the unfunded new liability (UNL) according to a formula that penalizes plans with low funding ratios by increasing their current contributions. The unfunded new liability is the excess of the unfunded current liability over the unamortized unfunded old liability (without regard to the value of an unpredictable contingent event benefit[43] (UCEB) for an event that has occurred):

$$UNL = (CL - AVA) - (\text{unamortized } UOL + \text{value of } UCEB \text{ for which event has occurred})$$

Panel B of table 4.2 provides the plan's current liability ($12 million) and adjusted value of assets ($9.5 million) as of January 1, 1990. The difference of $2.5 million represents the unfunded current liability at that time. To determine the unfunded new liability though, the remaining balance of the unfunded old liability determined above must be subtracted.[44]

---

[41] The unfunded old liability amount may have another 18-year amortization component reflecting benefits added by an amendment pursuant to a collective bargaining agreement ratified before October 17, 1987.

[42] Any plan amendment increasing liabilities and adopted after

October 16, 1997 is ignored. However, there is special treatment for later amendments adopted pursuant to collective bargaining agreements ratified before October 17, 1987.

[43] See footnote 38.

[44] The example assumes there is no UCEB.

Conceptually, this process is similar to that involved in computing the unpaid balance on an 18-year mortgage. From the beginning balance of $2 million, subtract the first year's amortization payment of $209,564. This leaves a balance of $1,790,436, which is carried forward at the discount rate of 9 percent to leave a balance of $1,951,575 at the beginning of 1990. Subtracting this amount (which can be thought of as the remaining balance from the old liability) from the total liability gives the unfunded new liability of $548,425.

The percentage of the unfunded new liability recognized depends on the funded current liability percentage, defined as the ratio of the plan's adjusted value of assets to its current liability:

$$UNLA = .3 - .25(maximum[0, \{AVA/CL\} - .35]) * UNL$$

If this ratio is 35 percent or less, the percentage of the unfunded new liability recognized is 30 percent. For every percentage point by which the funded current liability percentage exceeds 35 percent, the percentage of unfunded new liability recognized declines by 25 percent. Thus, in this example, the funded current liability percentage equals $9.5 million divided by $12 million or 79.2 percent. The percentage of the unfunded new liability that will be recognized equals 19 percent:

$$30\% - .25 \times (79.2\% - 35\%) = 19\%.$$

Multiplying this percentage by the unfunded new liability produces an unfunded new liability amount of $104,201.

At this point, the deficit reduction contribution can be determined by adding the unfunded old and new liability amounts for a total of $313,765. Netting out the amortization charges and credits from table 4.1 for the initial unfunded liability and plan changes produces a value of $250,000. Subtracting this amount from the deficit reduction contributions provides the additional amortization total of $63,675.

## Required Annual Payment

Minimum funding contributions must be made on a quarterly basis. The final payment is due 8.5 months after the close of the plan year.[45] Interest on unpaid quarterly installments is charged in the funding standard account at a rate equal to the larger of 175 percent of the federal mid-term rate or the rate of interest used to determine costs by the plan.

## Full-Funding Limitation

Basically, two provisions determine the maximum amount an employer can contribute and take as a deduction to a qualified pension plan in any one taxable

year. The first of these rules permits a deduction for a contribution that will provide, for all employees participating in the plan, the unfunded cost of their past and current service credits distributed as a level amount or as a level percentage of compensation over the remaining future service of each such employee. If this rule is followed, and if the remaining unfunded cost for any three individuals is more than 50 percent of the total unfunded cost, the unfunded cost attributable to such individuals must be distributed over a period of at least five taxable years. Contributions under individual policy pension plans are typically claimed under this rule.

The second rule, while occasionally used with individual policy plans, is used primarily in group pension and trust fund plans. This rule permits the employer to deduct the normal cost of the plan plus the amount necessary to amortize any past service or other supplementary pension or annuity credits in equal annual installments over a 10-year period. However, the maximum tax-deductible limit cannot exceed the amount needed to bring the plan to its full-funding limit. The full-funding limit is defined as the lesser of 100 percent of the plan's actuarial accrued liability[46] (including normal cost) or 150 percent of the plan's current liability, reduced by the lesser of the market value of plan assets or their actuarial value. The plan's funding standard account credit balance is subtracted from the asset value before determining the full-funding limitation.

If amounts contributed in any taxable year are in excess of the amounts allowed as a deduction for that year, the excess may be carried forward and deducted in succeeding taxable years, in order of time, to the extent that the amount carried forward to any such succeeding taxable year does not exceed the deductible limit for such succeeding taxable year. However, a 10 percent excise tax is imposed on nondeductible contributions by an employer to a qualified plan. For purposes of the excise tax, nondeductible contributions are defined as the sum of the amount of the employer's contribution that exceeds the amount deductible under sec. 404 and any excess amount contributed in the preceding tax year that has not been returned to the employer or applied as a deductible contribution in the current year.

---

[45] This deadline does not extend the time limit for making a contribution for tax deduction purposes.

[46] If the plan's actuarial cost method does not generate an accrued liability, the value that would be generated by the entry age normal method is used.

## Penalties for Underfunding

If the funding standard account shows a deficit balance, called the accumulated funding deficiency (minimum contributions in essence have not been made), the account will be charged with interest at the rate used to determine plan costs. Moreover, the plan will be subject to an excise tax of 10 percent of the accumulated funding deficiency (if the deficiency is not then corrected, the excise tax is increased to 100 percent of the deficiency). All members of the employer's controlled group are liable for payment of the minimum contribution and excise tax, with a lien on the employer's assets imposed for a deficiency in excess of $1 million. In addition to the excise tax, the employer may be subject to civil action in the courts for failure to meet the minimum funding standards.

## Penalties for Overfunding

An excise tax will be imposed on an underpayment of taxes that results from an overstatement of pension liabilities. A 20 percent penalty tax is imposed on the underpayment of tax if the actuarial determination of pension liabilities is between 200 percent and 399 percent of the amount determined to be correct. If the actuarial determination is 400 percent or more of the correct amount, the penalty tax is increased to 40 percent. If the tax benefit is $1,000 or less, no excise tax will be imposed.

# Funding Governmental Plans

## Justification for ERISA's Governmental Plan Exemption

ERISA was enacted to remedy long-standing abuses and deficiencies in the private pension system, including insufficient assets to assure payment of future benefit obligations. ERISA's legislative history offers several justifications for the exemption of governmental plans from the funding requirements noted in the previous section. The legislature considered the ability of the governmental entities to fulfill the obligation to employees through their taxing powers an adequate substitute for minimum funding standards. Also, there was concern that imposition of the minimum funding standards would entail unacceptable cost implications to the governmental entities (Davidson and Litvin, 1991).

## State and Local Plans

Unlike the private plans discussed in the previous section, public employee plans are not covered by ERISA and Congress has been concerned about whether public plan beneficiaries have protection under state laws comparable to ERISA protections for private plans. An ERISA-mandated congressional study, published March 15, 1978, concluded that serious problems existed at all levels of government in funding standards for public pension plans and that federal regulation was necessary and desirable. However, due to the potential constitutional conflict and because many experts believe that funding decisions are more appropriately made by the sponsoring state and local governments, the legislative proposals for regulating public plans have been limited to reporting, disclosure, and fiduciary standards (Bleakney and Pacelli, 1990).

In the absence of specific legal funding requirements, governments are not required to prefund their pension plan liability, and may opt to pay retirement benefits as they become due. However, in a 1990 report, the U.S. General Accounting Office (GAO) reviewed public pensions in four states[47] and found "the boards use actuarial valuations to determine the contributions necessary to fund earned benefits" (p. 2). They also concluded that "the plans' enabling statutes require that employees and employers make annual contributions on an actuarially sound basis. Generally the statues either (1) specify the contribution rates or (2) prescribe a range, floor, or ceiling rate of contributions" (p. 4).

In most instances the contribution includes the normal costs[48] and an amount that amortizes the supplemental liability over a period ranging from 20 to 40 years. In addition, gains and losses due to the differences between the past actuarial assumptions and the plan's actual experience are also usually amortized (Zorn, 1990). Chart 4.6 provides a distribution of the years to amortize unfunded pension obligations obtained from a Greenwich 1987 survey of 290 state and municipal pension plans (Greenwich Associates, 1988).

Although Mitchell and Smith (1991) determined that state and local pension plans had relatively small deviations in their assumptions of expected future rate of wage growth and the rate of return on pension fund investments in the late 1980s, it appears that recently several public systems were able to markedly decrease their contributions through changes in assumptions. For example, in 1991 Louisiana saved $11 million in contributions to its teachers retirement

---

[47] The report responded to a congressional request for information on public plans in the four states. The U.S. General Accounting Office was prohibited from publicly disclosing the identity of the plans.

[48] The majority of the respondents to the 1991 Public Pension Coordinating Council survey used the entry age normal actuarial method (Zorn, 1990).

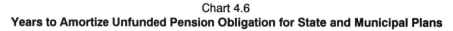

**Chart 4.6**
**Years to Amortize Unfunded Pension Obligation for State and Municipal Plans**

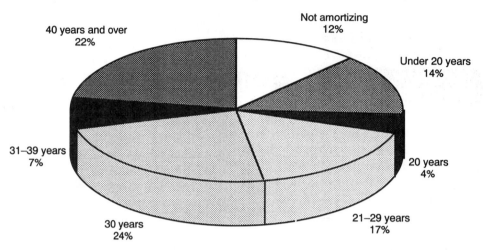

Not amortizing
12%

Under 20 years
14%

40 years and over
22%

20 years
4%

31–39 years
7%

21–29 years
17%

30 years
24%

Source: Greenwich Associates, *On Target, 90%: Public Pension Funds 1988* (Greenwich, CT: Greenwich Associates, 1988).

system by increasing the projected return from 7.5 percent to 8.25 percent. Missouri decreased contributions by $20 million by going from 8 percent to 8.5 percent in 1991 on its state employees' fund. New York City increased its rate of return assumption for city employees from 8.25 percent to 9 percent in 1990 and saved $40 million for the Transit Authority alone (Deutchman, 1992).

Even if a public pension plan has an actuarially required contribution, there is the distinct possibility that it may not be made.[49] Governmental contributions to public retirement plans are generally subject to the appropriation process within the employing government. Consequently, the plans compete with other governmental programs for funds. As one noted expert on public pension plans states: "actuaries can have all the numbers in the world, but the people who control the purse strings are the people who decide whether they're going to pay the money or not" (Bleakney, 1991).

The experience in the state of Illinois with regard to this process has been documented in some detail:

> State law did declare that the systems were to be funded on an actuarial basis, but the plan never acted on this. It did regularly contribute the cash to cover each years payouts until 1982, when it abandoned even that minimal contribu-

[49] There is also the potential for money already contributed to the fund to be seized for nonretirement purposes.

tion of discipline in the face of a recession and budget shortfall of hundreds of millions of dollars. Governor Thompson chopped the states contribution to the various retirement systems to as low as 60 percent of the 1982 payout. It was supposed to be a one year phenomena but it was stretched into ten years with the state contribution varying between 80 and 45 percent of the annual benefit payout. In 1989 Illinois wrote into law a funding schedule with a 40 year amortization, to be phased in during the following seven years. However the schedule was never followed. In April of 1991, a class action lawsuit was filed charging Illinois and its five retirement systems with violating the law (Hawthorne, 1992).

The average annual contribution amounted to 89 percent of that actuarially required for the 42 plans evaluated for 1988 by Mitchell and Smith (1991). Those plans that undercontributed in 1988 had a history of underfunding in past years, and fiscal pressures were a factor in the plans' funding practices.

GAO (1993) analyzed contribution data reported for 189 plans in the 1991 Public Pension Coordinating Council survey. They found that plan sponsors contributed only 80 percent of the amount actuarially required. The sponsors of the 40 percent of the plans that failed to contribute the full amount required contributed only 38 percent of the actuarially required amount. Chart 4.7 shows the distribution of plans by the percentage of required contributions actually made.

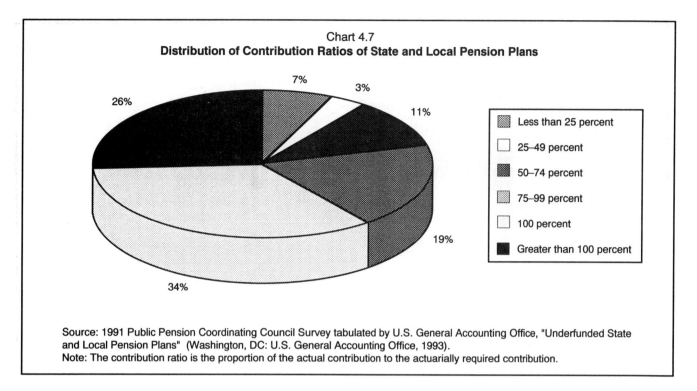

**Chart 4.7**
**Distribution of Contribution Ratios of State and Local Pension Plans**

7%
3%
26%
11%
19%
34%

Less than 25 percent
25–49 percent
50–74 percent
75–99 percent
100 percent
Greater than 100 percent

Source: 1991 Public Pension Coordinating Council Survey tabulated by U.S. General Accounting Office, "Underfunded State and Local Pension Plans" (Washington, DC: U.S. General Accounting Office, 1993).
Note: The contribution ratio is the proportion of the actual contribution to the actuarially required contribution.

## Federal Plans

*Civil Service Retirement and Disability Fund*[50]—
The Civil Service Retirement and Disability Fund contains two tiers of defined pension benefits (CSRS and FERS). Most employees covered by the CSRS contribute 7 percent of basic pay. Each employing agency matches the employee contributions. The total contributions for most employees is close to the static[51] normal cost of the benefits. Most employees covered by the FERS contribute a percentage of basic pay equal to 7 percent minus the OASDI rate. Agencies contribute the difference between the full "dynamic" normal cost of FERS coverage and the employee contribution.

Under the Civil Service Retirement Amendments of 1969, the Treasury makes the following payments to the fund:
- a 30-year amortization of any increases in the CSRS unfunded liability[52] that result from new or liberalized benefits,[53] increases in pay, or extension of coverage to new employee groups

- a payment of 5 percent interest on the CSRS statutory unfunded liability[54]
- a payment of the estimated cost of benefit attributable to CSRS military service less the value of certain deposits made by employees for such service

The Federal Employees' Retirement System Act of 1986 provides for separate financing of all benefits attributable to FERS, including those benefits attributable to frozen CSRS service for employees who elect FERS, based on a dynamic entry age normal funding method. Any supplemental liability under FERS are to be amortized over 30 years by the Treasury (except for liabilities attributable to Postal employees).[55]

The fund's investments consist solely of U.S. Government securities. The fair value of special government securities equals the par value since they are always redeemable at par regardless of the date of redemption or the interest rate. The fair value of U.S. Treasury bonds is determined by using the over-the-counter quotes.

---

[50] Unlike other federal agencies, the U. S. Postal Service is required to make three additional payments under Public Laws 93-449, 99-335, and 101-508.

[51] The CSRS uses static economic assumption of a 5 percent annual interest rate and no future salary inflation or cost-of-living increase in annuity.

[52] The unfunded liability is the estimated excess of the present value of all benefits payable from the fund to employees, former employees, and their survivors, over the sum of the present value of deductions to be withheld from future basic pay of employees and of

future agency contributions to be made in their behalf; plus the present value of the remaining 30 early amortization payment which had previously been scheduled; plus the fund balance as of the date the unfunded liability is determined.

[53] Automatic cost-of-living adjustments are excluded.

[54] This amount was $195.1 billion as of September 30, 1991.

[55] The supplemental liability as of 1988 is being amortized by annual payments of $419 million from the Treasury. In addition, increases in the supplemental liability during 1989 and 1990 are being amortized by annual payments of $16 million and $24 million, respectively.

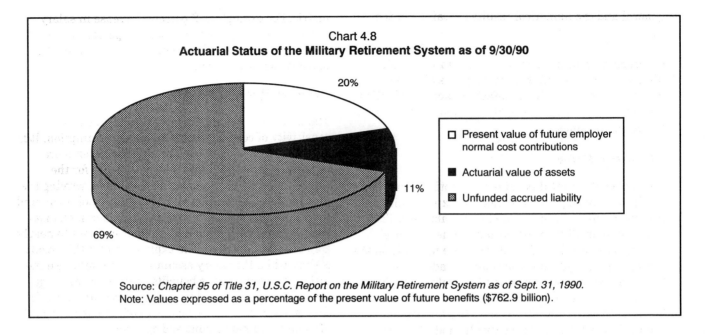

**Chart 4.8**
**Actuarial Status of the Military Retirement System as of 9/30/90**

20%

11%

69%

☐ Present value of future employer normal cost contributions

■ Actuarial value of assets

▨ Unfunded accrued liability

Source: *Chapter 95 of Title 31, U.S.C. Report on the Military Retirement System as of Sept. 31, 1990.*
Note: Values expressed as a percentage of the present value of future benefits ($762.9 billion).

*Military Retirement System*—There are three distinct benefit formulas within the military retirement systems. Retirement benefits are based on final basic pay (FINAL PAY) for personnel entering the Armed Services before September 8, 1980 and are based on the average of the highest 36 months (HI-3) for those entering after this date. Additionally, members first entering the Armed Services on or after August 1, 1986 are subject to a reduction (REDUX) if they retire with fewer than 30 years of service.

Public Law 99-661 mandates that two separate normal cost percentages be used for the valuation of the military retirement system. One is for active duty personnel (full time) and the second is for drilling reservists (part time).

The 1991 Fiscal Year normal cost percentages based on the aggregate method are summarized below:

| Benefit Formula | Full Time | Part Time |
|---|---|---|
| FINAL PAY | 49.6% | 14.6% |
| HI-3 | 43.6 | 13.4 |
| REDUX | 36.8 | 12.1 |

There was an initial unfunded liability as of September 30, 1984 of $528.7 billion. The amortization method is currently set up so that the amortization will be completed in the year 2043 (for a total of 60 annual payments). Changes in the unfunded liability arising because of modification in the benefit formulas, change in actuarial assumptions, and deviation in actual experience from expected experience are amortized over

30 years by payments that increase in absolute value at the same rate as the annual long-term basic pay scale assumption (currently 5.75 percent).

The actuarial status of the Military Retirement System as of September 30, 1990 is summarized in chart 4.8.

# Sensitivity Analysis of Alternative Actuarial Assumptions

The first section of this paper contained a description of the process used by sponsors to determine which of several values to choose for each of the actuarial assumptions required in the plan funding process. However, the impact of choosing one value versus another was not described and, as will be demonstrated in this section, the overall pension cost of a plan is more sensitive to some assumptions than others. This has become increasingly important in a public policy context as the solvency of PBGC has been debated. For example, a January 1993 report by GAO found that the PBGC's exposure to unfunded liabilities is much larger than plans have indicated on their annual reports.

The problem with performing any sensitivity analysis of this type is that the results will typically be limited to those of an extremely small number of plans. This is particularly true for the demographic assumptions due to the lack of detailed information reported on the 5500 forms. As a result, the principal set of comparisons in this section is based on a hypothetical pension plan described in Winklevoss (1977). Readers should be cautioned that these results are not necessarily applicable to plans and participant populations in general and the numerical results contained in the charts are based on active employees only.

The one variable that does not suffer from lack of sufficient information is the plan's interest rate (discount assumption). Fortunately it is also the assumption that has the greatest impact on valuation results. Thus, it will be analyzed in more detail than the other variables.

## Mortality Rates

The higher the mortality rates assumptions, the shorter will be the participants assumed life expectancies and the lower will be the calculated plan liabilities. The impact of mortality on the present value of future benefits is shown in chart 4.9. The rate multiple on the horizontal axis indicates the change made to the baseline assumption. For example, a rate multiple of 1.5 indicates that the annual mortality rate at each age has been increased by 50 percent. The impact of a change in mortality has a relatively modest impact. A change of 50 percent in either direction results in less than a 25 percent increase in costs.

## Termination Rates

Chart 4.10 shows the results of various termination rate assumptions, including a point which eliminates the assumption entirely (a rate multiple of zero). The impact of a 50 percent change in this assumption is approximately the same as for the mortality rates. It should be noted however that while a 50 percent swing (either way) in mortality rates would be viewed as a relatively uncommon event, a change of this magnitude in the termination rates could result from mergers and acquisitions or downsizings.

## Disability Rates

Chart 4.11 shows that pension costs are virtually invariant to substantial changes in the disability rates. This is due to the fact that as disability rates decrease, the increase in costs from retirement benefits are virtually completely offset by corresponding decreases in the disability benefits paid by the plan.

## Salary Rates

The upward sloping line in chart 4.12 shows the sensitivity of costs to the salary assumption for the hypothetical plan. Variations in the baseline value of approximately[56] 7 percent are significant and asym-

---

[56] The merit component of the salary scale in this example changes with age but is approximately 2 percent.

metric. For example, a 2 percent decrease in salary decreases costs by approximately 20 percent while a 2 percent increase in salary results in more than a 30 percent increase in cost.

## Interest Rates

The downward sloping line in chart 4.12 shows the sensitivity of costs to the interest rate assumption. It is immediately obvious that plan costs are even more sensitive to this assumption than they are for the salary rates discussed above. For example, varying the interest rate assumption by 2 percentage points around the 7 percent baseline results in pension cost changes ranging from more than a 60 percent increase to nearly a 40 percent decrease. The explanation for this result is that, while the salary assumption will influence the cost of the participant's benefits until retirement age, the interest rate is used to compute present values for the remainder of the participant's lifetime (or the joint lifetime of the participant and spouse).

This point is illustrated in more detail in chart 4.13, which shows the impact of changing the interest rate and the salary assumption simultaneously. This is accomplished by varying the rate of inflation, which is treated as a component of both rates. Pension costs decrease as the inflation assumption increases and the interest rate and salary rate increase beyond the 7 percent baseline. An increase in the inflation rate of 2 percentage points will decrease costs in this plan by nearly 20 percent.

As mentioned earlier, the sensitivity of the pension costs to any of these actuarial assumptions is a function of the age distribution of the participants. As a result, the impact of a change in interest rates will differ among plan sponsors. Schoenly (1991) provides the following comparisons to illustrate how the age distribution and weighting of liabilities will affect these adjustments. The last two columns show how a 1 percentage point increase in the interest rate will decrease the present value (pv) of each liability:

| Age | Type of Liability | pv @ 7% / pv @ 6% | pv @ 8% / pv @ 7% |
|---|---|---|---|
| 25 | deferred life annuity commencing at age 65 | 64.2% | 64.7% |
| 25 | temporary life annuity at age 65 | 89.7% | 90.5% |
| 45 | deferred life annuity commencing at age 65 | 77.5% | 77.9% |
| 45 | temporary life annuity to age 65 | 93.5% | 93.8% |
| 65 | life annuity | 93.5% | 93.8% |

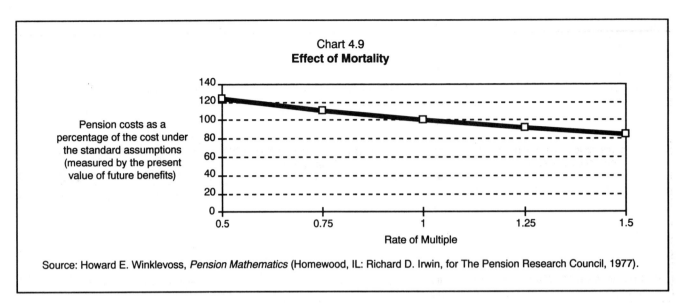

Chart 4.9
**Effect of Mortality**

Pension costs as a percentage of the cost under the standard assumptions (measured by the present value of future benefits)

Rate of Multiple

Source: Howard E. Winklevoss, *Pension Mathematics* (Homewood, IL: Richard D. Irwin, for The Pension Research Council, 1977).

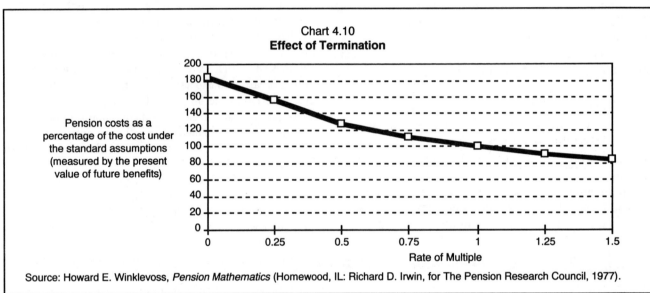

Chart 4.10
**Effect of Termination**

Pension costs as a percentage of the cost under the standard assumptions (measured by the present value of future benefits)

Rate of Multiple

Source: Howard E. Winklevoss, *Pension Mathematics* (Homewood, IL: Richard D. Irwin, for The Pension Research Council, 1977).

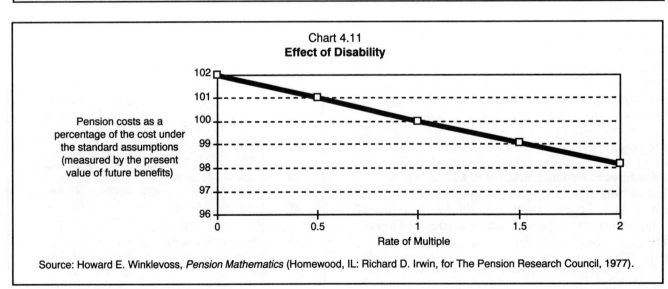

Chart 4.11
**Effect of Disability**

Pension costs as a percentage of the cost under the standard assumptions (measured by the present value of future benefits)

Rate of Multiple

Source: Howard E. Winklevoss, *Pension Mathematics* (Homewood, IL: Richard D. Irwin, for The Pension Research Council, 1977).

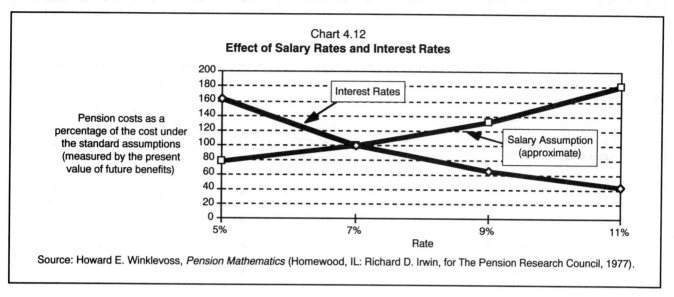

Chart 4.12
**Effect of Salary Rates and Interest Rates**

Pension costs as a percentage of the cost under the standard assumptions (measured by the present value of future benefits)

Interest Rates

Salary Assumption (approximate)

Rate

Source: Howard E. Winklevoss, *Pension Mathematics* (Homewood, IL: Richard D. Irwin, for The Pension Research Council, 1977).

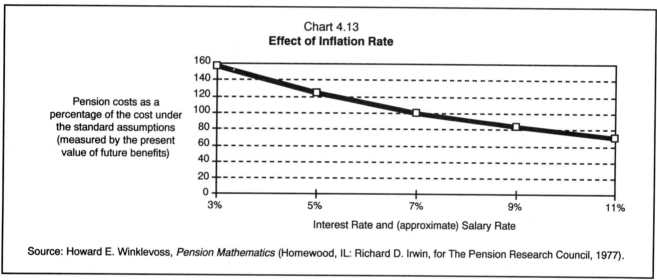

Chart 4.13
**Effect of Inflation Rate**

Pension costs as a percentage of the cost under the standard assumptions (measured by the present value of future benefits)

Interest Rate and (approximate) Salary Rate

Source: Howard E. Winklevoss, *Pension Mathematics* (Homewood, IL: Richard D. Irwin, for The Pension Research Council, 1977).

GAO (1993) developed a model to perform sensitivity analysis on the liabilities of pension plans from information found in the Form 5500 filings. They found that a 1 percentage point increase in the interest rate assumption will generally lead to about a 10 percent to 20 percent decrease in calculated plan liabilities. This is an aggregate estimate, the same 1 percentage point increase would lead to a decrease in the liability estimate for *nonretired* participants of anywhere from 6 percent to 65 percent, while for retired participants the same interest rate changes decrease the liability estimate by only 7 percent or less.

They also found that adjusting the discount rate for 44 plans[57] that terminated from 1986 to 1988 to the PBGC rate increased the liabilities by 31 percent. These plans calculated their liability using an interest rate assumption that was one-third larger than the rate used by PBGC.[58]

GAO also applied these adjustments to a sample of over 17,000 plans filing 1987 Form 5500 reports. They found that 16.1 percent of the sample was

---

[57] These plans accounted for 96 percent of the claims against PBGC for the period.

[58] The fact that PBGC interest rates were significantly lower than plan sponsor assumptions is at least partially due to the inherent difference between ongoing and termination assumptions. Sponsors' assumptions reflect the best estimate of the plan's *future* experience, which is not necessarily strongly tied to current market interest rates. Moreover, they are only set once each year and there is a preference for stability in this assumption to help the plan sponsors anticipate their yearly pension costs. In contrast, PBGC assumptions by definition focus on *current* experience in the annuity markets, especially for the portion of the liabilities attributed to retirees. An "immediate" rate is used to value these liabilities, a lower rate is used for liabilities attributed to other plan participants.

underfunded based on reported liabilities, but that number increased to 26.5 percent when the reported discount rates were decreased by 1 percentage point for each of the sample plans. Standardizing the discount rate to the PBGC rate in force on January 1987 had a similar effect with 24.7 percent of the sample plans being underfunded.

# References

Archer, Michael A. "Minimum Funding Requirements." In Martin Wald and David E. Kenty, eds., *ERISA: A Comprehensive Guide.* New York: John Wiley & Sons, Inc., 1991.

Bleakney, Thomas P. "Public Retirement Funds." *Record: Society of Actuaries,* Vol. 17, No. 3B. (1991): 1177–1197.

Bleakney, Thomas P., and Jane D. Pacelli. "Update of Retirement Systems for Public Employees." *Society of Actuaries Study Note* (1990) (BP).

Davidson, Stuart W., and Caren Litvin. "Private and Public Sector Benefit Plans — Differences and Similarities." In *Employee Benefit Issues 1991.* Brookfield, WI: International Foundation of Employee Benefit Plans.

Deutchman, Alan. "The Great Pension Robbery." *Fortune,* 13 January 1992, pp. 76–78.

Greenwich Associates. *On Target, 90%: Public Pension Funds 1988.* Greenwich Reports. Greenwich CT: Greenwich Associates, 1988.

Hawthorne, Fran. "Countdown in Illinois." *Institutional Investor* (December 1992): 73–81.

Itelson, Steven. "Selection of Interest Assumptions for Pension Plan Valuation." *Society of Actuaries Study Note,* 1991.

Knight, Ray A., Lee G. Knight, and Michael Winter, II. "Tax Planning for Pension Plans." *Management Accounting* (February 1992): 47–51.

KPMG Peat Marwick. Survey of Actuarial Assumptions for Pension Plan Accounting Costs: How Assumptions Are Chosen. March 1993.

McGill, Dan M., and Donald S. Grubbs, Jr. *Fundamentals of Private Pension Plans,* 6th edition. Homewood, IL: Richard D. Irwin for The Pension Research Council, 1989.

McGinn, Daniel F. "Over/Underfunded Pension Plans." *Employee Benefit Issues —The Multiemployer Perspective —1991.* Brookfield, WI: International Foundation of Employee Benefit Plans, 1992.

Mitchell, Olivia, and Robert S. Smith. *Pension Funding In The Public Sector.* NBER Working Paper No. 3898. Cambridge, MA: National Bureau of Economic Research, 1991.

Phillips, Kristen. "State and Local Government Pension Benefits." In John A. Turner and Daniel J. Beller, eds., *Trends in Pensions, 1992.* Washington, DC: U.S. Government Printing Office, 1992.

"Selecting Actuarial Assumptions." *Record: Society of Actuaries.* Vol. 17, no. 4B (1991): 2155–2170.

Schoenly, Stuart G. "Pension Topics." *Society of Actuaries Study Note* (1991).

U.S. General Accounting Office. *Public Plans in Four States Have Generally Similar Policies and Practices.* Washington, DC: U.S. Government Printing Office, 1990.

———. *Underfunded State and Local Pension Plans.* Washington, DC: U.S. General Accounting Office, 1993.

U.S. Office of Personnel Management. Retirement and Insurance Group. *Civil Service Retirement and Disability Fund: An Annual Report to Comply with the Requirements of Public Law 95-595.* Washington, DC: U.S. Office of Personnel Management, 1991.

Winklevoss, Howard E. *Pension Mathematics.* Homewood, Il: Richard D. Irwin for The Pension Research Council, 1977.

The Wyatt Company. *Accounting for Pensions and Postretirement Benefits.* Washington, DC: The Wyatt Company, various years.

Zorn, Paul. *Survey of State Retirement Systems Covering General Employees and Teachers.* Chicago, IL: Government Finance Officers Association and the National Association of State Retirement Administrators, 1990.

# Supplement: Actuarial Tables Used to Compute Normal Costs and Supplemental Liabilities

| Age | Salary Scale | Survival Probability | Discount Factor | TEBLA without Salary Scale | TEBLA with Salary |
|-----|-----|-----|-----|-----|-----|
| 65 | 14.603 | 1 | .747258 | 4.253 | 4.597 |
| 60 | 11.898 | .8592 | .417265 | 8.750 | 11.464 |
| 50 | 7.544 | .6646 | .311805 | 9.231 | 13.191 |
| 45 | 5.853 | .5248 | .232999 | 8.954 | 13.787 |
| 40 | 4.446 | .3809 | .130105 | 7.059 | 11.969 |
| 30 | 2.349 | .1416 | .097222 | 5.737 | 9.791 |
| 25 | 1.596 | .0643 | | | |

# V.   The Costs and Benefits of Pension Tax Expenditures

BY DALLAS L. SALISBURY

## Introduction

Pensions in their purest form are a means of providing income to individuals once they are no longer working. The primary reason that plans are established is to increase workers' economic security on reaching retirement age. Tax incentives are designed to encourage the expansion of pension coverage and increased saving levels and to provide a source of retirement income in addition to Social Security.

The provision of tax incentives to encourage pension coverage reflects a longstanding policy of the U.S. government. Under the Internal Revenue Code, an employer's contribution to a qualified plan is deductible within specified limits. Taxes on employer contributions and investment income are deferred for pension plan participants until the pension benefit is received and declared as income. Any individual who participates in a pension plan, whether he or she works for the federal government, a state or local government, or a private nongovernment organization, receives a deferral on income tax as the benefit accrues.

Individuals tend to focus on the immediate reduction in taxes that comes with pension tax treatment rather than on a calculation of the ultimate net tax gain or loss that will occur many years in the future. Because tax rates may be higher in the future than they are today, individuals may ultimately pay more taxes when they receive their benefit. Some people, as a result, would be better off never putting in the money. On the other hand, others may end up in a lower tax bracket in retirement than they were in when working, meaning they would have been better off in tax terms having received a pension rather than cash. In short, although it is generally assumed that everyone wins with lower tax payments when they invest in tax-deferred pensions, not everyone does.

Nevertheless, the federal government gives a value to this "gain from deferral," which is referred to as a "tax expenditure," that is, a tax the government does not get paid today because the value of the pension benefit accrual is not taxed as income today. Each year a set of tax expenditure estimates is developed by the Department of the Treasury and published as part of the federal budget. The total reported pension tax expenditure (which includes civil service, state and local, and private pension plans) is $56.5 billion for FY 1993. The magnitude of pension plan tax expendi-

tures estimates has attracted the attention of the media and public policymakers.

At the same time, pension funds and their taxation have come to the forefront because of the tremendous accumulation of pension assets in the economy. Private and public pension plans now hold more than $4 trillion in assets. Some policymakers have looked to this large pool of assets as a means to fund economic development projects such as infrastructure. Moreover, the ever-increasing federal budget deficit has caused policymakers to assess whether the "cost" of lost federal revenues, which is measured by tax expenditure estimates, is appropriate.

When we ask if pensions are worth the cost, we are focusing on the tax expenditures attributed to pensions. Are the tax incentives accorded to pensions meeting their public policy objectives? Do pensions provide enough benefit to individuals and the economy as a whole to justify the tax expenditure?

Several factors must be taken into account when evaluating the appropriateness of tax expenditures. First, analysts must determine what the numbers actually measure. It is especially important to distinguish between the types of plans represented by tax expenditure estimates. Often, pension tax expenditure estimates are referred to as if they only represent revenue associated with private pension plans. However, the number reflects all pension plans including civil service, military, state and local governments, and private plans.

Second, to assess whether pensions are worth the cost, it is important to recognize the impact that the funding practices of different plan types have on the revenue numbers. Because the tax expenditure estimates for pensions are calculated by the government on a cash flow basis, no value is placed on the pension promise itself, only on the advance funding of that promise. With the exception of Social Security and federal employee defined benefit plans, most pension plans now seek to advance fund as a means of assuring that promises made will be kept. Federal law requires private pension plans to set aside funds for the purpose of paying benefits as they become due. However, public pension plans may operate on a pay-as-you-go basis, distributing benefits from current receipts. Defined contribution plans are always fully funded for accrued liabilities by definition because the participants' pension benefit consists of the contributions and investment returns on these contributions.

This paper reviews the history of the relationship between government and pensions; analyzes the tax expenditure cost of pensions and the allocation of that tax expenditure across individuals, types of plans, and employment sectors; considers the methodology used to determine the tax expenditure; provides statistics on pension plans and the individuals earning benefits; and provides information on the assets and income streams produced by pension plans in return for the tax expenditure. This paper provides a basis for assessing pensions.

## Government and Pensions

The U.S. government has taken steps since its earliest days to assure that retirees have income: beginning in 1776, the government provided retired veterans with pensions; in 1914, the government allowed for-profit employers to deduct the cost of pensions paid to employees and allowed employers to deduct contributions to a pension trust for retirement income programs; in 1921 and 1926, the government acted to allow taxes on trust earnings to be deferred until benefits are paid; in 1935, Social Security was established to pay retirement benefits; and in 1974, the government established tax incentives for individuals to allow pre-tax contributions to individual retirement accounts (IRAs) and the deferral of tax in earnings until funds were removed as income.

To assure that pension plans do not discriminate in favor of highly compensated employees, Congress enacted the first nondiscrimination rules in 1942. Reporting and disclosure requirements were first enacted in 1947 and 1958. Keogh plans for self-employed individuals were established in 1962.

The Employee Retirement Income Security Act of 1974 (ERISA) made significant advance funding of private employer defined benefit pension plans mandatory, added new incentives for individuals to set aside funds in IRAs, established minimum standards in a number of areas to increase benefit entitlement, and established the Pension Benefit Guaranty Corporation (PBGC) to assure benefit security in private defined benefit pension plans. Prior to ERISA, many pension plans were operated on a pay-as-you-go basis. ERISA requires private pension plans to set aside funds for the purpose of paying benefits as they become due. Advance funding of private defined benefit pension plans was desired to (1) increase benefit security and (2) to increase the pool of savings in the economy.

To further encourage both employers and workers to save for retirement, the Revenue Act of 1978 added section 401(k) to the code, which allows employ-

ees to elect to have a portion of their compensation (otherwise payable in cash) contributed to a qualified defined contribution plan. The employee contribution is often treated as a pretax reduction in salary. Tens of thousands of these plans exist in both the public and private sectors. The Federal Employee Thrift Plan functions like a 401(k) plan.

The 1980s saw a shift in federal policy related to retirement income programs, after decades of expanding incentives and requirements to prefund pension promises. While the emphasis had traditionally been on employer action and encouragement of maximum funding, the 1980s brought a shift toward individual action, restrictions on the amount that could be contributed to employer-sponsored plans, and limits on the assets that could be maintained by a plan relative to benefits promised.

Enactment of the Tax Equity and Fiscal Responsibility Act of 1982 (TEFRA) represented the most dramatic shift from the decades long policy of expansion. TEFRA reduced contribution and benefit dollar limits for all private and state and local plans by nearly one-third. Further restrictions and reductions on allowable retirement plan contributions were included in the Deficit Reduction Act of 1984 (DEFRA) and the Tax Reform Act of 1986 (TRA '86). Finally, the Omnibus Budget Reconciliation Act of 1987 (OBRA '87) was enacted with a new "full-funding limitation" for defined benefit pension plans. The full-funding limit is essentially the lesser of roughly 100 percent of projected benefits (100 percent of benefits based on projected salary increases) or 150 percent of the plan's current liability, which essentially is all existing liabilities to employees and beneficiaries.[1] If sponsors contribute in excess of the full-funding limit, the amount will be treated as a nondeductible contribution subject to a 10 percent excise tax. Because many private defined benefit plans are fully funded according to this new standard, many private employers have not been able to make deductible contributions to defined benefit pension plans in recent years.

A defined benefit plan, like Social Security, promises a benefit based on a formula tied to years of service and/or earnings. To pay the benefit, the plan initially needs only enough funds to meet periodic cash flow. Initially, cash flow will be lower if the plan payments are made in the form of annuities rather than lump-sum distributions. Private employer defined benefit plans must make a current year contribution for

---

[1] A deduction is always allowed for a single-employer plan to make a contribution up to the level of its unfunded current liabilities if the plan has at least 100 participants.

the value of current year benefit accruals (normal cost) and amortize any liabilities attributable to past service over no more than 30 years.[2] However, the OBRA '87 full-funding limitation can act to prohibit the employer from making even the normal cost contribution if it would lead the plan to be more than 150 percent funded for current promised benefits. This legislation also substantially changed minimum funding for underfunded plans.

Critics of these post-1981 policy changes say that policymakers enacted them as a means to raise federal revenue at the expense of sound retirement policy. In any case, the changes have contributed to a substantial reshaping of retirement programs.

## Private Pensions

The number of private pension plans has grown significantly since the enactment of ERISA. From 1975 to 1989, the total number of tax-qualified employer-sponsored plans (both defined benefit and defined contribution plans) increased from 311,000 to 731,000, and gross participation (active workers, separated vested, survivors, and retirees) in such plans rose from 45 million to 76 million over the same period.[3]

Defined benefit plans have historically been the cornerstone of the private pension system. In a defined benefit plan, the employer agrees to provide the employee a nominal benefit amount at retirement, based on a specified formula, which is tied to years of service and compensation. The sponsor must decide how to pay for the plan. Traditionally these plans only paid an annuity at retirement age, but more of them now offer individuals the option of a lump-sum distribution when they leave the job.

This century saw the advent of defined contribution plans. In these plans, the employer makes specified contributions to an account established for each participating employee. The final retirement benefit reflects the total of employer contributions, any employee contributions, investment gains or losses, and possibly losses from forfeitures of employees terminating before achieving 100 percent vesting. The final account balance is generally paid to the individual as a lump sum when he or she leaves the job or retires. The individual will either receive more or less than was contributed, depending on investment experience.

In 1975, there were 103,000 defined benefit plans, with 33 million participants and $186 billion in assets. In 1989, there were 132,000 such plans, down from the peak of 175,000 plans in 1982 and 1983. The number of gross participants has remained in the 40 million–41 million range since 1983, and there was $998 billion in assets in 1989. Over the same period, the number of defined contribution plans increased from 208,000 to 599,000. The number of participants increased from 12 million to 38 million in 1987 and decreased slightly in 1989, to 36 million.

One of the most significant trends in pension coverage has been the tremendous growth of 401(k) plans over the past decade. Employee Benefit Research Institute (EBRI) tabulations of the May 1988 and May 1983 Current Population Survey (CPS) show that more than 27.5 million workers were covered by 401(k) plans in May 1988, up from 7.1 million in May 1983. These figures represented 24.2 percent and 7.1 percent of all workers, respectively. Participation grew from 2.7 million workers (2.7 percent of all workers) in 1983 to 15.7 million (13.8 percent of all workers) in 1988. And, in May 1988, the majority of 401(k) participants earned less than $30,000.[4]

There are many reasons for having each type of plan (Employee Benefit Research Institute, 1989 and 1990). The advantage to the individual of a defined benefit plan is shown most graphically when a president of the United States leaves office. The defined benefit is based on no more than eight years of service and is defined as the annual salary of a current cabinet member (about $145,000), or 72.5 percent of the presidential salary. The president is not taxed as the benefit accrues during his tenure but is taxed on the pension as it is paid. Even if the government put money aside in advance, it would not be treated as taxable income to the president.

Compare this to providing the president with a defined contribution plan. The law sets a maximum contribution of $30,000 per year, allowing $240,000 to be contributed over the eight years of a two-term president. Even with a high rate of investment return, the defined contribution plan would not fund two full years of retirement for the president. This example highlights the primary reason that defined benefit plans are valued: the ability to provide a targeted benefit at retirement based on a formula.

The second major difference is the ability to provide post-retirement inflation adjustments to

---

[2] Plans in existence at the time of ERISA could amortize past service liability over a 40-year period.

[3] Department of Labor, Pension and Welfare Benefits Administration, tabulations of the 1989 form 5500, unpublished (1993).

[4] The U.S. Bureau of the Census will collect similar data in April 1993, which should be available for Employee Benefit Research Institute (EBRI) tabulations in Winter 1994.

individuals who receive a monthly pension benefit check. This is not done for defined contribution plan recipients or for those who take lump-sum distributions from either type of plan. Many government employee plans provide for automatic inflation adjustments, while many private plans provide ad-hoc adjustments (Piacentini and Foley, 1992).

The final major difference is that younger workers who are likely to change jobs several times will do better with defined contribution plans. Once they are older and enter a last job, however, they will likely retire from that job in the best financial condition if it provides a defined benefit plan.

The future mix of traditional defined benefit plans, new defined benefit plans, and defined contribution plans is likely to constantly change. Plan choice will be affected by the average age of the work force, the relative desire of employers to get positive employee motivation today from plans, work force mobility, growth rates in sectors of the economy (including heavily unionized and older industrial sectors) in which traditional defined benefit plan coverage is most firmly established, federal tax laws, and the level of basic income tax rates.

Employers will have to assess their objectives over time as they experience work force, economic, and regulatory change.

# Pension Costs

## *The Value of Tax Expenditures*

The concept of tax expenditures was developed in the 1970s. The Congressional Budget and Impoundment Act of 1974 (section 3(a)(3)) defines tax expenditures as: ... "those revenue losses attributable to provisions of the Federal tax laws which allow a special exclusion, exemption, or deduction from gross income or which provide a special credit, a preferential rate of tax, or a deferral of tax liability . . ." (Employee Benefit Research Institute, 1983).

Pension, Keogh (pensions for self-employed individuals) and IRA tax expenditures are different from most other tax expenditures because they represent tax-deferred expenditures rather than tax-exempt expenditures. For example, payments for health benefits are never taxed, while pensions are taxed when paid to the individual.[5]

---

[5] For a full discussion of pension taxation, see Employee Benefit Research Institute, "Retirement Program Tax Expenditures," *EBRI Issue Brief* no. 17 (Employee Benefit Research Institute, April 1983); and "Pension-Related Tax Benefits," *EBRI Issue Brief* no. 25 (Employee Benefit Research Institute, December 1983).

The tax expenditure estimates for pensions are calculated by the government on a cash flow basis. This is significant because it has the effect of placing no value on the pension promise itself, only on the advance funding of that promise. First, the contributions made to plans and estimated investment earnings are treated as taxable wages. Second, benefits paid by the plans are treated as taxable income. Third, the tax to be paid on benefits is subtracted from the tax that would have been paid on contributions and earnings to get a net tax expenditure estimate. Thus, a "tax expenditure" is only considered to have occurred if advance contributions are made.

According to the FY 1993 federal budget, the pension tax expenditure is $56.5 billion for FY 1993. The tax expenditure number reported by the government should represent all types of pension plans—civil service, military, state and local, and private—because pension participants gain economic value and tax deferral regardless of where they work. However, the number reportedly does not currently include military plans. The estimate does cover both defined benefit and defined contribution plans.

The range of tax expenditures for employee benefits is presented in table 5.1. The total reported pension tax expenditure of $56.5 billion for FY 1993 has been broken down using the EBRI Tax Estimating and Analysis Model (TEAM) to show the numbers by sector (private, federal, state and local) and plan type (defined benefit and defined contribution). Based on present law and funded status of plans, the largest portion of the tax expenditure, $27.9 billion (or 49.4 percent), is attributable to public-sector defined benefit pension plans. Private sector defined contribution plans (such as 401(k) ) are next at $19.3 billion (34.2 percent), followed by private-sector defined benefit plans at $8.2 billion (14.5 percent) and public-sector defined contribution plans at $1.1 billion (2 percent). This compares with the tax expenditure for IRAs of $7.1 billion, $2.7 billion for Keogh plans, and $24.5 billion for the exclusion from taxation of a portion of Social Security and railroad retirement benefits.

In a recent article using unpublished data from the Department of the Treasury, Munnell (1992) broke out an estimated 1991 total pension tax expenditure of $48 billion as being $25.5 billion private (53 percent); $14.7 billion state and local (31 percent); and $7.8 billion civil service retirement (16 percent), for a public plan allocation of 47 percent. She notes that the military program was apparently not included by the Treasury. Using data from the 1991 report of the Military Retirement System (MRS) actuary, the program would have represented a tax expenditure of $5.5 billion in 1991. This would adjust the total to

Table 5.1

Table 5.1
Tax Expenditure Estimates by Budget Function, Fiscal Years 1993-1997

| Function | 1993 | 1994 | 1995 | 1996 | 1997 | Total 1993–1997 |
|---|---|---|---|---|---|---|
| | | | ($ billions) | | | |
| Income Security | | | | | | |
| Net exclusion of pension contributions and earnings | $56.5 | $58.8 | $61.3 | $63.8 | $66.0 | $306.4 |
| **Private defined benefit** | **8.2** | **8.5** | **8.9** | **9.3** | **9.6** | **44.5** |
| **Private defined contribution** | **19.3** | **20.1** | **21.0** | **21.8** | **22.5** | **104.7** |
| **Public defined benefit** | **27.9** | **29.0** | **30.3** | **31.5** | **32.6** | **151.3** |
| **Public defined contribution** | **1.1** | **1.1** | **1.2** | **1.2** | **1.3** | **5.9** |
| Individual retirement plans | | | | | | |
| (exclusion of contributions and earnings) | 7.1 | 7.4 | 7.6 | 7.9 | 8.2 | 38.3 |
| Keogh plans | 2.7 | 2.9 | 3.1 | 3.3 | 3.4 | 15.4 |
| Social Security and Railroad Retirement | | | | | | |
| Exclusion of untaxed Social Security | | | | | | |
| and railroad retirement benefits | 24.5 | 25.7 | 27.0 | 28.3 | 29.7 | 135.4 |
| Health/Medicaid | | | | | | |
| Exclusion of employer contributions | | | | | | |
| for medical insurance premiums and medical care | 46.4 | 51.3 | 56.9 | 63.0 | 69.6 | 287.2 |
| Medicare | | | | | | |
| Exclusion of untaxed Medicare benefits: | | | | | | |
| hospital insurance | 7.6 | 8.4 | 9.3 | 10.4 | 11.6 | 47.3 |
| supplementary medical insurance | 4.4 | 4.9 | 5.6 | 6.5 | 7.6 | 28.9 |

Source: Employee Benefit Research Institute (EBRI) and EBRI estimates by plan type using the EBRI Tax Estimating and Analysis Model (TEAM); and EBRI tabulations of data from U.S. Congress, Joint Committee on Taxation, *Estimates of Federal Tax Expenditures for Fiscal Years 1993-1997* (Washington, DC: U.S. Government Printing Office, 1992).

$53.5 billion and the public plan share to 52.3 percent.

The EBRI-TEAM numbers presented in table 5.1 assume the inclusion of military retirement and allocate the tax expenditure on that basis, finding a public plan total for 1993 of 51.3 percent of the total pension tax expenditure of $56.5 billion.

Generally, the pension tax expenditure number is discussed as if it only applies to private employer plans, and then sometimes only to private defined benefit plans. As the foregoing discussion makes clear, the number covers all plans, with a near equal split between the tax expenditure for private and public employees.

In 1983, pension tax expenditures were estimated at $25.8 billion in the federal budget; however, those same tax expenditure items were reestimated at $43.5 billion in the 1984 federal budget—an increase of 75 percent for the year—without a word of explanation. The change primarily reflected the addition of state and local workers and federal civilian workers to the estimate (Employee Benefit Research Institute, 1983).

As a result, the tax expenditure attributed to private pensions has often been exaggerated. Public pension plans are seldom mentioned as part of the equation. More often than not during a call for private pension plan "reform" an advocate states that change

must be made because of the "$56 billion tax expenditure." Would this be less compelling if the number was limited to the $8.2 billion for private defined benefit plans? Suddenly the elements of the total pension tax expenditure would be significantly smaller relative to that for mortgages, medical premiums, capital gains at death, or accelerated depreciation. It would also show that the number attributable to private plans had grown little from the number published in the 1983 budget and earlier as the tax expenditure for pensions. Finally, it would show that the tax expenditure for private defined benefit plans had declined significantly as the system matured.

It would put the discussion of pension policy issues on a more informed basis if the tax expenditure were broken down by plan type in government publications so that policymakers could clearly see the distribution of tax incentives.

## What Is the Value Per Participant?

Breaking out tax expenditure numbers by plan type and sector also provides another way to focus on the more than 66 million individuals covered by pension plans, in addition to the millions now retired (Piacentini and Foley, 1992).

The better funded the plan and the larger the annual benefit payments relative to annual contributions and investment earnings, the lower the tax expenditure per employee/participant as currently calculated by the government.

Taking estimated tax expenditure numbers and dividing by the number of employees provides a per capita value. There were about 6.5 million active participants in federal civilian and military pension plans in 1991 (table 5.2). Based on present contributions, earnings, and benefits paid by these plans, the tax expenditure represents approximately $1,900 per active participant. Were federal plan funding to accelerate to pay off present liabilities over the next 40 years, the tax expenditure would increase to over $4,000 per active participant, and the tax expenditure number presented in the budget would leap upward by several billion dollars.

There are 11.4 million active participants in state and local government pension plans. For these plans the tax expenditure is equal to about $1,152 per active participant. For the 28 million active participants in private defined benefit plans the value would be a tax expenditure of about $292 per capita. For private defined contribution plans, with about 29 million active participants, the per capita tax expenditure is about $665 (table 5.2).

Because public plans generally include a post-retirement inflation adjustment of benefits, the value of accruals and the necessary level of contributions are likely to be higher in the future than those for private pension plans. In addition, federal plans have such large unfunded liabilities that funding them will require larger contributions. As a result, we are likely to see a growing proportion of the tax expenditure coming from public-sector pension plans.

## Private Expenditures for Retirement Income

Private employers contributed $24 billion to defined benefit and $13 billion to defined contribution plans in 1975, growing to $25 billion to defined benefit plans and $71 billion to defined contribution plans in 1989. Defined contribution plans represented 35 percent of contributions in 1975 and 74 percent in 1989. Private employer contributions represented 3.9 percent of wages and salaries in private organizations, with a range, depending upon industry, of 1.8 percent in retail trade to 5.6 percent in transportation and utilities (Piacentini and Foley, 1992). Private retirement plans have about 78 million active, separated, and retired participants.

Private employer contributions to defined benefit plans grew to $48 billion in 1982 as plans responded to ERISA's funding requirements. Excellent investment returns during the 1980s, combined with federal legislation during the decade that placed limits on funding and benefits, have caused contributions to decline. More than 85 percent of private defined benefit plans are fully funded today, compared with less than 25 percent when ERISA was enacted (Goodfellow and Schieber, 1993). Contributions to defined contribution plans can generally be viewed as a percentage of income. As incomes have increased and as the number of workers given the opportunity to participate has grown, contributions have grown as well (Salisbury, 1989).

PBGC was created under ERISA to strengthen retirement security by guaranteeing some benefits for defined benefit plan participants. PBGC is funded by premiums paid by private defined benefit plans sponsors. PBGC has been the focus of attention during the past two years because of a present single-employer program deficit of $2.7 billion and a potential 40-year

### Table 5.2
### Per Capita Tax Expenditures, 1991

| | Gross Participants (millions) | Active Participants (millions) | Tax Expenditures ($ billions) | Tax Expenditure per Active Participants |
|---|---|---|---|---|
| Civil Service Retirement System | 4.014 | 1.654 | $ 3.5 | $2,116 |
| Federal Employees Retirement System | 1.367 | 1.279 | 2.2 | 1,720 |
| Military | 3.763 | 2.130 | 4.0 | 1,877 |
| Thrift Savings | 1.625 | 1.419 | 2.7 | 1,902 |
| State and Local | 16.684 | 11.357 | 13.1 | 1,152 |
| Total Public | 27.419 | 17.868 | 29.0 | 1,623 |
| Private Defined Benefit | 41.000 | 28.000 | 8.2 | 292 |
| Private Defined Contribution | 37.000 | 29.000 | 19.3 | 665 |

Source: Employee Benefit Research Institute tabulations.

exposure of $40 billion (Yakoboski, Silverman, and VanDerhei, 1992). Some have questioned whether a general taxpayer bailout might be necessary if the liabilities exceed assets. Table 5.3 shows the present single-employer defined benefit plan liabilities faced by PBGC in underfunded plans. The numbers demonstrate the general strengthening of funding in these plans that has resulted from federal legislation. The overall defined benefit system currently has $1.3 trillion in assets to cover $900 billion in liabilities. Therefore, while there is significant underfunding within individual plans, there are also sufficient resources available within the defined benefit system itself—the payers of PBGC premiums—to cover this underfunding.

The ERISA requirements for pension plan funding have generally provided the benefit security sought by the law.

## State and Local Expenditures for Retirement Income

State and local governments generally provide defined benefit pension plans to their work force. About 12 million active employees and another 5 million former employees, retirees, and survivors are covered. Employer contributions to these plans grew from $15 billion in 1975 to an estimated $47 billion in 1990. Most of these plans have been advance funded, resulting in significant investment earnings in addition to contributions. Total assets reached $916 billion in 1992 (table 5.4). There are pockets of underfunding in some state and local plans (Government Finance Officers Association and U.S. General Accounting Office, 1992).

### Table 5.3
### Exposure Levels of Single Employer Plans Facing the Pension Benefit Guaranty Corporation, 1978-1991

| Year | Exposure (in 1991 dollars) |
|------|---------------------------|
| | ($ billions) |
| 1978 | $145 |
| 1979 | 157 |
| 1980 | 91 |
| 1981 | 52 |
| 1982 | 49 |
| 1983 | 44 |
| 1984 | 32 |
| 1985 | 40 |
| 1986 | 61 |
| Average | 75 |
| 1987–1989 | a |
| 1990 | 32 |
| 1991 | 40 |

Source: Data for 1978 to 1986 are from Employee Benefit Research Institute compilations based on Richard A. Ippolito, *The Economics of Pension Insurance* (Philadelphia, PA: Pension Research Council, Wharton School, University of Pennsylvania, 1989); data for 1990 are from the Pension Benefit Guaranty Corporation's *Annual Report* adjusted to 1991 levels; data for 1991 are from the Pension Benefit Guaranty Corporation, "Pension Underfunding Growth Continues in PBGC's Top 50 List," News release, 19 November 1992.
Note: Figures are adjusted to 1991 levels using the Consumer Price Index for All Urban Consumers (CPI-U).
aNot available.

## Federal Direct Expenditures for Retirement Income

The most significant retirement income programs funded by the federal government are Social Security, the military retirement programs, and the civil service retirement programs. This paper focuses on the latter two, the pension programs provided to federal workers. These federal employee programs include about 6.5 million active participants and 4 million participants who are retired or have left federal employment but will receive a benefit at a later date. These programs represent a sizable liability to the federal government and thus to the American taxpayers.

Budgeted outlays (inclusive of interest paid on bonds held as assets by the plans) for these employee pension programs grew from $21 billion in 1975 to $73 billion in 1991 and are projected to grow to $92 billion in 1997 (U.S. President, 1992).

The Civil Service Retirement and Disability Fund consists of two programs that are part of both the pension tax expenditure and the direct federal outlays. The Civil Service Retirement System (CSRS) covers those hired as federal civilian employees prior to 1984, and the Federal Employees Retirement System (FERS) covers those hired after 1984. Table 5.5 indicates that the programs represent a larger future obligation for taxpayers than cash outlays imply. These two programs had an unfunded liability of $870 billion in 1992, compared with $831 billion in 1990. Combined contributions were just enough to cover benefit payments in both years, with the unfunded liability growing as a result of new benefit accruals. The unfunded liability of the two plans increased by $6 billion in 1992. The present unfunded liability for CSRS is equal to $468,000 per active CSRS participant.

Table 5.4
**Financial Assets of Private and Government Pension Funds, 1983-1992**

| Year | Single Employer | | Multi-employer | Private Insured | Federal Government Retirement | State and Local Government | Total |
|------|-----------------|------------------|-----|------|------|------|------|
| | Defined benefit | Defined contribution | | | | | |
| | | | ($ billions) | | | | |
| 1983 | $ 526 | $286 | $ 79 | $252 | $112 | $311 | $1,566 |
| 1984 | 535 | 322 | 81 | 291 | 130 | 357 | 1,716 |
| 1985 | 643 | 392 | 121 | 347 | 149 | 405 | 2,057 |
| 1986 | 739 | 447 | 143 | 410 | 170 | 469 | 2,378 |
| 1987 | 770 | 471 | 148 | 459 | 188 | 517 | 2,553 |
| 1988 | 857 | 522 | 170 | 516 | 208 | 606 | 2,879 |
| 1989 | 1010 | 623 | 200 | 572 | 229 | 735 | 3,369 |
| 1990 | 965 | 584 | 194 | 636 | 251 | 752 | 3,382 |
| 1991 | 1,208 | 780 | 238 | 678 | 276 | 877 | 4,057 |
| 1992 | 1,266 | 886 | 256 | 720 | 303 | 916 | 4,347 |
| | | | (percentage of total pension assets) | | | | |
| 1983 | 34.0% | 18.1% | 5.5% | 15.8% | 7.0% | 19.5% | 100.0% |
| 1984 | 31.7 | 19.0 | 5.5 | 16.4 | 7.3 | 20.1 | 100.0 |
| 1985 | 31.7 | 18.9 | 6.2 | 16.7 | 7.2 | 19.4 | 100.0 |
| 1986 | 31.1 | 18.8 | 6.0 | 17.3 | 7.2 | 19.8 | 100.0 |
| 1987 | 29.4 | 18.7 | 5.8 | 18.2 | 7.5 | 20.5 | 100.0 |
| 1988 | 28.9 | 17.9 | 5.8 | 18.4 | 7.4 | 21.6 | 100.0 |
| 1989 | 29.0 | 17.9 | 5.6 | 17.7 | 7.1 | 22.7 | 100.0 |
| 1990 | 27.8 | 16.9 | 5.3 | 19.4 | 7.6 | 22.9 | 100.0 |
| 1991 | 29.1 | 18.1 | 5.3 | 16.9 | 7.3 | 23.2 | 100.0 |
| 1992 | 29.1 | 20.4 | 5.9 | 16.6 | 7.0 | 21.1 | 100.0 |

Source: Employee Benefit Research Institute, *Quarterly Pension Investment Report,* second quarter 1992 (Washington, DC: Employee Benefit Research Institute, 1992); Board of Governors of the Federal Reserve System, *Flow of Funds Accounts: Assets and Liabilities Outstanding First Quarter 1992* (Washington, DC: Board of Governors of the Federal Reserve System, June 1992). All 1992 numbers are preliminary estimates.

Table 5.5
**Civil Service Retirement and Disability Fund, September 30, 1991–September 30, 1992**

| | CSRS[a] | FERS[b] | 9/30/92 Total | 9/30/91 Total |
|---|---|---|---|---|
| | | ($ billions) | | |
| Actuarial Value of Future Benefits | $1,031 | $128 | $1,159 | $1,126 |
| Assets | 256 | 32 | 288 | 261 |
| Unfunded Termination Liability | 774 | 96 | 870 | 864 |
| Normal Cost as a Percentage of Payroll (Dynamic) | | | | |
| Employer Civil Service Retirement System | | | 28.29% | 28.29% |
| Employer Federal Employees Retirement System | | | 13.7% | 13.7% |
| Cost to Fund Plan as a Percentage of Pay (40-year amortization) | | | 65.6% | 68.1% |
| Actual Contributions as Percentage of Pay | | | 36.5% | 36.9% |
| Undercontribution as Percentage of Pay | | | 29.1% | 31.2% |
| Contributions | 30.1 | 5.7 | 35.8 | 34.0 |
| Investment Income | 22.0 | 2.3 | 24.3 | 22.7 |
| Benefit Payments | 32.8 | 0.3 | 33.1 | 33.1 |
| Participants (millions) | 1.8 | 1.3 | 3.1 | 3.2 |
| Annuitants (millions) | 2.2 | c | 2.2 | 2.2 |

Source: Employee Benefit Research Institute compilation from *An Annual Report to Comply with the Requirements of Public Law 95-595. Sept. 30,1992, RI 10-27, March 1993.*
[a]Civil Service Retirement System.
[b]Federal Employees Retirement System.
[c]$29,900.

For the federal civilian plans, the actual contributions being made as a percentage of pay are substantial at 36.5 percent (table 5.5), compared with a reported 3.9 percent for private employers. However, the federal government would need to contribute 65.6 percent of pay in order to amortize the unfunded liability over 40 years, or an added $35 billion. Funding for the value of one year's growth in promised benefits for present workers ("dynamic normal cost") requires a contribution equal to 21.3 percent of pay in the CSRS and 12.9 percent of pay in the FERS.

MRS presents a future financial challenge for taxpayers and policymakers as well. However, the MRS's unfunded liability decreased slightly between 1991 and 1992. MRS had an unfunded liability of $633.1 billion at the end of FY 1992, compared with $627.0 billion at the end of FY 1991 (table 5.6). This decrease of $0.1 billion, when combined with the federal civilian pension plans, resulted in a combined FY 1992 decrease in unfunded liabilities of $0.1 billion. The actual contributions to MRS were substantial— 66.9 percent of pay, compared to MRS normal cost of 39.7 percent of pay. Funding the plan over the next 40 years would require contributions of 126 percent of pay. For FY 1992 this would have meant an added contribution of $24 billion.

Direct federal expenditures for retirement income are substantial. Were taxpayers funding these promises as fast as private employers are required by ERISA to fund theirs, the annual outlay—and either taxes or borrowing—would have to increase by at least

$53 billion: nearly the reported tax expenditure for all public- and private-sector employer pension plans. This would have meant added direct taxes of $53 billion to fund contributions plus an added $14.6 billion in reported tax expenditures, using the Treasury methodology. Adjusting Munnell's numbers to reflect MRS and a minimum required contribution with 40-year amortization would have increased the total tax expenditure to $68.1 billion, with civil service and MRS accounting for $27.9 billion, or 41 percent, of the total. Combined with state and local plans, the public share would climb to $42.6 billion, or 62.5 percent of the total pension plan tax expenditure (if public plans were required to meet ERISA funding standards).

Many analysts write as if every dollar of tax expenditure increases the federal deficit. When one looks at the tax expenditure represented by civil service and military plans, one sees that it is more complicated. When a pension promise is made to a civilian or military employee, a liability is created that effectively increases the federal deficit because it represents a promise taxpayers must eventually pay. However, it creates no tax expenditure and is not reported as part of the deficit because of cash accounting. Only if a contribution is made to secure the benefit will a tax expenditure arise or the reported deficit be affected. The future taxpayer's obligation has in theory been reduced because a contribution has been made and the plan now has lower liabilities and more assets. Yet, in the case of the CSRS and other federal plans, most of the assets are Treasury securities that repre-

Table 5.6
**Military Retirement System Actuarial Status Information as of September 30, 1992 and September 30, 1991**

| | September 30, 1992 | September 30, 1991 |
|---|---|---|
| | ($ billions) | |
| Present Value of Future Benefits | $733.1 | $726.8 |
| Actuarial Value of Assets | $106.1 | $93.7 |
| Unfunded Termination Liability | $627.0 | $633.1 |
| Normal Cost as a Percentage of Pay | 39.7% | 40.6% |
| Cost to Fund Plan and Liabilities as Percentage of Pay (40-year amortization) | 126.0% | 129.0% |
| Actual Contributions as a Percentage of Pay | 66.9% | 66.2% |
| Underfunding as a Percentage of Pay[a] | 59.1% | 62.8% |
| Normal Cost Contribution | $16.3 | $17.2 |
| Investment Interest Income | $10.0 | $9.0 |
| Capital Gains | $6.7 | $8.6 |
| Unfunded Liability Amortization | $11.2 | $10.8 |
| Benefit Payments | $24.5 | $23.1 |
| Participants | 1.9 million | 2.1 million |
| Annuitants | 1.5 million | 1.5 million |

Source: Employee Benefit Research Institute compilation from *Chapter 95 of Title 31, U.S.C. Report on the Military Retirement System as of Sept. 30, 1992,* unpublished report.
[a]Underfunding is defined here as the difference between the contribution necessary to fund the plan in 40 years and the actual contribution made to the plan.

sent a liability of the federal taxpayer, which means the nation accounts for the liability explicitly.

Federal employees may have implicit benefit security because the promise is made by the federal government, which is expected to be here to pay its bills. However, the magnitude of the liabilities of the plans now in place, and the level of future payments required, justify concern.

For the taxpayer, there should be an annual discussion of the increase in the growth of the federal pension obligation along with discussion of the tax expenditure for pension plans.

### What Would Taxpayers Save by Ending Federal Pensions?

Because federal pensions are not being funded at the rate ERISA requires for private plans, the tax expenditure that would otherwise be attributable to them is quite low. Ironically, a higher contribution would produce both a higher direct federal expenditure and a higher reported tax expenditure. Were federal civilian employees provided only with Social Security, the 1991 employer payroll tax payment would have been less than $6 billion. This compares with the actual contribution to just the CSRS plan of $29 billion (21.29 percent of pay). If applied to the federal government, ERISA would have required a CSRS contribution in excess of $64 billion. This higher contribution would have increased the pension tax expenditure number in the budget by $8.5 billion, or more than 15 percent.

The military contribution for Social Security in 1991 would have been about $2.5 billion (6.2 percent of pay), compared with a normal cost pension contribution of $16.3 billion (42.7 percent of pay). An additional $11.1 billion was contributed to help pay off the plans' unfunded liability (26.3 percent of pay). To meet the ERISA funding requirement for private plans, the total contribution would have been more than 130 percent of pay and more than an additional $28 billion in contributions. Adding in this contribution by the military plan would have increased the pension tax expenditure in the budget by an additional $6.5 billion, or more than 11 percent.

The size of the foregone revenues would indeed be large, but would the taxpayer be better off making no contributions to public pension plans? Lower contributions would lower the reported tax expenditure, but it would in no way reduce what must eventually be paid in taxes to provide the promised pension benefits. Taxpayers must eventually pay for public employee pension promises. Focusing on the tax expenditure for pensions makes much less sense than focusing on whether pension promises should be made, and if they

are, how and when should they be paid for. For all pension participants it is better to know that there is already "money in the bank" than to depend on future goodwill.

## Who Benefits?

### Who Benefits from the Tax Incentives?

The benefits of the pension system can be viewed in many ways, and the same numbers can be presented as positive or negative indicators. An analysis of who benefits most from the system based on the earnings distribution of participants finds most of the coverage going to those earning between $10,000 and $50,000 per year. An analysis of the system based on rates of participation reinforces this finding.

The Joint Committee on Taxation publishes statistics on taxpayers and tax expenditures, including the distribution of returns and taxes paid (table 5.7). Using the EBRI TEAM, the pension tax expenditure was allocated across taxpayers in the same way (column G). (The government last published its own income distribution of the pension tax expenditure in 1983.) Table 5.7 also shows the proportion of all taxes paid by each income group represented by the pension tax expenditure. Columns I and L show by how much income taxes would increase if pension tax incentives were eliminated and individuals received cash income that could not be tax sheltered.

One percent of all tax returns report income above $200,0000; these taxpayers pay 26 percent of all individual income taxes (U.S. Congress, 1992b). Table 5.7 allocates the value of pension tax incentives by income class and shows that high income taxpayers obtain 6.7 percent of the value of total pension tax expenditures (column H). If this group of taxpayers were to lose pension tax incentives, they could experience a 3 percent tax increase (column I).

Seven percent of the value of tax expenditures is received by taxpayers with income between $20,000 and $29,999, who pay 6 percent of all individual income taxes. This group could experience a tax increase of 14 percent if pension tax incentives were removed.

Middle-income households gain the most from pension tax incentives. Taxable returns showing income between $30,000 and $50,000 (29 percent of taxable returns) paid 18 percent of taxes, received 28 percent of the pension tax incentive value, and could experience an 18 percent tax increase if the incentives were removed. Upper middle income households at $50,000 to $100,000 (24 percent of taxable returns) paid 33 percent of taxes, received 43 percent of the tax expenditure, and could experience a 15 percent tax

Table 5.7
**Distribution of Income by Class of All Returns, Taxable Returns, Tax Liability, and Pension Tax Expenditures at 1992 Rates, 1992 Law,[a] and 1992 Income Levels**
[Money amounts in millions of dollars, returns in thousands]

| | A | B | C | D | E | F | G | H | I | J | K | L |
|---|---|---|---|---|---|---|---|---|---|---|---|---|
| | All Returns | | Taxable Returns[b] | | Tax Liability | | Value of Pension Tax Exp. | | | Tax Accruals vs Distributions | | |
| Income Class[c] | No. | % | No. | % | $ | % | $ | % | % of taxes | $ | % | % of taxes |
| Less than $10,000 | 22,449 | 19.7% | 4,501 | 5.4% | -$ 1,780 | 0.0% | $ 335 | 0.0% | 0.0% | $ 457 | 0.0% | 0.0% |
| $10,000-$19,999 | 24,260 | 21.3 | 13,924 | 16.8 | 8,156 | 1.7 | 775 | 1.4 | 9.5 | 1,425 | 2.1 | 17.5 |
| $20,000-$29,999 | 19,039 | 16.7 | 16,694 | 20.1 | 28,980 | 6.1 | 4,000 | 7.1 | 13.8 | 6,092 | 9.1 | 21.0 |
| $30,000-$49,999 | 24,245 | 21.2 | 23,826 | 28.7 | 86,347 | 18.2 | 15,870 | 28.1 | 18.4 | 21,062 | 31.3 | 24.4 |
| $50,000-$99,999 | 19,583 | 17.2 | 19,472 | 23.5 | 157,965 | 33.2 | 24,210 | 42.8 | 15.3 | 27,145 | 40.4 | 17.2 |
| $100,000-$199,999 | 3,452 | 3.0 | 3,436 | 4.1 | 72,150 | 15.2 | 7,550 | 13.4 | 10.5 | 7,500 | 11.2 | 10.4 |
| $200,000 and over | 1,114 | 1.0 | 1,111 | 1.3 | 123,759 | 26.0 | 3,760 | 6.7 | 3.0 | 3,568 | 5.3 | 2.9 |
| Total | 114,142 | 100.0 | 82,959 | 100.0 | 475,577 | 100.0 | 56,500 | 100.0 | 11.9 | 67,249 | 100.0 | 14.1 |

Source: Employee Benefit Research Institute tabulations from the EBRI Tax Estimating and Analysis Model and other data from U.S. Congress, Joint Committee on Taxation, *Estimates of Federal Tax Expenditures for Fiscal Years 1993-1997* (Washington, DC: U.S. Government Printing Office, 1992).
[a]Tax law as in effect on January 1, 1992, is applied to the 1992 level and sources of income and their distribution among taxpayers. Excludes individuals who are dependents of other taxpayers.
[b]Includes filing and nonfiling units. Filing units include all taxable and nontaxable returns. Nonfiling units include individuals with income that is exempt from federal income taxation (e.g., transfer payments, interest from tax-exempt bonds, etc.).
[c]The income concept used to place tax returns into classes is adjusted gross income (AGI) plus: (1) tax-exempt interest, (2) employer contributions for health plans and life insurance, (3) inside buildup on life insurance (4) workers' compensation, (5) nontaxable Social Security benefits, (6) deductible contributions to individual retirement arrangements, (7) the minimum tax preferences, and (8) net losses, in excess of minimum tax preferences, from passive business activities.

increase with the end of pension incentives. These relationships hold for public and private sector pensions.

## What If We Used Accruals for Tax Expenditures?

Using pension contributions, earnings, and benefits to calculate tax expenditures produces a low number if low contributions are made. Because federal plans make low contributions relative to the benefit being earned, they are not "charged" with as much tax expenditure as they would be if they contributed at a faster rate. Using the benefit being earned—the benefit accrual—as the basis of calculation would lead to a different distribution of value. Table 5.7 shows that using accruals would have produced a tax expenditure of $67.2 billion (column J) rather than $56.5 billion (column G).

This approach shows that the actual value of pensions is distributed more heavily at the middle and lower end of the income spectrum than the present method of calculating tax expenditures implies.

Pension plans are distributing more benefits to lower- and middle-income individuals than tax expenditure numbers imply. Those between $30,000 and

$50,000 represent $15.9 billion of the cash flow tax expenditure, while earning $21 billion in accruals. Were all public and private pensions being fully advance funded, the numbers would be the same.

## Pensions Primarily Benefit Those with Income Below $50,000

According to EBRI tabulations of the March 1992 CPS, the number of civilian workers covered by pensions (working for an employer with a plan) grew to 66.6 million. Active participants (currently earning a benefit) grew to 52.0 million (table 5.8). EBRI tabulations of the May 1988 CPS show that the number of entitled participants (those with a vested and irrevocable right to a benefit) exceeded 32 million in May 1988. Entitled participants represented 68 percent of all participants in May 1988, compared with 52 percent in May 1979.

Pension coverage and participation rates increase with income. Because of the income distribution of the population, most of those earning pensions are at lower income levels. As shown in table 5.8, among those earning less than $25,000 per year, 33.9 million were covered and 21.7 million participated. While this represents relatively low coverage and

**Table 5.8**
**Pension Coverage and Participation of the Civilian Nonagricultural, Wage and Salary Work Force by Earnings, Firm Size, and Age, and the ERISA Work Force, 1991**

| | Work Force | | Pension Coverage | | | Pension Participation | | |
|---|---|---|---|---|---|---|---|---|
| | No. (millions) | % of work force | No. (millions) | % of covered | % of group | No. (millions) | % of participants | % of group |
| General Work Force[a] | 119.8 | 100.0% | 66.6 | 100.0% | 55.6% | 52.0 | 100.0% | 43.4% |
| Annual earnings | | | | | | | | |
| less than $10,000 | 36.1 | 30.2 | 10.4 | 15.7 | 28.9 | 3.6 | 7.0 | 10.1 |
| $10,000-$24,999 | 42.1 | 35.1 | 23.5 | 35.3 | 55.9 | 18.1 | 34.9 | 43.1 |
| $25,000-$49,999 | 32.4 | 27.1 | 25.3 | 38.0 | 78.1 | 23.3 | 44.8 | 71.8 |
| $50,000-$74,999 | 6.4 | 5.3 | 5.2 | 7.8 | 81.8 | 5.0 | 9.5 | 77.5 |
| $75,000-$99,999 | 2.7 | 2.2 | 2.0 | 3.1 | 76.1 | 1.9 | 3.7 | 71.5 |
| $100,000 or more | 0.1 | 0.1 | 0.1[b] | 0.1 | 75.8 | 0.1[c] | 0.1 | 64.8 |
| Firm size | | | | | | | | |
| fewer than 25 workers | 28.5 | 23.8 | 5.5 | 8.2 | 19.2 | 4.1 | 7.9 | 14.3 |
| 25-99 workers | 16.7 | 14.0 | 6.8 | 10.2 | 40.5 | 5.1 | 9.9 | 30.7 |
| 100-499 workers | 18.3 | 15.3 | 10.9 | 16.4 | 59.6 | 8.4 | 16.1 | 45.9 |
| 500-999 workers | 7.2 | 6.0 | 5.1 | 7.7 | 70.8 | 4.0 | 7.7 | 55.7 |
| 1,000 or more workers | 49.1 | 41.0 | 38.4 | 57.6 | 78.1 | 30.3 | 58.4 | 61.8 |
| Age | | | | | | | | |
| Under 25 years | 21.7 | 18.1 | 7.2 | 10.9 | 33.4 | 2.7 | 5.2 | 12.5 |
| 25-44 years | 63.6 | 53.1 | 37.6 | 56.5 | 59.2 | 30.3 | 58.2 | 47.6 |
| 45-64 years | 30.9 | 25.8 | 20.2 | 30.4 | 65.5 | 18.0 | 34.7 | 58.3 |
| 65 years and over | 3.6 | 3.0 | 1.5 | 2.3 | 42.3 | 0.9 | 1.8 | 26.6 |
| Work status | | | | | | | | |
| Full time[d] | 94.1 | 78.6 | 58.3 | 87.5 | 61.9 | 48.8 | 93.9 | 51.8 |
| Part time[e] | 25.7 | 21.4 | 8.3 | 12.5 | 32.4 | 3.2 | 6.1 | 12.3 |
| ERISA Work Force[f] | 70.9 | 100.0% | 47.2 | 100.0% | 66.6% | 41.5 | 100.0% | 58.5% |

Source: Employee Benefit Research Institute tabulations of the March 1992 Current Population Survey.
[a]Civilian, nonagricultural, wage and salary work force.
[b]Equals 84,000.
[c]Equals 71,728.
[d]Employees reporting that they usually worked 35 or more hours per week at this job.
[e]Employees reporting that they usually worked fewer than 35 hours per week at this job.
[f]Civilian, nonagricultural wage and salary workers aged 21 and older with at least one year of tenure who reported in March 1992 that they worked 1,000 or more hours in 1991. A proxy for tenure was created because the March Current Population Survey does not include that variable. An employee is assumed to have at least one year of tenure if he or she reported having only one employer in the previous year and had worked 50 or more weeks during that year.

participation rates of 43 percent and 28 percent of all such persons, these workers represented 51.0 percent of all covered persons and 41.9 percent of all participants. Among those earning between $25,000 and $49,999 per year, 25.3 million were covered and 23.3 million participated. They represented 38.0 percent of those covered and 44.8 percent of participants. Among those earning between $50,000 and $74,999 per year, 5.0 million participated, representing 9.5 percent of all participants (table 5.8).

The average coverage and participation rates are highest in the range of income from $25,000 to $74,999, at 80.0 percent and 75.0 percent. Among those earning between $75,000 and $99,999, 1.9 million participated, or 3.7 percent of all participants. Above $100,000, 71,728 individuals participated in pension

plans, or 0.1 percent of all participants (table 5.8).

Another major factor of variation in pension coverage and participation is age, with 12.5 percent of those under 25 participating, compared with 47.6 percent of those between age 25 and 44 and 58.3 percent between age 45 and 64. This low rate among the young holds down the rate for the total work force, even though the inevitability of aging means that millions will move into covered jobs and become participants (table 5.8).

In firms with fewer than 25 workers, 19.2 percent of workers (5.5 million) were covered, and 14.3 percent (4.1 million) participated in an employer-sponsored plan in 1991. By comparison, in firms with 1,000 or more workers, 78.1 percent (38.4 million) were covered and 61.8 percent (30.3 million) participated.

The small employer issue is very significant in assessing the prospects for the future of pension coverage. EBRI tabulations of the March 1992 CPS reveal that employers with fewer than 100 workers accounted for 37.8 percent of all workers in 1991 (table 5.8). Policymakers would like small employers to establish pension plans, but most did not when marginal tax rates were high, regulation limited, and competition less strenuous. For these employers, the cost of Social Security is also a significant expense. As a result, retirement policy should probably assume that there will never be significant voluntary pension growth among small employers.

Rising health costs assure that this will be even more true in the future, because employees and employers place a higher priority on health protection for today than on retirement savings for tomorrow (Snider, 1992). The Medicare payroll tax will continue to rise, and there is the prospect of mandatory expenditures for worker health care. This moves small employer pension sponsorship with employer contributions even further away as an achievable policy objective.

## *People Not Percentages*

Most analysts focus on the proportion of those at given income levels who participate in pension plans and declare that this indicates that pensions favor high-income persons. Looking again at table 5.8, among workers earning less than $10,000, 10.1 percent participated in pensions in 1991, or 3.6 million persons. This compares with a participation rate of 64.8 percent for those earning above $100,000, but this group includes only 71,728 people, according to EBRI tabulations. Eighty-nine percent of those covered by pensions and 86.7 percent of participants had earnings below $50,000 in 1991.

In addition, analysts have focused on retiree's share of income as represented by pension payments (U.S. Congress, 1992c). The foregoing analysis points out that Census surveys treat only annuity payments from pensions as pension income. As a result, lump-sum distributions paid prior to retirement are not "credited" to the pension system. For 1989, this resulted in a major difference in the number reported by the Social Security Administration as retiree pension income and the number reported by the Commerce Department in the National Income and Product Accounts as pension benefit payments (Salisbury, 1993).

As a result of current tax laws and methods of data collection, an assessment of the results of the pension system must focus primarily on the current work force, rather than the retiree population. This is

in fact an unfortunate result and may argue for both policy change and for much improved data collection.

## *Pension Plans and Benefit Payments*

Pension plans have had a history of significant increases in benefit payments. Pension plans paid more in benefits in 1990 ($234 billion) than Social Security retirement ($223 billion).

Employer pensions are an important source of retirement income and are growing. The data available understate pension plans' contribution to retirement income because they do not include lump-sum distributions made prior to and at retirement. In spite of this, the number of retirees with pension income continues to grow. Fifty-seven percent of married couples and 34 percent of unmarried persons aged 65 and over (representing 44 percent of all aged households) reported pension income in 1990 (Grad, 1992). According to the 1991 Advisory Council on Social Security, the percentage of elderly families receiving income from employer-sponsored pensions is expected to increase from the current 44 percent to 76 percent by the year 2018 (Reno, 1993). Among married couples currently aged 45 to 59, nearly 70 percent are earning a pension right, and others who are not now participating in pension plan report a pension right from a former employer (Goodfellow and Schieber, 1992).

In 1990, private pension benefits, estimated by the Department of Commerce at $141.2 billion, accounted for 31 percent of the $457.3 billion in total estimated retirement benefit payments (table 5.9).[6] By comparison, private pension benefits totaled $7.4 billion in 1970. Combined with benefits paid by the federal civilian and military retirement system and state and local government employee retirement systems, employer payments of $234.3 billion accounted for 51 percent of total benefits in 1990. Social Security benefits for retirees and their spouses and dependents totaled $223 billion and accounted for the other 49 percent of total benefits. Actual private benefits in 1989 were closer to $164 billion than the $133.6 billion reported for 1989 (table 5.9). This surge of benefit payments appears to be the result of lump-sum distributions paid by plans as part of early retirement programs, including growing use of such lump sums by defined benefit plans.

Pension payments to individuals have increased over the years as the pension system has matured. Table 5.10 shows the maturity of the pension

---

[6] Department of Commerce estimates of private pension benefit payments lag actual data by three years.

## Table 5.9
## Retirement Benefit Payments from Private and Public Sources, Selected Years 1970-1990

| Source of Benefit[a] | 1970 | 1975 | 1980 | 1985 | 1986 | 1987 | 1988 | 1989 | 1990 |
|---|---|---|---|---|---|---|---|---|---|
| | ($ billions) | | | | | | | | |
| Private Pensions | $7.4 | $15.9 | $36.4 | $97.7 | $120.2 | $120.8 | $124.1 | $133.6 | $141.2 |
| Federal Employee Retirement[b] | 6.2 | 14.5 | 28.0 | 41.1 | 42.2 | 44.9 | 48.1 | 50.6 | 53.9 |
| State and Local Employee Retirement | 4.0 | 8.2 | 15.1 | 25.5 | 28.4 | 31.2 | 34.1 | 36.6 | 39.2 |
| Subtotal | 17.6 | 38.6 | 79.5 | 164.3 | 190.8 | 196.9 | 206.3 | 220.8 | 234.3 |
| Social Security Old-Age and Survivors Insurance Benefit Payments[c] | $28.8 | $58.5 | $105.1 | $167.2 | $176.8 | $183.6 | $195.5 | $208.0 | $223.0 |
| Total | $46.4 | $97.1 | $184.6 | $331.5 | $367.6 | $380.5 | $401.8 | $428.8 | $457.3 |
| Total | 100.0% | 100.0% | 100.0% | 100.0% | 100.0% | 100.0% | 100.0% | 100.0% | 100.0% |
| | (percentage of total) | | | | | | | | |
| Private Pensions | 16.0 | 16.4 | 19.7 | 29.5 | 32.7 | 31.8 | 30.9 | 31.2 | 30.9 |
| Federal Employee Retirement[b] | 13.4 | 14.9 | 15.2 | 12.4 | 11.5 | 11.8 | 12.0 | 11.8 | 11.8 |
| State and Local Employee Retirement | 8.6 | 8.4 | 8.2 | 7.7 | 7.7 | 8.2 | 8.5 | 8.5 | 8.6 |
| Subtotal | 37.9 | 39.8 | 43.1 | 49.6 | 51.9 | 51.8 | 51.3 | 51.5 | 51.2 |
| Social Security Old-Age and Survivors Insurance Benefit Payments[c] | 62.1 | 60.3 | 56.9 | 50.4 | 48.1 | 48.3 | 48.7 | 48.5 | 48.8 |

Source: Employee Benefit Research Institute tabulations based on U.S. Department of Commerce, Bureau of Economic Analysis, *Survey of Current Business, January 1992* (Washington, DC: U.S. Government Printing Office, 1992); *The National Income and Products Accounts of the United States: Statistical Supplement, 1959-1988*, Vol. 2 (Washington, DC: U.S. Government Printing Office, 1992); and U.S. Department of Health and Human Services, Social Security Administration, *1991 Annual Report of the Board of Trustees of the Federal Old-Age and Survivors Insurance and Disability Insurance Trust Funds* (Baltimore, MD: Social Security Administration, 1991).
[a]Includes only employment-based retirement benefits.
[b]Includes civilian and military employees.
[c]Includes payments to retired workers and their wives, husbands, and children.

system, with 44 percent of retirees reporting pension income in 1990, compared with 31 percent in 1976.

These numbers represent annuity payments only, so that the billions of dollars now paid each year in lump-sum distributions and taken into income would result in earnings reported as asset income. As the pension system continues to change, it will become increasingly important to find a way to identify this pension-created wealth. The growth in the numbers in table 5.10, it should be stressed, would be significantly greater if all income attributable to past pension distributions could be documented.

## Pensions and Savings

Pension plans that are advance funded serve to expand total savings (VanDerhei, 1992). The magnitude has been debated, and studies show wide variation, from a low of $0.32 per $1.00 of pension savings to a high of $0.84. At either level, this translates into billions of dollars each year, with total pension assets exceeding

$4 trillion in 1991. As previously noted, federal pension plans have combined unfunded liabilities of more than $1.6 trillion. If federal plan participants have saved less because of the pension income promise, then federal plans may have served to decrease personal savings, as private and state and local plans have served to increase personal savings with substantial advance funding.

Another way to assess the degree to which a pension plan assists individuals with total savings is whether or not they report income other than earnings that would suggest other than pension savings. EBRI tabulations show that the lowest earners are likely to have only earned income. In 1991, 14.1 million persons with no interest income participated in their employer's pension plan, and 38.7 million persons with no dividend income participated (table 5.11). While these percentage participation levels and rates are lower than would be desirable, the number of people is significant. These individuals will likely be better off economically than the 36 million reporting no interest income and no

Table 5.10
**Percentage of Single Individuals and Married Couples[a] Aged 65 and Over with Income from Specified Sources, Selected Years 1976-1990**

| Source of Income[b] | 1976 | 1978 | 1980 | 1982 | 1984 | 1986 | 1988 | 1990 |
|---|---|---|---|---|---|---|---|---|
| | | | | (millions) | | | | |
| Number | 17.3 | 18.2 | 19.2 | 19.9 | 20.8 | 21.6 | 22.3 | 23.1 |
| Percentage with | | | | | | | | |
| Retirement benefits | 92% | 93% | 93% | 93% | 94% | 94% | 95% | 95% |
| Social Security[c] | 89 | 90 | 90 | 90 | 91 | 91 | 92 | 92 |
| Retirement benefits other | | | | | | | | |
| than Social Security | 31 | 32 | 34 | 35 | 38 | 40 | 42 | 44 |
| railroad retirement | 3 | 3 | 2 | 2 | 2 | 2 | 2 | 2 |
| government employee pensions | 9 | 10 | 12 | 12 | 14 | 14 | 14 | 15 |
| private pension or annuities | 20 | 21 | 22 | 23 | 24 | 27 | 29 | 30 |
| Earnings | 25 | 25 | 23 | 22 | 21 | 20 | 22 | 22 |
| Income from assets | 56 | 62 | 66 | 68 | 68 | 67 | 68 | 69 |
| Veterans' benefits | 6 | 5 | 5 | 4 | 5 | 5 | 5 | 5 |
| Public assistance | 11 | 10 | 10 | 16 | 16 | 7 | 7 | 7 |

Source: Susan Grad and Karen Foster, *Income of the Population 55 and Over, 1976*, U.S. Department of Health, Education, and Welfare, pub. no. 13-11865 (Washington, DC: U.S. Government Printing Office, 1979); Susan Grad, *Income of the Population 55 and Over*, 1978, 1980, 1982, and 1984, U.S. Department of Health and Human Services, Social Security Administration, pub. no. 13-11871 (Washington, DC: U.S. Government Printing Office, 1981-1985); and Susan Grad, *Income of the Population 55 or Older, 1986*, U.S. Department of Health and Human Services, Social Security Administration, pub. no. 13-11871 (Washington, DC: U.S. Government Printing Office, 1988); Susan Grad, *Income of the Population 55 or Older, 1988*, U.S. Department of Health and Human Services, Social Security Administration, pub. no. 13-11871 (Washington, DC: U.S. Government Printing Office, 1990); and Susan Grad, *Income of the Population 55 or Older, 1990*, U.S. Department of Health and Human Services, Social Security Administration, pub. no. 13-11871 (Washington, DC: U.S. Government Printing Office, 1992).
[a]Couples are included if they are married, living together, and at least one is aged 65 or over.
[b]Receipt of sources is ascertained by a yes/no response to a question that is imputed by the Current Population Survey for 1976-1986. A married couple is counted as receiving a source if one or both persons are recipients of that source. Data for 1988 and 1990 are from the Survey of Income and Program Participation.
[c]Recipients of Social Security may be receiving retired-worker benefits, dependents' or survivors' benefits, transitionally insured, or special age 72 benefits. Transitionally insured benefits are monthly benefits paid to certain persons born before January 2, 1987. The special age 72 benefit is a monthly benefit payable to men who reached age 72 before 1972 and to women who reached age 72 before 1970 and who do not have sufficient quarters of coverage to qualify for a retired worker benefit either under the fully or transitionally insured states provisions.

pension participation, or the 61.1 million reporting no dividend income and no pension participation. Whether advance funded or not, for millions of individuals with an accrued pension benefit but no interest or dividend income, the pension may well be the only income producing savings they have as they approach retirement.

## The Need for More Complete Presentations

Some analysts and policymakers have suggested raising revenue by imposing taxes on pension funds. Often, however, they have not considered the potential effects that changing the tax treatment could have on the availability and extent of pension benefits, the financial markets, and the U.S. economy.

A recent Congressional Research Service (CRS) analysis includes the following paragraph: "To tax defined benefit plans can be very difficult since it is not always easy to allocate pension accruals to specific employees. It might be particularly difficult to allocate accruals to individuals not vested. This complexity would not, however, preclude taxation of trust earnings at a specified rate." (U.S. Congress, 1992c)

No further analysis or discussion is provided in the CRS analysis. Policymakers would also need to consider (1) the implications for the federal budget and state and local budgets (and benefit security) of requiring the payment of a portion of accumulated assets as an excise tax by public pension plans; (2) the implications for PBGC of decreasing the assets in private defined benefit plans by taxing them away (they might suggest an increase in the PBGC premium payment instead) at a time when the agency says that it has insufficient income and the plans it insures have insufficient assets; and (3) the implications for plan terminations and ultimate retirement income if defined benefit assets are taxed but the assets of defined contribution plans are not.

When making changes in the pension system,

Table 5.11
**Pension Coverage and Pension Participation of the Civilian, Nonagricultural Wage and Salary Work Force, by Earnings and Interest and Dividend Income, 1991**

| | Total | Pension Coverage | | Pension Participation | |
|---|---|---|---|---|---|
| | (millions) | (millions) | (percentage) | (millions) | (percentage) |
| Total | 119.8 | 66.6 | 55.6% | 52.0 | 43.4 |
| Less than $10,000 | 36.1 | 10.4 | 28.9 | 3.6 | 10.1 |
| $10,000-$24,999 | 42.1 | 23.5 | 55.9 | 18.1 | 43.1 |
| $25,000-$49,999 | 32.4 | 25.3 | 78.1 | 23.3 | 71.8 |
| $50,000-$74,999 | 6.4 | 5.2 | 81.8 | 5.0 | 77.5 |
| $75,000-$99,999 | 2.7 | 2.0 | 76.1 | 1.9 | 71.5 |
| $100,000 or more | 0.1 | 0.1 | 75.8 | 0.1 | 64.8 |
| Without Interest Income | 50.1 | 20.8 | 41.5 | 14.1 | 28.1 |
| Less than $10,000 | 21.5 | 5.3 | 24.4 | 1.7 | 8.0 |
| $10,000-$24,999 | 19.7 | 9.4 | 47.6 | 6.9 | 34.9 |
| $25,000-$49,999 | 7.9 | 5.5 | 69.8 | 4.9 | 62.3 |
| $50,000-$74,999 | 0.7 | 0.5 | 69.6 | 0.5 | 62.3 |
| $75,000-$99,999 | 0.2 | 0.1 | 53.1 | 0.1 | 45.8 |
| $100,000 or more | 0.1 | a | 100.0 | a | 100.0 |
| Without Dividend Income | 99.8 | 51.6 | 51.8 | 38.7 | 38.8 |
| Less than $10,000 | 33.4 | 9.3 | 27.7 | 3.2 | 9.5 |
| $10,000-$24,999 | 37.6 | 20.4 | 54.3 | 15.5 | 41.2 |
| $25,000-$49,999 | 24.3 | 18.6 | 76.2 | 16.9 | 69.5 |
| $50,000-$74,999 | 3.4 | 2.6 | 78.5 | 2.5 | 73.1 |
| $75,000-$99,999 | 1.1 | 0.8 | 69.8 | 0.7 | 65.7 |
| $100,000 or more | a | a | 74.9 | a | 49.9 |

Source: Employee Benefit Research Institute tabulations of the March 1992 Current Population Survey.
aLess than 50,000.

these interrelationships should be considered before policy actions are taken. And, the primary objective of pensions—economic security—should not be overlooked.

## Conclusion

A 1991 *National Tax Journal* article concluded with the following: "Whereas the case for employer-sponsored pensions as an institution is strong, the case for a major tax expenditure is weak . . . given the demands on the budget, eliminating a tax expenditure that benefits a declining and privileged proportion of the population should be given serious consideration."[7]

This paper has shown that the proportion of workers with entitlement to a pension has been growing—from 24 percent in 1979 to 28 percent in 1988— and the number increasing—from 23 million workers to 32 million—during the same period—while the proportion of workers with coverage and participation has flattened (Piacentini, 1989). Entitlement is growing

because of the earlier participation and shorter vesting periods required by ERISA and TRA '86. A mobile and aging work force promises continued improvement in benefit entitlement, the true test of a pension system.

This paper has shown that the primary value of pensions accrues to middle- and lower-income taxpayers (tables 5.7 and 5.8). Elimination of the tax expenditure by taxing individuals would place the greatest burden on these individuals.

Some analysts have suggested recovering the tax expenditure by levying a 2.5 percent tax on pension reserves. Applied to private defined benefit pension plans insured by PBGC, a 2.5 percent levy would amount to $35 billion rather than the $8.2 billion tax expenditure attributed to private plans. Taxation of insured assets held by insurance companies for annuities purchased by pension plans would raise an additional amount of more than $15 billion, but it would also assure losses for the insurers because the tax would not have been anticipated when the annuities were priced. The tax in PBGC-insured plans could increase PBGC's problems. It might be better to increase the premiums these plans pay to PBGC than to tax away reserves. However, a number of analysts

---

[7] See Alicia H. Munnell, "Are Pensions Worth the Cost?" *National Tax Journal* (September 1991): 393-403.

and some members of Congress have argued that an increase in premiums might cause employers to terminate plans. A tax that is bigger than PBGC premiums could be expected to do the same, eliminating plans paying premiums to PBGC in the process. It is interesting to note that total premiums paid to PBGC are less than $1 billion per year, compared with the $35 billion trust tax that advocates suggest be taxed away from PBGC-insured plans.

Recovery of the $19.3 billion tax expenditure associated with private defined contribution plans could be achieved by a 2.5 percent levy on reserves. Given the individual account nature of the plans and the level of interest rates relative to inflation today, this tax could cause many individual accounts to have no real investment return or a negative return. The annual loss of account balance could significantly reduce the ultimate account balance and discourage saving in the first place. And, for any participant making an early withdrawal and paying the 10 percent excise tax, the loss would be even more significant. In hindsight, investment of after tax-dollars in tax-exempt municipal bonds would look like what the individual should have done.

Recovery of the $28 billion tax expenditure associated with public employee defined benefit pension plans through an excise tax would be constitutional but would require increased future contributions by taxpayers to the plans to compensate for the loss of investment earnings on the money taxed away.

For the federal government the levy would simply increase what it ultimately had to contribute to the plans to pay benefits. A solution that sounds simple and is labeled "feasible" by some analysts may not prove to be so.

Legislative actions of the 1980s that reduced the amounts that could be contributed to public and private pension plans have reduced the tax expenditure for pensions. They have also served to increase the level of pension promises that are unfunded and, thus, not fully secured. This paper has used the funding of federal pension plans to show that the pension tax expenditure number currently is, and in the future will be, influenced by contributions made to the federal civil service and military pension plans. The federal plans underline the potentially misleading nature of the tax expenditure number. The federal worker is being promised a future benefit, to be paid for by taxpayers, whether or not advance contributions are made. If an advance contribution is made, a tax expenditure is recorded, which is said to increase the deficit. Yet, the real deficit, the obligation that something must be paid by future taxpayers, was increased with the promise. At minimum, this argues for presentation of pension tax expenditures in government documents by sector

and, ideally by plan type. Ideally, we would also begin to see more focus on the financial status of the public pension plans.

This paper has also sought to clarify that the debate over whether or not funded pensions add to national and individual savings is a debate over magnitude. For millions of low-income Americans the value of the pension they are entitled to may represent the only income producing savings they have.

The paper has also sought to underline the need for much better data on pension distributions and what individuals do with them. As more private defined benefit and most public and private defined contribution plans pay benefits as a single lump-sum distribution when the employee leaves, issues of "erosion in the value of vested pension credits after job termination" and "the erosion of benefits after retirement" become less important than issues of preservation of distributions and retirement planning.

The goal of economic security in retirement is shared by all. Pensions play a role in achieving that goal.

## Bibliography

Altman, Nancy. "Rethinking Retirement Income Policies: Nondiscrimination, Integration, and the Quest for Worker Security." Reprint. *Tax Law Review* (Spring 1987): 433-508.

Altman, Nancy J., and Theodore R. Marmot. "ERISA and the American Retirement Income System." *The American Journal of Tax Policy* (Spring 1988): 31-46.

_____. "The Reconciliation of Retirement Security and Tax Policies: A Response to Professor Graetz." *University of Pennsylvania Law Review* (May 1988): 1419-1445.

Andrews, Emily S. *The Changing Profile of Pensions in America.* Washington, DC: Employee Benefit Research Institute, 1985.

Bodie, Zvi, and Alicia H. Munnell, eds. *Pensions and the Economy: Sources, Uses, and Limitations of Data.* Philadelphia, PA: Pension Research Council, Wharton School of the University of Pennsylvania and University of Pennsylvania Press, 1992.

Employee Benefit Research Institute. "Changing the Tax Treatment of Health Benefit Programs." *EBRI Issue Brief* no. 5 (Employee Benefit Research Institute, 1982).

_____. "Federal Pensions: An Island of Privilege in a Sea of Budget Austerity." *EBRI Issue Brief* no. 10 (Employee Benefit Research Institute, July 1982).

_____. *Fundamentals of Employee Benefit Programs.*

Fourth edition. Washington, DC: Employee Benefit Research Institute, 1990.

_____. "Individual Saving for Retirement—The 401(k) and IRA Experiences." *EBRI Issue Brief* no. 95 (Employee Benefit Research Institute, October 1989).

_____. "Pension Fund Taxation: Examining the Issues." *EBRI Issue Brief* no.105 (Employee Benefit Research Institute, August 1990).

_____. "Pension-Related Tax Benefits." *EBRI Issue Brief* no. 25 (Employee Benefit Research Institute, December 1983).

_____. "Retirement Program Tax Expenditures." *EBRI Issue Brief* no.17 (Employee Benefit Research Institute, April 1983).

_____. *What Is the Future for Defined Benefit Pension Plans?: An EBRI Roundtable.* Washington DC: Employee Benefit Research Institute, 1989.

Feldstein, Martin. *The Effects of Tax-Based Saving Incentives on Government Revenue and National Saving.* Working Paper No. 4021. Cambridge, MA: National Bureau of Economic Research, Inc., 1992.

Goodfellow, Gordon P., and Sylvester J. Schieber. "Death and Taxes: Can We Fund for Retirement Between Them ?" Paper. Washington, DC: The Wyatt Company, forthcoming.

_____. "The Role of Tax Expenditures in the Provision of Retirement Income Security." In Richard V. Burkhauser and Dallas Salisbury, eds., *Pensions in a Changing Economy.* Washington, DC: Employee Benefit Research Institute and the National Academy on Aging, 1993.

Graetz, Michael J. "The Troubled Marriage of Retirement Security and Tax Policies." *University of Pennsylvania Law Review* (April 1987): 851-907.

_____. "Retirement Security and Tax Policy: A Reply" *University of Pennsylvania Law Review* (April 1989): 1239-1245.

Grad, Susan. *Income of the Population 55 and Older 1990.* U.S. Department of Health and Human Services, Social Security Administration, pub. no. 13-11871. Washington DC: U.S. Government Printing Office, 1992.

Hustead, Edwin C., Toni Hustead, and Robert H. Selles. *OBRA 1987: The Impact of Limiting Contributions to Defined Benefit Plans.* Prepared by Hay/Huggins, Inc. for the Department of Labor. Washington, DC: U.S. Department of Labor, 1989.

Hurd, Michael D. "Research on the Elderly: Economic Status, Retirement and Consumption and Saving." *Journal of Economic Literature* (June 1990): 565-637.

Korczyk, Sophie M. *Retirement Security and Tax Policy.* Washington DC: Employee Benefit Research Institute, 1984.

Kosterlitz, Julie. "Promises to Keep." *National Journal* (August 29, 1987): 2138-2144.

Lazear, Edward P. "Some Thoughts on Saving." Conference Paper. Cambridge, MA: National Bureau of Economic Research, 1992.

Metz, Joseph G. *The Federal Taxation of Public Employee Retirement Systems: A Handbook for Public Officials.* Washington, DC: Government Finance Research Center of the Government Finance Officers Association, 1988.

Munnell, Alicia H. "Are Pensions Worth the Cost?" *National Tax Journal* (September 1991): 393-403.

_____. "Current Taxation of Qualified Pension Plans: Has the Time Come?" Prepared for the American Law Institute-American Bar Association Pension Policy Invitational Conference, October 25-26, 1991, Washington, DC.

_____. "It's Time to Tax Employee Benefits." *New England Economic Review* (July/August 1989): 49-63.

Pension Benefit Guaranty Corporation. *Annual Report 1991.* Washington, DC: Pension Benefit Guaranty Corporation, 1991.

Piacentini, Joseph S. "Pension Coverage and Benefit Entitlement: New Findings from 1988." *EBRI Issue Brief* no. 94 (Employee Benefit Research Institute, September 1989).

Piacentini, Joseph S., and Jill D. Foley. *EBRI Databook on Employee Benefits.* Washington DC: Employee Benefit Research Institute, 1992.

Poterba, James M., Steven F. Venti, and David A. Wise. "401(k) Plans and Tax-Deferred Saving." National Bureau of Economic Research conference paper, May 1992.

Reno, Virginia P. "The Role of Pensions in Retirement Income: Trends and Questions." In Richard V. Burkhauser and Dallas L. Salisbury, eds., *Pensions in a Changing Economy.* Washington, DC: Employee Benefit Research Institute and the National Academy on Aging, 1993.

Salisbury, Dallas L. *Economic Survival in Retirement: Which Pension Is for You?* Washington DC: Employee Benefit Research Institute, 1982.

_____. "Policy Implications of Changes in Employer Pension Protection." In Richard V. Burkhauser and Dallas L. Salisbury, eds., *Pensions in a Changing Economy.* Washington, DC: Employee Benefit Research Institute and the National Academy on Aging, 1993.

_____. *Why Tax Employee Benefits?* Washington DC: Employee Benefit Research Institute, 1984.

Salisbury, Dallas L., Ed. *Retirement Income and the Economy: Policy Directions for the 80s.* Proceedings. Employee Benefit Research Institute-Education and Research Fund policy forum, May 6, 1981, Washington DC.

Snider, Sarah. "Public Opinion on Health, Retirement, and Other Employee Benefits. *EBRI Issue Brief* no. 132 (Employee Benefit Research Institute, December 1992).

U.S. Congress. Congressional Budget Office. *Tax Policy for Pensions and Other Retirement Saving.* Washington DC: U.S. Government Printing Office, 1987.

_____. House. Committee on Ways and Means. *Overview of Entitlement Programs.* Washington, DC: U.S. Government Printing Office, 1992a.

_____. Joint Committee on Taxation. *Estimates of Federal Tax Expenditures for Fiscal Years 1993-1997.* Washington DC: U.S. Government Printing Office, 1992b.

_____. *Simplification of Present-Law Rules Relating to Qualified Pension Plans.* Joint Committee Print. Washington, DC: U.S. Government Printing Office, 1990

_____. Senate. Committee on the Budget. *Tax Expenditures.* Prepared by Congressional Research Service. Washington, DC: U.S. Government Printing Office, 1992c.

U.S. Department of Defense. *Military Retirement System as of September 30, 1990.* Unpublished report. Washington DC: Department of Defense, 1990.

_____. *Military Retirement System as of September 30, 1991.* Unpublished report. Washington DC: Department of Defense, 1991.

Texas Association of Public Employee Retirement Systems. *Federal Taxation of Retirement Savings and Trusts.* Houston, TX: Texas Association of Public Employee Retirement Systems, 1992.

U.S. Department of Health and Human Services. Social Security Administration. Office of Research and Statistics. "Pension Coverage Among Private Wage and Salary Workers: Preliminary Findings from 1988 Survey of Employee Benefits." *Social Security Bulletin* (October 1989).

U.S. Department of Labor. Pension and Welfare Benefits Administration. John A. Turner and Daniel J. Beller, eds., *Trends in Pensions*, second edition. Washington, DC: U.S. Department of Labor, 1992.

U.S. Department of the Treasury. Office of the Secretary. *Report to the President: Tax Reform for Fairness, Simplicity, and Economic Growth.* Washington, DC: U.S. Government Printing Office, 1984.

U.S. Federal Retirement Thrift Investment Board. Office of Benefits and Program Analysis. "Thrift Savings Fund Financial Statement, December 1991."

U.S. General Accounting Office. *Tax Policy: Effects of Changing the Tax Treatment of Fringe Benefits.* Washington, DC: U.S General Accounting Office, 1992.

U.S. Office of Personnel Management. Retirement and Insurance Group. *Civil Service Retirement and Disability Fund.* Washington, DC: Office of Personnel Management, 1991.

U.S. President. *The President's Tax Proposals to the Congress for Fairness, Growth and Simplicity.* Washington, DC: U.S. Government Printing Office, 1985.

_____. Office of Managment and Budget. *Budget of the United States: Fiscal Year 1993.* Washington, DC: U.S. Government Printing Office, 1992.

VanDerhei, Jack. "Pensions, Social Security, and Savings. *EBRI Issue Brief* no. 129 (Employee Benefit Research Institute, September 1992).

Woyke, John F. "Taxing Pension Funds—Is the U.S. Next?" *Employee Relations Law Journal* (Winter 1992-1993): 517-524.

Yakoboski, Paul, Celia Silverman, and Jack VanDerhei. "PBGC Solvency: Balancing Social and Casualty Insurance Perspectives." *Issue Brief* no. 126 (Employee Benefit Research Institute, May 1992).

# VI. Fat Cats, Bureaucrats, and Common Workers: Distributing the Pension Tax Preference Pie

BY SYLVESTER SCHIEBER AND GORDON GOODFELLOW[1]

## Introduction

Critics of the current preferences favoring retirement savings programs in the U.S. federal income tax system argue that these preferences are not meeting their goal. For example, Alicia Munnell has argued in several places that: "The goal of federal tax policy since 1942 has been to encourage, through favorable tax provisions, the use of tax-qualified pension and profit-sharing plans to ensure greater retirement security for all employees, not just highly paid executives."[2,3,4] She then proceeds through an analysis of cross-sectional data to prove that pensions do not cover all employees and that all retirees are not getting pension benefits and reaches her oft-stated conclusion that: "Broad provision of private retirement income across income classes has not been achieved, given the pattern of pension coverage and distribution of benefits."[5] Jane Gravelle, in testimony before the Senate Budget Committee regarding tax preferences aimed at income security programs, stated that: "About 80 percent of the tax expenditures in this category in the tax expenditure budget are associated with pension plans which disproportionately benefit higher income individuals who are more likely to be covered by pension plans, are recipients of larger benefits, and whose tax rates are higher."[6]

These sweeping conclusions by Munnell and Gravelle and others have totally ignored the true goals of the tax preferences encouraging employers to establish retirement programs, the documented characteristics of the programs covering workers today, and the actual distribution of tax and retirement benefits accruing under them.

## Goals of Retirement-Oriented Tax Incentives

Although pension coverage for everyone may be a desirable goal, it is patently absurd to assert that federal tax incentives must improve the retirement income security of "all employees" to be successful. If Congress intended that employers' tax-deductible contributions to pensions should apply to all employees, it would legislate a mandatory employer-based pension program covering all workers. For all practical purposes, Congress has legislated such a program, which we all know as Social Security. Indeed, the analysis by the Committee on Economic Security in 1935 based the development of Social Security on the lack of universality of employer-sponsored pension programs.[7] At the time the Social Security Act was passed in 1935, policymakers realized that companies "may wish to supplement the stipulated benefits" provided by Social Security.[8]

While Congress has chosen not to mandate pension programs, it has recognized the desirability of employer-sponsored pensions. Professor Dan McGill has written that from the earliest days of the income tax system in the United States, reasonable employer pension payments to retirees or contributions to trust funds were tax-deductible expenses. The 1921 Revenue Act eliminated current taxation of income for stock bonus and profit-sharing plans established by employers to benefit some or all of their workers. Initially, these provisions were extended to pension trusts by administrative ruling, and they were established in law in the 1926 Revenue Act. The 1928 Revenue Act allowed employers to make reasonable tax-deductible

---

[1] The authors comments and opinions expressed in this paper are solely their own and do not necessarily represent the opinions of The Wyatt Company or any of its other associates.

[2] Alicia H. Munnell, "Are Pensions Worth the Cost?" *National Tax Journal* (September 1991): 397.

[3] Alicia H. Munnell, "Current Taxation of Qualified Pension Plans: Has the Time Come?" Prepared for the American Law Institute-American Bar Association, Pension Policy Invitational Conference, Washington, DC, October 25–26, 1991.

[4] Alicia H. Munnell, "Current Taxation of Qualified Pension Plans: Has the Time Come?" *New England Economic Review* (March–April 1992): 16.

[5] Alicia Munnell, "Current Taxation of Qualified Pension Plans: Has the Time Come?" Prepared for the American Law Institute-American Bar Association, Pension Policy Invitational Conference, Washington, DC, October 25–26, 1991; "Current Taxation of Qualified Pension Plans: Has the Time Come?" *New England Economic Review* (March–April 1992): 16.

[6] Jane G. Gravelle, Statement before the Committee on the Budget, U. S. Senate, February 3, 1993.

[7] Committee on Economic Security, *Social Security in America* (Washington, DC: Social Security Board, 1937): 167–178.

[8] Ibid., p. 178.

contributions to their pension plans to fund previously unfunded accrued liabilities. The 1938 Revenue Act modified the revocability of pension trusts and required that a retirement trust be for the exclusive benefit of the employees covered until all liabilities are met under a plan. The 1942 Revenue Act and amendments to it in the 1954 Internal Revenue Code (IRC) modified the standards for tax qualification of plans and precluded plan sponsors from discriminating in favor of a sponsor's owners and officers. In 1974, the Employee Retirement Income Security Act (ERISA) established requirements that employers actually fund benefit promises as they accrue, set standards to assure that broad groups of workers covered by pensions would be offered the opportunity to participate in them and ultimately receive benefits, and limited the extent to which high-paid workers could benefit from the tax incentives accorded to pensions.[9]

During the 1980s, ERISA and the tax provisions favoring employer-sponsored retirement programs were modified on several occasions. The Tax Equity and Fiscal Responsibility Act reduced the limits that had been established under ERISA on the benefits that could be provided on a tax-favored basis and required that minimum benefits be paid to low-wage workers covered by plans. The Deficit Reduction Act further restricted the limits on allowable benefits. The Retirement Equity Act established more rigorous standards for plan participation and vesting than those included in ERISA originally. The Tax Reform Act again reduced the limits on allowable benefits and expanded discrimination standards that employer-sponsored plans are required to meet. The Omnibus Budget Reconciliation Act of 1987 amended the prior provisions on funding of benefits as they accrue and pushing the funding of benefits for many workers until later in their careers. Virtually every one of these pieces of legislation was followed by additional legislation to clean up technical problems introduced in the increasingly complicated body of law affecting employer-sponsored retirement plans.

Nowhere in any of the legislation dating back to the earliest regulation of pension and profit-sharing programs is there a stipulation that the tax incentives accorded these plans be distributed to "all employees"

in the national economy. While individual policy analysts may stipulate criteria that evaluate the distribution of retirement program tax incentives against a measure of universal participation, these criteria are inconsistent with a body of tax law and regulation that dates back 80 years. The success of other government programs and incentives is not judged on the basis of universal participation.

The problem of less than universal participation in federal programs where participation is not mandated is that even under the best of circumstances, not everyone eligible takes advantage of the benefits offered by most federal programs. For example, only about 65 percent of the individuals eligible for cash assistance from the Supplemental Security Income (SSI) program run by the Social Security Administration take it.[10] Likewise, only 66 percent of the individuals eligible for food stamps actually receive them.[11] Among all farm operations, only 36 percent benefit from the distribution of direct government payments to farm operators.[12] Among undergraduates who are dependents of parents with family incomes below $10,000, 34 percent receive no direct federal aid, although 21 percent of those in families with incomes between $40,000 and $50,000 receive such aid, and 9 percent with incomes between $70,000 and $80,000 do.[13] As long as we depend on individuals choosing to take advantage of the opportunities presented to them, we will have incomplete success in attaining universal utilization in any program, be it an incentive or direct benefit. While less than universal participation in every public endeavor to provide benefits to members of society raises questions about horizontal equity, it is inappropriate to scrap them all simply because some of those eligible to benefit from them fail to participate.

Pure equity concerns were not the motivation for pension reforms in the 1980s as evidenced by lawmakers' protection of their own self-interests relative to restrictions they have imposed on other citizens. In the passage of ERISA, Congress had established maximum funding standards, limiting the amount of benefits that could be funded for highly compensated workers. In the initial consideration of the provisions of ERISA, Congress considered exempting government workers from these limits, but it struck the

---

[9] Dan M. McGill, *Fundamentals of Private Pensions*, Fourth edition (Homewood, IL: Richard D. Irwin, Inc., 1979).

[10] John F. Sheils, et. al., *Elderly Persons Eligible for and Participating in the Supplemental Security Income Program*. Report prepared for the U.S. Department of Health and Human Services by Lewin-ICF (Washington, DC: U.S. Government Printing Office, 1990).

[11] Pat Doyle and Harold Beebout, *Food Stamp Program Participation Rate*. Report prepared for the U.S. Department of Agriculture, Food

and Nutrition Service (Washington, DC: Mathematica Policy Research, 1988).

[12] James Duncan Shaffer and Gerald W. Whittaker, "Average Farm Incomes: They're Highest Among Farmers Receiving the Largest Direct Government Payments," *Choices* (Second Quarter 1990): 31.

[13] National Center for Education Statistics, *National Postsecondary Student Aid Study: Estimates of Student Financial Aid, 1989–1990* (Washington D C: U.S. Department of Education, 1991).

— Pension Funding and Taxation

exemption from the final legislation.[14] In passing the Tax Reform Act of 1986 (TRA '86), Congress lowered the maximum level of benefits private plans could fund for early retirees but exempted themselves and other government and nonprofit workers from the new lower limits. In a similar vein, Congress exempted the federal government from having to meet the actual deferral percentage (ADP) tests in its own 401(k) type savings plan that it requires of all private employers. If lawmakers were truly interested in equity, this is an odd way of delivering it.

## The Pension Anomaly: Declining Coverage and Expanding Protection

While many of the changes imposed by ERISA have had positive effects on pension programs and provided many benefits to their participants, in recent years federal law and regulations have been changing so frequently and have become so complicated that they are making the establishment and maintenance of plans extremely difficult.

The overbearing burden of new pension legislation and regulation during the 1980s required employers that sponsored retirement plans to modify them repeatedly. In addition, plans are now required to do

additional complex discrimination testing that was not previously necessary for the operation of their plans. Plan modifications and added compliance testing have made plans more expensive to administer. Robert Clark and Ann McDermed have focused on the implications of these new regulatory requirements for the establishment and maintenance of plans. They conclude:

The series of regulatory initiatives have raised the cost of providing defined benefit pensions and lowered the value of the pension contract. In response to the regulations, the incidence of defined benefit coverage has declined. These post-ERISA regulations have increased the administrative and reporting costs of all pensions, especially for defined benefit plans. They have reduced the value of defined benefit pension contracts to firms thereby limiting their options to use pensions as incentives to influence employee turnover and retirement. This means that the cost of a dollar of future pension benefits to the worker in terms of foregone earnings has risen. In response to these changes, fewer workers and firms will want to pay the extra costs associated with defined benefit plans.[15]

---

[14] Senator Lloyd Bentsen's (D-TX) comments in *Legislative History of the Employee Retirement Income Security Act of 1974*, prepared by the Subcommittee on Labor of the Committee on Labor and Public Welfare, U.S. Senate (Washington, DC: U.S. Government Printing Office, April 1976).

[15] Robert L. Clark and Ann A. McDermed, *Regulatory Impact on Defined Benefit Pension Plans* (Washington, DC: The American Enterprise Institute, forthcoming).

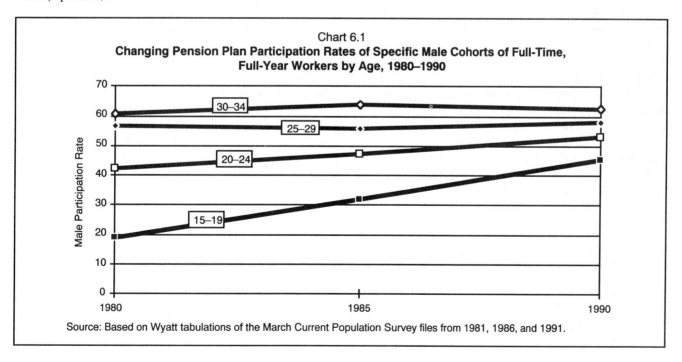

Chart 6.1
**Changing Pension Plan Participation Rates of Specific Male Cohorts of Full-Time, Full-Year Workers by Age, 1980–1990**

Source: Based on Wyatt tabulations of the March Current Population Survey files from 1981, 1986, and 1991.

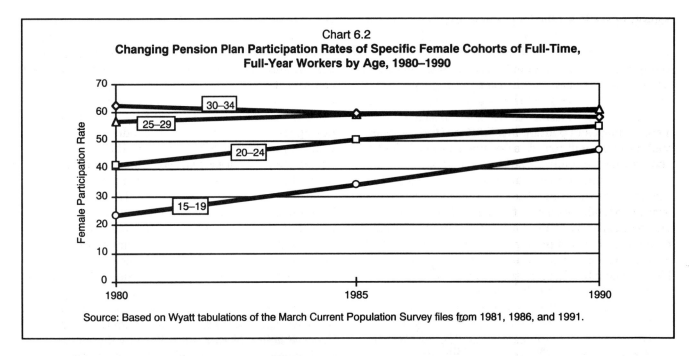

Chart 6.2
Changing Pension Plan Participation Rates of Specific Female Cohorts of Full-Time,
Full-Year Workers by Age, 1980–1990

Source: Based on Wyatt tabulations of the March Current Population Survey files from 1981, 1986, and 1991.

Corresponding with the increasing cost and complexity of administering a retirement plan, the levels of pension coverage in the economy began to decline. Our earlier research, tracing the matriculation of the baby boom generation into the work force, documents the phenomenon.[16] Charts 6.1 and 6.2 are derived from that analysis. The purpose of our analysis then was to show that pension participation of younger workers tends to increase as they move into their working careers. We focused this analysis on the pension participation rates of full-time, full-year workers from the baby boom cohorts of the population in 1980, 1985, and 1990.

Each line of chart 6.1 compares a 5-year cohort of male workers' progression into the pension system over a 10-year period. For example, considering men aged 15 to 19 in 1980, 19.1 percent were participating in a pension. By 1985, 31.9 percent of the full-time, full-year male workers in this cohort were participating in a plan. By 1990, the pension participation rate for full-time, full-year male workers in the cohort was up to 45.5 percent.

Chart 6.2 shows similar information for the female cohorts of the baby boom generation. For women in the younger cohorts of the baby boom generation, the increases in their pension participation rates were even steeper than they were for men.

One disturbing finding in our earlier analysis was that participation rates for individuals of equivalent ages in 1980 and 1990 had fallen significantly. For example, we found that a comparison of the pension partipation rate of men who were aged 25 to 29 in 1980 with men who were aged 25 to 29 in 1990 showed a decline of 11 percentage points. The pattern was consistent for men aged 30 to 34 and for women in both age groups. Our finding of the declining pension participation rates among this relatively restricted group of workers over the 1980s corresponds with that of David E. Bloom and Richard B. Freeman, who considered the general decline in the pension participation rates over the decade. They found that pension coverage fell most heavily for younger and less educated men.[17] In other words, the various legislative and regulatory efforts aimed at broadening the distribution of employer-sponsored retirement benefits during the 1980s may have had exactly the opposite effect.

While the general news on pension coverage during the 1980s was not good, the overall prospects of pension recipiency rose markedly over the decade. To a large extent, this is because of the increased expectations of women under employer-sponsored retirement programs. As recently as the early 1980s, fewer than one in four of all retired women, and 31 percent of recently retired women, were receiving a pension or

---

[16] Gordon P. Goodfellow and Sylvester J. Schieber, "The Distribution of Tax Benefits for Pensions and the Provision of Retirement Income Security" (Washington, DC: National Academy on Aging, 1992): 1113.

[17] David E. Bloom and Richard B. Freeman, *The Fall in Private Pension Coverage in the U.S.* (Cambridge, MA: National Bureau of Economic Research, 1992). The authors find that pension coverage fell most heavily on younger and less educated men.

**Pension Funding and Taxation**

expecting one.[18] While the pension system may have provided little or no benefit to the large majority of women in the past, the future potential of women under the system is vastly different. Women themselves now have a much greater likelihood of earning a pension benefit in their own right than their mothers or grandmothers had in the past. In addition, since the early 1980s, changes in pension law increase the likelihood that a woman will receive a pension as a dependent of a spouse who is eligible for pension benefits.

Earning a significant pension entitlement requires a substantial attachment to the work force over an extended period of time. Simply because women's exposure to the work force is so much greater today than it was in prior generations, their potential for earning a pension in their own right has to be much higher. The labor force patterns of women today suggest that the improvements in pension coverage that are now beginning to take place could continue well into the future. To understand this, consider the variations in the labor force participation patterns of women on the basis of their age.

For women aged 65 to 69 in 1992, chart 6.3 shows their labor force participation rates at various points in their lives. Data are not available in this form to reflect the earliest part of their working careers, but

the pattern reflected there is consistent with what we know about our mothers' and grandmothers' attachment to the work force outside the home. Most of them did not work during the years in which they had young children at home. Some of them, certainly not all, did enter the labor market after their children grew to the point of not needing full-time supervision, especially during the period in which their children were of college age. In many families, the mothers' wages during the children's college years were a major resource that made advanced education possible. For some of these women, the need for added income to meet the financial demands their children's college education required was the primary motivation for working outside the home. When their children graduated, they again became full-time homemakers.

Chart 6.3 shows that this group of women had a rising labor force participation rate for roughly 20 years, peaking at around 55 percent as they approached age 50 and then declining gradually until they reached age 60 and more steadily thereafter. Slightly less than one-half of these women were in the work force during the five years prior to turning age 60, and only one-third were there in the five years prior to turning age 65. Even if 60 percent or 70 percent of these older working women were covered by a pension over the last 10 years leading up to age 65, only about one-quarter of all women in this age group would qualify for their own pension on the basis of a job just prior to retirement.

---

[18] John R. Woods, "Retirement-Age Women and Pensions: Findings from the New Beneficiary Survey," *Social Security Bulletin* (December 1988): 7.

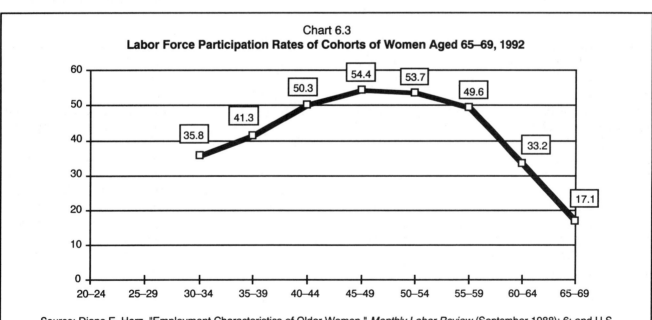

Chart 6.3
Labor Force Participation Rates of Cohorts of Women Aged 65–69, 1992

Source: Diane E. Herz, "Employment Characteristics of Older Women," *Monthly Labor Review* (September 1988): 6; and U.S. Department of Labor, *Employment and Earnings*, February 1992–January 1993 (Washington, DC: U.S. Government Printing Office, February 1992–January1993).

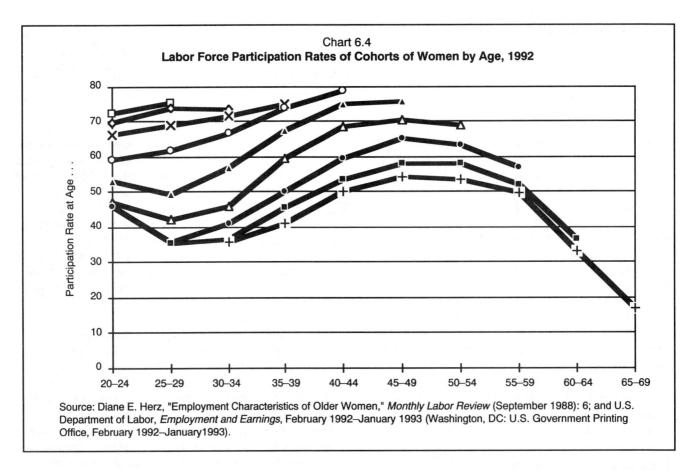

Chart 6.4
**Labor Force Participation Rates of Cohorts of Women by Age, 1992**

Participation Rate at Age . . .

Source: Diane E. Herz, "Employment Characteristics of Older Women," *Monthly Labor Review* (September 1988): 6; and U.S. Department of Labor, *Employment and Earnings*, February 1992–January 1993 (Washington, DC: U.S. Government Printing Office, February 1992–January1993).

Chart 6.4 shows the same type of information as chart 6.3 on successively younger cohorts of women. The bottom line in chart 6.4 replicates the single line in chart 6.3, offering a frame of reference against which the labor force participation of younger women can be compared. What is particularly striking in the figure is that each successive five-year cohort under age 60 in 1992 shows a noticeable increase in labor force participation over prior cohorts, at every attained age. The long-term implication of this changing work pattern of women is that the sustained participation can be best understood by reflecting back on chart 6.2 shown earlier. There we saw that the pension participation rates of younger women who were working on a full-time basis were basically equal to those of younger men who were working full time. If women continue to sustain the higher participation rates that are reflected in chart 6.4, undoubtedly their own pension recipiency rates will increase significantly in the future, although the process will be gradual as it has been in Social Security.

Table 6.1 shows a historical pattern of growth in the percentage of women aged 62 or over who received Social Security benefits on the basis of their own entitlement as retired workers. As the labor force participation rates of women have risen, the percentage

of elderly women receiving a Social Security benefit has gradually increased. The percentage receiving benefits does not rise as rapidly as the increase in labor force participation rates, because the older cohorts of women who received benefits as dependents of entitled workers remain in the total beneficiary pool for a long time. The same is the case with employer pensions. The oldest women who are in the retirement pool today never worked outside the home, or if they did, worked in a time when pensions were less prevalent.

One thing that continues to distinguish men from women relative to participation in pensions is their split between part-time and full-time work. Among all men over age 15 in the labor force at sometime during 1990, 68 percent worked full-time throughout the year, compared with 51 percent of the women. While women who were working part-time were more likely to participate in a pension plan than men who were working part-time, the pension participation rates of part-time workers are generally less than one-half those of full-time workers. Thus, the prevalence of part-time work by women reduces their overall pension participation rate below that of their male counterparts.

While women may not yet be earning pension protection in their own right to the extent men are, another reason more women can expect to receive a pension in the future is the passage of the Retirement Equity Act in 1984. Until that time, a married man earning a pension had the right to select a benefit that did not provide survivor protection without notifying his spouse. The Retirement Equity Act required that, in the future, workers had to get their spouses' signatures acknowledging the selection of a benefit that did not provide for survivors' benefits before such a benefit could be paid. Also, the new law made provision for the splitting of pension accruals in cases of divorce. In the past, it was far more likely that women were victimized than men when it came to loss of survivor benefits or sharing in any kind of pension benefits in cases of divorce. Thus, the provisions of the Retirement Equity Act, raising the likelihood that spousal benefits will be paid, will continue to be an important basis for women's pension benefit entitlements in the future.

## Estimated Distribution of Tax Benefits Across the Income Spectrum

One way of determining whether or not the preferences in the tax code for retirement programs are creating

vertical or horizontal equity problems is to focus on the accumulation of benefits under the plans. The analysis cannot merely look at the cross-sectional distribution of the benefits at a point in time because the benefits are accumulated at varying rates over a lifetime. This is true of both defined benefit and defined contribution plans. In the case of defined benefit plans, two individuals covered by the same plan can have widely different increments in their accumulated benefits during a given year because of differences in their age, pay, and tenure under the plan.

In the case of defined contribution plans, an individual participating in the plan for several years will typically have a larger accumulation under the plan than one who has only been a participant for a year or two. While both participants may make an identical contribution to the plan in a particular year, the one with the larger balance will have the extra benefit of return on accumulated assets to raise his or her accrual relative to workers with shorter tenure. But the mere fact that a worker is young and has a small accrual under one or the other plans this year does not mean he or she will not ultimately age into an accrual comparable to the accrual an older, longer tenured worker enjoys today.

The tax preferences accorded retirement

---

Table 6.1
**Percentage of Women Over Age 62 Receiving Social Security on the Basis of Their Own Work History**

| Year | Percentage |
|------|-----------|
| 1960 | 43.3% |
| 1970 | 50.6 |
| 1980 | 56.9 |
| 1988 | 59.7 |

Source: Barbara A. Lingg, "Women Beneficiaries Aged 62 or Older, 1960–1988," *Social Security Bulletin* (July 1990).

---

Table 6.2
**Distribution of Federal Income Taxes, Pension Accruals, and Federal Tax Expenditures Attributed to Pensions, by Family Income Level after 1986 Tax Reform Act**

| Income Level | Federal Income Tax Distribution | Pension Accruals Distribution | Tax Expenditure Distribution | Ratio of Tax Expenditure Share to Income Tax Share |
|---|---|---|---|---|
| Less than 5,000 | 0.15 | 0.04 | 0.01 | 0.04 |
| $5,000–$9,999 | 0.98 | 0.18 | 0.06 | 0.06 |
| $10,000–$14,999 | 2.31 | 1.07 | 0.52 | 0.23 |
| $15,000–$19,999 | 3.76 | 5.22 | 3.51 | 0.94 |
| $20,000–$29,000 | 9.74 | 11.76 | 10.09 | 1.04 |
| $30,000–$49,999 | 22.10 | 43.67 | 44.72 | 2.02 |
| $50,000 or more | 60.96 | 38.06 | 41.09 | 0.67 |
| Total | 100.00 | 100.00 | 100.00 | |

Source: Sylvester J. Schieber, *Benefits Bargain: Why We Should Not Tax Employee Benefits* (Washington, DC: Association of Private Pension and Welfare Plans, 1990). Tax rates and distribution of taxes paid are from Michael E. Weber and Laura Y. Prizzi, "Individual Income Tax Returns for 1988: Selected Characteristics from the Taxpayer Usage Study," *Statistics of Income Bulletin* (Fall 1989): 13. Pension participant tabulations by the author from the May 1988 Current Population Survey conducted by the U.S. Census Bureau, Department of Commerce, for coverage statistics. The pension accrual distribution and tax expenditure distribution were derived by the author.

programs benefit both workers in the above examples. In any given year, they benefit an individual with a larger accrual more than they benefit one with a smaller accrual, other things being equal. But what holds for any particular year may not hold over a lifetime. In order to get a true sense of the beneficial nature of the tax preferences accorded pensions, it is important to focus on the long time-horizon over which retirement benefits are earned and consider the aggregate accumulation of tax benefits on that basis. One of the problems in developing such an analysis is in finding lifetime retirement plan participation records on large cross-sections of individuals that would be representative of the population. While such data are not generally available, there have been attempts at estimating the distribution of the retirement plan tax preferences from this broader perspective.

In the first of these analyses,[19] Schieber developed estimates of the accrual rates under plans sponsored by a sample of approximately 750 large- and medium-sized firms. He then developed estimates of the number of workers who were also retirement plan participants in each of seven income class ranges. The number of participants in each income class was multiplied by the midpoint of the income class and the relevant accrual factor. The accrual factors for the lower income classes were adjusted to account for the greater turnover among workers at lower pay levels. The resulting products were summed, and the estimate of the distribution of pension benefits accruing to each income class are shown as the share of the total pension accruals in table 6.2.

The results in table 6.2 suggest that the largest beneficiaries of the benefits that derive from the plans and the largest beneficiaries of the tax preference are workers with family incomes between $15,000 and $50,000 per year. These families accounted for 35.6 percent of all federal income tax collections, but derived 60.7 percent of the estimated pension accruals. At the high-income end of the distribution, those workers in families with incomes of $50,000 or more accounted for 61.0 percent of the federal taxes but only 38.1 percent of the pension accruals.

Schieber also estimated the share of the pension-related tax expenditures going to each of the income classes as shown in table 6.2. The higher tax rates in the upper-income brackets heavily weight the distribution of the tax incentives toward the middle- and upper-income workers. At the time the analysis was developed, a dollar of pension accrual for someone

in the $50,000 bracket was attributed three times the pension-related tax benefit of a dollar of pension accrual for someone in the $10,000 to $15,000 bracket, and roughly twice that of someone in the $20,000 to $30,000 bracket. This strictly reflects variations in the marginal tax rates that were applicable in the various income classes. Because tax rates are higher for higher-income workers, the distribution of the tax incentives is skewed more toward upper-income workers than is the distribution of the benefits themselves. For example, while those workers in families with incomes between $15,000 and $30,000 accounted for 17.0 percent of the benefit accruals, their share of the estimated tax incentives is only 13.6 percent of the total. Workers in families with more than $50,000 in income were attributed with 38.1 percent of the benefits but 41.1 percent of the tax incentive.

The right-hand column on table 6.2 further documents the relationship between the share of pension-related tax incentives each of the income classes receives and its share of personal income taxes paid. A ratio that is less than 1.0 suggests that that income group is getting a smaller share of the tax incentive than their share of the federal income tax burden. The results suggest that workers living in families with incomes below $15,000 are getting relatively little from the tax incentives for pensions. They suggest that workers in families between $15,000 and $30,000 are relatively close to breaking even on the tax incentives. Workers in families with earnings between $30,000 and $50,000 are heavy beneficiaries of the tax incentives relative to the share of the federal income taxes they pay. And, finally, workers in families with incomes over $50,000 get less than their share of pension-related tax incentives in comparison to their relative share of the federal tax burden.

In a more recent analysis,[20] Dallas Salisbury used estimated tax expenditures for employer-sponsored retirement programs developed by the Joint Committee on Taxation. He then utilized the Employee Benefit Research Institute (EBRI) tax estimating and analysis model to allocate these tax expenditures across the taxpaying public. The results of his analysis are shown in table 6.3. While the income classes shown in table 6.3 are different than those in table 6.2, and range across a broader range of the income spectrum, the two analyses lead to similar results.

Salisbury estimates that the ratio of the share of tax benefits from retirement plans to the share of income tax liability in the $10,000 to $19,999 income

---

[19] Sylvester J. Schieber, *Benefits Bargain: Why We Should Not Tax Employee Benefits* (Washington, DC: Association of Private Pension and Welfare Plans, 1990).

[20] Dallas Salisbury, "Pension Tax Expenditures: Are They Worth the Cost?" *EBRI Issue Brief* no. 134 (Employee Benefit Research Institute, February 1993).

## Table 6.3
### Distribution of Income by Class of All Returns, Tax Liability and Pension Tax Expenditures at 1992 Rates and 1992 Income Levels

| Income Class | Total Tax Returns | | Tax Liability | | Value of Tax Expenditure | | Tax Ex % Inc Tax % |
|---|---|---|---|---|---|---|---|
| | Number | Percentage | Amount | Percentage | Amount | Percentage | Ratio |
| Less than–$10,000 | 22,449 | 19.7% | $ (1,780) | 0.0 | $ 335 | 0.0% | NA |
| $10,000–$19,999 | 24,260 | 21.3 | 8,156 | 1.7 | 775 | 1.4 | 0.8 |
| $20,000–$29,999 | 19,039 | 16.7 | 28,980 | 6.1 | 4,000 | 7.1 | 1.2 |
| $30,000–$49,999 | 24,245 | 21.2 | 86,347 | 18.2 | 15,870 | 28.1 | 1.5 |
| $50,000–$99,999 | 19,583 | 17.2 | 157,965 | 33.2 | 24,210 | 42.8 | 1.3 |
| $100,000–$199,999 | 3,452 | 3.0 | 72,150 | 15.2 | 7,550 | 13.4 | 0.9 |
| $200,000 and over | 1,114 | 1.0 | 123,759 | 26.0 | 3,760 | 6.7 | 0.3 |
| Total | 114,142 | 100.0% | $475,577 | 100.0% | $56,500 | 100.0% | 1.0 |

Source: Dallas Salisbury, "Pension Tax Expenditures: Are They Worth the Cost?" *EBRI Issue Brief* no. 134 (Employee Benefit Research Institute, February 1993).

Note: Percentages may not total 100 percent due to rounding.

class is 0.8. Schieber breaks that income class into two components and finds that the ratio in the $10,000 to $14,999 income class is 0.2 and in the $15,000 to $19,999 income class is 0.94. The next two higher income classes in each of their analyses are identical. In the $20,000 to $29,999 income class, Salisbury estimates the ratio of tax expenditures to taxes is 1.2, compared with Schieber's estimate of 1.0. In the $30,000 to $39,999 income class, Salisbury's estimate of the ratio is 1.5, compared with the Schieber's estimate of 2.0. Schieber aggregates everyone above $50,000 and estimates a benefit to tax ratio of 0.7, whereas Salisbury breaks this income class into three separate groups, estimating a ratio of 1.3 for the income class $50,000 to $99,999; 0.9 for the income class $100,000 to $199,999; and 0.3 above that amount.

Both of these analyses lead to the conclusion that the tax benefits accorded to employer-sponsored retirement programs are distributed most heavily across the middle-income segments of the work force. The share of the pension-related tax benefits being received are significantly less than the share of income taxes being paid at the highest income levels. These tax preferences clearly are not accruing disproportionately to the "fat cats" that have often been the focus of critics of existing pension policy. In an earlier paper, we included an analysis of the tax preferences that accrue under both pensions and Social Security and found that the tax benefits accruing to higher-wage workers under

pensions are often more than offset by their less than fair return from Social Security.[21] This more holistic view of the retirement system makes an even stronger case that the tax preferences included in our retirement system are less than proportionately distributed toward high-wage workers.

# The Distribution of Pension Tax Preferences: Another View

We have argued elsewhere that the current method of estimating the value of the tax expenditures accruing to individuals participating in employer-sponsored retirement programs wildly exaggerates the value of these tax preferences.[22] In developing that analysis we estimated the tax expenditures related to pensions, attempting to replicate the Treasury Department's methodology for estimating the value of the preferences based on contributions to plans, the income earned on the assets in the plans, and their distributions of benefits.

In the case of employer-sponsored pension and savings plans, the tax expenditure estimates developed by the Treasury Department treat a given year's contributions to pension trusts as taxable wages, and treat the return on assets in the trust funds as taxable income accruing to participants in the plans. The tax rate used in estimating the lost tax revenues on contributions to the funds and the fund income is

---

[21] Gordon P. Goodfellow and Sylvester J. Schieber, "Death and Taxes: Can We Fund for Retirement between Them?" In Ray Schmitt, ed.,

*The Future of Pensions in the United States* (Philadelphia, PA: University of Pennsylvania, forthcoming).

[22] Ibid.

23.5 percent, a weighted average marginal tax rate for covered workers. The estimated tax revenues collected from benefits paid by employer-sponsored plans is calculated using a 20.0 percent weighted average marginal tax rate for beneficiaries.

We applied this method of calculating pension-related tax expenditures for 1990 in an effort to roughly replicate the estimated $46.8 billion in forgone federal revenues for fiscal year 1990 as presented in the fiscal 1992 budget. We calculated the net tax expenditure in two ways: (1) using the traditional method of treating inflationary returns to pension trusts as taxable; and (2) using the more reasonable method of treating only real returns to pension trusts as taxable for purposes of developing the tax expenditure estimates. Our results are presented in table 6.4.

The tax expenditure estimates that we derived for 1990 using published government statistics on actual plan financial operations did not come close to the estimated numbers included in the federal budget submitted to Congress for 1990. Our estimates of the total tax expenditure using the conventional measure was only $17.0 billion for that year. The reason our estimate of the 1990 pension tax expenditure was so different from the Treasury estimate is that they use an estimated rate of return that is relatively constant over time, to estimate the interest return and capital gains on pension assets. Estimates developed by the conventional measure of tax expenditures for pensions for 1988 and 1989 yield estimates that are somewhat higher than the published tax expenditure estimates—$64 billion and $87 billion, respectively. The estimate for 1987 would be $44 billion using this methodology. Over the four years for which there are data since the passage of tax reform, the estimated average tax expenditure would be $53 billion using the conventional measure. We included the Military Retirement System (MRS) in our calculations, which apparently the Treasury Department does not. Thus, our estimates are relatively close to the estimates developed by the Treasury Department.

In our analysis, we developed a modified calculation procedure that is more consistent with the concept of having workers defer consumption during their working lives in order to help meet their consumption needs during their retirement years. Under this alternative, fairer concept of the tax expenditure, only the tax preference accorded to real returns on pension assets is considered. Using this alternative concept, the average tax expenditure estimate for the first four years after tax reform would be $27 billion.

One noteworthy result in table 6.4 was the

## Table 6.4
### Pension Balances and Flows and Estimated Tax Expenditures for 1989-1990

|  | Private Plans | State and Local Plans | Federal Plans | Total Plans |
|---|---|---|---|---|
|  | ($ billions) | | | |
| 1989 Balance | $1,749.1 | $734.9 | $298.6 | $2,782.6 |
| 1990 Employer Contributions | 52.5 | 32.7 | 58.4 | 143.6 |
| 1990 Employee Taxable Contributions | N/A | 14.0 | 4.4 | 18.4 |
| 1990 Interest Earned[a] | 105.8 | 1.0 | 21.2 | 128.0 |
| 1990 Benefits Paid | 141.2 | 39.2 | 53.6 | 234.0 |
| 1990 Balance | 1,766.3 | 743.4 | 328.9 | 2,838.6 |
| Nominal Return Rate | 6.0 | 0.1 | 6.7 | 4.6 |
| Total Interest Plus Pretax Contributions | 158.3 | 33.7 | 79.6 | 271.6 |
| Taxes on Benefits Paid | 28.2 | 7.8 | 10.7 | 46.8 |
| Forgone Taxes[b] on Contributions and Fund Earnings | 37.2 | 7.9 | 18.7 | 63.8 |
| Tax Expenditure – Nominal Basis | 9.0 | 0.1 | 8.0 | 17.0 |

Sources: The 1989 and 1990 balances held by private plans and state and local plans are based on Federal Reserve Flow of Funds data from *EBRI Quarterly Pension Investment Report*, Third Quarter, 1991 (Washington, DC: Employee Benefit Research Institute, 1992); federal plan data are from the annual reports submitted in compliance with Public Law 95-595 for the Federal Reserve Bank, the Public Health Service, the Army-Air Force Exchange Service, the Coast Guard, the Military Retirement System, and the Civil Service Retirement/Federal Employee Retirement Systems.
    Private-sector employer contributions to private pension and profit-sharing plans and the benefits paid by these plans are taken from U.S. Department of Commerce, Bureau of Economic Analysis, *Survey of Current Business*, January 1992. Contributions and benefits from federal retirement programs were aggregated from the respective P.L. 95-595 reports.
[a]Derived from beginning and ending balances, contributions made to the plans, and benefits paid by them.
[b]Calculated at a rate of 23.5 percent; taxes collected were calculated at a rate of 20.0 percent, which is consistent with rates reportedly used by the U.S. Treasury in estimating tax expenditures.

relative magnitude of the estimated tax expenditures attributable to public plans in general and federal plans in particular. Over the first four years following the passage of the Tax Reform Act of 1986 (TRA '86), we estimated that one-half of the retirement plan-related tax expenditures were attributable to public employer plans. In other words, one-half of the estimated tax expenditures related to pensions can be attributed to return on assets related to inflation, and one-half of that has nothing to do with plans sponsored by taxable entities. It turns out our estimates may be conservative.

Munnell has estimated the distribution of $48 billion in tax expenditures related to employer-sponsored retirement plans for 1991.[23] She estimates that $25.5 billion of this was attributable to private pension participants, $14.7 billion to state and local plans, and $7.8 billion to federal civilian retirement programs. But she also notes that the Treasury Department had not included MRS. During fiscal 1991, the federal government made a normal cost contribution of $16.3 billion to the MRS plus an amortization payment of $10.6 billion on unfunded prior obligations. The plan realized $7.8 billion in investment income and $8.6 billion in capital gains. MRS paid out $23.2 billion in benefit payments.[24] Applying the Treasury's 23.5 percent forgone tax rate on contributions and earnings and subtracting their 20 percent rate on benefit payments would have yielded an added $5.5 billion in retirement-related tax benefits accruing

---

[23] Alicia Munnell, "Are Pensions Worth the Cost?" *National Tax Journal* (September 1991): 394.

[24] *Chapter 95 of Title 31, USC. Report on the Military Retirement System as of September 30, 1991,* Table 5, p. 17, Table 6, p. 19, Table 7, p. 20, unpublished report as cited in Dallas Salisbury, "Pension Tax Expenditures: Are They Worth the Cost?" *EBRI Issue Brief* no. 134 (Employee Benefit Research Institute, February 1993).

to federal workers in 1991. In other words, the total tax expenditure would have been $53.5 billion, with 25 percent of it accruing to federal workers, 27 percent to state and local workers, and 48 percent to private-sector workers.

EBRI has taken the retirement plan tax expenditures for public- and private-sector plans and estimated the per capita value of the benefits that are accruing under the various major types of plans. The results of these calculations are shown in table 6.5. Assuming that the typical worker participating in a retirement plan in the private sector is participating in both a defined benefit and a defined contribution plan, the combined value of the tax expenditure is about $960. By comparison, the tax expenditure related to the defined benefit plans covering federal workers are twice that amount. On top of that, the estimated value of the tax expenditure related to the thrift-savings plan for federal workers is nearly the equivalent of the tax expenditure related to the defined benefit plans covering them. The value of the tax benefits accruing under MRS are shown to be slightly less in the table than those that accrue to federal civilian workers under their defined benefit plans. However, the table only includes $4.0 billion of the $5.5 billion in total tax expenditures related to the program. If the full $5.5 billion is used in the calculation, the MRS per capita tax benefit would have been $2,582 for 1991. The state and local plans would appear to be providing benefits that are more in line with the benefits being provided by private-sector employers than those provided by the federal government.

Every bit of evidence that we have looked at leads us to conclude that the people employed in the governmental bodies legislating and regulating pensions are benefiting to a greater extent, on average, from the preferential tax treatment accorded pensions

---

Table 6.5
**Per Capita Tax Expenditures for Employer-Sponsored Retirement Plans, 1991**

| | Active Participants (millions) | Tax Expenditures ($ billions) | Tax Expenditures per Active Participant (dollars) |
|---|---|---|---|
| Civil Service Retirement System | 1.826 | $ 3.5 | $1,917 |
| Federal Employees Retirement System | 1.136 | 2.2 | 1,936 |
| Military Retirement System | 2.130 | 4.0 | 1,877 |
| Federal Thrift Savings Plan | 1.419 | 2.7 | 1,902 |
| State and Local | 11.357 | 13.1 | 1,152 |
| Private Defined Benefit | 28.000 | 8.2 | 292 |
| Private Defined Contribution | 29.000 | 19.3 | 665 |

Source: Dallas Salisbury, "Pension Tax Expenditures: Are They Worth the Cost?" *EBRI Issue Brief*, no. 134 (Washington, DC: Employee Benefit Research Institute, February 1993).

than are the individuals in the private sector who are being regulated. While it is possible to cite examples of rich plans providing generous benefits in the private sector, the limits on benefits and discrimination standards that apply to private-sector plans limit the extent of benefits that can be provided to higher income private sector workers. The fact that federal lawmakers have exempted themselves from these regulations because they would limit benefits under federal pension plans or limit contributions to their savings programs leads us to conclude that the biggest beneficiaries of these preferences are the bureaucrats who are setting the rules.

## Closing Observation

Critics of the tax preferences accorded pensions often pretend that eliminating them would raise an additional $50 billion in federal revenues each year. Munnell in her writings has suggested revenues in this order of magnitude could be raised by taxing the contributions and earnings on pension trusts each year. While the arithmetic arriving at the estimates of potential revenues to be raised by taxing retirement trusts is straightforward, actually collecting the revenues would be a far more complicated proposition. The substantial share of the tax preferences accruing to workers in the public sector means that new taxing

provisions on pensions would raise much less revenue than the tax expenditure estimates in the annual federal budgets imply. If the federal government taxes its own pension funds, it would merely be creating an expense on the one hand that would exactly offset the extra revenue collected on the other. Its power to tax the trusts established by state and local government raises constitutional issues that would have to be resolved before any added federal revenues could be raised. The only pension trusts that are clearly vulnerable to proposals like Munnell's are those held by private plans.

Today, more than one-half of the tax preferences accorded retirement plans are accruing to less than 10 percent of the work force, namely public-sector workers. To further curtail the retirement benefits that private-sector workers can accrue under their plans without addressing the relative preferential treatment accorded public-sector workers under TRA '86 will merely exacerbate the existing inequities. Full elimination of the preferential tax treatment accorded pensions would raise less than one-half the revenue implied by the tax expenditure estimates included in the annual federal budgets. The burden of such a policy would fall solely on the back of private-sector workers. It is time to quit pretending that these proposals are being made in the interest of improving the equitable application of the federal tax sytem.

# PART TWO

# WHAT ARE THE IMPLICATIONS OF TAX POLICY CHANGE?

# VII. Changing Private Pension Funding Rules and Benefit Security

BY MICHAEL J. GULOTTA

This article discusses changing funding rules for private defined benefit pension plans and their effect on benefit security. After examining the concept of benefit security, it focuses on the single-employer plans that are tax qualified, covers what is known about the effect of recent changes in funding rules, and discusses prospective rules changes.

## Defining Benefit Security

Benefit security means different things to different people. One viewpoint looks at the benefits promised to each individual if the plan were to terminate. It essentially asks: Does the plan have enough money to insure payment of current benefits? Under this definition, a participant is secure in his or her benefit if the plan, the plan sponsor, or an outside agency will pay all the benefits due to the participant should the plan terminate.

A second view of benefit security looks less to the insurance aspects of the plan and more to the participant's expectation of benefits. Under this definition of benefit security, continuation of the plan is the key question; benefit expectations are secure only if the pension plan remains both affordable and in the employer's and employee's mutual best interest. As the question of funding changes for private pension plans is discussed, two concepts should be kept in mind:

- Security of payment of benefits accrued at the time of plan termination; and
- The sponsor's ability to continue the plan in a fashion that meets the sponsor's needs and satisfies employees' benefit expectations.

## Tax Deduction Rules Matter—Tax Reform of 1986

Analysis of the effect of funding rules on benefit security needs to include not only minimum funding requirements but also the effect of tax deduction rules on employer actions that affect benefit security. Tax deduction rules became important as a result of changes in pension funding rules put into place with the Tax Reform Act of 1986 (TRA '86). Prior to 1986, plan sponsors could prepay future years' contribu-

tions—they would not receive a tax deduction until the contributions would otherwise have become due, but no tax penalties would apply. While relatively rare, some plan sponsors funded plans on this basis, believing that the need to adhere to a specific funding philosophy outweighed the deferral of the tax deduction. With TRA '86, penalty taxes were imposed on sponsors who prefunded pension contributions before the contributions were deductible. The specific penalty was a 10 percent excise tax to be paid by the plan sponsor on the excess contribution each year until the contribution becomes deductible.[1]

With this new tax, the effect of maximum deduction rules became much more important in the calculation of the plan sponsor's reaction to funding rule changes. Suddenly, maximum tax deduction rules affected even more stringently the sponsor's ability to create a coherent and consistent strategy for funding the plan.

## Other Changes in TRA '86

The effects of other changes imposed by TRA '86 are still working their way through the pension system. Because of the delay in issuing regulations interpreting the changes in the law and also the incremental nature of these changes, some of these effects are yet to be felt. Major changes put into place by TRA '86 were designed to limit the use of pension plans by highly compensated individuals. While intended to ensure that the pension deduction benefits primarily nonhighly compensated individuals, these changes often have the effect of breaking the link between the vast majority of pension plan participants and the senior managers who make decisions about benefit design and plan funding. Primary among the new rules were changes in the maximum benefit that can be paid from a qualified pension plan (the 415 limit)[2] and in the maximum pay on which benefit calculations may be based (the 401(a)(17) limit).[3] These limits affect pension benefit security in two ways.

---

[1] Internal Revenue Code (IRC) sec. 4972.
[2] IRC sec. 415.
[3] IRC sec. 401(a)(17).

First, the limits affect benefit security through the mechanical operation of the funding rules. By law, the maximum benefit limits and the maximum pay for pension calculations are to be indexed for inflation. But, under tax deduction rules, companies cannot reflect the future indexation of these limits. Thus, the pure mechanics of the funding process do not allow companies to prefund on a basis that reflects anticipated inflation in these limits, even though, in the funding calculations, benefits subject to the limits are discounted at an interest rate that anticipates future inflation.

Second, and more important, these limits break the bond between executives, who decide on funding policy for these plans, and the vast majority of plan participants. Under these rules, the benefits of executive decisionmakers will primarily come from sources other than the qualified pension plan. Indeed, executive pensions will be primarily paid from the corporation's general resources and subject to risk if the company should fail. It is increasingly difficult to argue that qualified pension plan participants should be secure in all of their benefits, given that the executive pension is largely subject to risk. While it may be argued that, to some extent, the greater exposure of executive pension to risk of failure may motivate better corporate performance, that argument may then be further applied to participants in the qualified pension plan.

The vast majority of current pension underfunding is in negotiated, or union, plans.[4] It is quite rare for a plan that covers management pension decisionmakers to be underfunded to the same degree as a union plan. Union plan underfunding appears to be due to both of the same factors outlined above but in a greater degree:

- Mechanically, most of the underfunded union plans do not anticipate any increase in benefits due to future pay increases or to future negotiations.
- Most of the underfunded plans are separate from the plans covering management decisionmakers.

## 1987 Changes in Funding Rules

In 1987, the Reagan administration proposed reform of the rules governing minimum required contributions to tax qualified pension plans. The reforms also included a number of other proposals including:

- allowing withdrawals from overfunded plans in certain circumstances;
- tightened requirement for waivers of minimum pension funding rules;
- allowing transfer from overfunded pension plans to retiree health trusts;
- revisions to the deductibility rules so that a plan could contribute current underfunding to the pension plan, even if the contribution would otherwise be too large to be deductible in a single year; and
- indexing the Pension Benefit Guaranty Corporation (PBGC) premium and adding a component that varies with the amount of plan underfunding.

The administration's proposals were designed to address both sides of the benefit security question. By strengthening funding rules primarily for plans that were not adequately funded to insure current benefit commitments, the proposals addressed the ability of the plan to make benefit payments on plan termination. By allowing for withdrawals from an overfunded plan, without requiring a plan termination, the program looked to encourage the continuance of pension plans so as to meet participants' benefit expectations. The administration proposal proved to be only the opening salvo. Each of the four congressional committees with pension jurisdiction came up with different proposals to revise minimum funding rules.[5] Not to be outdone, private-sector industry groups floated at least six other alternative proposals. Many of the key concepts of the various proposals were outlined in the initial administration proposal. They included the following minimum funding rules:

- *The complement rule.* This rule required faster funding of underfunded current benefit liabilities. Under the rule, the speed of funding was inversely related to the degree of funding. Thus, a severely underfunded plan would be forced to fund any underfunding over a shorter period than a mildly underfunded plan. A version of this rule was adopted in the final legislation.[6]
- *Funded ratio maintenance rule.* Here, the basic idea is to define the funded ratio as the liability for accrued benefit promises divided into the current assets of the trust; this funded ratio is not allowed to decrease. In the 1987 administration proposal, any decrease in the funded ratio was required to be made up over the succeeding three

---

[4] Pension Benefit Guaranty Corporation, *Annual Report 1992*, p. 10.

[5] Separate, and conflicting, bills from the House Education and Labor Committee, House Ways and Means Committee, Senate Labor and Human Resources Committee, and Senate Finance Committee were

passed by the respective chambers, and all four bills were reconciled in the 1987 Budget Reconciliation Act Conference.

[6] IRC sec. 412(l).

years. Other proposals mandated annual improvement in the funded ratio. Problems with these proposals included the disproportionate effect of gains and losses, making required contributions very volatile, and the speed of funding for amendments. Also, any requirement that mandated annual improvement in the funded ratio would need to be carefully structured to preserve the ability to pay several years' contributions at once. Otherwise, plan sponsors would be discouraged from contributing in excess of the minimum required.

- *Cash flow rule.* This type of rule requires that an underfunded plan dedicate its investment earnings to improving the plan's funded status and paying for amendments by requiring all, or a stated fraction, of benefit payments to be repaid to the pension fund via the annual contribution. Special rules apply to lump-sum payment of benefits; these rules are designed so that full repayment of the lump sum is not required, but a sufficient contribution must be made so that the plan's funded ratio is not harmed by the lump sum payment. Opponents argued that this rule would force too fast an acceleration of funding and might be too volatile when a plan has a lump-sum benefit option already in place. (Internal Revenue Service rules would generally not permit the removal of the lump-sum option for benefits already accrued.[7])

Final legislation in 1987 adopted modified versions of several of these rules. The complement rule was adapted so that it applies only to the funding of new events. For underfunded benefits already promised at the date of the Omnibus Budget Reconciliation Act of 1987 (OBRA '87), somewhat faster amortization of underfunding was adopted, spreading costs of these underfunded current promises over 18 years. Rather than adopt a funded ratio maintenance rule, faster funding was specifically adopted for pension plan losses (spread over 5 years rather than the previous 15-year requirement) and new amendments (through the application of the complement rule). The cash flow rule was not adopted. In addition, Congress rejected the concept of allowing withdrawals from ongoing plans or allowing the transfer of excess pension assets to fund retiree medical benefits. Other concepts adapted from the Reagan administration proposal included:

- tightened requirement for waivers of minimum pension funding rules;[8]
- revisions to the deductibility rules so that a plan could contribute current underfunding to the pension plan, even if the contribution would otherwise be too large to be deductible in a single year;[9] and
- reformulating the PBGC premium to add a component that varied with the amount of plan underfunding.[10]

Other parts of OBRA '87 required:

- collateralization of amendments in severely underfunded plans. In order to amend a plan that is less than 60 percent funded for current benefits on plan termination, the sponsor must put up collateral, which then becomes available to PBGC in the event of a subsequent plan termination;[11]
- increased protections for PBGC when plans near or enter bankruptcy;[12]
- increased contributions for shutdown benefits after the shutdown occurs;[13]
- phase-in rules that tended to mitigate the impact of the OBRA '87 rules over the near future. Steel companies received special extended compliance schedules for the new funding rules. The collateralization rule was set up to exclude underfunding in effect at the time of enactment;[14]
- a new full funding limit was imposed, eliminating contributions to plans that had assets exceeding 150 percent of the liability for current benefit promises, regardless of the status of funding for future benefit promises;[15] and
- a defined range of interest rates, based on 30-year Treasury bond rates, was mandated for determining the value of current benefit promises.[16]

## Subsequent Legislation

Since OBRA '87, various pieces of pension legislation have been passed. Most significant for our purposes is OBRA '90, which revived some of the proposals regarding use of excess assets by plan sponsors. OBRA '90 allowed sponsors with fully funded plans to use assets in excess of 125 percent of liability for current benefits to pay retiree health benefits. This proposal was significantly less valuable to plan participants than the 1987 administration proposal, as it allows the sponsor

---

[7] IRC sec. 411(d)(6).
[8] IRC sec. 412(d).
[9] IRC sec 404(a)(1)(D).
[10] Employee Retirement Income Security Act of 1974, sec. 4006(a)(3)(E).
[11] IRC sec. 401(a)(29).

[12] OBRA '87 sec. 9312, 9313, and 9314.
[13] IRC sec. 412(l)(5).
[14] OBRA '87 sec. 9303(e)(3) and IRC sec. 401(a)(29).
[15] IRC sec. 412(c)(7)(A)(i)(I).
[16] IRC sec. 412(b)(5)(B).

to transfer assets to pay only one year's worth of benefits at a time, rather than to prefund the entire retiree medical liability. Further, the provision is only for a limited number of years, expiring at the end of 1995. In tandem with the retiree health asset transfer proposal, further restrictions were placed on plan sponsors' ability to recover assets by terminating pension plans.

# What Has Been the Effect of the OBRA '87 Changes?

As discussed, many of the changes made by OBRA '87 were phased in and did not immediately change funding requirements. To the extent that rules were not phased in, there are some data on the effects of the changes in the law.

## Full Funding

Many plan sponsors ceased to contribute to their pension plans after the new full-funding limit of OBRA '87 went into effect. A 1989 survey by Mercer-Meidinger-Hansen predicted that an additional 19 percent of pension plans would be fully funded for 1988 due to the new full-funding limit imposed by OBRA '87.[17]

Tabulations by the U.S. Department of Labor through 1988 show pension contributions to defined benefit plans hit a post-ERISA (Employee Retirement Income Security Act of 1974) low point of $18.4 billion in 1988, from a high of $40.8 billion in 1982.[18]

A study of the effects of OBRA '87 on pension plan funding performed by Hay Huggins demonstrated that pension plan contributions would be less predictable for plan sponsors after OBRA '87 was effective.[19]

Clearly, the increased volatility of required contributions makes defined benefit pension plans less attractive to corporate sponsors of the plans. Further, by limiting contributions based on a multiple of current pension benefits only, sponsors may be unable to fund benefit programs on a level basis. Both of these factors detract from the security of benefit expectations.

## Minimum Funding Rules

Improvements in pension funding have not yet substan-

[17] William M. Mercer-Meidinger-Hansen, *The Effect of OBRA on Pension Plans, A Survey* ( New York, NY: William M. Mercer-Meidinger-Hansen, 1989).

[18] J. A. Turner and D. J. Beller, eds., *Trends in Pension 1992*, U.S. Department of Labor, Pension and Welfare Benefits Administration (Washington, DC: U.S. Government Printing Office, 1992).

[19] Hay/Huggins Co. Inc., *OBRA 1987: The Impact of Limiting Contributions to Defined Benefit Plans* (New York, NY: Hay/Higgins Co., Inc., 1989).

tially improved PBGC's relative position. For instance, the most recent PBGC listing of the top 50 underfunded plans notes that underfunding in the list increased from $13.5 billion in 1988 to $24.2 billion in 1991. Average funded ratios have dropped in the four years from 77 percent to 74 percent.

Several explanations are advanced for the lack of improved funding:

- Transition rules in the 1987 act have deferred the effect of some of the most powerful rules to improve funding. For instance, old underfunding is paid off over 18 years; only new underfunding is scheduled for faster payment. The special transition rules for steel companies may also have a deferred effect (see charts 7.1 and 7.2). The collateralization rules for amendments also have not yet shown any effect, because the threshold for their application is so low (applying only to plans less than 60 percent funded, with a transition rule for pre-OBRA '87 underfunding).

- OBRA '87 sped up the amortization of losses, to protect against the use of overly optimistic assumptions by underfunded plans. At the same time, amortization of gains was sped up symmetrically. This has the effect of allowing good asset returns to offset most of the additional funding requirement due to the amendments. Because gains are taken into account so quickly, plans can avoid increased funding, even when granting significant pension improvements (see charts 7.3 and 7.4).

- Similarly, OBRA '87 does not protect against the effect of a change to more optimistic assumptions. A change in assumptions may often be used to offset the effect of an increase in funding requirements due to plan amendments.

- The evolving application of the law of bankruptcy to PBGC claims has circumvented provisions designed to apply creditor pressure for funding of plans near bankruptcy.

In summary, OBRA '87 has increased the volatility of pension plan contributions. This increased volatility decreases the attractiveness of defined benefit pension plans for all plan sponsors (of both overfunded and underfunded pension plans). Thus, OBRA '87's increased volatility detracts from the overall security of benefit expectations for participants in these plans. The requirements of OBRA '87 for underfunded plans do not appear to have substantially improved the funded status of these plans to date, due to transition rules, the adaptability of the bankruptcy bar, and flaws in the funding rules.

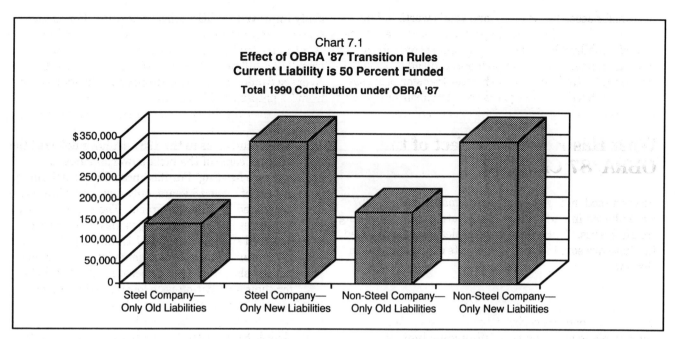

Chart 7.1
**Effect of OBRA '87 Transition Rules**
**Current Liability is 50 Percent Funded**

**Total 1990 Contribution under OBRA '87**

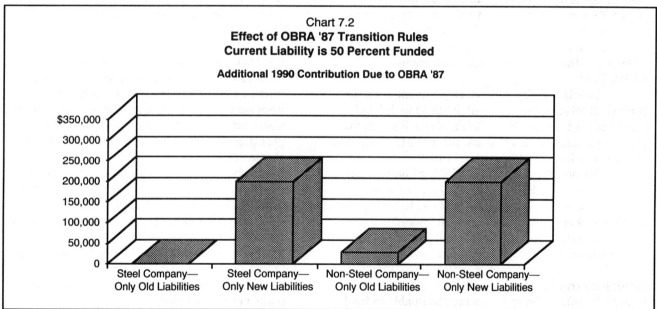

Chart 7.2
**Effect of OBRA '87 Transition Rules**
**Current Liability is 50 Percent Funded**

**Additional 1990 Contribution Due to OBRA '87**

Notes on the charts

Charts 7.1 and 7.2 are illustrations of sample plans that are 50 percent funded on a current liability basis as of January 1, 1990. The plans are:

- A steel company that under IRC sec. 412(l) has only unfunded old liability,
- A steel company that under IRC sec. 412(l) has only unfunded new liability,
- A nonsteel company that under IRC sec. 412(l) has only unfunded old liability, and
- A nonsteel company that under IRC sec. 412(l) has only unfunded new liability.

For purposes of the illustration, the current liability of each of the plans is $2,000,000; they are mature plans, in which the current liability for the retired population is equal to that of the active population. Benefit payments are assumed to be 10 percent of the retiree current liability. The interest rates used for current liability and funding purposes are 9 percent and 10 percent, respectively. As of January 1, 1990, the average remaining years for amortizing unfunded accrued liability is 20 years for each of the plans. The average past service of the active population is 13.8 years. For the plans that have unfunded old liability, the balance of such unfunded liability is $1,000,000 as of January 1, 1990. The plans are assumed to be funded on a unit credit funding method. For simplicity, the plans are assumed not to have experienced any gains or losses or assumption changes.

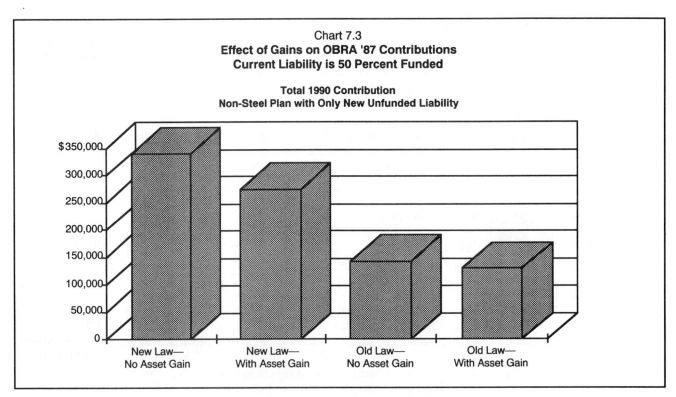

Chart 7.3
**Effect of Gains on OBRA '87 Contributions**
**Current Liability is 50 Percent Funded**

**Total 1990 Contribution**
**Non-Steel Plan with Only New Unfunded Liability**

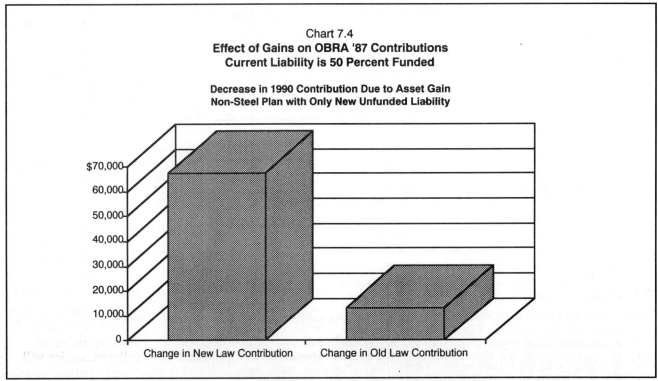

Chart 7.4
**Effect of Gains on OBRA '87 Contributions**
**Current Liability is 50 Percent Funded**

**Decrease in 1990 Contribution Due to Asset Gain**
**Non-Steel Plan with Only New Unfunded Liability**

Charts 7.3 and 7.4 are illustrations of the effect of gains and losses on the contribution rate before and after the changes of OBRA '87. They are based on the sample non-steel plan with only new unfunded liability illustrated above. The gain is assumed to have increased assets by 10 percent above the level that otherwise would have obtained. Thus, plans with a gain have assets of $1.1 million. Chart 7.3 shows the total contribution; chart 7.4 compares the decrease in contribution due to an asset gain under old law and OBRA '87.

# Public Policy Proposals[20]

## Funding and Guarantee Reform

In 1992, the Bush administration proposed new reform of the rules governing pension funding, guarantees, and the liability of bankrupt companies to PBGC. Rep. J.J. Pickle (D-TX) introduced a bill with features similar to the administration's funding proposals.[21] The 1992 proposals included the following changes to funding rules:

- *A cash flow rule.* This rule would be similar to that proposed in 1987 and would phase in over a four-year period.
- *Contributions in each year.* The administration argued that a contribution should be required in each year that a plan is underfunded, i.e., that it should not be possible for an underfunded plan to live off its prior contributions. Opponents of this proposal argued that many underfunded plans are sponsored by employers in highly cyclical industries. If a sponsor can make three years of contributions in one year and then make no contribution in the next two years, the plan will be better funded in years one and two than it otherwise would have been. Opponents further argued that if a plan cannot use prior contributions in excess of those required to offset requirements in lean years, then sponsors will avoid ever contributing more than the minimum.
- *Redefinition of liabilities to be funded.* The 1992 administration proposal redefined the measure of accrued benefit promises to be the plan actuary's best estimate of liabilities at plan termination. In effect, this gave the actuary the ability to use different assumptions (e.g., retirement rates, mortality, etc.) for calculating this value than are used for the long-term funding of the plan. It removed current restrictions on the interest rate to be used and left all decisions to the actuary. Rep. Pickle's bill, on the contrary, used the definition of current liabilities now in the law but narrowed the range of permissible interest rates to be used to value the liability, cutting off the upper half of the range of interest rates that are currently allowed. Another alternative would be to require plans to establish liability on the basis of PBGC assumptions. Arguments against the last idea include the fact that PBGC assumptions are generally more conservative than those of insurers; a requirement to use PBGC rates would in effect force all plans to be overfunded on termination, when annuities are purchased from an insurer. Whether more discretion is needed by the actuary, to measure actual termination liabilities, or less discretion is advisable, given the potential client pressures brought to bear on the actuaries of underfunded plans, is an argument that continues to evolve.

The administration proposal also included a change in the guarantee of participants' benefits and in rules regarding PBGC's rights to recover from the bankrupt sponsor of an underfunded plan. In essence, no benefits due to amendments would be guaranteed by PBGC unless the plan was fully funded for current benefits at some point between the grant of the amendment and the date of a subsequent plan termination. The bankruptcy provisions, to some extent, merely conformed the bankruptcy code to legislative provisions of OBRA '87. Other proposals would increase PBGC's right to recover from the bankruptcy estate by a steadily increasing percentage. Rep. Pickle's bill did not include the bankruptcy provisions, although a separate bill containing similar provisions was introduced. Also, there was no reduction in guarantees in the Pickle bill; instead the rule requiring collateralization of plan amendments in an underfunded plan was considerably strengthened. Rep. Pickle has reintroduced his bill in 1993. [22]

Both the 1992 administration proposal on changes in the guarantee and the requirement of increased collateralization are subject to criticism for the effect they produce on benefit security. The 1992 administration proposal has been criticized for not recognizing improvements in funding for any amendment until funding has been completed for all current benefit promises. This detracts from benefit security, viewed as insurance of current benefit promises. The collateralization proposal, on the other hand, will likely prevent any future amendments to an underfunded plan. This is because it essentially requires a company with an underfunded plan to perform the financial equivalent of funding most of the value of a plan amendment—plus all of its accumulated underfunding—in the year a plan amendment is next granted, without any ability to spread the cost over time. Thus, collateralization will restrict participants' ability to be secure in their benefit expectations.

---

[20] Since the time that this paper was prepared, the Clinton administration proposed the Retirement Protection Act of 1993 to reform the PBGC. The proposal addresses four main areas: funding, premiums, compliance, and participant protection. Appendix A contains an article that describes the Clinton proposal.

[21] The Bush administration proposal was introduced as H.R. 4200. Rep. Pickle's bill was introduced as H.R. 5800.

[22] H.R. 298.

## Changes in the Maximum Pay To Be Reflected in Pension Calculations

Recent proposals by the Clinton administration to further reduce the maximum pay that may be used in calculating pension benefits will only exacerbate the harmful effects of changes made by TRA '86. Again, under tax deduction rules, companies cannot reflect the provisions of the law that provide for indexation of the limit on pensionable pay. Thus, on the mechanical level, pension funding will be even more closely linked to the volatile funding of current liabilities rather than to the smooth funding of projected liabilities. Further, by pushing the maximum pay level farther down the corporate chart, yet more pension decisionmakers will be exposed to greater risk and will identify less with the rank and file pension participants.

# Where Do We Go From Here?

Before outlining a view of the future, I would like again to review our definitions of benefit security. I have talked about benefit security from two perspectives:
- The ability to provide the value of benefits promised to date, and
- Providing a climate in which benefit expectations can continue to be met.

Let us look first at the security of benefits already accrued. It is clear that ERISA as currently formulated has not operated to clear up all instances of underfunding. However, ERISA has operated over time to reduce the number of underfunded plans to a relatively small minority of plans. Thus, changes to ERISA to improve security of benefit promises on plan termination should be incremental, not sweeping. I believe that changes should be made to the ERISA funding scheme that incorporate the following broad principles:
- New amendments to underfunded plans should be funded on a faster basis. Some mechanism is also needed to ensure that funding for these amendments is in addition to the funding that would otherwise have taken place and that gains and assumption changes do not remove the urgency of funding every plan up to at least the level of current benefit promises.
- The system of PBGC guarantees must be rationalized to reflect the moral hazard inherent in allowing guarantees to take effect before funding is required. ERISA already recognizes that it is unsound policy to allow guarantees to take effect before funding is required for substantial owners of pension plans. The experience of the past 16 years has shown that it is not only substantial owners that have the power to shift liabilities onto the PBGC insurance system before the beneficiaries have made the appropriate financial sacrifices to fund the benefit promises. Clearly, parties in collective bargaining have demonstrated similar abilities to shift liabilities onto the guarantee system. Plan improvements should be guaranteed only as money is required to be put aside to fund those benefits.
- The Bankruptcy Code must be conformed to ERISA provisions. Plan contribution requirements should be treated just as are post-petition salary and other benefit costs.
- Tax rule obstacles to funding of underfunded plans must be removed. These include an exemption to the combined limit on deductibility of pension and profit-sharing contributions so that sponsors need not bargain away a savings plan contribution in order to adequately fund the pension plan.

Looking at the second definition of benefit security, it is clear that the private pension system must be strengthened to protect sponsors' ability to continue benefits, fund their programs, and meet benefit expectations. To this end, I propose the following changes:
- Repeal of the branch of the full-funding limit that limits contributions solely on the basis of current benefit accruals, without thought for the future. This will allow sponsors to fund plans on a level basis and so encourage long-term continuation of benefit programs.
- Maximum dollar limits on pay to be used in calculating pension plan benefits, and the maximum dollar limits on benefits payable from a qualified pension plan should be removed for plans that are :
  - not top-heavy and
  - meet the nondiscrimination requirements of Internal Revenue Code (IRC) secs. 410(b) and 401(a)(4).

This should realign the interests of pension plan decisionmakers with those of the majority of plan participants.

It is important that changes be made in the benefit system to encourage adequate funding of current benefit promises on plan termination. However, for the vast majority of plan participants, benefits are currently secure and would be fully provided in the event of plan termination. For these participants, the important goal is to ensure that the current level of benefit expectations is not endangered by short-sighted policies that strangle the sponsor's interest and ability to preserve the promised level of benefits by continuing the plan.

# VIII. Changing Public Pension Funding Rules

BY FIONA E. LISTON AND ADRIEN R. LABOMBARDE

## Introduction

Tight state and local government budgets during recent years have brought the funding of public pension funds into sharper focus. Long-term policies come into conflict with short-term crises, with some governments deciding that a distant funding target will not be put beyond reach if one or two current contributions are missed or delayed. Others find apparent magic in the actuarial assumptions underlying the funding. Frequently one small change in an actuarial assumption can claim to win some very large budget battles. Meanwhile, accountants and creditors peer at the governments' pension books, dubious about exactly how well or poorly funded the pensions really are. As recent struggles in California amply illustrate, the issues here are not merely academic ones. Knowledgeable command over pension funding decisions is increasingly the key to control over much of a government's overall budget.

Governmental decision makers can find their general budget policies influenced by their pension funding practices in three direct aspects:

- the effect of the pensions' funded level on the credit rating of the public unit's debt;
- potential financing of local projects through selective investment of pension assets; and
- the amount of annual pension expense included in the budget itself.

Beyond these issues that are directly related to a government's budget, pension funding concerns will have myriad indirect effects on other critical governmental decisions, notably on the design of pension programs and overall compensation policies.

Looking at public pension funding in the limited context of the current year or the immediate, short-term future can have severe consequences. Certain decisions—e.g., changing the investment policy for the plan's assets or modifying benefit formulas—will actually affect the program's ultimate cost. Other decisions—e.g., modifying the actuarial assumptions or methods used to determine plan costs—will technically modify only the timing of the funding, accelerating or delaying the incidence of the cost. In either case, the effect on current costs and funded levels can only be properly understood in the context of the long-term cost. Temporary cost "savings" used to ease through a

current budget crisis could backfire if the ultimate result is to impose future pension cost burdens that would be untenable or unacceptable.

Public pension plan funding is conducted in a special setting that distinguishes it from private employers' pension plan funding. First, the tax-exempt status of the employer removes one of the primary incentives for pension funding. Public pensions are not backed by the Pension Benefit Guaranty Corporation (PBGC) and are not subject to the minimum funding requirements of the Employee Retirement Income Security Act of 1974 (ERISA). Even the accounting rules for reporting the funded status to creditors and others are not as strict. Finally, the nature of the employer itself can have a bearing on the pension funding question, as the governmental sponsor must look to future generations of taxpayers—rather than to income from new products and services—for support of projected pension costs.

## Background Considerations in the Public Pension Funding Decision

Many public pension plans were originally funded on a pay-as-you-go basis. No money was put aside during employees' active service to prefund future benefits. Instead, retirement payments were made from the general coffers when the benefits actually came due. In large part because of the risk of bankruptcy of the plan sponsor, minimum funding standards have been imposed that prohibit a tax-favored private-sector pension plan from using the pay-as-you-go approach. Although bankruptcy of a governmental employer is not as remote a risk as used to be believed, generally the public plan sponsor is perceived to be a permanent entity with relatively strong control over the source of funds (i.e., the tax base). Hence, one of the most compelling arguments for advance funding of pension benefits—the need for an independent fund that could survive the plan sponsor—has little persuasive force in the public plan arena.

With some justification, taxpayers could resist strong advance funding on the premise that the pension funding process diverts tax dollars from other governmental functions into investments that have no direct bearing on the operation of the locality. If local taxes must then be increased to fund the local functions, or if the cost of borrowing is greater than the return on the pension fund assets, then the governmental entity and its taxpayers have lost out.

Conversely, the accumulation of a large pension fund provides a temptation during hard times to divert that money to other local uses, frequently without the same controls generally exercised for the general budget. The recent ruckus in California is a case in point, where the governor used a fund set up to provide cost-of-living increases to make the state's regular pension contribution. The strong emotions that these issues can arouse among the popular citizenry was witnessed this past election, when California voters approved a petition that installs controls against any future "raids," such as granting the board of trustees sole and exclusive power over actuarial services, a function that had previously been given to the governor under the law.

Finally, payment of pension benefits without advance funding would save on administrative expense. There would be no need to hire expensive pension professionals, such as investment advisers, investment brokers, and pension actuaries.

Nevertheless, there are many compelling reasons for governmental units to advance fund pension benefits. Perhaps the strongest argument for advance funding is intergenerational taxpayer equity. Pension benefits are a significant part of the entire compensation package for public employees. Taxpayers pay for the current salary and health care benefits of their public servants while they are performing their duties. These same taxpayers, then, should be providing for the retirement benefits accruing for those employees during the period when services are being rendered. To defer the cost of providing an element of compensation is, effectively, to pass on the cost to the next generation of taxpayers. Such intergenerational transfers can operate in equilibrium (i.e., the burden passed by the current generation to the next generation is comparable to the burden received from the previous generation) only in very large systems such as Social Security, where factors (e.g., employee-to-taxpayer ratio) are relatively stable from generation to generation and the social contract is subject to strong governmental control. In contrast, an intergenerational transfer at the local governmental level might usually be little more than a temporary "fix," a perceived easy way out of a current budget crisis. If the government cannot afford to compensate its employees at the current level, then on what basis is it assuming that the children will be able to do so?

Building a pension fund to pay for the accruing benefits also provides a measure of security to the employees who have been promised a benefit. In these times when government budgets are strained, employees can feel more secure about their future benefits if there is an independent fund dedicated to that specific purpose. Indeed, we might now be witnessing cutbacks of previously accrued benefits if there were no public pension funds. The economic value of benefit security is difficult to measure but is nonetheless quite real. Certainly it could be expected that the cost of labor for a public employer would be higher if its employees had less certainty about the security of future benefits; otherwise, skilled employees would simply tend to move to other employers with whom the benefit security is higher.

A strong pension fund can be invested, thereby defraying future costs by earning interest. Although this income must be considered offset by the cost to the governmental unit of borrowing amounts for other public purposes, the long-term nature of the pension funding process generally serves to keep the government in the black. The governmental employer can best control this balance by closely coordinating projected pension outlays with its general budget and borrowing needs, rather than simply determining pension costs independently in a vacuum solely on the basis of the benefits themselves.

Of course, prefunding pension benefits does permit more flexibility in cash flow than pay-as-you-go. Without prefunding, the sponsor must meet benefit payout commitments as they occur. If pension benefits are prefunded, there is a certain degree of flexibility that can be built into the funding method. As long as funding targets are met in the long run, governments can adjust current contributions to ease through times of economic trouble.

## Is There a Problem with Current Public Plan Funding?

A report recently issued by the General Accounting Office (GAO) on the funding practices of state and local governments raises some concerns that pension contributions by state and local governments are not being made, that actuarial assumptions are being manipulated in order to reduce required plan contributions, and that many state and local plans are less than fully funded.

We doubt that the public pension funding picture is as gloomy as GAO has painted it. Their report shows an average funding ratio of 85 percent across all state and local plans. This ratio compares the funds' assets to an actuarial funding target known as accrued liability. In the private sector, when a pension plan has reached this target it is not allowed to contribute any more until the target has outgrown the assets. In other words, the accrued liability forms an *upper bound* on where the assets should be if the company is following a responsible funding pattern. The GAO report indicates that 61 of the 189 plans studied have reached this target. If these were private sector plans, they would be considered very well funded.

The remaining state and local plans averaged a 76 percent funded ratio. This funded level is a significant improvement over the 51 percent average funded ratio reported by the Pension Task Force on Public Employee Retirement in its 1978 report. Even with the recent economic problems, the trend in funded ratios can be expected to continue increasing.

The GAO report claims that 75 of the 189 plans contributed less than the actuarially required amount in 1988. Because there are no minimum funding standards for public plans, the significance of this simple count is unclear and potentially misleading. The GAO report also claims that 27 percent of the plans in a Greenwich Associates' study changed their actuarial assumptions in 1989. Although the report goes on to mention that changing actuarial assumptions is not necessarily inappropriate behavior, again the significance of the GAO's tally requires further inspection before any conclusions can be formulated.

Generally, an employer is being tagged an "under-contributor" against an actuarial standard previously set for prior years' contributions, either on the basis of previous actuarial assumptions or previous actuarial methods or both. In some instances, emerging experience might demonstrate the previous funding target to be too conservative, in which case a change in the target itself, resulting in lower future contributions, would be appropriate. If the contribution change is being accomplished primarily because of external budget pressures, then the long-term implications for pension decision making are troubling. Even so, any decision to adjust the flow of money into the fund cannot be judged outside of the context of the entire funding equation, including the current funded level, expected future net cash flows, and certain expected external factors.

## How Do We Solve the Public Plan Funding Dilemma?

Similar problems regarding the funding of private-sector plans were identified in the 1960s. The federal government "solved" those problems with the enactment of ERISA. Yet after more than a decade of development and many compromises, the minimum funding standard of ERISA still failed to work well for private

plans. The PBGC crisis during the mid-1980s focused attention on the weakness of the funding standard. A patch was stitched over the funding standard with the deficit reduction contribution enacted by the Omnibus Budget Reconciliation Act of 1987; but even that effort was so watered down through the political process that it has had barely any effect on underfunding in the private sector.

Today, the federal government's rules for private plans restrain some plans to an arbitrary full-funding limitation, while gaping holes still permit other plans to go insolvent. Certainly, this funding standard could not be expected to provide the solution to the concerns over the funding of state and local governmental pensions. Serious constitutional questions surround the question of whether the federal government should even attempt to impose a pension funding standard on local jurisdictions, because the issue is so closely bound up in each government's budget and taxation authority. Perhaps the furthest the federal government might ever be able to reach into the public plan funding question would be an imposition of fiduciary standards on decisions pertaining to plan assets (e.g., possibly establishing federal control over the questions raised in the recent California situation).

Should state and local governments codify their own pension funding standards? The states of Florida and Pennsylvania have done so. Some states and counties mention funding methods and amortization periods in their statutes. Other jurisdictions that have not gone as far as codifying their contribution schemes have nevertheless made serious funding commitments and have seen their funding ratios increase to more comforting levels.

Even so, the mere codification of a minimum funding standard cannot be seen as the solution to the funding question. First, instead of adding credibility, the codification can actually eliminate accountability. This apparent anomaly is most easily witnessed with severely underfunded private plans: the plan can continue toward insolvency while plan sponsors pretend that all is well as long as the minimum required contribution has been made.

Some basis for comparing the funding among different public plans—as well as for comparing the funding of public plans with that of private plans—might help the plan sponsors to make their funding decisions in a more informed setting. To some degree, albeit without directly establishing an absolute benchmark, such comparability is one of the principal aims of the effort by the Governmental Accounting Standards Board (GASB) to develop a standard for the reporting of public pension cost.

Yet even a GASB accounting standard would

offer little more than a crude starting point for judging the issue. First, the long process of seeking a consensus among GASB constituents is likely to leave the standard rather loose, effectively considering comparable all plans within a very wide band of funded ratios measured according to various methods and assumptions. More importantly, the GASB standard will deal with only part of the public plan funding equation as though it exists in isolation. To complete the equation—and thereby to gain an understanding of whether a particular public pension plan is being adequately funded—a projection that closely coordinates the pension plan's net cash flow with the jurisdiction's overall budget—in particular, including future anticipated tax receipts—is necessary. The pension side of this projection should examine the degree to which the plan's past funding has pushed the funding for previously accrued benefits into contributions expected for future periods, while the overall budget side of the projection should gauge the ability of the emerging tax base to support that transfer.

# IX. Decreasing the Compensation Cap for Pensions: Consequences for National Retirement Policy

BY FIONA E. LISTON AND ADRIEN R. LABOMBARDE

## Introduction

The Omnibus Budget Reconciliation Act of 1993 (OBRA '93) included a provision that lowered the cap to $150,000 for compensation that may be taken into account during 1994 for tax-qualified pension or profit-sharing plans. In 1993, the compensation cap was $235,840. Thus, counting the cost-of-living increase in the cap that would have otherwise taken effect in 1994, for the highest-paid employees the modification could slice the amount of compensation used to determine pensions by as much as 40 percent.

A primary stated objective of the compensation cap reduction relates to potential discrimination with respect to highly compensated employees. Even if employers respond by amending the design of their pension plans, reducing the compensation that can be used to determine benefits or contributions will generally shift the balance of tax-qualified benefits more in favor of nonhighly compensated employees. Of course, it is recognized that a strong driving force behind the provision relates not so much to social policy as to the harsh realities of a federal budget deficit that continues out of control. The net near-term effect of the compensation cap reduction is anticipated to be increased taxes through the lower deductions that employers will be able to take for contributions to tax-qualified plans.

Ultimately, *both* objectives may be lost. Any gains for nonhighly compensated employees will be negligible or nonexistent: as some pension plans are terminated, other plans are amended to approximate the pre-1994 balance, while any "lost" benefits for highly compensated employees are simply paid in other forms of compensation. Meanwhile, the costs in permanent damage to national pension policy—for example, by delaying funding of benefits—may within a very short period of time exceed the very temporary jolt of revenues the provision might raise.

The decrease in the compensation cap could affect qualified pension and profit-sharing plans in three distinct ways:

- *Lower qualified benefits or contributions* for the high-level highly compensated employees;[1]
- *Tighter results for numerical nondiscrimination tests* that include high-level highly compensated employees; and
- *Delay of funding for projected benefits* of intermediate-level and high-level employees (including young nonhighly compensated employees).

It is worth emphasizing at this point that if the employer does not react to the compensation cap decrease by amending or terminating its tax-qualified plans, the *only* employees who will be most significantly hurt in any direct way (i.e., by losing entitlement to tax-qualified retirement savings) will be the high-level highly compensated employees. Other highly compensated employees might suffer lost tax-qualified savings potential under a 401(k) cash or deferred arrangement, but in most cases these losses are likely to be relatively minor. Although the *funding* of projected benefits for certain nonhighly compensated employees will be significantly delayed, those employees will not actually receive lower benefits on account of the compensation cap decrease (again, presuming no change in the plan). The distinctions made within this paragraph do *not* mean, however, that the nondiscrimination objective of the legislation can be achieved. The disruptive effects of the compensation cap decrease make it highly unlikely that the critical assumption underlying these observations (i.e., no change in the pension plan itself) will be maintained. These disruptive effects are real enough and serious enough to ultimately threaten the viability of pension and profit-sharing plans in their current forms, particularly within the very firms most essential to U.S. economic growth and competitiveness.

---

[1] Within this paper, reference to "high-level" highly compensated employees denotes an employee (or, in the case of family aggregation of certain highly compensated employees, the family unit) who earns more than $150,000 during the initial year of application of the reduced compensation cap. Ultimately, this class could include some employees initially earning slightly less than $150,000, because pay increases for employees at these levels are typically at rates higher than the cost-of-living increases subsequently granted to the compensation cap.

# Lower Qualified Benefits for High-Level Highly Compensated Employees

Assuming future compensation increases to be at the same rate as future increases in the compensation cap, virtually any employee (regardless of age or service) who is currently earning more than $150,000 will see lower benefits under an unamended qualified defined benefit plan than would otherwise have been expected.[2] Similarly, any high-level highly compensated employee will see lower contributions under an unamended defined contribution plan.

Actually, the threshold for the affected group will probably be somewhat lower than $150,000, because the rate of compensation increases for these employees is typically higher than the average rate that would be used for the cap. Moreover, under the final legislation, the rate of increase for the new compensation cap may be restrained below the rate of increase for average compensation during periods of high inflation, further expanding the potential group for whom benefits or contributions are exposed to curtailment.

*Example.* An employer's integrated profit-sharing plan is currently designed to grant employees an employer contribution equal to 5 percent of all compensation up to the compensation cap, plus an additional 5 percent of any such compensation that is in excess of the Social Security wage base (for 1993, equal to $57,600). If the compensation cap decrease to $150,000 had been effective during 1993, the following illustrates the effect that would be realized for any employee earning more than the current cap of $235,840.

|  | Old Cap | New Cap |
|---|---|---|
| Includable Compensation | $235,840 | $150,000 |
| 5 percent of Total Compensation | 11,792 | 7,500 |
| 5 percent of "Excess" Compensation | 8,912 | 4,620 |
| Total Contribution | 20,704 | 12,120 |
| Percentage Decrease |  | 41.5% |

Of course, the degree of the "cut" in qualified plan benefits or contributions will depend upon how much an employee's earnings exceed the compensation cap. For example, an employee earning just over $150,000 will ultimately not be severely affected (although, as discussed below, funding of the benefit may be materially delayed even for these employees). The degree of cut for an employee may also depend on the plan design. For example, under a plan with benefits or contributions that are integrated with Social Security (as in the illustration shown at the right), a cut of 40 percent in the included compensation would reduce retirement benefits for the highest paid by slightly more than 40 percent. Finally, for a defined benefit plan, the degree of benefit cut could depend on an individual's age and service. For example, a very highly paid employee who is already near retirement would probably not accrue any additional benefits but would have previously accrued benefits protected under transition rules, so that the eventual benefit might not be as significantly lower as would be expected for a young employee who experiences the full effect of the lower target.

In most cases (i.e., unless the pension plan is already generous enough to be encountering other benefit limitations in the tax code), a plan could pre-serve the benefit expectations of its top wage-earner by modifying the benefit formula (e.g., increasing the expected cumulative accrual rate by 40 percent if the top employee is earning more than the 1993 cap).[3] Technically, if the employer objectives underlying the benefit or contribution design were to be very precise, such a redesign would probably need to be updated from time to time (e.g., since the Social Security wage base does not increase at the same rate as the compensation cap would).[4] Of much more critical practical interest are two other problems. First, the rebalancing implicit in a redesign that preserves the benefits of the highest wage earner within the group cannot possibly retain the balance for any significant portion of the remainder of the group without violating nondiscrimination rules. Hence, the employer's compensation policy would be distorted by the higher benefits or contribu-

---

[2] The exception (i.e., high-level highly compensated employees who would receive no less a pension benefit than before the compensation cap decrease) occurs primarily in the case of transition rules protecting benefits that had accrued previously to reductions in other limits under the law, specifically in those cases for which the employee could not have anticipated ever seeing further accruals even under the current compensation cap (e.g., employees now near normal retirement who had accrued the full $136,425 permissible prior to the 1982 changes in the benefit limitations under sec. 415 of the tax code).

[3] For the defined contribution plan shown in the illustrative example, the 1993 contributions could have been preserved for the highest

paid employees by amending the plan to provide a 10.3 percent contribution for all compensation up to the new compensation cap, plus a 5.7 percent contribution for all such compensation over the Social Security wage base.

[4] For employers who either maintain only a traditional defined contribution plan or whose defined benefit plan has been essentially frozen (either by will or in effect through the past decade of decreases in various limits applicable to the plan), one way to at least approximate a preservation rebalancing would be through conversion to what is commonly referred to as an "age-weighted" profit-sharing plan.

tions for other employees (including both the nonhighly compensated employees and any highly compensated employees who earn less than the reference point used for the rebalancing). The second problem follows from the first: such rebalancing would be extremely expensive.[5] An intermediate form of rebalancing (i.e., not fully preserving amounts for the highest paid, while only partially increasing amounts for the nonhighly compensated) might deal with the cost problem, although the shifting of compensation objectives would remain a concern.

Of course, proper full appraisal of the effect of any benefit decreases in the context of national retirement policy should ultimately take into account the likelihood that—at least for large employers—any "lost" benefits or contributions for many of the high-level highly compensated employees might simply be replaced though nonqualified benefits or other forms of compensation.[6]

For defined benefit plans, reduced benefit expectations for the class of employees earning over $150,000 will be directly reflected in a lower funding target. Of course, most of the reduced funding in this instance has to be sharply distinguished from the funding delay discussed in a later section in this paper. Here, we are not referring to a deferral of funding for benefits that will eventually accrue; rather, there is the elimination of benefits needing to be funded. In fact, to the extent that previous funding has relied on the higher benefit expectations before the cap reduction, there will temporarily be a degree of overfunding (again, "real" surplus rather than the temporary "imaginary" surplus of the funding delay discussed later) vis a vis the new funding target. Some plans of private employers might now be constrained by the full-funding limit; others already at the full-funding limit will see the period of "contribution holidays" extended further.

For national pension policy and each employer's own compensation policy, there are dangers lurking in this disruption of the incidence of pension cost, when too many years elapse without any charge for pensions. Strictly on the financial and actuarial basis, however, this particular portion of the "lower funding" arising from the cap reduction is consistent with the lower benefits that will actually accrue. Another way of expressing this same point is to observe that any lower funding arising from the lower benefit expectations will not be direct cause for any concern on the part of the Pension Benefit Guaranty Corporation (PBGC), which insures private employers' underfunded pensions. In fact, for some plans PBGC could very well benefit from this aspect of the compensation cap reduction: amounts that had been accumulated toward higher benefit expectations that will now not be possible under the qualified plan will in effect be available to fund other benefits under the plan, increasing the overall funded level of the plan in real terms over the coming years as the higher-waged employees' expectations "wear away."

## Tighter Results for Numerical Nondiscrimination Tests

For ratios used in various tests to gauge possible discrimination in favor of highly compensated employees, the compensation used in both the numerator—which essentially tracks actual accruals under the plan—and the denominator—which is used to set the standard against which discrimination is judged—must be limited to the compensation cap. Lowering the cap to $150,000 will typically have the effect of making it more likely that the tests would be failed.

For example, in the simplest instance of testing potential discrimination in a plan's definition of compensation (e.g., base pay, excluding overtime), for a group that includes any employees who currently earn more than $150,000, lowering the cap will increase the average ratio of included compensation for the highly compensated employees without affecting the average ratio of included compensation for nonhighly compensated employees. Another example arose in test computations conducted by the authors on a defined benefit plan with a primary insurance account (PIA)-offset benefit formula. For that plan, the general nondiscrimi-

---

[5] Of course, for an isolated case that *does* aggressively pursue the rebalancing despite the direct increase in employer cost (e.g., preserving overall compensation objectives through other means, such as lower direct compensation for those who receive higher qualified benefits or contributions), the proposal's nondiscrimination objective would be satisfied. If, however, any significant segment of the qualified plan universe were to pursue such rebalancing, it is doubtful that the proposal's revenue objective would be achieved.

[6] A special transition rule that is being proposed for public plans would permit a government to essentially exempt all public employees in service as of a 1995 cutoff date from the change in the compensation cap. However, any new public employees after the cutoff date would have to be subject to the new compensation cap. In addition to permitting public employers to avoid conflict with local laws, reliance on this special transition rule would significantly minimize the immediate threat of reduced benefit expectations, although of course the reductions remain a problem in the design of the benefit package for new employees. For public employers, the absence of viable alternatives for replacing "lost" amounts with nonqualified deferred compensation makes any restriction from the cap—even if only for future employees—a major concern.

nation test could be satisfied under the 1993 compensation cap. If that compensation cap were decreased to $150,000, then even after taking account of lower benefits for the high-level highly compensated employees as discussed in the first section of this paper, the general nondiscrimination test would not have been satisfied.[7]

A plan that would have previously been considered nondiscriminatory could therefore be more vulnerable to the tests with a lower compensation cap. Depending on the circumstances, this exposure could influence design of the benefits, perhaps encouraging a decrease in the accrual rate for highly compensated employees or an increase in the accrual rate for nonhighly compensated employees. Preliminary research suggests, however, that it would be unlikely that the overall effect on nondiscrimination test results would be significant for most cases, except in the instance of the special tests discussed in the following paragraph.

The special nondiscrimination test under tax code sec. 401(k) applicable to deferrals under a qualified cash or deferred arrangement, and the corresponding special nondiscrimination test under tax code sec. 401(m) applicable to employer matching contributions and employee contributions, merit special attention. As the following series of charts illustrate, the effect of the compensation cap decrease will depend largely on the average level of deferral or contribution being made by or for the nonhighly compensated employees (NHCEs). For various illustrative NHCE levels of deferral under a 401(k) arrangement, the charts show the maximum amounts that could be deferred for highly compensated individuals over the range of various compensation levels. In all instances where the two lines diverge, the higher line indicates the deferral amount using the 1993 compensation cap, while the lower line indicates the deferral amount using the new, lower compensation cap.

For simplicity purposes, these ceilings assume that all highly compensated employees not otherwise restricted will contribute at a uniform rate of compensation. In practice, if some highly compensated employees contribute less than that rate, then other highly compensated employees would be able to contribute at higher rates. Therefore, the ceilings implied by these

illustrations are "soft," indicating the basic pattern of the deferrals. For typical cases, however, the trends will remain similar to those indicated by the illustrations.

For the 401(k) nondiscrimination test, the nature of the effect of the compensation cap decrease can be seen to shift dramatically around a breakpoint of about 4 percent average rate for the NHCE deferrals, equivalent to a permissible average rate of about 6 percent for the highly compensated employees.[8] For plans below the breakpoint, with lower levels of deferral, the effect of the compensation cap decrease is isolated among the high-level highly compensated employees (i.e., those earning over the cap). For plans that have higher deferral rates, the shift is rather striking: the high-level highly compensated employees are not affected at all by the compensation cap decrease, while lower-level highly compensated employees share a moderate degree of decrease in permissible deferral.

## Delay of Funding for Projected Benefits of Intermediate-Level Employees

For defined benefit plans, the compensation cap can actually be viewed as two separate limitations: first, the cap on the current amount of compensation taken into account for currently accruing the pension; second—almost separately—a ceiling on the amount of projected compensation taken into account in funding the projected benefits expected to be earned under a plan. The second aspect of the limit—the inability to take future increases of the cap into account in current funding—will tend to delay the funding of some of a plan's benefits. The lower funded levels that could emerge from this phenomenon must be distinguished from the lower funding levels discussed in the first section of this paper. Rather than lower funding attributable to ultimately lower benefits, the inability to project future increases in the cap means that the plan will have to delay the funding for benefits that *will* ultimately be paid. Instead of the constant rate as a percentage of compensation—a typical budgeting and financial objective for the employer—the pension costs

---

[7] Except in the case of the special nondiscrimination tests under sec. 401(k) and 401(m) of the tax code, an employer could generally avoid exposure to this concern by operating a plan with broad coverage (i.e., not requiring application of the average benefit percentage test) that complies with a nondiscrimination safe harbor on the basis of a safe harbor definition of compensation. Numerous employers will find these particular design constraints to be either too tight or simply inappropriate as a response to any compensation cap decrease.

[8] This estimated 6 percent breakpoint emerges due to the relationship between the dollar limitation on 401(k) deferrals—equal to $8,994 in 1993—and the compensation cap of $150,000. If, for example, the cap decrease was changed to $200,000 (on a 1993-equivalent basis), then the breakpoint for the different 401(k) effects would be at an NHCE average deferral rate of about 2.5 percent correlating to a 4.5 percent permissible average deferral rate for highly compensated employees.

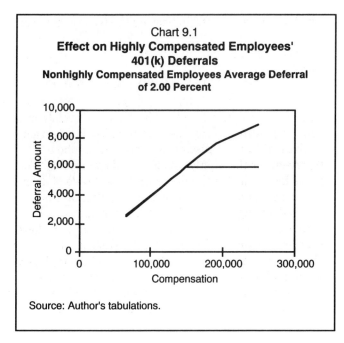

**Chart 9.1**
**Effect on Highly Compensated Employees'**
**401(k) Deferrals**
**Nonhighly Compensated Employees Average Deferral**
**of 2.00 Percent**

Source: Author's tabulations.

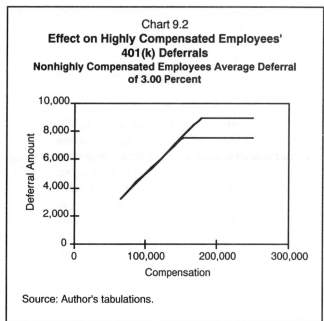

**Chart 9.2**
**Effect on Highly Compensated Employees'**
**401(k) Deferrals**
**Nonhighly Compensated Employees Average Deferral**
**of 3.00 Percent**

Source: Author's tabulations.

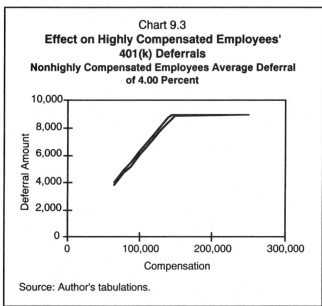

**Chart 9.3**
**Effect on Highly Compensated Employees'**
**401(k) Deferrals**
**Nonhighly Compensated Employees Average Deferral**
**of 4.00 Percent**

Source: Author's tabulations.

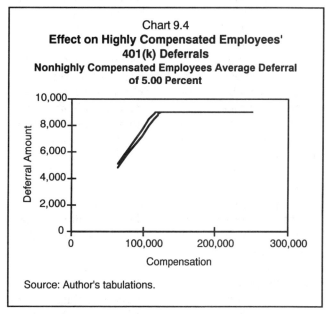

**Chart 9.4**
**Effect on Highly Compensated Employees'**
**401(k) Deferrals**
**Nonhighly Compensated Employees Average Deferral**
**of 5.00 Percent**

Source: Author's tabulations.

will be lower in earlier years, eventually to be made up by higher costs in later years.

For a salary-related plan, generally accepted accounting practice regards the portion of benefits arising from future compensation increases but attributable to benefits that have been earned through past service to be a current liability. Both the minimum and maximum funding standards applicable to private plans recognize this almost as a central tenet of the funding of a salary-related plan. With a nonprojected compensation cap in place, however, the funding methods for purposes of the minimum funding and

maximum deductible costs for private employers are directly constrained. The accounting rules for private employers do not follow the lead of these funding rules, requiring future compensation cap levels to be projected in order to determine the costs and liabilities reported on financial statements.[9]

The identification of the employees with respect to whom the funding must be delayed under a

_____

[9] For public employers, this issue is a subjective question of comparability and credibility, because the funding and accounting rules are more flexible.

frozen compensation cap is primarily sensitive to the employees' age and secondarily sensitive to the rate of increase anticipated for future compensation. With a 3 percent anticipated rate of increase, any 20-year-old employee with compensation greater than about $40,900 are included in the group that gives rise to delayed funding. If the anticipated rate of increase is 5 percent, the 20-year-old threshold drops to about $17,500. For any 20-year-old earning less than this threshold, funding remains unaffected by the compensation cap. For any 20-year-old earning between this threshold and the $150,000 cap, funding of a portion of ultimate benefits is delayed because of the inability to project the cap. For 20-year-old employees earning over $150,000, the funding target is decreased as discussed above in connection with lower permissible benefits, and the portion of benefits attributable to compensation between the threshold and the cap is funded on the delayed basis.

Although worthy of serious concern with respect to funding objectives, a threshold such as $17,500 can be dangerously misinterpreted if taken out of context. First, it should be reiterated that for employees between this threshold and $150,000, no actual benefits are curtailed, presuming the continued existence of the plan and the continued ability of the plan sponsor to meet its pension funding obligations. Second, the strong age sensitivity of the threshold cannot be ignored. While certainly the majority of the work force

is above a $17,500 threshold, that line applies only to 20-year-old employees. Using a 5 percent assumed increase rate, the threshold for a 35-year-old employee is about $36,400, for a 50-year employee about $75,800. While employees above these thresholds are certainly not uncommon, they are a significant minority, rather than the pervasive majority implied by simply citing the 20-year-old threshold.

Two further observations tend to further dilute any emphasis on a threshold such as the 20-year-old 5 percent increase figure of $17,500. First, the effect on funding for any employee actually earning near the threshold is negligible. An employee must earn about 10 percent higher than that threshold—in this instance, a 20-year-old at more than about $19,250—in order to see a 10 percent decrease in the projected benefit obligation with respect to that employee in the first year. This slope is more gradual as an employee progresses through funding; for example, for the projected benefit obligation to be 10 percent lower than without a frozen cap five years into funding, an employee would need to have a compensation about 30 percent higher than the basic threshold. Second, because of the extremely low actuarial cost factors for younger ages, the cost and liability implications of employees who exceed the thresholds below around age 35 tend to have virtually no impact on the aggregate results for the full plan. Although the lines are far from clearly drawn, it would not be too much of an exaggera-

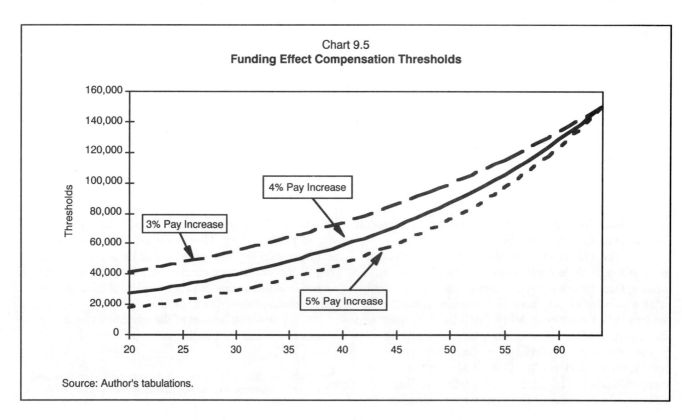

**Pension Funding and Taxation**

tion to generalize that any funding effect from the inability to project the compensation cap tends to be restricted to the funding of portions of benefits for middle-aged employees who are highly compensated (i.e., in 1993 earning more than $64,245) or older employees who are super-highly compensated (i.e., in 1993 earning more than $96,368).

On the contrary, it would be very dangerous to dismiss the funding delay as imaginary because real benefit decreases might not be at stake, or to minimize the potential danger in those cases for which the demographics give rise to larger delays. In particular, it is worth pointing out that if a plan terminates in an underfunded position that has been exacerbated by this funding delay, *all* employees—not merely the ones over even the lowest thresholds discussed above, and certainly not merely the highly compensated employees—are hurt, because unfunded liabilities are not allocated among employees on any basis that would take the delay into account for the various classes of employees.

For employers in conventional businesses (e.g., with established, rank-and-file industrial work forces), preliminary research suggests that the reduction in the projected benefit obligation attributable solely to the inability to project the $150,000 compensation cap might rarely be in excess of 5 percent. Rather trouble-some, however, is the portrait of the employer that would suffer most from this effect: one characterized by a young or middle-aged work force with a competitive compensation structure and a low ratio of higher-paid employees to lower-level staff. This pattern could easily describe a typical professional-oriented service organization (e.g., banks, legal and accounting firms, etc.) or an industrial "hi-tech" employer. For such employers, the reduction in the funding target can easily range from 15 percent to 25 percent.

For plans with employees affected by the funding delay, the annual pension costs could temporarily be materially—almost severely in some cases—affected as the plan shifts to the new funding target. Over the long run, however, the difference in pension cost (as compared with projection of the caps) may be relatively small for an ongoing plan, as employees for whom costs need to increase to make up for previous funding delays offset newer employees for whom funding delays are still in the early stages. Typically, problems with severely accelerated costs attributable to this issue would emerge only in maturing plans. Such problems will most likely occur in relatively small firms with top-heavy plans benefiting primarily aging highly compensated employees. Although any delay of funding should generally be studied skeptically and avoided if at all possible, it is doubtful that this particular funding constraint would, for example, pose any immediate, material new threat to the solvency of PBGC's insurance program.

# X. Implementing Basic Tax Changes: Income Versus Consumption Tax Treatment[1]

BY RICHARD A. IPPOLITO[2]

## Introduction

Retirement income that is generated outside the Social Security system is financed by individuals postponing current consumption in favor of consumption later in life, when more uncertainty surrounds their ability to work. The decision concerning how much to save depends on the tradeoff between current and future consumption. This tradeoff depends on at least two important factors: price and the rate of time preference.

By the "price" of postponing consumption, I mean the value of current consumption sacrificed in order to have an extra dollar of consumption later in life. The price is lower, the higher the rate of return on investment monies. Apart from price, some individuals attach less value to later consumption *just because it occurs in the future.* High discounters attach less value to future events and thus save less. Low discounters attach more value to future events and thus save more.

Public policy is intertwined with these issues. Clearly, the government can increase the price of future consumption by increasing taxes on savings. In effect, tax rules that penalize savings encourage low discounters to act like high discounters. In addition, as long as low discounters accept the responsibility of financing part of the old-age consumption for those who do not save, they have a stake in the "free-market" savings decisions of high discounters. This discussion first addresses the price issue, then incorporates the externality caused by high discounters' inclination to ignore their need for future consumption.

## Impact of Pension Tax Policy on the "Price" of Future Consumption

As a general rule, contributions to a pension trust fund are tax deductible to the firm, and investment earnings are tax exempt. Pension benefits are taxed as ordinary income during retirement. This policy is often referred to as *consumption tax treatment* because wages saved for later consumption are taxed once when they are spent.[3] This policy is in sharp contrast with ordinary income tax rules. Under income tax rules, wages saved for later consumption are taxed once when earned, and *again* in the form of taxes on earnings during the accumulation process. The so-called double tax biases individuals toward current consumption and away from postponed consumption.

### The Economic Relevance of "Two" Tax Rates on the Same Level of Income

The compelling case for tax treatment of savings is that the effective tax rate on wages does not depend on the period in which the earnings are used to support consumption. Income tax treatment encourages workers to ignore their consumption requirements in the future, a problem of special magnitude during older ages when workers' productive capabilities typically wane.

One way to characterize income tax treatment of savings is as an extra income tax on wages at the time they are earned.[4] In effect, there is a two-tier tax rate. If earnings are used to support *current* consumption, they are assessed a tax rate equal to the statutory rate prescribed in the Internal Revenue Code (IRC). If earnings are used to support *future* consumption, they are assessed at the statutory rate *plus* some increment.

Consider a worker 25 years from retirement. Suppose the real interest rate is zero. The income tax rate specified in the IRC is 33 percent. If the worker saves $1 per year in real terms over 25 years, his after-tax pension at retirement under a consumption tax is $16.67 ($25 minus 33 percent tax). Under income tax rules, if the nominal interest rate is 10 percent, the worker's after-tax pension is only $11.33 ($25 minus $8

---

[1] This discussion summarizes portions of my book, *An Economic Appraisal of Pension Tax Policy in the United States* (Homewood, IL: Irwin, 1990).

[2] The views expressed herein are my own and do not reflect the official positions of the Pension Benefit Guaranty Corporation.

[3] Discussions of consumption tax systems can be found in D. Bradford, *Blueprints for Basic Tax Reform* (Washington, DC: U. S. Department of the Treasury, 1977); N. Kaldor, *An Expenditure Tax* (London: Allen and Unwin, 1955); R. Hall and A. Rabushka, *The Flat Tax* (Stanford, CA: Hoover Press, 1985); and C. Walker and M. Bloomfield, *The Consumption Tax: A Better Alternative* (Cambridge, MA: Ballinger, 1987).

[4] See Richard Ippolito, *An Economic Appraisal of Pension Tax Policy in the United States* (Homewood, IL: Irwin, 1990).

in tax during accumulation[5] for a net of $17, less the 33 percent tax on pension income). The tax rate is not 33 percent but 54.6 percent (chart 10.1).

Consider two identical workers earning the same wage income, both 25 years from retirement. The high discounter saves nothing and thus relies on public support of his consumption during old age. The federal government assesses a tax rate against his wage income of 33 percent. The low discounter saves a portion of his wages to support his own consumption during old age. He faces two tax rates. On the portion of his income immediately consumed he pays a 33 percent tax. On the portion he saves for consumption at age 65, he pays a 54.6 percent tax.

In some sense, there is a special "second-tier" income tax levy of 21.6 percent on top of the 33 percent statutory tax rate *if and only if* income is used to support future consumption. The second-tier tax is higher, the higher the nominal interest rate, the higher the statutory marginal income tax rate, and the longer the period of accumulation.

By expressing income tax treatment of wages and savings as a two-tier tax scheme on wage income at the time it is earned, it is easy to compare the differences between consumption tax treatment and income tax treatment of savings even assuming a zero interest rate. This approach greatly simplifies the exposition yet retains the essence of the economic impact of pension tax policy. In this form, I demonstrate in the appendix that, if consumption financed by savings is taxed disproportionately, workers react by spending more of their lifetime income on consumption during their working years and reducing their anticipated standard of living during retirement. In addition, because consumption is taxed disproportionately when workers are in their leisure-intensive retirement period, leisure becomes more expensive; and thus the individual retires later.[6]

Chart 10.2 shows the impact of income versus consumption tax treatment on consumption rates and the retirement age. Chart 10.3 illustrates the value attached to these distortions. In the latter figure, the demand schedules for consumption during work and retirement years are identical. They are downsloping owing to diminishing marginal utility of consumption. The income tax artificially increases the cost of con-

---

[5] A contribution in the amount of $1 per year (increased for inflation at 10 percent per year) that accumulates at an after-tax rate of return of 6.67 percent, amounts to $207.35 in nominal terms after 25 years. This amount expressed in real terms is $17.02. Thus, the individual has $25 minus the $8 he or she pays in taxes during the accumulation period. In addition, he pays the usual 33 percent tax on his remaining $17, leaving him with a net income of $11.33.

[6] If workers can control the amount of work effort during their work years, they also will react by taking more leisure during their career in anticipation of less leisure later. See Richard Ippolito, "Income Tax Policy and Lifetime Labor Supply," *Journal of Public Economics* (April 1985): 327–347.

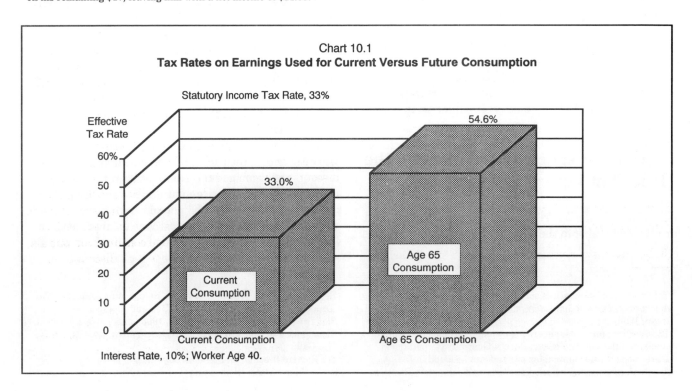

Chart 10.1
**Tax Rates on Earnings Used for Current Versus Future Consumption**

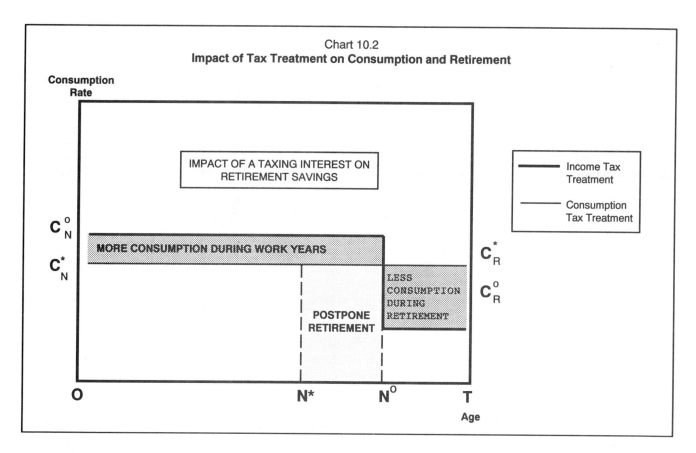

Chart 10.2
**Impact of Tax Treatment on Consumption and Retirement**

Consumption Rate

IMPACT OF A TAXING INTEREST ON RETIREMENT SAVINGS

——— Income Tax Treatment

——— Consumption Tax Treatment

$C_N^o$

$C_N^*$

MORE CONSUMPTION DURING WORK YEARS

$C_R^*$

LESS CONSUMPTION DURING RETIREMENT

$C_R^o$

POSTPONE RETIREMENT

O          N*     N$^o$     T

Age

sumption during retirement. The distortion causes the worker to forego consumption during retirement, which has relatively high marginal value, for more consumption during work years, which has lower marginal value. The sum of the shaded areas represents the reduction in welfare owing to the distortions of the tax on relative consumption rates.

The worker reduces the magnitude of the distortion by working more periods and retiring later in life. On the margin, workers reduce the value of the distortion by giving up leisure to obtain a lower cost of consumption. Thus, in equilibrium, the distortion caused by the double taxation on savings is manifested in both later retirement and a lower standard of living in retirement.[7]

## Pension Externality: Including Some High Discounters in the Pension Plan

Under current pension rules, except for small savings

limits in individual retirement accounts, the tax advantages of pensions are limited to firm-sponsored pensions. The tax qualification rules encourage similar pension coverage across workers in the firm.[8] As a result, it is likely that low discounters in the firm save less than their desired amount, and high discounters save more. If the plan pays benefits in an annuity form, it is likely that substantial amounts of retirement income are received by high discounters who otherwise would not have this income in a market in which individuals decided on their own level of savings for retirement.

This outcome has some positive externalities to low discounters because, to the extent that some high discounters are forced to save more than they would otherwise, they impose less burden on low discounters during retirement. That is to say, if high discounters do not save for retirement, low discounters are forced to finance not only their own old-age consumption but also part of the consumption of old-age high discounters.

---

[7] If hours worked are permitted to be a variable instead of a constant, it is straightforward to show that another substitution would occur from leisure during retirement to leisure during work years. See Richard Ippolito, "Income Tax Policy and Lifetime Labor Supply," *Journal of Public Economics* (April 1985): 327–347.

[8] Firms may have separate pension plans for some types of workers, for example, union versus white collar, and for different plant

locations, but they may not structure pension coverage so as to award disproportionate benefits to the highly paid. See Everett T. Allen, Joseph J. Melone, Jerry S. Rosenbloom, and Jack L. VanDerhei, *Pension Planning: Pensions, Profit Sharing, and Other Deferred Compensation Plans*, Seventh edition (Homewood, IL: Irwin, 1992).

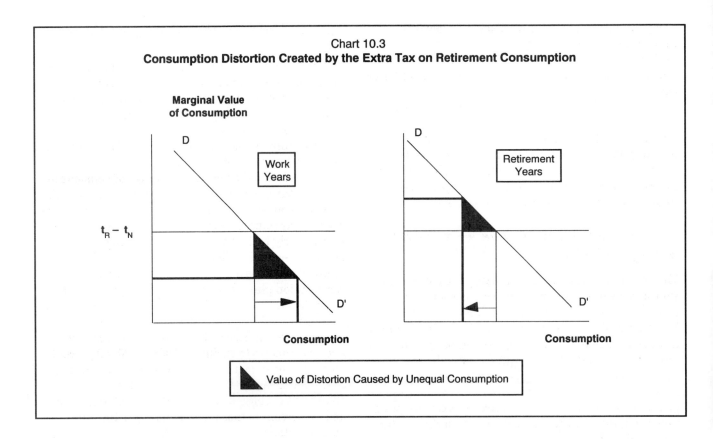

**Chart 10.3**
**Consumption Distortion Created by the Extra Tax on Retirement Consumption**

Marginal Value of Consumption

D

Work Years

$t_R - t_N$

D'

Consumption

D

Retirement Years

D'

Consumption

Value of Distortion Caused by Unequal Consumption

To the extent that firms offer a lump-sum option in their pension plans, the forced savings effect of pensions is diminished. As high discounters change employers, they can take the lump sum and spend it immediately.[9] Even if they stay until retirement, if they take their benefits as a lump sum, high discounters are not likely to have a substantial amount left to finance retirement during older ages.

### Pension Externality: Capital Stock and Wages

The impact of imposing a second-tier tax on postponed consumption makes it apparent that the capital stock in the economy is lower under a comprehensive income tax. The amount of capital accumulated by retirement age is smaller because workers are encouraged to enjoy less consumption during a shorter retirement period. The observed savings rate itself would not fall by as

much as the capital stock. But part of the savings is taken in increments by the federal government for current spending, and thus only a portion of savings is actually invested in productive capital. As the capital stock falls, the capital-labor ratio, and thus overall wages, also fall across the economy. Thus, even though only *some* individuals save, *all* workers benefit to some extent from the capital accumulation, even if those who save nothing themselves.

## Consideration of Alternative Tax Rules

The obvious alternative to the current special tax policy toward pensions is to equalize tax treatment on all savings. This alternative can be affected in two dramatically different ways. First, the consumption tax treatment could be extended to all forms of savings. Second, pensions could be stripped of their special tax status.

### Broad Consumption Tax

If all savings enjoyed consumption tax treatment, pensions no longer would be special. There would be no reason for pensions to exist, except insofar as they provided either production efficiencies for firms or

---

[9] The data suggest that 88 percent of preretirement lump-sum distributions are rolled over into individual retirement accounts. See J. Piacentini, "Preservation of Pension Benefits," *EBRI Issue Brief* no. 98 (Employee Benefit Research Institute, January 1990). I have argued elsewhere that high discounters are most likely to quit defined contribution firms. See Richard Ippolito, "Selecting and Retaining High-Quality Workers: A Theory of 401k Pensions," unpublished paper (Washington, DC: Pension Benefit Guaranty Corportion, 1993).

group annuity benefits for workers.[10] In general, pension assets and coverage would fall substantially. Individuals would be free to set up a variety of savings schema to satisfy their particular desires to save for old age.

Low discounters probably would save more under this arrangement because there would be no constraint on the amount of savings under a broad consumption tax. High discounters would save less. Overall capital accumulation could be higher or lower. All the benefits of extending the consumption tax treatment to pensions would be maintained.

## Treating Pensions Like Other Tax-Exposed Savings Vehicles.

The obvious alternative to equalizing tax policy is to subject pensions to comprehensive income tax treatment.[11] In this model, pensions as an institution would be dramatically smaller, and the inefficiencies embedded in the double tax on savings would be spread to all retirement savings. All individuals would be encouraged to act more like high discounters, consuming more during younger ages and less during retirement. Thus, individuals' target wealth for retirement consumption would fall, thereby causing a reduction in the capital stock and wages.

Finally, since the income tax imposes a double tax on all postponed consumption, it would be more costly for firms to use deferred wages. Even though pensions might be considered a useful tool to defer wages to encourage long tenure, they would more likely be discarded, regardless of the efficiency implications, due to their higher cost.

# Likely Drift in Pension Tax Policy

The probability that a consumption tax will be introduced to displace the current comprehensive income tax in the United States is remote. It is equally unlikely that the special tax treatment of pensions would be eliminated. The trend in pension tax policy, however, has gradually worked in the direction of reducing the net tax advantages of pensions.

I define the net tax advantage of pensions as the total tax savings over conventional savings vehicles, *minus* the attendant regulatory costs. Some of the new regulations impose more restrictive funding rules (particularly to defined benefit plans), and some enhance derivative IRC provisions for qualified plans. These changes have encouraged the growth of defined contribution plans, particularly 401(k) plans, at the expense of defined benefit plans,[12] and indirectly have contributed to the decline in pension coverage.[13]

A recent survey by the American Academy of Actuaries shows that, during 1988–1990, 59 percent of terminations of plans with 1–24 participants mentioned government regulation as a cause for termination, 46 percent of those with plans with 25–99 participants, and 36 percent of those with plans with 100–499 participants.[14]

The growth of defined contribution plans has gradually changed the main benefit form of pension payments from annuities to lump sums. For low discounters, this trend has no important implications for retirement income.[15] High discounters who happen to work for firms that sponsor pensions will likely spend their pension monies before they reach old age.[16]

The net decrease in the tax advantage of

---

[10] That is, if it is important to the firm to discourage quitting and to encourage retirement over particular age ranges, then some pensions could survive, even though other savings vehicles also were exempt from taxation during the accumulation period. Similarly, some pensions could be maintained if there was an advantage to pooling workers for annuities. That is, pensions that pay annuities as the required form help workers avoid adverse selection at the time of retirement and reduce the cost of individual annuities for the group as a whole.

[11] This proposal has been made by Alicia Munnell, "Current Taxation of Qualified Pension Plans: Has the Time Come?" *New England Economic Review* (March 1992): 12–25..

[12] See Hay Huggins Company, *Pension Plan Expense Study for the Pension Benefit Guaranty Corporation* (Washington, DC: Pension Benefit Guaranty Corporation, 1990); R. Clark and A. McDermed, *The Choice of Pension Plans in a Changing Environment* (Washington, DC: American Enterprise Institute, 1990); *What Is the Future of Defined Benefit Pension Plans?* (Washington, DC: Employee Benefit Research Institute, 1989); and Richard Ippolito, *An Economic Appraisal of Pension Tax Policy in the United States* (Homewood, IL: Irwin, 1990).

[13] A recent study finds that, in 1988, pension plans were offered to almost the same percentage of the work force as in 1980, but that the participation rate declined for young men. The study attributes the lower participation rates to the spread of 401(k) plans. See W. Even and D. MacPherson, "Why Have Pension Coverage Rates Declined during the 1980s?" unpublished paper (Oxford, OH: Miami University, 1993).

[14] American Academy of Pension Actuaries, *The Impact of Government Regulation on Defined Benefit Pension Plan Terminations* (Washington, DC: American Society of Pension Actuaries, 1993).

[15] If they leave the firm before retirement age, they can transfer the monies into an IRA to continue accumulating tax free until age 59.5. However, if they choose to convert the monies to annuities, they face the adverse selection and nongroup cost structures associated with individual purchase prices from insurance firms.

[16] To the extent that they leave the firm before retirement age, they likely will spend their lump sums before retirement. If they collect their lump sum upon retirement, they likely will spend these monies early in retirement.

pensions may also help explain the trend toward less pension coverage in small firms. Restrictions on the funding of higher-wage employees are not easily circumvented by changes in other actuarial assumptions in small firms. Regulatory costs are also felt disproportionately by small firms.[17] According to the American Academy of Actuaries' survey, fully 58 percent of pension plan sponsors that terminated defined benefit plans in the 1–24 size group did not replace the plan with any new plan; about 33 percent of those that terminated plans with 25–499 participants did not install a replacement plan, and 16 percent of those with larger groups did not do so. Of the firms that offered a replacement plan, virtually all were defined contribution plans.

There is a temptation to increase taxation on pensions on the assumption that pensions are demanded predominantly by low discounters, and that, despite the higher tax, these individuals will still save sufficiently to finance their own retirement without imposing additional demands on the public pension system. But this trend in policy likely is partly to blame for the drift toward defined contribution plans and less pension coverage. The long-run consequence of these trends is that a higher portion of high discounters will have no private pension annuity during old age. If the tax advantage of pensions erodes sufficiently, a larger portion of low discounters will begin behaving like high discounters. The encouragement to spend imposes more burden on a Social Security system that already is projected to be under financial stress when the baby boom generation begins to enter retirement in less than 20 years.

# Mathematical Appendix

In this appendix, I demonstrate the impact of eliminating special tax policy on retirement savings. I can express the problem in a way that has a familiar solution.[18] Consider an individual with a constant real wage over N working years. Suppose the hours of work during work years are a given, and that death occurs with certainty at age T. Also, suppose that utility is a log function of consumption and leisure, intertemporally independent and additive in consumption and leisure. The individual's internal discount rate is zero.

I specify two consumption tax rates: $t_N$ is applied to consumption during work years ("current consumption"), and $t_R$ is applied to consumption during retirement years ("postponed consumption"). This two-tier tax scheme mimics the impact of an income tax on investment earnings.

Recalling that utility is a log function of consumption and leisure, utility at age j is

(1) $U_j = \log(C_j) + \log(L_j)$,     $U(C_j)' > 0$,     $U(C_j)'' < 0$,

where $C_j$ and $L_j$ are consumption and leisure during period j. I can assume without consequence that after retirement, leisure is abundant and during work years, it is zero. Thus,

(2) $L_j = 0$,     j=1,...,N     and
    $L_j = L$     j=N+1,...,T.

Since the wage rate and hours of work are constant over the work life, and there is neither discounting nor uncertainty, it is straightforward to show that the solution involves a single consumption rate during work years, $C_N$, and a single constant consumption rate during retirement years, $C_R$. I assume that the wage rate per period is a constant, w. Thus, the savings rate, $w - C_N$, is also constant during work years.

The individual maximizes lifetime utility

(3) $U = N \log(C_N) + [T-N][\log(C_R) + \log(L)]$,

subject to a lifetime income constraint that total consumption equals total after-tax earnings:

(4) $wN = N[1+t_N]C_N + [T-N][1+t_R]C_R$,

where $t_N$ and $t_R$ are the tax rates on consumption during work and retirement periods.

It is easy to show that the solution to this problem is characterized by the following two conditions:[19]

(5) $C_R(1 + t_R) = C_N(1 + t_N)$,     and
(6) $N/T = 1 / [\log(C_R) - \log(C_N) + \log(L)]$

Consider the nature of the solution with consumption tax treatment of earnings. In this model, the consumption tax scheme is characterized by equal tax rates on current and postponed consumption, $t_N = t_R$. It is apparent from (1) that consumption during work and retirement years are equal. The age of retirement is solved directly from (2) using this condition. Using an asterisk to denote an optimal solution in this case, we have:

(7) $C^*_N = C^*_R$     and
(8) $N^*/T = 1 / \log(L)$,     if $t_R = t_N$.

---

[17] See Hay Huggins Company, *Pension Plan Expense Study for the Pension Benefit Guaranty Corporation* (Washington, DC: Pension Benefit Guaranty Corporation, 1990).

[18] The solution parallels the analytics of progressive taxation on income. See Richard Ippolito, "Income Tax Policy and Lifetime Labor Supply," *Journal of Public Economics* (April 1985): 327–347.

[19] Substituting (5) into the budget constraint (4), yields
    $w / C_N(1 + t_N) = T / N$.
Finally, differentiating lifetime utility subject to the income constraint with respect to retirement age and using 5, we have
    $w / C_N(1 + t_N) = \log(L) + \log(C_R) - \log(C_N)$.
Combining these conditions yields condition 6.

Now consider the solution if an income tax is applied to retirement savings. In this case, the effective tax rate on retirement consumption is higher than the tax rate on current consumption: $t_R > t_N$. Under this condition, it is apparent from (4) that workers reduce retirement consumption and increase current consumption, so that $C_R < C_N$. This unequal consumption directly implies from (4) that retirement is postponed. Using the notation $i^o$ to denote the optimal value of $i$, we have:

(9)    $C^o_R < C^o_N$ ;

(10)   $N^o/T = 1 / [\log(C^o_R) - \log(C^o_N) + \log(L)] > N^*/T$,
       if $t_R > t_N$.

# PART THREE
# WHAT DO PEOPLE THINK IT ALL MEANS?

# XI. Pension Funding and Taxation: Achieving Benefit Security

EBRI/ERF POLICY FORUM

[Editor's note: *The following discussion is based on selected interactions and comments from the proceedings of the Employee Benefit Research Institute/Education and Research Fund's policy forum held on May 5, 1993 at the Grand Hotel, 2450 M Street, N.W., in Washington, D.C.*]

## Pension Taxation

**MR. SCHMITT**: I think this is a very important forum. The papers are very, very helpful in focusing attention on the tax expenditure number and showing that it does include public plans. I guess we all can agree now that the methodology behind that computation of tax expenditures is somewhat faulty and could be criticized.

I'm a neutral person in this debate. But I think that the critics are going to keep focusing on all tax filers to see what are they getting for that tax expenditure, and it really isn't too much if you look at the tables presented in the papers. It's certainly not a fat cat benefit either. It's going to middle income people, predominantly.

But if the government were to look at the tax expenditure, they would view it as a spending program. In other words, they look at what we are getting for that expenditure. So as long as you have pension coverage numbers that show that under $20,000, or even under $30,000, which might be the median income, workers are not really getting much benefit from the pension tax expenditure, it is always going to be a subject of criticism.

But at the same time, it's important to say, how do we measure that tax expenditure? To keep in mind that public plans are getting half of it, and really it requires a lot of sorting out, and I think today's program, notwithstanding health insurance as being a big, hot topic today, it's something that we've really got to get a grasp on.

We really have to forge ahead and come together with some kind of consensus of where we agree and where we disagree on this one because it is very critical to the future of private pensions.

**MR. SCHIEBER**: When we look at these tax expenditures and their distribution, we often overlook that one

of the reasons they tend to be so low at the lower income level is low marginal tax rates on low incomes. Multiply anything by a small number and it comes out being a small number. Maybe we can change the laws of arithmetic and resolve that problem.

There is also another issue that Gordon [Goodfellow] and I have been raising in the work that we've been doing. There is a broadly stated goal, on some people's part, that pensions really ought to be dipping down into the very bottom end of the income spectrum. If you looked at people who get to retirement with a lousy earnings record throughout their career, they are people who most years of their working lives had very low earnings. They tend to be people who have extremely erratic work habits, they do seasonal work, they have many jobs, typically with very low tenures over their careers.

An employer-based pension tends to be proportional. Even if you could capture somehow a portion of low-wage workers' earnings in each and every year and invest them in something that would give you a reasonable rate of return, it is going to provide a very small absolute benefit in retirement—an insignificant benefit.

If we need to enhance the income security of people at the very bottom end of the income spectrum, there has to be a more efficient way of doing that than investing more money in pensions or condemning pensions because of their failure to provide for low-income workers.

Now, having said that, it seems to me that pensions are a particularly efficient vehicle for delivering benefits to a broad cross-section of the middle income classes. It's regrettable that people at $20,000 aren't getting a tax expenditure. But I just don't think it's a practical possibility.

**MR. PAUL**: Syl [Schieber] made a point in his remarks that I think we ought to take into account as we consider this question, which is that you have to factor Social Security into this as well. The lower-paid worker gets a Social Security benefit that is disproportionately high in relation to his payroll tax, while the higher-paid worker who is getting the pension tax expenditure gets a disproportionately low Social Security benefit in relation to his payroll tax. Am I correct, Syl?

**MR. SCHIEBER**: That is correct.

MR. PAUL: So I think that as we talk about this question, we should factor that analysis into our argument and make sure that, in fact, if you want to do something for the lower paid worker, why don't we simply raise the Social Security minimum benefit and be done with it, and stop discussing this question as though the private pension system should do everything.

The second piece that I think we should look at is that the people who earn under $20,000 are disproportionately younger than the rest of the population. People who start out in jobs under $20,000 gravitate to higher paying jobs before their career is over.

MR. SCHIEBER: In some of the other work we've done, we have argued that you need to focus on the accrual of pensions over a life perspective as opposed to just doing a cross-sectional snapshot because of various phenomena that you mentioned.

MR. PIACENTINI: I think that one of the things that critics do is calculate the tax expenditure slightly differently from the numbers that are presented here. If you start from Table 3 in your paper, that's taken from Dallas' [Salisbury] work[1], you can calculate a per capita column, dividing the value of the tax expenditure by the number of tax returns in each group, with the understanding, of course, that many individuals in the lower income groups are getting no tax expenditure. And you end up with numbers that increase very sharply from $15 at the low end to more than $3,000 on the high end.

I think that the critics want to focus on that and say that fat cats do benefit disproportionately. Now, of course, none of that refutes a more overriding point that most of the aggregate benefit is concentrated in the middle income areas where you find most of the tax base.

I am certainly very persuaded, Syl [Schieber], by your point that we need to look at this over the life cycle because people do change income classes in many cases. And by your point that we need to look holistically, not just at the pension tax expenditure but at Social Security as well and, arguably, I think at the whole tax system.

I recall that in an earlier paper you showed that if you choose some ideal distribution of the tax burden, and then you superimpose pension tax expenditures over that, with just a small tweak in tax rates, you can get back to your ideal distribution of the tax burden.

___

[1] Dallas Salisbury, "Pension Tax Expenditures: Are They Worth the Cost?" *EBRI Issue Brief* no. 134 (February 1993): 14.

And I think, arguably, as I think you've pointed out before, that may be exactly what has happened in our democratic process.

MR. SCHIEBER: The problem I have with the fixation on an absolute number that a specific individual might get is that the number can be fairly large, and it tends to ignore what else is going on in the tax system.

I think one of the problems we have had with tax policy over the last 10 to 15 years is that we have more and more divested the interest of senior management in the pension system. We have taken their self-interest out of their pension plan.

And as we take their self-interest out of their pension plans, being the financially astute people that they are and having fiduciary responsibilities to a lot of other groups, it seems to me that there has to be a natural tendency to ratchet the system down.

I think our fixation on these big numbers, without consideration of other elements of the tax system, and without consideration of what happens when people lose interest in these endeavors has been wrong-headed policy.

MR. STEUERLE: A fundamental question with pension benefits would be to pick someone at a given income level to ask whether this particular tax preference for that person is the best way to assess the same amount of taxes on that person. To favor the pension benefit you've got to come to the conclusion that it's worthwhile to raise that person's tax rate on wages and other capital income in order to finance the pension benefit.

Should that pension tax policy increase savings more than a lower tax rate then you might come out in favor of it. Were the opposite of that true, you might not.

This comes up when people advocate, for instance, a consumption tax. They think a consumption tax results in the nontaxation of capital income, which is often asserted to be roughly equivalent to the value of pension tax preferences. But this raises an interesting question. Where would pensions, with their emphasis on encouraging saving for retirement, fit into that type of world?

I think sometimes the pension tax issue is really taken out of context. You really want to ask if for a particular person this particular tax benefit is the best way to spend the money? That is the basic efficiency issue that has to be addressed.

MR. SNYDER: The one point that the EBRI brief that just came out, and other studies have shown, is that much of the growth of the defined contribution plans is in what I call "second-tier plans" or "add-on plans."

I've often wondered why that didn't become a focus of those who want to go after the tax breaks that are afforded pensions. If you look at the pension as supposedly adding a second tier of income, especially for the higher wage workers who lose Social Security benefits as their income grows, it's not clear that the American taxpayer should support a third layer to that.

**MR. HINZ**: I've got a couple of observations. One, I was also struck with the size of the subsidy attributed to the federal plan, but it seems to me that focusing on that is a bit of a red herring in this debate. Assuming that federal employees have some effective or reasonably effective ability to discount their total compensation package back to its present value, this is more of an accounting phenomenon than anything that has to do with the subsidy.

If we take away the tax subsidy to federal plans, Uncle Sam is still on the hook over the long run and, presumably, would simply adjust pay or other benefits over the short term.

More defined contribution plans and more churning in the workforce are going to give workers a lot more choice in when to make their savings at those periods in their life cycle, in their career, when they have higher income.

Perhaps it shouldn't concern us quite as much that the tilt looks like it's in those high earning years because the old paradigm of the steady accrual of a benefit over a long career with a single employer may be getting awfully tired as we get into the next century.

**MR. SCHIEBER**: The point we were attempting to make on the federal and state and local plans is the opposite of the point you took, Richard [Hinz]. It's not that we need to focus necessarily on these numbers and say the federal plans are bad. It's that you should not be making private pension policy when you're adding these numbers into the equation. You ought to take them out.

If you want to look at the tax expenditure for private plans, you ought to be looking at the tax expenditure for private plans. It's only about half of the potato.

## Implications of Tax and Funding Rules on Plan Sponsorship (401(a)(17)[2] and 415 limits[3])

**MR. PIACENTINI**: I'd like to raise a question about what we call the "link" between the interest of executives and those of rank and file workers in company pension plans. Some have argued that that link has been weakened as the tax benefits available to the higher paid have eroded. And as such, the higher paid people who tend to be decision makers are now less inspired to set up plans at their companies.

My question has to do perhaps with the relationship between this issue and a question of whether pensions are sort of an add-on that management grants to workers, or the competing view, that they are deferred pay that workers would have received if the pension plan hadn't been in place?

I think if you subscribe to the former view, then certainly this erosion in shared interest would mean pension plans would be provided much less frequently.

On the other hand, if you subscribe to the latter view, that pensions are deferred pay, I think that even if the manager's ability to benefit personally from the tax preference were sharply curtailed, they might still want to offer a pension plan as simply the most tax effective way to compensate their employees in the labor market.

Now, of course, all of this is not relevant to proposals which, while purported to curtail benefits only for highly paid people, in fact can reach down into the lower paid ranks as the 415 limits can under certain circumstances and as the proposed scale-back of 401(a)(17) includable compensation would, as Jack documented in his background paper.[4]

**MR. WRAY:** I subscribe to the view that defined

---

[2] The sec. 401(a)(17) limit refers to the annual compensation limit that can be considered for calculating benefits and contributions under qualified retirement plans. At the time of the policy forum, participants were discussing a provision of President Clinton's proposed budget that would lower the limit from $235,840 in 1993 to $150,000 in 1994. The provision was enacted as part of the Omnibus Budget Reconciliation Act of 1993, which was signed into law on August 10, 1993.

[3] The Employee Retirement Security Act of 1974 imposed limits on the benefits and contributions that can be provided under qualified plans. For a defined benefit plan under Internal Revenue Code sec. 415, the annual employer-provided benefit for an employee cannot

exceed a stipulated dollar amount or, if lesser, 100 percent of the employee's average annual pay (within limits) for the three consecutive years of highest pay. The dollar limit was initially established at $75,000, to be adjusted annually to reflect increases in the consumer price index (CPI). By 1982, this limit had reached $136,425. However, under changes made by the Tax Equity and Fiscal Responsibility Act of 1982, this limit was rolled back to $90,000, beginning in 1983. It is adjusted for future increases in the CPI, reaching a level of $115,641 in 1993.

[4] See, Jack L. VanDerhei, "Implications of Lowering the Compensation Limit for Qualified Retirement Plans, *EBRI Notes*, Vol. 14, No. 5 (Washington, DC: Employee Benefit Research Institute, 1993).

contribution retirement benefits are deferred compensation. When you look at the system in this context, it's clear that its success rides on offering high-paid executives—especially the owners of small companies—incentives to offer plans to their workers, because they are the people who drive the system.

Operating a retirement plan takes time and costs money. If we continue to reduce the tax benefits of these plans to highly paid people, they're not going to bother with them. Instead, they'll distribute cash bonuses that employees can save in IRAs. I think our failure to connect executives to these plans is one of the reasons why we've seen a net decrease in the number of plans in the United States.

**MR. CONAWAY**: One thing that we do, obviously, is dilute the incentive for an employer to maintain the plan in the first place. There's a reduction in the tax benefit, in effect.

I think looking outside the qualified fund, there's another set of issues. Do we care, as a country, about the security of benefits on compensation above $150,000? And I think we have a situation, where you're going to have benefits replaced, in effect, on a non-qualified basis, on an unfunded basis.

That raises retirement policy issues. To the extent that we care about benefits at that level as a country in terms of encouraging those benefits and whether we care about the security of those benefits.

Companies aren't going to stop providing these benefits, they will just provide them on an unfunded basis. Maybe we don't care. I don't know what the answer is, but that's going to be the fact. I've talked with several people about this proposal, and they like it because it will reduce their required contributions.

There may be an opportunity here to argue that there could be a secured non-qualified vehicle to enable employers to replace these benefits on a non-tax-favored, but secured, basis.

**MR. HALPERIN**: It seems to me that with respect to the section 401(a)(17) limit, you have to distinguish between its effect on current benefits and the effect on future funding. The effect on future funding can be pretty silly.

I see no argument against being able to project increases in both the section 415 and 401(a)(17) limits in order to estimate what the limits will be at the time of retirement. The result of a failure to do so is to allow a defined contribution plan to be funded much faster than a defined benefit plan designed to provide comparable benefits. That seems to me to be clearly ridiculous.

As to the effect on current benefits, the issue is more complicated. Even if you conclude that adequate replacement at retirement of earnings in excess of $150,000 is not a concern of public policy, you still must consider the effect of a reduction in the section 401(a)(17) limit on an employer's willingness to continue to maintain a qualified plan.

Without a better feel for what will happen if tax benefits are reduced, it is impossible to determine whether it makes sense to reduce the section 401(a)(17) limit. It is possible, however, that much of the existence of qualified plans is a result of the fact that it enables employers to provide retirement benefits, which it desires to do for nontax reasons, while providing the employee with security against the financial failure of the employer still without current tax on the amount set aside. If it is these unique advantages rather than the tax-free build-up of investment earnings that drives the existence of qualified plans, it may mean that a change in the section 401(a)(17) will have a smaller effect.

**MR. GULOTTA**: I think that we're fooling ourselves if we believe that benefits in excess of 415 limits and benefits based on compensation in excess of 401(a)(17) limits are not going to be delivered to senior executives. They will be. I also think that we're going to see a greater interest in securing those benefits through non-qualified means.

We're creating a rift between the interests of the highly paid and the average plan participant. Increased security of executive benefits will lead to even less attention on funding benefits for the average worker.

I also agree with the point that it is silliness to use those limits for purposes of determining what is deductible and what is not deductible for funding purposes.

**MR. SCHIEBER**: It seems that the limits are high enough that benefits above them will be delivered. There has been a fairly long-term trend, with these limits gradually creeping downward. Certainly one of the CBO [Congressional Budget Office] options—not a recommendation—they always point out—is to go ahead and lower the 415 limits to the Social Security taxable maximums. I submit at some juncture the limit is going to get low enough that the people in the corporation are going to look at the magnitude of the liability, that they're not able to fund, and it is undoubtedly going to affect benefits.

We're not just talking about senior-level executives. There are some companies already where sizable numbers of average income people are being affected.

**MR. GLAZE:** The overall objective of the reconciliation bill, at this point, is to focus the tax hits, if you will, on those who are the most wealthy. That is, of course, the theme of this revenue raising provision.

But I think there are a lot of influential people in the pension area who understand that the way the pension system works is that if you take away the incentives for the more wealthy taxpayers in the pension system, then you tend to squeeze the middle income and the lower income guys out of their pension plans. You don't provide the incentive for the more wealthy people to sponsor plans. And that is a concern.

I think that the 401(a)(17) issue has some of that effect. I'm not sure how much. I have one pension expert who I talk to in my state of Arkansas who says that this proposal will shut down 40 percent of his small business pension plans. That seems rather dramatic to me. If that were the case nationwide, it would certainly be a disaster. But I'm not sure I know that would be the case at this point. I have no idea. It's hard to measure the impact that some of these provisions have on the middle and lower income people. It's very hard to educate members, taxpayers, and the voters about the impact.

## Private Pension Plan Funding

**MR. SNYDER:** Mike Gulotta mentioned varying contributions over the cycle of the corporation. That would conflict with our goals to enhance funding in underfunded plans. Would you exempt underfunded plans from cyclical contributions?

**MR. GULOTTA:** I would give them the opportunity to fund when they are in the part of their business cycle which enables them to do so and not limit the contributions to, say, 25 percent of compensation.

**MR. SNYDER:** If our goal is to have underfunded plans speed up their funding, then we'd like to see them contribute each year.

**MR. GULOTTA:** I don't think you want to create a straight jacket situation that requires funding in each and every year. If a sponsor is permitted to fund three years' worth of contributions in year one, then clearly participants are better off than if the contribution had to be spread over three years. If you give underfunded plans greater flexibility, the system is better off.

**MR. CONAWAY:** Perhaps it's incompatible with the voluntary tax-based retirement system to insist on high standards of achievement in terms of social goals. It

may be difficult to insist on legislation with no transition rules.

I'm not sure how where you're trying to toughen a funding rule with respect to an existing unfunded liability, you get from X to Y without a transition period.

**MR. GULOTTA:** I agree. From a practical point of view it would be difficult to implement legislation that does not address transitional issues, including significant unfunded liabilities that exist today.

We don't want to increase the cashflow burdens of corporations that are on a financial brink. I understand that fully. I think what Congress should move us toward is opposed to liberal transition rules.

**MR. HINZ:** Maybe we ought not to focus only on overfunded and underfunded defined benefit plans. I suspect there are a number of circumstances where we still see underfunded defined benefit plans that are not getting much funding, and fairly significant contributions to 401(k) plans and other types of arrangements from the same employer.

An alternative solution to some of these problems is to aggregate all of the plans in the firm and prevent significant cash going into 401(k) plans until defined benefit plans have been funded.

## Public Pension Plan Funding

**MR. MADDEN:** We deal with about 150 public funds. One, there are limits, in many cases, on what these state entities or public funds can invest in. In the past they were extremely restrictive and they still exist. For example, in the State of Mississippi there is a 35 percent limit on investing in equities. In one case we demonstrated to them that they could save $100 million over the next 10 years if they would just change the investment restriction, but the legislative block was so big that they opted not to. More commonly, investments in equities are limited to a maximum of 60 percent.

With one major pension fund in the Midwest, we saw assets grow dramatically through the '80s as they went from 20 percent to 40 percent in equities. I wrote a report that said the plan is extremely well funded and was told to take that out of the presentation because the press would get a hold of it and criticize the actuary because the same amount of money continued to be contributed through all of those times.

**MR. SNYDER:** GAO [General Accounting Office] recently looked at the funding levels of a fairly large sample of state and local plans covering about

70 percent of assets in the plan universe. We found that there is wide distribution in funding. About one-third of the plans are 100 percent funded, while another 60 percent are over 50 percent funded but not 100 percent funded. At the other extreme, under 10 percent of these plans are very poorly funded. Portland, Oregon has one fund for firemen and police that is 2 percent funded, and they understand that they have a pay-as-you-go system.

I'd just like to point out that Portland is a local jurisdiction that does not contribute to Social Security. They are avoiding the Social Security tax, and they are avoiding pension contributions. There is a free lunch somewhere for a short period of time, but there is going to be a catch-up.

There is also a group of seriously underfunded state plans in West Virginia, Oklahoma, and Maine. There are a number of local government plans, including the District of Columbia, that are not very well funded.

**MR. SCHMITT**: Public pension plans are entitlements, and future legislators can renege on the deals that were made by previous legislators. In the case of Oregon, maybe the benefits will have to be reduced because there isn't any funding.

I think it's important that when we criticize the funding of federal pensions or state and local pensions we recognize that these promises can be changed. It's going on right now with the federal plan in the budget reconciliation process where Congress might be cutting back on cost-of-living increases.

On one hand we might argue that the plans are generous, but on the other hand, you're at the whim of Congress or the state legislature to keep those benefits in the future. That's a big question mark now.

**MR. LINDEMAN**: Should we care about public pension plan funding? You have funding rules because you want to diversify the assets backing pension funds to minimize risk, especially from insolvency. You do it for greater recognition of the costs up front. Also, employees want it as a way of protecting their accrued benefit.

**MR. SNYDER**: I think it's good financial practice to pay your bills when you accrue them.

**MR. LINDEMAN**: I'm asking if you think there's a significant bankruptcy risk on the part of state and local governments? I'm also asking if you think the accounting rules are forcing the recognition of the future costs in any way?

**MR. SNYDER**: Well, the accounting rules are an

interesting conflict. The Accounting Standards Board is about to issue an exposure draft in which they're going to change the position held previously which was that state and local governments must report public plan financial data using a consistent actuarial method to value their liabilities. The revised exposure draft will let state and local governments use whatever method they want to use, which will add a lot of complexity to interpreting financial statements. To answer Dave's [Lindeman] first question, the risk of bankruptcy is there in Bridgeport, Connecticut and Kalkaska, Michigan.

**MR. FOY**: The District of Columbia, in the late 1960s hired a very large number of police officers because of riots and growth of the city. The pension fund was pay-as-you-go, so they didn't have to put any money aside for those police officers. Twenty years later comes, suddenly you've got policemen retiring at a rapid rate, and all of a sudden their pension cost, which is pay-as-you-go, is going through the roof. So when the governments don't prefund and don't pay for the benefits as they accrue, they're going to get burned later.

**MR. SCHMITT**: I agree that funding public plans makes sense from an accounting, budgetary, and intergenerational tax equity standpoint.

**MR. SCHIEBER**: The federal government, hopefully, is an employer in a relatively unique position. At some juncture, the accrued liabilities under these plans have to be paid.

The one thing that would be valuable in terms of funding the federal plans is that people would realize the true cost of the plans. Issues could then be debated in a timeframe when people could make adjustments. If we don't adjust these plans until people get to retirement and present us with the liabilities, then for all of the people who worked under the plans there is no time to save enough to make up for losses.

**MR. SCHMITT**: I think they're adjusting to the cost issue now. I think we are seeing the end of the rainbow with the generosity of federal plans.

**MS. LISTON**: I think, certainly, on a state plan basis those adjustments have been happening for a while because you've got different layers of benefits, you have people in tier 1, tier 2, tier 3. And a lot of the remaining unfunded liabilities in these plans is attributable to the tier 1 employees, and it is being funded. It's not being necessarily added to at the same rate that it was. So the problems are being recognized and dealt with in many cases.

**MS. KORCZYK**: I think it is very important to fund state and local government plans for reasons that are qualitatively different from federal plans. State and local tax bases are mobile, and the federal tax base essentially isn't very mobile. So you're getting at not only an intergenerational mismatch between who is paying and who is benefiting from the government spending, but you're also going to have some intragenerational mismatches. States don't have a way of going after you if you lived in Minnesota in 1963 and now you live in California. There's really no way of finding you to fund the liability based on the services you received in 1963.

Another important reason for funding the state and local plans is the lack of the legal safeguards that ERISA imposes on private plans. The benefits aren't inherently as secure.

**MS. RAPPAPORT**: I support funding for all the reasons stated, and I think there is an additional issue: the demographics of the population. At exactly the same time that all of these benefits are going to have to be paid out, even if the groups don't go bankrupt, there's going to be an increased demand for all sorts of public services because of the population aging, and that's going to be extremely difficult.

**MR. SALISBURY**: The federal government could extend funding requirements to public plans. Back when *National League of Cities v. Usery* came down in the LEAA [Law Enforcement Assistance Association] cases, there was a strong argument that it was not possible for "ERISA-fication" of public plans. There have been Supreme Court cases since then that go in the opposite direction. It might be politically infeasible, but it is not legally infeasible. Whether or not federal, state, and local plans should be pre-funded increasingly has to rest on the issues of intergenerational transfers and long-term liabilities.

If Ross Perot really wants to focus on "the true federal deficit," in terms of what has been committed to people that taxpayers will have to pay, he should not stop with the outstanding bonds of the federal government. He should add to that the unfunded liability of Medicare. He should add the unfunded liability of Social Security. He should add the unfunded liability of military and federal pensions. By rough estimates, he'd get to $15 trillion before he even moves to state and local governments and other entitlements programs.

That's a lot of promises out there that taxpayers will have to pay for or promises will have to be broken. Benefit cutback rules that do apply to private sector plans do not currently apply to state and local plans or to military and civil service retirement plans.

Things that can't be done in a Draconian way by private employers to strip away instantaneously past benefit promises for prior service, can be stripped away very, very quickly in the public sector.

Benefit security is the strongest reason that plan participants and beneficiaries should want public pension promises advance funded.

**MR. SNYDER**: The overriding theme is benefit security, the issue of ERISA-fying public sector plans is something that concerns state and local governments. I might add that ERISA protections have appeal when you look at vesting provisions and the other protections that private sector workers have for those tax breaks. I emphasize that it's a disproportionately low level of protection that many public sector workers have. However, we must ask, "What does the taxpayer think about pre-funding pensions?" There was a recent election in Newfoundland where the candidate ran on the platform of cutting $70 million out of the pension plan. That is, using contributions to balance the budget. He won overwhelmingly and is taking that as a mandate—cut pension promises.

## Economically Targeted Investments

**MR. GULOTTA**: In New York, Governor Cuomo is appealing the court decision that the Controller has the responsibility for selecting the funding method. The obvious intent is to go to a lesser cost funding method.

Also, there seems to be a trend toward what are called "ETIs" or economically targeted investments. What's the impact of ETIs on the funded status of the plans?

**MS. LISTON**: We have not been asked to analyze economically targeted investments. One plan is doing so with a very small portion of their fund and they realize that it's almost the same as venture capital. They have made the decision that they want to invest a certain portion of the fund in economically targeted investments. They've decided that they're willing to risk a lower rate of return on that for the social good. They are very aware of what they're doing.

**MR. GRANT**: If an ETI has a lower rate of income return on an investment, they're not being done properly. There's a good body of evidence that indicates that ETIs are competitive. In many cases, ETIs return a higher rate of return than similar assets in the class. As long as they have a competitive return, they're not having any negative impact on funding and could be positive.

MR. MADDEN: We've been asked by a number of our public funds what we think about ETIs. We look at it on a pay now or pay later basis. You can increase local taxes to pay for infrastructure, or you can take it out of the pension fund and possibly increase taxes later to make up the benefit.

MR. HEALEY: I have two comments on ETIs. First, I spend about half of my time with public pension funds, and I would underscore that we may be understating the amount of pressure on all of the large public pension funds for economically targeted investments. The funds inherently operate in a very political environment. Governors and treasurers of states get reelected because voters like what they do. Economically targeted investments get page one news. The pressure, I submit, is astonishing, and it's going to increase.

Second, the better question is: "Whose money is it really?" Is it the money of the pensioners who are going to get it, or is it the money of the taxpayers who provided it initially?

Massachusetts, Wisconsin, Colorado, and others, have a decade-long history of very attractive returns on economically targeted investments. But you have Kansas and Oregon and probably a number of others who have records of hundreds of millions of dollars lost in a 12-month period from poorly conceived or fraudulently conceived economically targeted investments.

MR. SCHIEBER: About three or four years ago I was in China for a pension conference. In the municipal sector, they're starting to set up a centralized Social Security program and many of the employers want to establish pension programs. One of the problems they have with their pensions is that all of the deferred monies are invested in socially desirable investments, and they are getting abnormally low rates of return. They tried to figure out how they could get completely out of the social investing scheme.

MR. GRANT: It argues for a diversification of the fund. Neither is the right solution. All or nothing. Neither is the right solution.

MR. GLAZE: The issue is whether this is a voluntary or involuntary requirement to make funds invest their dollars in infrastructure. My sense is that we're not ready to push forward with legislation that would require pension funds to have a certain percentage of their dollars invested in public infrastructure. I can't see that today we would make pension funds spend their money a certain way. I think that it is incumbent,

at this point, for Congress and the administration to look at ways to make those types of investments attractive. And, hopefully, that would be the course that we would be set upon at this point.

MR. KASS: I am struck by the prospect of an increasing tension between fiduciary standards and conditions on the continued availability of tax preferences.

To open up the investment process more to infrastructure investments where the benefits socially are not just incidental but potentially primary does not appear to be an immediate risk to the system. However, I do think that the pressure will increase, or the tension will increase, between fiduciary standards, and the desire of lawmakers to see this very large pool of capital deployed in ways that are viewed as benefiting the economy generally, and perhaps benefiting the economy in ways that investments in publicly traded securities don't.

I think a potential source of concern is that the continued availability of the tax benefits favoring pension plans will somehow be connected to the relaxation of what have been historic standards of prudence. I think that's a risk that we need to pay close attention to over the next decade.

## Saving for Retirement

MR. IPPOLITO: There are two kinds of people in this life: high discounters and low discounters. High discounters don't care about the future and don't save. Low discounters care about the future and tend to save. If high discounters don't save, low discounters know that they're going to have to finance their own retirement consumption *and* contribute to support the consumption of the high discounters as well.

Karen Ferguson [executive director of the Pension Rights Center] is concerned that the high discounters aren't going to have enough income when they get older. She wants to find a way to get them more income.

I am less concerned about high discounters. I think they should be faced with the consequences of their own proclivity to avoid savings. Though I am disproportionately concerned with low discounters, I come to the same conclusion as Karen: we need to be concerned about the trend toward defined contribution plans. First, high discounters will evade savings in 401(k) plans. Second, they will spend their pension monies long before they grow old.

The problem with the defined contribution/401(k) plans is that it is very easy to opt out or lump out. People who change jobs tend to take the lump sum; and only between 12 percent and 25 percent of the people who take a pre-retirement lump sum avail themselves of the opportunity to roll it over into an IRA to evade the excise tax on the distribution.

Furthermore, even if high discounters stay in the firm until age 58 or 62, I think it's pretty apparent to most of us that a high discounter isn't going to sit down and say, "Oh, I think I'm just going to arrange my monies so I'll have an annuity for life." I think it's more likely that they're going to spend the money while they're young-old, as Emily Andrews likes to talk, and have none left when they're old-old.

I yearn for a world in which we could let everyone have their free choice, and if everyone had to face the consequences of their apathy, it's clearly the optimal solution. But we live in a world in which the savers face the consequences of spenders' rash behavior.

It's nice to be cavalier about the idea that we're losing pension coverage and having more people covered by plans that are going to provide lump sums rather than annuities. But I think that the low discounters are going to have face the consequences in the long run of less retirement income being delivered by the pension system. It means that there's going to be more pressure on the public systems at the very point at which we're expecting the Social Security system to already be under significant financial pressure.

**MR. PIACENTINI**: I have one comment and one question for Dick [Ippolito]. First, I wonder whether there is some kind of meaningful relationship between income levels and behavior. That is, in terms of affordability, if you can't afford to save for your retirement, that might make you behave like Dick's "high discounter." However, contrary to Dick's characterization, it's not so much that you don't want to save for your retirement, but it's that you find it difficult.

Second, Dick, what, if any, effect on this analysis would you presume from access to credit markets? If you have a defined benefit pension that doesn't offer you a lump sum, and you're a "high discounter," you may reach retirement with more savings than you would have chosen on your own. But if you have access to credit markets, you could borrow and end up there with more debt somewhere else. So you're in the same net position that you would have been if your participation in the pension plan had been voluntary.

**MR. IPPOLITO**: Well, I think we don't have to worry about the latter point because high discounters, by definition, don't save, and thus have no collateral to secure borrowing. In a perfect world, a high discounter would never work for pension firms. In reality, people

choose their jobs for a lot of reasons, and thus high discounters may end up in a pension job. This is not an optimal outcome because they'd prefer to have the cash. But low discounters benefit because fewer high discounters will require income assistance when old.

In regard to the former point, I think the individual discount rate would have to be correlated positively with income level and wealth. If you have a high discount rate, you're not going to want to invest in either physical or human capital. You're not going to go to school or engage in training, et cetera. As a consequence, high discounters are much more likely to have low income.

For some people this rationale doesn't work because, for example, their parents might force them to go to school. So even though they have a high discount rate, they end up with a college education and earn a little bit more. I think some of the people in this room might have some friends who fall into that category. They earn a fair amount of money, but they never keep it. The United States is unique in the world for having no savings at low income levels. In other countries they have savings at all income levels. People who study savings behavior across the world attribute the zero savings to the fact that all our social programs are means-tested in the United States. These rules discourage people at low income levels from accumulating wealth. Elsewhere in the world, you have no choice but to save something. Otherwise, how are you going to live when you get old?

**MR. WRAY**: The data you quoted does not include people who chose to leave their money in their employer's plan, people who roll their money over into other qualified plans, or people who use their lump-sum distributions in ways that enhance their future security, such as paying down debt or purchasing a primary residence. According to a Gallup study commissioned by the Profit Sharing Research Foundation, 61 percent of people who receive lump sums save their money in one way or another. Approximately 30 percent roll their money over into IRAs.

401(k) plans are one of the most efficient ways for individuals to save because they can invest their money in professionally managed portfolios. For some people, unmatched 401(k) plans alone may not be enough to ensure retirement security, but they do offer a good way to save for the future.

**MR. SALISBURY**: EBRI just got some preliminary tabulations from the Internal Revenue Service. The 1990 income tax returns reported $126 billion as lump-sum distributions; $76 billion of that was rolled over.

About 25 percent of all individuals who got a

lump-sum distribution chose to roll over the lump-sum distribution; 75 percent chose not to roll it over, accounting for about $50 billion that was taken directly into income. There are some low discounters out there.

**MR. WRAY**: The issue really is how much leakage the system can tolerate. It's clear that most lump-sum distributions are maintained in tax-deferred status, and, as I said earlier, a lot of people leave their money in their employer's plan or roll it over into other qualified plans. Perhaps more important is data from a new Gallup study commissioned by John Hancock that shows that people won't contribute to 401(k) plans if they can't have access to their money before they retire, even though most don't take advantage of that access.

**MR. GOODFELLOW**: I'd just like to take issue with the statement that the returns to the 401(k) plans are so good because the money is professionally managed. If people manage their own money, they tend to put it in low-risk investments.

The Wyatt Company has a survey in which 50 percent of the money is in GICs [guaranteed investment contracts]. There's a concern, at least in the benefits community, that people are going to have less at the end than they would if that money were put in DB [defined benefit] plans.

**MR. WRAY**: Professionally managed doesn't mean wisely allocated. 401(k) plans allow people to invest more efficiently than they can on their own because they benefit from the professionally managed aggegration of money. For example, GICs offer much better returns than bank savings accounts.

**MR. GOODFELLOW**: If the alternative is a passbook savings account and a 401(k) plan, you're correct. But if the difference is between a 401(k) plan and the DB plan, DB plans will do better.

**MR. CONAWAY**: Dick [Ippolito], in the current situation the availability to save for an individual is contingent largely on the type of plan and the level of benefit that the employers set up. The sense I was getting from your comments was that you might not look adversely at a situation where the employer is, in effect, taken out of the arrangements and the tax-favored vehicles are available at the individual level.

**MR. IPPOLITO**: The employer linkage doesn't make a lot of sense, particularly when you're talking 401(k) plans. You're just running through an agent to get access to a savings vehicle that, presumably, you could

have on your own directly with the mutual fund, for example.

The problem with all of the voluntary systems is that there is an externality. With more flexibility in pensions, we get more freedom in the short run. Low discounters get a chance to save more, and in the short run are better off. But in the long run, we have to realize that there is an increasing portion of the population that is going to end up with no savings, which implies a higher burden for low discounters in the long run.

**MS. KORCZYK**: We know that pension coverage is closely correlated with income and real income growth virtually evaporated during the 1980s. As a result, the pension system has stagnated. And so long as society keeps tinkering with the pension system to improve coverage, we're pushing on a string.

We need to look at the whole tax system together. We need to restart economic growth before the pension system is going to get back in shape.

**MS. ANDREWS**: Dividing the world into savers and spenders oversimplifies the matter. We need to focus on the specific uses of funds in particular situations. For example, it is an oversimplification to ignore the life-cycle aspects of saving and investment. In particular, younger persons who do not roll over their lump-sum distributions still may be savers. Incentives to save differ at different ages. Younger persons who are savers may use their lump-sum distributions to pay for a down payment on a home or to finance further investment in education.

Such possibilities point to the need for a continuing source of empirical evidence with which to analyze the actual uses of lump-sum distributions. Current Population Survey benefit supplements provide such evidence. These data tell us how funds are used upon distribution and the age at which the distribution occurred. We must carefully study the investment patterns of different age groups before we casually divide the population into savers and spenders.

**MR. IPPOLITO**: The existence of dichotomous savings behavior, while oversimplified in a model with low and high discounters, should provide some motivation to the staffers on the Hill who have perpetrated a lot of these changes in the law that have discouraged defined benefit plans in the U.S. I think the motivation has been that they're trying to keep the higher income people from getting too many of the benefits of pensions. Ironically, people at the low income levels who ordinarily wouldn't be doing much saving are going to end up with less retirement income in the long run. Low discounters are probably going to still have a fair amount of income when they're old regardless of the laws enacted by Congress. That's the point.

**MR. LINDEMAN**: I suggest that we don't forget that individuals can dissave by borrowing against their home or otherwise. To what extent should we also constrain that behavior—borrowing—to achieve some greater amount of self-protection from spenders? To what extent does it make sense, either in that context or under current law, to force lump sums to be annuitized? And doesn't that just lead to greater tax arbritrage given the deductibility of home equity loans?

**MR. KASS**: Concerning the investment behavior of participants in defined contribution plans, I think it is likely to continue to be the case, for a variety of reasons, that defined contribution plan participants will exhibit different investment behaviors than agents of defined benefit plans do, whatever their level of sophistication. Partly it's a function of the fact that the defined benefit plan exists in perpetuity and can adopt a consistent investment posture through time that an aging participant in a defined contribution plan can't. And, obviously, that participant will be exhibiting a higher liquidity preference, among other conservative tendencies, as that participant ages, so that the realizable investment returns over a working lifetime will never, in the best of circumstances, approach those that at least are projected in defined benefit plans.

Therefore, we face the inescapable prospect of replacement ratios declining even if contribution rates in defined contribution plans approximate those that are being experienced in defined benefit plans, which have higher expected rates of return. This presents an enormous dilemma. On the one hand, workforce mobility and other issues clearly favor portability of pension benefits. The only scheme that can feasibly provide portable pension benefits is a defined contribution scheme. For that reason, among others, these plans are likely to grow in popularity.

On the other hand, defined contribution plans are likely to erode through time the level of wealth that individuals carry into retirement. You can be the lowest discounter in the world and find yourself poorer than you would have been in the traditional defined benefit

programs. They had the effect of providing secure, stable, and relatively high levels of retirement income for rank and file workers, high discounters and low discounters included.

**MR. PAINE**: There's some way out of this. If you think of a typical defined benefit system, it has invested in long-term securities, usually with a significant percentage of equities. When we get to that moment when someone retires, nothing happens. Instead, the funds continue to be invested for the long term, and we pay the benefit out. I see the dilemma when you say, "Well, if we do this on a defined contribution basis, doesn't this mean that we don't have a way to keep investing" — at least if the individual has any responsibility over it. And besides which, when he gets to old age, then the risk of making the short-term wrong decision gets to ruin part or all of what was the good, long-term accrual period. I wonder if we haven't missed a bet by not looking at the annuity market as a way to solve this problem.

I've seen some of these systems of variable payment. For example, let's assume someone invested in a portfolio during active employment which was one of these long-term investment systems. Let's further assume that there was an annuity portfolio that matched it. Let's assume that the unit price to buy this annuity would go up and down with the value of that portfolio.

One person would get out of his defined contribution plan when the values were high and so was the annuity price. Someone else would go out when the values were low, but so would be the annuity price. If we can have a unit price system and two equal portfolios, we can extend to the defined contribution saver the same idea of a defined benefit plan that, in effect, uses the same investment pre- and post-retirement.

So I think there are ways to do it, but we don't seem to be investigating those. And with the increasing emphasis on defined contribution plans, which we've all acknowledged is occurring, I think we need to pay more attention to that. For without some kind of a lifetime income guarantee with some mortality underwriting taking place, then I'm not sure the private pension systems are doing what this government tax support is asking for it to do.

# Appendix A: PBGC Reform Proposed in Retirement Protection Act of 1993

BY CELIA SILVERMAN, PAUL YAKOBOSKI, AND KATHY STOKES MURRAY

## Introduction

In response to concern regarding the Pension Benefit Guaranty Corporation's (PBGC) long-term financial health, Secretary of Labor Robert Reich appointed last March an interagency task force to examine the issue and recommend any necessary changes. The task force included representatives from the National Economic Council, the Office of Management and Budget, and the Departments of Treasury, Commerce, and Labor, as well as PBGC. The task force's recommendations are contained in the Clinton administration's Retirement Protection Act of 1993, which was submitted to Congress on October 26.

PBGC was created under the Employee Retirement Income Security Act of 1974 (ERISA) to strengthen retirement security by guaranteeing some benefits for employer-sponsored defined benefit pension plan participants. Although PBGC has always operated with a net deficit, recent large terminations have increased the agency's net deficit to $2.7 billion for 1992. PBGC acknowledges that it is not in any immediate danger of financial failure, as it has positive cash flow. However, the proposals in the Retirement Protection Act are designed to deal with its problems while they are still manageable.[1] They address four main areas: funding, premiums, compliance, and participant protection.

## Funding

ERISA required all pension plans subject to its minimum funding requirements to establish a "funding standard account" that provides a comparison between actual contributions and those required under the minimum funding requirements. The main purpose of the funding standard account is to provide some flexibility in funding by allowing contributions greater than the required minimum, accumulated with interest, to reduce the minimum contributions required in future years. Although the 1974 rules were designed to reduce underfunding, many plans continued to have plan liabilities in excess of plan assets. This often occurred because the plans were able to amortize new liabilities, created by plan amendments, over a period of 30 years.

The Omnibus Budget Reconciliation Act of 1987 (OBRA '87) established additional minimum funding requirements for plans covering more than 100 participants that are not at least 100 percent funded for current liabilities. In general, the current liability is the plan's liability determined as if the plan were to terminate today. A plan's unfunded current liability is calculated by subtracting the actuarial value of assets, less the credit balance in the funding standard account, from the current liability. Plans that have an unfunded current liability based on this calculation must pay an additional minimum funding contribution called the deficit reduction contribution.

Although the OBRA '87 modifications undoubtedly increased the minimum funding requirements for many underfunded plans, there were several provisions that allowed some underfunded plans to (legally) circumvent the law's objective. The new proposal focuses on improving underfunded defined benefit plans' funding status by attempting to change these provisions, accelerating funding for underfunded plans, and removing some impediments to provide additional funding.

First, the new proposal would strengthen the deficit reduction contribution by accelerating funding of certain liabilities (referred to as "new" liabilities) accrued after the effective date of OBRA '87. The new liability is funded at a rate of 30 percent per year for plans with a funding ratio (assets divided by current liabilities) less than or equal to 35 percent. For every percentage point by which the funding ratio exceeds 35 percent, the percentage of unfunded new liability recognized declines by 0.25 percent. The proposal would increase the current 35 percent threshold to 60 percent.

Current law allows, but does not require, employers to recognize benefit increases negotiated in collective bargaining immediately for funding purposes. The proposal would require that negotiated benefit increases be treated as if they were benefit increases amended to the plan at the time of the collective

---

[1] For a comprehensive discussion of the issues concerning the Pension Benefit Guaranty Corporation's financial solvency, see Paul Yakoboski, Celia Silverman, and Jack VanDerhei, *EBRI Issue Brief* no. 126, "PBGC Solvency: Balancing Social and Casualty Insurance Perspectives" (Employee Benefit Research Institute, May 1992).

bargaining agreement.

The proposal also attempts to correct an aspect of the OBRA '87 minimum funding requirements that in many cases minimized the impact of the deficit reduction contribution. Under the OBRA '87 calculations, a plan's gains are counted twice: once in the value of the assets used to calculate the plan's underfunded position when determining the deficit reduction contribution and again as an amortization credit used to reduce the minimum required contribution under the funding standard account. The proposal attempts to correct this problem for underfunded plans by eliminating the double counting of gains.

Current law allows plan sponsors to select interest rate assumptions within a corridor of 90 percent to 110 percent of the four-year weighted average of interest rates on 30-year Treasury securities for the purposes of calculating current liability. Plan sponsors are also able to choose their own mortality tables. This flexibility in assumptions allows plan sponsors to reduce current liability by maximizing interest rate assumptions (within the corridor) and choosing a set of mortality rate assumptions that will result in a reduced value of plan liabilities. The proposal would reduce the upper bound of the interest rate corridor to 100 percent of the weighted average and mandate the use of a single specified mortality table.

Since the implementation of the OBRA '87 modifications, it has been observed that, even with the additional funding required by the deficit reduction contribution, plans with a heavy concentration of retirees relative to the number of active participants may find themselves in a position where benefit payments exceed the minimum required contributions to the plan. The proposal provides for a plan solvency rule that would require payment of quarterly contributions by underfunded plans with insufficient cash and marketable securities to pay for three years' worth of pension distributions to bring plan assets up to this sufficient level. The disbursements include administrative expenses, benefit payments, and a portion of lump-sum distributions and annuity purchases and are based on the lesser of disbursements made during the previous 36 months or three times the distributions made during the last 12 months. The proportion of lump-sum distributions and annuity purchases that will be included in this calculation would be tied to the funding ratio, decreasing proportionately as the funding ratio increases. Plans that are required to make the plan solvency contribution but do not do so would be prohibited from paying plan participants any benefits that are greater than what they would receive from a straight life annuity until the contributions are made. Plans making benefit payments exceeding this limit would be

subject to a penalty.

The proposal also includes several provisions intended to remove impediments to funding by eliminating the excise tax on some nondeductible contributions and repealing quarterly contributions for fully funded plans.

All funding proposals would be effective for plan years beginning in 1995 and would include benefit increases negotiated in 1993 and 1994. Transition rules would also be provided for up to a seven-year period. The transition rule would vary according to the plan's funding ratio—generally limiting the required contribution to an amount that would increase the plan's funding ratio by three percentage points annually for plans with a funding ratio of 75 percent or less and 2 percent for plans with a funding ratio of 85 percent or greater. Plans with a funding ratio between 75 percent and 85 percent would be required to contribute an amount that would increase the funding level by between 2 percent and 3 percent.

## Premium Reforms

Premiums consist of a flat rate charge of $19 per participant and a variable rate charge for underfunded plans of $9 per $1,000 of unfunded vested benefits. The variable rate payment is capped at $53 per participant. The proposal would eliminate this cap over a three-year phase-in period. Premium payments would thus rise for some underfunded plans. The goal of this change is to provide underfunded plans with an increased incentive to reduce their underfunding while allowing them time to adjust to the change.

## Compliance Reforms

The proposal would give PBGC the means, other than plan termination, to protect the funding of pension benefits from potentially threatening corporate transactions. Toward this end, the proposal would enable PBGC to obtain a court order requiring that departing controlled group members[2] remain responsible for pension underfunding for a limited time or post security for part of the liabilities; require plans underfunded by more than $50 million to provide advance notice of transactions that may negatively impact pensions; require employers, in addition to plan administrators, to inform PBGC of "reportable" events such as

---

[2] The employer's controlled group consists of the employer's parent corporation and any corporations of which the parent owns at least 80 percent.

bankruptcy; and require increased financial reporting on underfunded plans and their sponsors and their controlled group members if underfunding exceeds $50 million or there is an outstanding lien for missed contributions or an outstanding funding waiver of more than $1 million.

In addition, the proposal would grant ongoing plans a claim for pension underfunding against liquidating sponsors or controlled group members; prohibit benefit increases in underfunded plans during bankruptcy; allow PBGC to enforce minimum funding requirements when missed contributions exceed $1 million; and enable PBGC to immediately file liens against an employer's assets on behalf of a plan for the full amount of missed contributions if the employer fails to make a contribution of more than $1 million.

Finally, the proposal would require companies undergoing bankruptcy reorganization to continue making pension contributions as an administrative priority expense and grant PBGC membership on creditors' committees.

## Disclosure to Participants

Currently, employers must provide plan participants with a summary annual report and a summary plan description, which are often too complex and not understood by participants. The proposal would require plan administrators of certain underfunded plans to notify participants of the plans' funding status and the degree of guaranty provided by PBGC. The information would be written in a format prescribed by PBGC with the intent of being comprehensible to the average plan participant. The proposal would also require employers to provide assets to PBGC to fund missing participants' benefits on termination of fully funded plans. PBGC would pay the benefit to the participants should they be located or contact PBGC.

## Other Proposals

The proposal includes miscellaneous other changes that would provide more flexible remedies for PBGC to address noncompliance in standard termination procedures; change the guarantee of benefits of substantial owners; modify the maximum guarantee of disability benefits; clarify the definition of contributing sponsor; repeal the average recovery ratio (payment of unfunded nonguaranteed benefits would be based on actual recoveries in all size plans); and extend the first distress test of ERISA sec. 4041(c)(2)(B) to include liquidation under federal laws similar to Title 11.

## Funding for Retirement Protection Act

The proposal is intended to be revenue neutral and would be funded by the increase in premiums; the exemption of quarterly contributions for fully funded plans; the elimination of cross testing age-weighted profit-sharing plans based on benefits; and the rounding down of cost-of-living adjustments for limits on defined benefit levels that may be funded on a tax-deferred basis, limits on contributions to defined contribution plans, and limits on employee elective deferrals under a sec. 401(k) plan. The cost-of-living adjustments would be rounded down in specific increments, with subsequent upward adjustments made by the same increment.

## Legislative Outlook

The administration sent the legislative language for its PBGC reform proposal to Congress on October 26. Reps. William Ford (D-MI) and Dan Rostenkowski (D-IL) introduced the bill for the administration on October 28. H.R. 3396 was referred to the Education and Labor and the Ways and Means Committees of the House. Despite strong objections from some plan sponsors, the bill retains language that would effectively eliminate age-weighted profit sharing plans. The Treasury Department, Labor Department, and the Internal Revenue Service reportedly stand firm in their united opposition to age-weighted profit sharing plans. Certain key members of Congress support these plans and are likely to strongly object to their inclusion in the legislation. Other members of Congress have objected to the removal of the cap on the variable rate premium as too risky for the financial stability of firms with severely underfunded plans. Thus, the bill is likely to be heavily debated in Congress.

With regard to timing, Rep. Dan Rostenkowski (D-IL), chairman of the House Ways and Means Committee, and Sen. Bill Bradley (D-NJ), a member of the Senate Finance Committee, have both announced their intention to turn to pension reform as the next major issue for their respective committees once legislative action on the North American Free Trade Agreement (NAFTA) and health care reform is completed. Given the contentiousness of both NAFTA and health care reform, action on PBGC reform legislation is not likely until 1994 at the earliest. Furthermore, PBGC legislation raises jurisdictional disputes between the tax and labor committees, which is likely to further delay action. In the meanwhile, should there be a major termination, a clear financial reason for reform will arise, along with publicity to encourage action. Barring large terminations during 1994, and assuming the PBGC's deficit continues to decline with continued low interest rates, action could well be pushed into 1995 as PBGC's balance sheet improves.

# Appendix B: Policy Forum Participants

**Moderator**

William S. Custer
Employee Benefit Research Institute

**Authors and Speakers**

Harry Conaway
William M. Mercer, Inc.

David T. Foy
Milliman & Robertson

Gordon Goodfellow
The Wyatt Company

Steve Glaze
Office of Senator David Pryor

Michael J. Gulotta
Actuarial Sciences Associates, Inc.

Richard L. Hubbard
Arnold & Porter

Richard Ippolito
Pension Benefit Guaranty Corporation

Adrien R. LaBombarde
Milliman & Robertson, Inc.

Fiona E. Liston
Milliman & Robertson, Inc.

Thomas Paine
EBRI Fellow

Dallas Salisbury
Employee Benefit Research Institute

Sylvester J. Schieber
The Wyatt Company

Celia Silverman
Employee Benefit Research Institute

Jack VanDerhei
EBRI Fellow, Temple University

Paul Yakoboski
Employee Benefit Research Institute

**Discussants**

David Gustafson
Pension Benefit Guaranty Corporation

Thomas J. Healey
Goldman Sachs & Company

Richard Hinz
U.S. Department of Labor

Dennis Kass
J.P. Morgan Investment Management

Ray Schmitt
Congressional Research Service

Donald C. Snyder
U.S. General Accounting Office

**Participants**

Nancy Altman
Consultant

Keith Ambachtsheer
Keith Ambachtsheer & Associates, Inc.

Mitchell Anderman
Sun Company, Inc.

Joe Anderson
Capital Research Associates

W. Michael Andrew
Social Security Administration

Emily Andrews
Mathematica Policy Research, Inc.

Shinji Asonuma
Japanese Ministry of Health & Welfare

Harsh Bansal
United Technologies Corporation

Paul S. Berger
Arnold & Porter

Chris Bowlin
National Association of Manufacturers

Doug Burnette
American Society of Pension Actuaries

David Certner
American Association of Retired Persons

Robert Clark
North Carolina State University

Carolyn Cridler-Smith
Pennsylvania Blue Shield

Marianne Duluca
Pacific Telesis Group

John N. Feldtmose
A. Foster Higgins, Inc.

Karen Ferguson
Pension Rights Center

Jay Foreman
United Food and Commercial Workers Int'l Union

Robert Friedland
National Academy of Social Insurance

George A. Fromme
AT&T

Michael Gersie
The Principal Financial Group

Richard Grant
AFL-CIO

Janice Gregory
The ERISA Industry Committee

Daniel Halperin
Harvard Law School

Donald Harrington
AT&T

Frederick D. Hunt
Society of Professional Benefit Administrators

Kathy Ireland
Investment Company Institute

Melissa Kahn
American Council of Life Insurance

Michael Kahn
National Education Association

James A. Kaitz
Financial Executives Institute

James Klein
American Association of Private Pension and Welfare
Plans

Sophie M. Korczyk
Analytical Services

Steve Kraus
American Council of Life Insurance

Shawn Lapenae
Merrill Lynch

Robert Leonard
NYNEX Corporation

William Link
The Prudential Insurance Company of America

William B. Madden
SEI Company

John Markson
Mobil Oil Corporation

Allan C. Martin
Bankers Trust Company

Juanita Mast-Faeth
Bristol-Myers Squibb Company

John J. McCormack
TIAA-CREF

James Merrill
General Motors Investment Management Corp.

Curtis Mikkelsen
Morgan Guaranty Trust Company

Ed Miner
Kemper Financial Services, Inc.

Jim Moberg
Pacific Telesis Group

Joyce Morrissey
Quantum Chemical Corporation

David Nearpass
Buck Consultants, Inc.

Peter Neuwirth
Godwins, Inc.

J.W. O'Toole
Phillips Petroleum Company

Robert D. Paul
The Segal Company

Joseph Piacentini
Aetna Life and Casualty

Anna Rappaport
William M. Mercer, Inc.

Marcia Richards
Towers Perrin

Melvyn Rodrigues
Atlantic Richfield Company

Ellin Rosenthal
Hewitt Associates

Stan Ross
Arnold & Porter

Paula Ryan
John Hancock

Peter Schmidt
Arnold & Porter

Robert Sheridan
Fidelity Investments

David Skovron
Kwasha Lipton

Lisa Sprague
U.S. Chamber of Commerce

Richard Tomlinson
The Upjohn Company

Donald Torey
Chase Manhattan Bank

John Turner
U.S. Department of Labor

Thomas Vasquez
KPMG Peat Marwick

Barry Voichick
IBM Corporation

Ronald Walker
William M. Mercer, Inc.

Howard Weizman
The Wyatt Company

Thomas E. Wood
J.L. Kellogg Graduate School of Management

David Wray
Profit Sharing Council of America

**Employee Benefit Research Institute Staff**

Althea Alexander
Michael Anzick
Sarah Boyce
Sabrina Cabada
Patsy D'Amelio
Deborah Holmes
Jeanette Hull
Nora Super Jones
Ken McDonnell
Stacey Nowland
Debra Oberman
Cindy O'Connor
Carolyn Piucci
Sarah Snider

# Index

benefit security, 1
compensation cap reduction effects, 133
contributions and benefits, *24, 26*
effect of regulations on cost, 107
effects of reducing compensation cap, 134–137
funding levels, 25–27, 29
mandatory employee contributions, 50
minimum funding limits, 46–48
participation rates, 18, *18, 19*
private, 86–87
tax principles, 45–47
trends, 1, 15, 17–18, *18, 19*
Defined contribution plans
advantages and disadvantages, 87–88
investor preferences, 38–39
mandatory employee contributions, 50
minimum funding requirements, 47
participation rates, 18–19, *20, 21*
trends, 1, 18–19, *20*
types, 47
Department of Commerce, 9
Department of the Treasury, 46, 71, 113
Disability benefits
actuarial assumptions, 61–62
Disability rates, *62*, 79, *80*
Disclosure requirements, 44, 163
Distribution of tax benefits, 111–116, *113*
Distribution statistics, *37*
District of Columbia, 154

## E

Early retirement, 62–63
EBRI. *See* Employee Benefit Research Institute
Economic Recovery Tax Act of 1981, 52
Elderly. *See also* Retirees
sources of income, *13, 14*
Eligibility, 44
Employee Benefit Research Institute, 7
Employee contributions, 49–51
Employee Retirement Income Security Act of 1974, 3,
43, 52
effects, 126
justification for governmental plan exemption, 75
minimum funding requirements, 161
pension contribution level, 122
purpose, 44, 106
Employee stock ownership plans, 47
Employer contributions, 49
deductibility, 44
full-funding limitation, 74
limits, 45
minimum funding requirements, 46
simplified employee pensions, 53
Employment-based plans. *See also names of specific
types of plans*

coverage and participation, 7, *8, 38*
Equity holdings, 31, *35*
ERISA. *See* Employee Retirement Income Security Act
of 1974
ERTA. *See* Economic Recovery Tax Act of 1981
ESOPs. *See* Employee stock ownership plans
Estate and survivor benefits, 55
Excise taxes
minimum funding requirements for single employer
plans, 46–47
nondeductible employer contributions, 45–46, 74
prefunding, 119
termination, 45
Executive pensions, 120, 152. *See also* High income
individuals; Top heavy plans

## F

Federal Employee Retirement System, 27, 91
Federal Employee Thrift Plan, 86
Federal Employees' Retirement System Act of 1986, 77
Federal government's role in policy development, 1–2
Federal plans
financial trends, 24
funding, 77
potential tax savings by ending, 94
types, 20, 27, 29
FERS. *See* Federal Employees' Retirement System Act
of 1986
Financial assets of pension funds, *30, 92*
401(k) plans, 50, 87
description, 51
high income individuals' referrals, 135
lump-sum distributions, 55
maximum deferral, 53
nondiscrimination tests, 134
participant loans, 56
participation levels, 87
Florida, 129
Forfeiture provisions, 48, 49
Full-funding limitation, 74, 86, 87, 122
current benefit accruals, 126
Reagan administration proposals, 121
Funding delays, 134–137
Funding levels
federal defined benefit plans, 27, 29
private defined benefit plans, 25–27
state and local defined benefit plans, 29
Funding ratios, *27*
maintenance rule, 120–121
Retirement Protection Act of 1993, 161
state and local plans, 128–129
Funding rules, 119–120
public plans, 127, 128
Funding standard accounts, 71–72, 161–162

Minimum benefits for low-income workers, 106
Minimum funding requirements, 120–121. *See also*
    Underfunded plans
  defined benefit plans, 46–48
  exemptions, 71
  OBRA '87 changes, 122
  required annual payment, 74
  single-employer plans, 46
  standards, 70–71
  underfunded plans, 72–74
  waivers, 47, 71, 120
Money purchase plans, 47
Mortality rates, 61, *61*, 78, *80*
MRS. *See* Military Retirement System
Multiemployer plans
  interest rules, 46
  minimum funding waivers, 47
Multiple plan participation, 47

# N

National Income and Product Accounts, 35
NIPA. *See* National Income and Product Accounts
Nondiscrimination
  compensation cap reduction effects, 131
  effects of reducing compensation cap, 133–134
  first rules enacted by Congress, 86
  private plans, 3
  requirements, 126
  simplified employee pensions, 53
  testing, 107
Nondiversion rule, 43–44
Nonqualified plans. *See also names of specific types of
    plan*
  deductibility, 48
  employer contributions, 49
  ERISA requirements, 49
  tax principles, 48

# O

OASDI. *See* Old-Age, Survivors, and Disability Insur-
    ance
OBRA. *See* Omnibus Budget Reconciliation Act of 1987;
    Omnibus Budget Reconciliation Act of 1990;
    Omnibus Reconciliation Act of 1993
Old-Age, Survivors, and Disability Insurance, 1
Omnibus Budget Reconciliation Act of 1987
  amortization periods, 121, 122
  changes in actuarial assumptions, 46
  effect of gains on contributions, *124*
  full-funding limitation, 86, 122
  minimum funding requirements, 122, 161
  timing of benefit funding, 106
  transition rule effects, *123*

Omnibus Budget Reconciliation Act of 1990
  minimum funding requirements for underfunded
      plans, 72–74
  retiree health benefits, 121–122
  reversion to employer, 45
Omnibus Budget Reconciliation Act of 1993
  compensation cap, 131
Oregon, 154, 156
Overfunded plans, 75, 120. *See also* Maximum funding
    limits

# P

Part-time work, 110
Participant loans, 55–56
Participation rates, 7, *8*, 9, *38*, 95–96, *96*, *100*
  defined benefit plans, 18, *18*, *19*
  defined contribution plans, 18–19, *20*, *21*
  men, *107*, 108
  private plans, 15
  public plans, 20–21
  women, 108, *108*, *109*, *110*
  younger workers, 108
Pay-as-you-go funding. *See* Current disbursement
    funding
PBGC. *See* Pension Benefit Guaranty Corporation
Pennsylvania, 129
Pension Benefit Guaranty Corporation, 99
  bankruptcy provisions, 125
  compensation cap reduction effects, 133
  establishment, 86
  explanations for lack of improved funding, 122
  indexing premium, 120
  purpose, 60
  Reagan administration proposals, 121
  Retirement Protection Act of 1993, 161–164
  solvency, 78, 90–91
  timing of guarantees, 126
Pension Task Force on Public Employee
    Retirement, 129
Prefunding, 85–86
  approaches, 59–60
  process, 60–61
  public plans, 127–128
  tax penalties, 119
Premium reforms, 162
President Kennedy's Committee on Corporate Pension
    Funds, 44
Private expenditures for retirement income, 90–91
Private-insured plans
  asset allocation, *33*
  investment mix, 30–31
Private plans, 87–88. *See also names of specific types of
    plans*